NUREMBERG

EVIL ON TRIAL

NUREMBERG
EVIL ON TRIAL

James Owen

headline
review

First published in Great Britain in 2006
by Headline Review

An imprint of Headline Publishing Group

1

Cataloguing in Publication Data is available from the British Library

Hardback: 10-digit ISBN 0 7553 1544 8; 13-digit ISBN 978 0 7553 1544 4
Trade paperback: 10-digit ISBN 0 7553 1599 5; 13-digit ISBN 978 0 7553 1599 4

Typeset in Aldine401 by Palimpsest Book Production Limited, Grangemouth,
Stirlingshire
Designed by The Flying Fish Studio Ltd
Picture section designed by The Flying Fish Studio Ltd
Printed and bound in Great Britain by Mackays of Chatham plc,
Chatham, Kent

Headline's policy is to use papers that are natural, renewable and recyclable
products and made from wood grown in sustainable forests. The logging and
manufacturing processes are expected to conform to the environmental
regulations of the country of origin.

HEADLINE PUBLISHING GROUP
A division of Hodder Headline
338 Euston Road
London NW1 3BH

www.reviewbooks.co.uk
www.hodderheadline.com

'On 5 October 1943 when I visited the building office at Dubno my foreman . . . told me that in the vicinity of the site, Jews from Dubno had been shot in three large pits . . . All of the 5,000 Jews who had still been living in Dubno before the action were to be liquidated . . .

'Thereupon I drove to the site . . . and saw near it great mounds of earth, about 30 metres long and 2 metres high. Several trucks stood in front of the mounds. Armed Ukrainian militia drove the people off the trucks under the supervision of an SS man . . . All these people had the regulation yellow patches on the front and back of their clothes and thus could be recognised as Jews . . .

'The people who had got off the trucks – men, women, and children of all ages – had to undress upon the orders of an SS man, who carried a riding or dog whip. They had to put down their clothes in fixed places, sorted according to shoes, top clothing, and underclothing . . . Without screaming or weeping these people undressed, stood around in family groups, kissed each other, said farewells, and waited for a sign from another SS man, who stood near the pit, also with a whip in his hand. During the fifteen minutes that I stood near I heard no complaint or plea for mercy. I watched a family of about eight persons . . . An old woman with snow-white hair was holding the one-year-old child in her arms and singing to it and tickling it . . . The father was holding the hand of a boy about ten years old and speaking to him softly; the boy was fighting his tears. The father pointed to the sky, stroked his head, and seemed to explain something to him. At that moment the SS man at the pit shouted something to his comrade and instructed them to go behind the earth mound . . .

'I walked around the mound and found myself confronted by a tremendous grave. People were closely wedged together and lying on top of each other so that only their heads were visible. Nearly all had blood running over their shoulders from their heads. Some of the people shot were still moving . . .'

Hermann Grabe, witness at Nuremberg

Contents

Preface: The way to Nuremberg

History is the prelude to myth. When what actually happened, in all its unsimplified and usually unsensational truth, is forgotten, we create legends for ourselves. Frequently this is because the facts are not exciting enough, or not properly understood, or because they are uncomfortable to live with. Few Britons, for instance, think of the retreat from Dunkirk in 1940 as the defeat that it was.

Five and a half years after that reverse, shall we call it, the once victorious leaders of Germany were charged as war criminals in a trial held at Nuremberg. The popular conception of the proceedings – the myth – is that they were a model act of justice in which those in the dock received their well-deserved fate, and which demonstrated that henceforth warmongers and tyrants would not be immune from prosecution. The reality was more complex, significantly so, and if history has a value it is in reminding us that the past ought not be backlit and airbrushed for ease of mass consumption. That, as the Nazis knew, is not history but propaganda.

The decision to hold the principal members of the German regime to account was novel and, from the start, contentious. There were no satisfactory precedents for the authorities of one country, or a coalition of nations, to judge those of another. After his final defeat, Napoleon had been exiled without a trial, an executive decision that had played out rather better than that agreed by the Allies in Paris after the First World War. There it was settled that an international court would arraign the Kaiser as a war criminal, but this plan was scotched when he sought sanctuary in Holland, which refused to be bullied into arresting him. In the hopes that it would hasten its return to normality, Germany's own courts were then allowed by the Allied Powers to pursue some 900 other potential defendants, but such was the internal opposition to the process that no more than a dozen were ever tried. Of those, just six were convicted, and several were sprung from jail by mobs soon after beginning their notably short sentences of imprisonment.

When the Allied Governments faced the same problem a generation later, there was a determination that things should be handled better, but no consensus had been established in the intervening years as to what the solution should be. Thus the various administrations acted as they always do when faced with a thorny question: they prevaricated. The British Cabinet had discussed reports of the massacre of Jews as early as 1942, and had agreed to set up a joint war crimes commission with the Americans, but it was not until Stalin, Roosevelt and Churchill met at Moscow in late 1943 that a formal intention to punish war crimes committed by the Axis was announced. Even then, with a Second Front still to be opened, their declaration had more about it of a campaign to occupy the moral high ground than any sense that a practical plan was in hand. The differences between the leaders' preferred method of dealing with the most prominent Nazis emerged at the Teheran summit a few weeks later, as has often been reported: Stalin proposed at dinner, only half in jest, that the foremost 50,000 be shot out of hand; Churchill was appalled by the suggestion, and so shocked when Roosevelt teasingly appeared to follow suit that he walked out. The significance of the episode, however, lies not so much in the exaggerated scale of the Soviet suggestion as in its demonstration of how far apart thinking on the point still was.

Yet it would be wrong to regard Churchill as being the defender of the rule of law on this issue. Ever keen on prompt, soldierly action, he in fact favoured for a long time summary execution of the leading Nazis after their capture, though rather fewer than Stalin might have contemplated. The sole exception he was considering was that Hitler should be sent to the electric chair. Few in the Government felt qualms at identifying as self-evident the guilt of the leading Axis figures, and the advice it had received from the Lord Chancellor and the Foreign Office was that submitting them to due process of law might throw up all manner of problems, among them opportunities for self-justification and claims that the court was conducting a show trial.

As in the war in general, the decisive moment came only when the Americans brought their resources to bear on the matter. The United States was converted late to the idea of the criminality of the Nazis. The persecution of the Jews in the 1930s and the rumours of mass killings afterwards had not penetrated the rather insular American consciousness. They had not endured German occupation, and in their initial campaigns in North Africa and Italy their troops had witnessed little evidence of war crimes or racial murder. The thirst in America for retribution was principally directed at the Japanese, who had struck without warning at Pearl Harbor and had brought the country into the war.

With victory in Europe ever more in sight, however, in 1944 plans began to be made within the Roosevelt administration to shape the post-war world. With one eye already on Soviet ambitions, many in government wanted a war crimes trial at which American conceptions of justice and democracy could be displayed against the values of a despotic dictatorship. Yet with an ailing President at the helm and an election pending, no firm decisions were taken. Although Roosevelt was safe in the White House by the time of the Yalta Conference in February 1945, Churchill and Stalin could still not be brought around to the notion of a trial, and only after the President's death in April, and Truman's succession, was some urgency injected into the process.

At the start of May, at the inaugural meeting of the United Nations in San Francisco, the British were finally persuaded of the merits of a tribunal. With both Mussolini and Hitler now dead, the stakes were a little less high, and, with other German leaders likely to be captured imminently, some decision as to their fate needed to be taken and conveyed to commanders in the field. The risk for the British, as the Americans made clear, was that if they did not join in they would have to watch while the Americans staged a trial alone. The reasons for the Cabinet's change of heart remain obscure, but certainly they would have understood the implications that remaining aloof from a trial would have for Britain's prestige. And all of a sudden, shooting those who no longer represented a threat seemed rather too like the behaviour of the Nazis themselves.

On 2 May, two days after Hitler's suicide, Truman appointed Robert Jackson to lead the American contribution to the proceedings. It was a fateful choice. Jackson was a Supreme Court Justice who owed his nomination to Roosevelt's patronage and combined his conception of the law with a decided sense of mission. There were stories that Jackson, regarded by some as rather vain and ambitious, had his sights on becoming Chief Justice of the Supreme Court, or even President himself, but it was not so much his personal aspirations that were to hamper the preparation and conduct of the trial as his lofty hopes for what it might achieve – the damning of totalitarianism. It caused him, and the team of American lawyers that he led, largely to neglect the humdrum essentials of a criminal trial: the demonstration from evidence of the guilt of the accused. The British, by contrast, would focus much more narrowly on the business in hand, the securing of convictions.

By late June, with the French and the Russians more or less won round too, Jackson and an American contingent travelled to London to lay the groundwork for the trial with representatives from the other Four Powers. It was they who had borne the brunt of the war effort, and the nineteen other nations in the Allied coalition ultimately agreed to delegate responsibility to them for seeing justice done. The task of effecting a workable compromise between four countries with separate legal systems, four imperial states that approached the conference in different strengths amplified by national pride (and, in the Soviet case, obliged to refer decisions to Moscow), demanded formidable diplomatic skills.

Jackson did not possess them. The negotiations proved difficult and lengthy, despite the best efforts of the British representative, the Attorney-General, Sir David Maxwell Fyfe. Eventually the location of the trial was settled. Berlin would have been the natural venue, but the shattered city had limited facilities to host such a sizeable undertaking. There would have been an additional complication for the Western Powers: the German capital was within the Soviet area of administration, and was itself inconveniently divided into four zones, each controlled by one of the Allies. Instead, Nuremberg emerged as the favoured choice, not for its associations with the Nazi Party rallies of the 1930s but because it had the largest courthouse still standing in Germany, and because the prison attached to it had survived the bombing that had reduced half of the city to rubble.

More problematic was the format of the trial itself. Without too much wrangling, it was decided that it should be conducted by judges sitting as a military tribunal, in effect a court martial, which would give it more flexibility and dispense with the need for a jury. It proved trickier to find an accommodation between the common-law system on which American and British justice is based, and the civil-law traditions of the French and Soviets. There are fundamental differences between the adversarial method employed in the former, in which lawyers for both sides call forth and challenge evidence given by witnesses in person, including the defendant, and the latter, where the judge acts more as an active inquisitor than as an umpire, working from bundles of pre-sworn statements and allowing the accused to make a statement in his defence without it being tested by the prosecution. In the event, a fusion of both traditions governed the trial, and largely successfully. It was adapted to rather better by the multi-national prosecution, however, than by the defence lawyers, all of whom were German and who mostly failed to exploit the novel possibilities offered them by oral examination of witnesses.

They also complained frequently – and not without reason – about what proved to be the most disputed aspect of the trial: the charges on which their clients were arraigned. When the trial was first discussed within the American administration, the leading Nazis had been conceived of as a criminal gang. It is easy to forget now, when so much is known about Hitler's Germany, how little was understood then about exactly how it was run, and indeed one of the most striking features of the trial was the testimony about the Fuehrer's dictatorial style.

In Washington in 1944, however, the main issue was seen as how to make the group in authority carry responsibility for criminal acts that had been carried out by subordinates, often at many removes and in locations geographically remote from where the original policy had been formulated. How, for instance, could one tie a specific massacre of prisoners of war in Belgium carried out by junior soldiers to a general directive given several years previously in Berlin by a minister they had never met?

The solution was seen to lie in the crime of conspiracy, which was familiar to American lawyers and had been successfully used by them in Stock Exchange and gang-busting cases. The attraction of conspiracy was that it gave criminal status to acts that were not themselves illegal, providing they had been done to further a subsequent breach of the law. Thus, the accomplice who lends his friend the burglar a ladder can be caught by a conspiracy charge if he knew or suspected to what use his loan would be put; and, said the Americans, the minister who puts his signature to an order can be prosecuted for the massacre carried out because of it by his nation's army.

Furthermore, the broad scope of conspiracy would permit the prosecution to catch within it a whole series of wrongs, not just the war crimes that had first been mooted. It would enable them to address crimes committed before the war, such as persecution of the Jews, thus allowing the entire Nazi legacy to be put on trial. A conspiracy indictment also seemed a neat way of tying the gang together, an apt charge for those who had – as the Americans believed – plotted as a team for years to take over Europe.

Jackson was convinced of the merits of conspiracy, and wanted to adopt it as the main thrust and binding element of the prosecution case. The other Powers were less persuaded of such a strategy. British diplomats were already briefing Maxwell Fyfe that Germany had not been governed as a collective and that Hitler had proceeded more in an opportunistic way than by following a grand strategy. Meanwhile the French, who had no law of conspiracy, were uneasy at the notion that someone who had not actively participated in a crime could be found guilty of it.

The Soviets were also cautious, though their attitude was always marked by a general suspicion of the Western negotiators and by some puzzlement at the care being taken over the rights of defendants. Their fate, they made little secret of showing, had long been determined, whatever appearances had to be kept up. Iona Nikitchenko, the chief Russian representative, already had extensive experience of political justice; it was he who in the 1930s had presided over the show trial of Grigory Zinoviev and other former leading Bolsheviks who had made the mistake of opposing Stalin.

Both the civil-law Powers also objected to the robust Anglo-Saxon tradition of the prosecution having the right to call surprise witnesses, but since it was the Americans who were committing by far the greatest part of the resources needed for the trial, it tended to be Jackson who got his way, even on conspiracy.

Thus on 8 August, when the Four Powers signed the London Charter that set out the rules of the trial and the categories of charges, conspiracy – or the Common Plan as it was called – was merely a subsection of Count One, Crimes against Peace, or the planning and initiating of aggressive war. Yet by the time that the defendants were indicted in October, conspiracy had detached itself to become not just a count in its own right, and the only one of which all the defendants were accused, but a charge that encompassed the commission of not simply Crimes against Peace but the other two counts in the Charter as well: War Crimes and Crimes against Humanity. It aimed at nothing less than blaming all the defendants for every invasion and atrocity of which the court would hear evidence.

Conspiracy had become the prosecution's main assault on the accused, and the focus of the American effort. In the final reckoning, so over-ambitious and unsatisfactory did the charge prove that the judges severely curtailed its application. Its use against the defendants probably did not make much difference to the verdicts, but it did have an appreciable effect on the Americans' conception and conduct of the trial itself.

Of the four charges now set out in the indictment, Count Two or Crimes against Peace seemed at first glance relatively straightforward. As the prosecution would later state, the heart of all that had happened in the previous six years – the raison d'être of the trial – was that Germany had invaded or occupied more than a dozen countries, from Austria in 1938 until the oft-forgotten takeover of Italy in 1943 after its Government had changed sides.

Yet, like the conspiracy charge, the idea that launching an aggressive war was a crime was a concept unknown to international law. The modern body of rules governing the actions of, and interactions between, sovereign states was in its infancy, and few lawyers could agree on their interpretation. In particular, there was no consensus as to whether various non-aggression treaties signed by Germany and other countries in recent years (most notably the Kellogg–Briand Pact of 1928, which was cited in the indictment) really had outlawed war.

In court, the defence – already discomfited by the broad sweep of the conspiracy allegation – argued strongly against the validity of Count Two. The inter-war treaties had provided no clear penalties for their breach, they said, and were thus never intended to make that action a crime. To set up a court to punish such a contravention of the agreements was to create crimes that were both new and retrospective in their application. If the German leaders had committed criminal offences, they could not have known that they were doing so at the time.

Moreover, said the defence with force, this was mere victors' justice. The Charter was drawn up and the Tribunal staffed only by the winning powers (and in some cases by the same people), with no semblance of neutrality. There was, for instance, to be no German judge. Nor, indeed, any mention of possible Allied war crimes or aggression. The morality of bombing Dresden and Hiroshima is eternally debatable, but it is rarely recalled that in 1941 Britain itself had occupied two independent states, Iceland and Persia, albeit in order to forestall perceived German invasions.

More blatantly, there was to be no assessment of the legitimacy of Russia's naked grab for territory in Finland in 1939 or its seizure of much of eastern Poland two weeks after the German occupation had begun. Both were consequences of the Nazi–Soviet Pact of non-aggression, signed in August 1939, but the court would try to prevent reference to that, and did refuse to admit evidence of Allied war crimes as mitigation or explanation of those committed by Germans.

Two other provisions of the Charter also distressed the defence by their novelty. It declared that it could not be an answer to the charges to plead obedience to the orders of a superior, and it also stripped the defendants of any immunity afforded them by virtue of their ministerial office. The effect of this, coupled with the decision to go after the leading Nazis, was the most radical and ultimately most influential step in the proceedings. For the first time, individuals were to be held responsible for decisions, such as declaring war, that had hitherto been regarded as acts of the State itself.

In their closing speeches to the court, the prosecution countered these points by arguing that the Charter had done no more than give substance to sanctions that were already widely accepted by the international community. The trial and punishment of leaders of states might be new, but only because it had not been done before. Agreement that it could be done existed, albeit in implied and unwritten form. It was a notion familiar to British lawyers, used to prosecuting crimes born and defined by precedent rather than by Acts of Parliament yet still recognised by the courts.

Hitler and his followers, of course, may have had a different opinion of the point, had they shown more interest in international law than they did: Goering happily admitted to the prison psychologist that 'of course, we thought your treaties so much toilet paper'. Yet, at the last, the arguments of the defendants' lawyers about the validity of the Charter's articles carried only moral weight. As the sovereign power in Germany, the Allies now had the right to make its domestic laws, and the Charter had been incorporated into them.

Count Three of the indictment, War Crimes, proved far less contested, although its scope was also radical. In the Charter, it had been intended to cover principally breaches of well-recognised customs of war, such as the mistreatment of military prisoners – three million Soviet POWs died in German captivity – rather than what might now be termed ethnic cleansing: the deliberate extermination of civilians on racial grounds. Soldiers had often been prosecuted before for war crimes, but what was novel in the Charter was that the Allies sought to make their superiors bear responsibility for those acts as well.

By the time that the indictment itself was drawn up, however, the War Crimes charge had expanded to take in what had originally been the province of the charter's last count, Crimes against Humanity. It was this category that was intended to deal with the Nazis' racially motivated murders, and by giving it a separate count to denote something of the scale and systematic nature of their slaughter of other populations. Though it was to be at Nuremberg that the figure of six million victims was first heard, the murder of the Jews was not, however, initially given especial prominence in the charter. It is important to remember that the trial began only six months after the surrender of Germany, and though there had been much press coverage of the liberation of the concentration camps, the wider public had yet to take on board the unique nature of the Holocaust.

To an extent, that was true of the prosecutors too, wading as they were through a morass of documents in which they were endeavouring to see paths and patterns.

The existence of the planned nature of the Final Solution was still emerging during the trial itself, and Rudolf Hoess, the commandant of Auschwitz, was interrogated by representatives of the prosecution during it.

The revised Count Three of the indictment, now embracing race crimes, therefore specifically mentioned Poles and Gypsies as well as Jews. All of them were stated to have been subject to an unfamiliar term: genocide. The word had recently been coined by a Polish–Jewish émigré lawyer, Raphael Lemkin, although since he defined it as the attempt to exterminate a nation, such as the Armenians, who had been persecuted by Turks during the First World War, he did not include acts against the Jews. Nonetheless, the word was applied to them in the indictment, and war crimes thus came to have a sense much closer to the usage now.

Crimes against Humanity – Count Four as it had become – was to be largely reserved for dealing with the repression of opponents of the Nazis within Germany, both during and before the war, though the indictment made clear that the prosecution would use evidence of the crimes against the Jews to ask for convictions under this heading as well. Such duplication was evidence, too, of the decided woolliness that clothed much of the early thinking about the trial.

Now that that had been done, however, there remained only to choose its protagonists. Each of the Four Powers was to select a judge, and a deputy who would attend the hearings but vote only in case of illness. Truman's nominations both had some ulterior motive to them. Francis Biddle had been Jackson's successor as Roosevelt's Attorney-General, but he had not supported Truman's candidacy for the vice-presidency in 1944, and once in power the new President had demanded his resignation. Nuremberg was meant as a sop to his dignity. His alternate was to be John Parker, a Southern judge who had twice narrowly failed to be ratified as a Supreme Court Justice, largely on account of his conservative views on racial integration and employment rights. His second rebuff had occurred a few months earlier, and the trial of the Germans was meant as a consolation prize for him and his backers in Truman's own political heartland.

Attlee's Government had at first sounded out for the British post Sir Norman Birkett, a High Court judge and formerly one of the best-known criminal advocates at the Bar. He had accepted at once, only for the Foreign Office to suggest that such a high-profile trial merited the appointment of a more senior figure, not least so as to keep up Britain's standing among the other judges. An Appeal Court judge, Sir Geoffrey Lawrence, was duly prevailed upon and Birkett, inwardly fuming, agreed to go as his deputy.

In the event, the principal judges decided to elevate their alternates to the same status that they enjoyed, and Birkett took a leading part in both discussion and the eventual drafting of the judgment. It was the avuncular Lawrence, however, who was elected president of the court, a position that might well not have gone to the younger Birkett had he been the first British judge. Lawrence was not as sharp as his colleague, but his steadying manner proved invaluable in heading off many of the potential problems raised during the trial, not least cultural, legal and political differences between the judges. For instance, the Soviets – Nikitchenko himself and a rather enigmatic one-time film producer named Alexander Volchkov – proved reluctant to endorse any decision without prior approval from Moscow. The octet was completed by Henri Donnedieu de Vabres (inevitably known as 'Nom de Dieu'), a professor of international law, and Robert Falco, a rather pettifogging member of France's highest court, who like Nikitchenko had helped to frame the Charter in London. In general, however, the Tribunal harmonised as well as could be hoped during the long ten months that the trial lasted.

The idealistic Jackson was to be the chief prosecutor for the Americans, but though he proved a fine orator his lack of practice in cross-examination would have an important influence on the case, notably when he came to cross swords with the most prominent of the defendants, Hermann Goering.

Jackson was fortunate in having as his British counterpart a barrister with considerable experience of awkward witnesses. Maxwell Fyfe, who had been the youngest King's Counsel appointed in 200 years, was not in fact Britain's chief prosecutor. That was Sir Hartley Shawcross, who after the Conservatives' election defeat in the summer had become Attorney in the new Labour Government in Maxwell Fyfe's stead. Yet such was the pressure of work at Westminster, notably the scrutiny needed of the legislation creating the Welfare State, that Shawcross could be spared to make only the opening and closing speeches at Nuremberg, and as Maxwell Fyfe had been involved in much of the initial planning for the trial it was thought sensible that he handle the day-to-day prosecution of the case.

Having Rex Harrison for a brother-in-law had certainly not rubbed off on him. There was little showy about Maxwell Fyfe, who though politically ambitious was an effective team player. He, Shawcross and Birkett had once appeared together in a celebrated dismembered-body trial, and the small size and camaraderie of the London Bar engendered cohesion in the British case that made it more effective than that presented by the Americans, whose numbers at Nuremberg topped 650. The British knew better what admissions they were seeking from which witnesses, and what evidence must be adduced from which document in order to secure them.

For the sake of easing the workload, the four prosecuting nations decided to divide up the four counts between them, with the Americans taking the Common Plan (and, it turned out, as many of the issues that encompassed as possible). The British concentrated on the invasions, Crimes against Peace. The French, whose lawyers included a future French Prime Minister, Edgar Faure, and the Soviets, who employed a notably hectoring style in court, took joint charge of Counts Three and Four, apportioning crimes committed in Western and Eastern Europe between them. Despite the efforts made to impose clarity on the prosecution case, however, it did proceed to a somewhat unmethodical schedule, with witnesses and examinations being slotted in here and there. Jackson had opted to use evidence mainly from documents rather than from witnesses as being more reliable, but the sheer amount of paperwork cited – much of it repetitious – meant that proceedings tended to move at a leaden pace.

The final selection to be made, and one that continued to alter even once the trial had begun on 20 November, was that of the defendants themselves. There were to be no Italians tried at Nuremberg, it being deemed that the country had suffered enough already when under German rule, but as late as August there was no agreement among the Allies as to which of the Nazis they held should be arraigned. Those captured by the British or the Americans, sometimes in near-comic circumstances in the weeks after the surrender, sweated on their fate at the two camps where they were interned, pointedly codenamed Dustbin and Ashcan.

Many of the key figures – Hitler, Himmler, Goebbels – were dead, as were security chief Reinhard Heydrich and Fritz Todt, the forced-labour boss. Of those that remained, some were always likely candidates for trial, most obviously Goering, von Ribbentrop and Hess. The last named, once the Deputy Fuehrer, had been in British custody since 1941, when he had parachuted into Scotland in an attempt to forge a peace between Britain and Germany. It was a move that had taken both country's leaders wholly by surprise, but which was in keeping with his increasingly eccentric behaviour. The difficulty was that very little of substance was known about the lesser lights of the regime, men such as Ernst Kaltenbrunner, chief of the Reich Security Main Office, or Alfred Rosenberg, the Party's philosopher-in-residence and Minister for the Occupied Eastern Territories.

The desire of the Americans, however, to put the whole Nazi system on trial led to a number of compromises as to whom to indict. Many of these were unsatisfactory. Someone was needed to stand for Nazi propaganda and, as Goebbels was dead, Hans Fritzsche, a broadcaster and civil servant who was almost no one's idea of a leading war criminal, was selected. Someone was needed to symbolise anti-Semitism, so Julius Streicher, the editor of the near-pornographic rag *Der Stuermer*, was chosen, even though he had been under house arrest since 1941. Someone was needed to represent finance, so Hjalmar Schacht, the former Minister of Economics, was indicted, shortly after being found in the concentration camp where he had been sent on suspicion of plotting against Hitler.

Some obvious names were, in hindsight, omitted, such as Heinrich Mueller, head of the Gestapo, whose significance had eluded the Allies. That of Adolf Eichmann to the Final Solution was only just being learned. Ministers quite as important as the flaccid Walther Funk, Schacht's successor and now his fellow defendant, escaped charge, among them Walther Darré. The architect of the 'Blood and Soil' ecological policy and director of the Race and Resettlement Office was subsequently convicted at one of the dozen trials of Nazi officials and camp followers that took place at Nuremberg after that of the principal defendants.

The final list of twenty-four names indicted in October 1945 had rather the feel about it of a lucky dip. Alongside those men who had once shaken the world were several surprises, such as Albert Speer, the armaments minister whose advice had been much sought after by the Allies since the surrender, and Karl Doenitz, the former commander-in-chief of the Navy and briefly Hitler's successor. They were joined by two soldiers, Field Marshal Wilhelm Keitel and General Alfred Jodl, neither of them long-time Nazi Party members, who had clearly been chosen to personify German aggression. That Hitler himself had committed suicide, which had been doubted for some months and had thus led him to be included on early versions of the list, was now accepted, but another name on the bill was that of Martin Bormann, in effect the Fuehrer's private secretary, who had not been seen since the last days in the Bunker and was widely thought to be dead. He was nonetheless tried in absentia.

A number of the cases were clearly going to be hard to stand up: how involved in the war had been Constantin von Neurath, ousted as Foreign Minister in favour of Ribbentrop in 1938, and replaced by Heydrich as Governor of Bohemia and Moravia for being too soft? That against Gustav Krupp, the arms mogul, proved simply embarrassing. He had been chosen to represent the German munitions industry at the initial suggestion of the British. From early on, reservations were expressed as to what part he had played in launching the war, and these doubts turned to humiliation when, very belatedly, it was discovered that the proposed defendant was a senile septuagenarian who had been paralysed by a stroke in 1941.

Krupp was dropped from the bill of indictment by the court as being unfit to stand trial. When Jackson tried to substitute Krupp's son Alfred, who had really been running the firm during the war – and making use of slave labour – he was told shortly that this was a trial, not a football match. One other defendant also failed to take his place in the dock. Robert Ley, head of the Labour Front, the sole trade union in the Nazi State, committed suicide in late October.

In addition to the individuals named in the indictment, it listed seven other defendants. Bent on defining the entire Nazi system as rotten, the Americans had also decided to prosecute several of its key organisations, including the SS, the Gestapo and the General Staff and High Command of the Armed Forces. If they were found criminal, at a stroke so would be the hundreds of thousands of Germans who had been members, even though the organisations had been perfectly legal when they joined them.

The French and Soviets had had grave concerns about such corporate and retrospective declarations of guilt, and at the trial the case against the organisations proved perhaps the least satisfactory of any of its aspects. Not only did it generate an avalanche of affidavits – more than 190,000 of them – which necessitated pre-selection by a separate commission, but the scope of the case was again too wide and vague. Moreover, some of these defendants turned out to be rather different in nature from what the prosecutors had assumed; the important-sounding Reich Cabinet, for instance, had last met in 1938, and had played no role in determining government policy. With their patience by now exhausted, the Tribunal acted with exasperated stringency when faced with this part of the case, restricting those prosecuted to the top ranks of certain organisations, and dismissing entirely the accusations against others.

§

What follows is a selection of extracts from the transcripts of the trial and accounts of it written by those who took part, including judges, defendants and reporters. They are aimed at the general reader more than those with a detailed knowledge of the subject, and I have therefore provided some paragraphs of explanatory commentary where that might be helpful. Where possible, I have tried to let these voices from the past speak for themselves. The official record, including documents used in evidence, runs to more than forty volumes; I hope that this proves a representative and more readily accessible account of the proceedings.

The trial commanded the world's attention in 1945 and 1946, perhaps more so than any other single event of that immediate post-war period. It drew to it famous writers and journalists, including Martha Gellhorn, John Dos Passos, and Yevgeny Khaldei, the photographer who had taken the picture of two soldiers unfurling the Soviet banner on the Reichstag. Their words and images ensured that the watching public, including – however reluctantly – the Germans themselves, became aware of the full horror of the Nazis' reign. Evil remains the correct description of it, however banal its perpetrators were. Sixty years on, there is a danger that we think we are familiar with what happened at their behest. It has become a part of our cultural matrix, so often have we been exposed to it, and that perhaps has rather robbed it of its power to shock. Many of the extracts that follow can still do so. The trial may not have had many moments of drama – away from the cinema, court proceedings seldom do – but the testimony elicited remains the most raw and authentic insight available into the workings of a rogue state, and the suffering that results when a civilisation suspends its moral judgment.

October 1945: Preparations for the trial

By October of 1945, autumn had come to Nuremberg but, despite the importance and scale of the trial due to open there in just a few weeks' time, much still remained to be done. It was only on 6 October that twenty-four of the most prominent names in the Nazi movement and the German Army learned that it was they who would be the defendants. Now brought together and housed in spartan cells in the forbidding prison attached to the courthouse, they waited anxiously for another two weeks before discovering the details of the crimes with which they were charged. In the meantime, another group on whom there would soon be much attention – the eight judges – met each other for the first time.

Francis Biddle, the senior of the two American judges nominated by Truman to the Tribunal, was a liberal, from a prominent Philadelphia family, with a well-cultivated mind and literary interests. His wife, Katharine Garrison Chapin, was a poet, although in common with all those working at the trial he would have to put up with her absence for the foreseeable future, as Nuremberg was administered by the military and those serving there were not allowed initially to be accompanied by their spouses. Some years later, Biddle wrote his memoirs, and in them recalled the personalities of the judges appointed by the other three Powers.

Francis Biddle: The judges meet for the first time

The British representatives arrived just before us, and we had tea with them 8 October. They both wore wing collars, striped trousers, black coats. Mr Justice [Lord Justice, in fact] Geoffrey Lawrence, my opposite number and a few years my senior, said when we met – apparently not remembering his 'briefing', and confusing me with A.J. Drexel Biddle, Jr, who in London during the war had been ambassador to the governments in exile of eight of the countries conquered by the Germans – that he 'realised the advantage' of my 'diplomatic training' – he was 'nothing but a simple barrister and judge'. He looked like John Bull – rubicund, healthy, a twinkling eye and pleasant English humour, friendly and attractive. As time wore on we became close friends. At that time he was a member of the Court of Appeals and soon after the trial was made a Law Lord. He reminded me of Galsworthy's Soames Forsyte, I think on account of his instinctive feeling for art values, a fresh and discriminating enjoyment with no particular intellectual background or subtlety of informed taste. He was typical of an English tradition which has by no means disappeared – conservative, land-loving, sturdy. He raised Guernseys at his place, Hill Farm, Oaksey, near Malmesbury in Wiltshire. He had strength, an understanding of men that came from a human friendliness rather than any turn of shrewdness, and a very real personal dignity.

There was a ruddy, outdoor quality about Lawrence, which he must have inherited from his father, Alfred Tristram Lawrence, First Baron Trevethin, who had died when, trout fishing at the age of ninety-three, he had leaned forward from a stone in the bed of the stream, lost his balance and been swept down by the current and drowned before his gillie could reach him. He was appointed Lord Chief Justice by Lloyd George in 1921 to fill the vacancy caused by the resignation of Lord Reading to become viceroy of India, but served for only one year, it was said by an agreement he had first made with the prime minister.

Lawrence's alternate, Sir Norman Birkett, was very different. Lawrence was short and roundish, Birkett towered above him, six feet three, beak-nosed, reddish hair, lean, angular, hawklike. He had wit, was broadly read, particularly in poetry; was impulsive and generous.

I liked Birkett at once. He had left a large and lucrative practice as one of the leading barristers of England two or three years before to accept an appointment on the Court of King's Bench. He had often spoken in the United States at meetings of the American Bar Association and was very popular with our bar. Proof of his popularity at such occasions was afforded by a story which he liked to recount of a highly inebriated member, after one of the dinners, with an arm around Birkett's shoulders, assuring him that 'What I like about you, Sir Norman, is that you're not one of those condescending sons of bitches that they so often send over.' Birkett talked pithily, with an apt sense for a fitting quotation, and a well-stored and accurately catalogued memory. He had been the British Government's first choice as member, but when the matter had been referred to the Foreign Office, it had insisted that a Lord of Appeal should be appointed rather than a nisi-prius [more junior] judge, and the choice had fallen to Lawrence, Birkett gracefully agreeing to go as his alternate. I don't think the two men were close friends – temperamentally they were very different – but they appeared to get along well, their relationship marked by more than usually good manners . . .

The two Frenchmen also exhibited contrast. M. Donnedieu de Vabres was a short, stout professor from the École de Droits in Paris, with a quick, overbalanced, slightly uncertain gait. He was a recognised authority on international law, a little pedantic, with formal, old-fashioned manners, very courteous. He had great sweeping moustaches, which he liked to twirl upward with a flourish after speaking or eating. When his earphones were attached something warlike was added, and he looked like the drawings of Vercingetorix in school editions of *Caesar's Commentaries*. He was familiar with German, but knew only three or four words of English, usually out of context, but which on occasion he liked to exercise. When his wife joined him some weeks later I ran into them at the Grand Hotel; and with an old-world flourish he introduced me to her. 'Mon cher collègue permit me to introduce you to – my woman!' Madame Donnedieu de Vabres, who understood and spoke English, turned crimson.

The French alternate, Robert Falco, was a member of the Cour de Cassation, the highest court in France. He had been a captain in the First World War, and had been decorated for gallantry in action. Sceptical, ironic, hard-working, sharing my preference for understatement, he made a very pleasant companion as well as a resourceful associate.

Major-General Nikitchenko, vice-chairman of the Supreme Court of the USSR, was in his forties, the youngest member of the Tribunal. He was grave, dignified, thin-lipped, capable, I thought, of using cruelty when it seemed appropriate; restrained, subtle. He knew what the rest of us were like, knew the score, kept in mind a few essentials. After he got to trust us, or at least to understand us a little better, he did not bother quite so much with the meticulous passion for detail which the Russians felt called upon to exhibit during those first few slow weeks. Out of a limited and childlike sense of humour something apt now and then would emerge. Nuremberg had been selected largely because its immense Palace of Justice had hardly been touched in the concentrated bombing that almost destroyed the old city. As we walked by it together for the first time, Nikitchenko turned to me, saying, through his interpreter, 'I suppose your pilot must have had the trial in mind when he skipped the courts. You Americans think of everything!'

His alternate, Lieutenant-Colonel A.F. Volchkov, a member of the Soviet District Court, could carry on a limited conversation in English – he had lived in London for several years – and was a pleasant, easy-going Slav who became quite affectionate when he had dined pretty well. He had an unclear mind, and never seemed to grasp the point of what was going on. He bored Nikitchenko, and was a little afraid of him.

Biddle was the natural choice to be president of the court but, when the judges came to vote on the matter, he decided that as the Americans were, with their superior resources, going to dominate the trial, it would be better if the Tribunal were led by another nationality. The avuncular, level-headed Lawrence proved to be a happy solution.

§

By 19 October, just a month before the trial was due to begin, the indictment detailing the charges and evidence against the accused was ready. The responsibility of serving it on the defendants was given to the 29-year-old Airey Neave, a barrister and soldier then best known (before his entry into politics) for his wartime escape from Colditz. Accompanied by Burton Andrus, the American colonel in charge of the prisoners, Harold Willey, the General Secretary of the Tribunal, a priest and two soldiers struggling under the weight of the legal papers, Neave afterwards recalled in his account of the trial how, with some trepidation, he had made his way first to the cell that held Hermann Goering.

Airey Neave: The indictments are served

As the cell was unlocked, I braced myself to meet him. In a few seconds the door swung open. Andrus entered and Goering rose unsteadily to his feet. With his stick under his arm, Andrus stood stiffly to attention on my right. His polished helmet glinted in the sunlight from the small barred window. I stepped towards Goering and waited. To my left stood the interpreter and Mr Willey. Then came the two soldiers bearing documents. There was no room for the other witnesses of this macabre ceremony. They slowly assembled outside and I could hear their boots grating on the stone floor.

The cell was crowded and I felt shut in with Goering. Once again that urgent desire to break out came to me, as it had often done since my days in the town gaol of Colditz. My eyes searched the cell. There was a steel bed, a table, a chair. No piece of furniture was allowed within four feet of the window wall. The chair was removed at night and the bed fastened to the floor. There were signs of fresh plaster, where all bars and hooks had been removed from the window. It was a harsh place for any prisoner. I caught sight of the photographs of Goering's wife and small daughter on his table. They were carefully arranged beside a pile of books.

For a time, I shunned Goering's face. It seemed an age before the rest of the party came to a halt outside. I felt forced to take another look at the cell. It was about thirteen feet long and nine feet wide. Opposite was a water closet and a washbowl with running water.

I realised at this second glance, how good the conditions were. Far better than Plotsk in 1941. My eyes turned from the water closet back to the photographs of the little girl, Edda Goering. It was only a month since Sam Harris [a prosecution lawyer] and I had studied the Dechenschule concentration camp near Essen, where fifteen toilets were available for five hundred Krupp slaves.

The photograph of Goering's daughter, so like her father, touched me. Then I felt suddenly angry. It was impossible to forget the Krupp guards who caught a prisoner trying to keep a snapshot of his parents. They seized it, tore it up, and beat him till he bled.

My apparent diffidence, which puzzled Judge Biddle and Mr Willey, was gone. I turned and stared at Goering. It was his turn to look away from me towards Andrus to whom he insolently referred as 'the Fire Brigade Colonel'.

Goering was a mixture of bluff and moral cowardice. He refused to meet my eyes but I could see that his were small and greedy. Rebecca West, who studied him closely in the dock, likened him to those fat women with their sleek cats seen in the late morning in doorways along the steep streets of Marseilles. Certainly he had the look of a woman about him and I was reminded of his passion for jewels.

It was not that Goering seemed in the least homosexual, rather the reverse. He was, nevertheless, indefinably feminine. He appeared exquisitely corrupt and soft even amid the austerities of Nuremberg. My first impression was of meeting a dissolute Roman Emperor, game to the last.

Goering was now fifty-three. Since he had been in prison at Nuremberg in September, his weight had declined from twenty to fifteen stone and his grey uniform was too large. His drug intake was being reduced. His complexion was an actor's. It had a brownish tint like that of a veteran star inured to make-up and costume. Indeed, before the end of the Thousand-Year Reich, Goering was seen at official parties in a toga and sandals. When he first came into the hands of Colonel Andrus, he had been a decayed and gloomy voluptuary. By October, he was once more on the stage, his health and confidence returning.

Andrus had known Goering since May when the former Reichsmarschall had been detained at Mondorf-les-Bains after his capture. He used to describe how Goering arrived with sixteen monogrammed suitcases, a red hatbox and a valet. His fingernails were varnished red. He had been indiscreetly entertained by American officers and believed he was on his way to see Eisenhower. Andrus has also written that one of the suitcases contained 20,000 paracodein pills.

At last, Goering turned to face me. I caught the full menace of his narrow, bright eyes. His wide lips suggested nameless appetites. I was no longer afraid of him, despite this air of evil. I was struck again by his small stature and the way in which his grey Air Force uniform tunic hung loosely. He wore no badges of rank, which had been stripped from him. The showmanship, the decorations, and the panoply of the Reichsmarschall of Greater Germany had vanished in the flames and dust.

This was the destined successor to Hitler; the Commander-in-Chief of the German Air Forces; the Prime Minister of Prussia and the President of the Reichstag. He now lived in a cell watched night and day by GIs. Instead of the stupendous rooms of scuttled Carinhall [Goering's estate outside Berlin], with its plundered wines and looted tapestries, he lived out of a GI mess tin. No knives or forks were allowed in the cells and all food had to be eaten with a spoon. Breakfast was oatmeal and bread. Lunch: soup, fried fish, tomato sauce, beet salad, rice and coffee. Supper: bean stew, bread and tea.

I was surprised to find my voice.

'Hermann Wilhelm Goering?'

The man was still the actor. He bowed to me and smiled. I noticed that despite his age, his hair was a thick, dark brown, another hint of Hollywood. When I first entered, his mouth had twitched nervously; he seemed unsteady. Now he was in possession of the stage again. There was a trace of geniality in those cruel eyes as he gestured with one fat white hand towards the bed. It was as if to say, 'I am afraid I cannot offer you a chair.'

On my next visit to his cell, on the following day, he used those very words in a fruity voice, as I called to discuss the choice of German counsel. This day he simply said:

'*Jawohl*.'

I repeated the words agreed with Mr Willey.

'I am Major Neave, the officer appointed by the International Military Tribunal to serve upon you a copy of the indictment in which you are named as defendant.'

Goering's expression changed to a scowl, the look of a stage gangster, as the words were interpreted.

I handed him a copy of the indictment which he took in silence. He listened as I said, 'I am also asked to explain to you Article 16 of the Charter of the Tribunal.'

A copy in German was handed to him.

'If you will look at paragraph (c). You have the right to conduct your own defence before the Tribunal or to have the assistance of counsel.'

My words were correct and precise. Goering looked serious and depressed as I paused.

'So it has come,' he said.

§

Goering had not expected to be treated as a war criminal when he surrendered to American soldiers at the end of the war, and he had spent some time regaling them with stories about his glory days before he was arrested, an event that came as a rude shock to him. By October, he had become reconciled to the prospect of a trial, but others named in the indictments still professed bewilderment at being held responsible for the invasions and atrocities listed in the indictment.

Among these was Franz von Papen, who had led the conservative Catholic Centre Party in the early 1930s. In Hitler, he believed he had found a tool to control the mob, and when von Papen became Chancellor in 1932, at the head of a minority government, he had passed measures that had helped his Nazi allies into power after him, such as lifting a ban on the SA, the movement's brown-shirted thugs. Once Hitler succeeded him as Chancellor, however, von Papen rapidly realised that he had been wrong to think of Hitler as a mere soapbox orator. Though he served as his deputy for eighteen months, he had little authority, and in the summer of 1934 he had resigned after Hitler, fearful of their strength and influence, had ordered the murder of Ernst Roehm, the SA leader, and hundreds of his followers.

Yet despite this, and the Nazis' assassination in July 1934 of the Austrian Chancellor Engelbert Dollfuss, von Papen had then accepted an offer to become German minister in Vienna, where he became closely involved in the events surrounding the Anschluss, the union of Austria with Germany in 1938, brought about largely by military pressure on Austria's Government. In 1939, he was relegated to the embassy in Turkey, where he saw out the war.

Von Papen was regarded by some as a wily political veteran whose protestations of innocence were merely a pose; during the First World War, when military attaché in then neutral Washington, he had been expelled from America for plotting sabotage. Yet in his memoirs, von Papen maintained his stance of being mystified as to why he had been indicted for acts carried out well before the war. He also recalled his apprehension at the handicaps he foresaw when it came to defending himself.

Franz von Papen: Contemplating my defence

I was faced by the problem of how best to counter these accusations. To all intents and purposes, there were two main points: first of all, I had to prove that my activities between 1932 and 1934 had not served to bring Hitler to power or strengthen his position. Secondly, I had to show that I had not attempted to undermine the Schussnigg Government by subversive methods but, on the contrary, had done all I could to combat the Nazis' plans for a forcible Anschluss, while seeking evolutionary methods of bringing about a union between Austria and Germany. How was I to set about it? There was a method, completely unknown to our own legal processes, of a defendant appearing as a witness in his own defence under oath. I felt that this provided the best opportunity of rejecting the accusation of evil intentions and exploring my true thoughts. However, I was under no illusions as to how much belief was likely to be given to my protestations. The general atmosphere in the months after Germany's collapse was such that the victorious powers regarded almost any German who had held an official appointment as a criminal whose word was not likely to be accepted. The problem was how to obtain objective proofs.

I had no archives or documents at my disposal. The files of the German Government had either been destroyed or were in the hands of the occupying powers. Almost all my own private files in Wallerfangen and Berlin had been lost or destroyed in the war. Germany's transport and communication systems had practically ceased to exist. There was no way of discovering the whereabouts of friends or acquaintances, or even of ascertaining if they were still alive. Some of my closest collaborators were dead, and we were not permitted to get in direct touch with foreigners. There was, in any case, the question of whether they would be prepared to testify in favour of a German. According to the rules of procedure, all our requests for witnesses had to be made through the prosecution, who then forwarded them to the Court with their own comments. Under the system, again outside our experience, of differentiating between prosecution and defence witnesses, most of Germany's leading personalities had been arrested and were being held as possible prosecution witnesses, and were therefore not at our disposal.

We had no means of knowing exactly what documents the prosecution possessed. In my own case, for example, they presented a series of reports concerning my activities in Austria, covering the period from August 1934 to the spring of 1938. I could only assume that they had a complete set, but our repeated requests that these reports should be placed at our disposal – I knew that they provided me with a complete defence – were rejected on the grounds that the prosecution had no further documents in their possession. I will leave it to the reader to judge whether it is likely that the prosecution had come by chance on only those particular documents which supported their own case. This shabby manoeuvre was shown up later when the very reports I had been asking for, which provided incontrovertible evidence of my continual fight with the illegal Nazi party in Austria, were produced by the prosecution in a later trial, as part of their case against Hitler's former emissary there, Wilhelm Keppler. We met with the same treatment over the minutes of the Cabinet meetings in 1933 and 1934. Only a few were presented by the prosecution and our requests for the remainder were again rejected on the grounds that the prosecution did not have them.

I have referred more than once to our unfamiliarity with the procedure adopted by the Court, which caused the German defence counsel much difficulty. The prosecution was at all times the dominating factor. To those accustomed to Continental methods, the Court played only a minor role. In any German criminal trial, it is above all the duty of the judge, by interrogation and enquiry, to extract the truth. Here it was a contest between the prosecution and the defence, in which the Court acted as a sort of umpire. According to the Statute [the Charter], both prosecution and defence had the same rights, but this equality existed only on paper. As I have described, the prosecution held all the trumps and the defence had nothing, being entirely dependent on the goodwill of the prosecution for the production of their evidence. The defence was greatly restricted in its efforts, whilst the prosecution could surprise them at any time with new witnesses and documents. The defence had to make all its requests for evidence weeks beforehand, thus providing the prosecution with ample time to counter their arguments. A request for a witness led in almost every case to that person being arrested and brought to Nuremberg, where they were first interrogated by the prosecution. Even if the defence finally obtained access to them, it was only in the presence of a representative of the prosecution. The result was that it became an imposition to require anyone to undergo this ordeal. Those who were produced did not know whether they might not be incriminating themselves, and in most cases tried to pin on other people the responsibility for anything that had happened.

There was also another fundamental point – the presence in the Court of a Russian member. Relations between the Soviet Union and the Western Powers still preserved a façade of amicable co-operation.

The result was that any attempt to refer to Russian policies, such as, for example, their joint attack on Poland in 1939, was forbidden. Today it would seem grotesque to have a Russian sitting in judgment on charges of waging aggressive war. In any normal criminal trial the fact that a judge himself participated in the crime before the court would act as an immediate disqualification. But at Nuremberg any attempt to suggest that the Russians, or, in specific circumstances, the Allies, had employed methods with which the Germans were now charged, was immediately ruled out of order. 'We are not interested in what the Allies may have done,' Lord Justice Lawrence used to say.

§

Like the survivors of a shipwreck threatened by a rising sea, the defendants each had their own and often unexpected way of dealing with the approaching trial. Goering was all blustery defiance, while von Papen was nobly stoic. Albert Speer, the Nazis' chief architect and the highly effective Minister of War Production, was one of the few to have already expressed remorse for his part in the conflict.

Speer had joined the Nazi Party in 1931 after being impressed by seeing Hitler speak. His architectural commissions for the Party soon brought him to the Fuehrer's notice, and their relationship had blossomed into one of close affinity that continued until the closing days of the war.

From the mid 1930s onwards, Speer had been the deviser of the contexts in which the Party displayed itself, from the spectacles of the Nuremberg Rallies to the Olympic Stadium for the 1936 Games. During the first part of the war he had concentrated on preparing the vainglorious urban projects that delighted Hitler, but in 1942 he had been appointed Minister for War Production.

By centralising decisions, reducing bureaucracy, concentrating manufacture and improving efficiency, Speer had transformed the German munitions industry. After the surrender, he had given the Allies much valuable information, but while many would come to see this co-operation as being more self-serving than a sign of repentance, at the time it came as a surprise to most observers when he was committed for trial. Thoughtful and sensitive, Speer took a keen interest in the reactions of his co-accused to their indictment, as he recalled in his autobiography.

Albert Speer: How we faced up to the trial

Along with the indictment we were presented with a long list of German lawyers, from whose ranks each of us could choose his defender if we had no proposals of our own. Much as I strained my memory, I could not recall a single lawyer. The names on the list were completely unknown to me, so I asked the court to make a choice. A few days later I was taken to the ground floor of the Palace of Justice. At one of the tables a slight man with strong glasses and a low voice stood up. 'I am supposed to be your lawyer, if you agree. My name is Dr Hans Flaechsner, from Berlin.' He had friendly eyes and an unassuming manner. When we discussed various details of the indictment, he displayed a sensible, unhistrionic attitude. Finally, he handed me a form. 'Take this with you and consider whether you want me for your defence attorney.' I signed it there and then and did not regret it. In the course of the trial Flaechsner proved to be a circumspect, tactful lawyer. But what mattered more to me, he felt a sympathy toward me out of which, during the ten months of the trial, a real mutual affection developed . . .

During the preliminary investigation the prisoners were prevented from meeting. Now this regulation was relaxed, so that we crossed paths more often in the prison yard, where we could talk without surveillance. The trial, the indictment, the invalidity of the international Tribunal, profound indignation at the disgrace – again and again as we walked our rounds of the yard I heard the same subjects and opinions. Among the twenty other defendants I found only one who shared my views. That was Fritzsche, with whom I could consider in detail the principle of responsibility. Later Seyss-Inquart also showed some understanding of this. With the others, the discussion was useless and wearing. We were speaking different languages.

On other questions also we naturally enough held divergent opinions. In what light we were going to describe Hitler's rule for purposes of this trial was acutely important. Goering, though he had strong reservations about some practices of the regime, was all in favour of whitewashing Hitler. Our only hope, he held, was to use this trial to promote a positive legend. I felt that it was unethical to deceive the German people in this way; I also thought it dangerous because it would make the transition to the future more difficult for the whole nation. Only the truth could accelerate the process of cutting free from the past.

I had a certain insight into Goering's real motives when he observed that the victors would undoubtedly kill him but that within fifty years his remains would be laid in a marble sarcophagus and he would be celebrated by the German people as a national hero and martyr. Many of the prisoners had the same dream about themselves. On other subjects Goering's arguments were less effective. There were no differences among us, he said; we were all sentenced to death from the start and none of us had a chance. It was pointless to bother about a defence. I remarked: 'Goering wants to ride into Valhalla with a large retinue.' In actuality Goering later defended himself more stubbornly than the rest of us did.

At Mondorf [the preliminary interrogation centre] and Nuremberg, Goering had undergone a systematic withdrawal cure which had ended his drug addiction. Ever since, he was in better form than I had ever seen him. He displayed remarkable energy and became the most formidable personality among the defendants. I thought it a great pity that he had not been up to this level in the months before the outbreak of the war and in critical situations during the war. He would have been the only person whose authority and popularity Hitler would have had to reckon with. Actually, he had been one of the few sensible enough to foresee the doom that awaited us. But having thrown away his chance to save the country while that was still possible, it was absurd and truly criminal for him to use his regained powers to hoodwink his own people. His whole policy was one of deception. Once, in the prison yard, something was said about Jewish survivors in Hungary. Goering remarked coldly: 'So, there are still some there. I thought we had knocked off all of them. Somebody slipped up again.' I was stunned.

My vow to accept responsibility for the entire regime could not be kept without some severe psychological crises. The only way of getting out of it was to escape the trial by suicide. Once I tried using a towel to stop the circulation in my sick leg, in order to produce phlebitis. Remembering from one of our lectures in Kransberg that nicotine from even a cigar, crumbled and dissolved in water, could be fatal, I kept a crushed cigar in my pocket for a long time. But from the intention to the deed is a very long way.

The Sunday divine services became a great support for me. Even as recently as my stay in Kransberg I had refused to attend them. I did not want to seem soft. But in Nuremberg I threw aside such prideful feelings. The pressure of circumstances brought me – as, incidentally, it did almost all the defendants with the exception of Hess, Rosenberg and Streicher – into our small chapel.

20 November 1945: The trial opens

Amid feverish excitement and tension, the trial began on 20 November in a courtroom specially enlarged to hold not merely the dozens of prisoners and, lawyers, but also several hundred spectators and reporters. The smell of fresh paint was still in the air. Among those waiting nervously in the dock for the formal entry of the judges was Hans Fritzsche.

A journalist who had made a career for himself in the new medium of wireless in the 1920s, Fritzsche had become head of the Government's radio news service in 1932, and had joined the Nazi Party the next year on being appointed chief of news in the Press Department of the recently established Propaganda Ministry.

For the next decade, his task was to disseminate the Government's announcements to the press both at home and abroad, steering editorial coverage as the regime found it necessary. He was, however, never more than a conduit for the information passed to him by Joseph Goebbels, the Nazis' principal propagandist.

From 1937, Fritzsche had become much more widely known as a broadcaster and the presenter of a weekly news round-up. In his capacity as a civil servant, however, he had been merely a functionary, but in the absence of Goebbels, who had committed suicide, he now found himself cast as representative of the Nazis' systematic distortion of the truth and, as he later wrote in his account of his ordeal, on trial for his life.

Hans Fritzsche: The scene in the courtroom

At seven a.m. on Tuesday, the 20th November, 1945, we were carefully shaved; at eight our best suits were given out to us, and at nine we were led forth by the guards. Once again we entered an empty hall; prisoners had, we learnt, to be always in their places before anyone else arrived on the scene. It was an integral part of that 'good impression' so dear to the Commandant's [Andrus] heart.

At half-past nine the main doors opened and defending counsel came in, some in black gowns, others in the purples and reds of the law schools. They were followed by the Prosecution among whom were a few familiar figures in civilian clothes standing out in the mass of uniforms. Here and there we recognised a familiar face: I watched Dr Kempner, a former fellow-countryman of mine, taking his seat among the leading members of the American prosecuting team . . .

I next scanned the press section, where I soon noticed many acquaintances from earlier days who, though they had once been glad enough to catch my eye, were now studiously looking in the opposite direction.

The presence of these compatriots in court, their attitude and the places they occupied was not the first intimation we had had that the trial was to be more than a conflict between nationalities; but it was the most convincing one. From thenceforward we understood that the line which divided prosecutor from prisoner, *us* from *them*, was not a national but an ideological frontier. This struck me so forcibly that on our first day in court I asked von Neurath, who was sitting next to me, whether he thought our line of defence – that the motive for our past actions had been the national interest, not the interest of a political party – would be accepted as legally relevant. I need not have worried: not one of us was able to hold to the original course of his argument in the stormy proceedings which followed – we were all driven like leaves before the hurricane of accusation launched at us.

I remember that in the middle of the turmoil of later days a little event occurred which both excited and steadied us, so eagerly did we grasp at any straw in that strange wind-blown existence. Dr Frick [Hitler's Minister of the Interior] recognised his wife sitting among the spectators in the public gallery. She made a gesture with her little parasol, so unobtrusively that no stranger could have recognised the movement as a greeting; but her husband, off his guard, stared as if he had been bewitched at this apparition from a world that had vanished when the prison doors closed upon him, and did not know whether to rejoice or tremble. Somebody must have noticed a trace of these conflicting emotions in the prisoner's demeanour and, suspecting that something unusual was happening, put two and two together; from then on all members of the prisoners' families were specifically debarred from the hearings. Jodl's plucky wife alone was able to gain permission to attend the court and she came in the capacity of assistant to her husband's counsel . . .

At length an order was given which brought to an end the lively commotion going on in front of our box, and Colonel Mays, Marshal of the Court, requested all present to take our seats. At once the chattering throngs dispersed and from the apparent chaos order emerged. The four groups of prosecutors with their women secretaries, the defence lawyers in their black and sanguine robes, the brightly dressed visitors, all stood out in bold contrast to one another as silence fell on the packed court.

There was a loud shout of '*Attention!*' Everybody rose to their feet, the guards stood to attention, and the officers on duty saluted as the members of the Tribunal filed in. We prisoners gazed tensely at the faces of the men who held our fates in their hands.

There were eight of them – four judges, each with his Assessor [the alternate judges] who acted as a sort of understudy so that if a member of the Tribunal were unavoidably absent, the trial could still go on. First came the French, wearing gold-coloured robes; they were followed by the Americans and British in plain dark gowns, while the Russian contingent in military uniforms brought up the rear. For a moment all remained standing; the English counsel acknowledging the Bench's greeting with their customary ceremonious and respectful salutations, the others with brisk polite bows. The Judges glanced across at the counsel for the Defence, whose reactions, I noticed, varied very considerably; then we all sat down again.

§

There was little drama on the first day, which was given over to the reading of the lengthy indictment. The next morning, the defendants were required to enter their pleas – Guilty or Not Guilty. Those who tried to use the opportunity to make a speech were abruptly cut off by Lawrence, who quickly imposed his authority on proceedings. The case against the senile Gustav Krupp, the arms tycoon, had been dismissed a week earlier, and all the remaining accused pleaded Not Guilty, with Rudolf Hess's little bark of 'Nein!' drawing a titter of laughter from those watching. Then the mood once more became solemn, as the bespectacled and bow-tied Robert Jackson, the United States' chief prosecutor, rose to his feet. His opening speech, which impressed all with its eloquence, outlined the rationale for holding such a trial, the difficulties facing the court, and the hopes that the eventual judgments would help to heal Germany's wounds.

Trial transcript, 21 November 1945: Robert Jackson's opening speech for the prosecution

May it please Your Honours:

The privilege of opening the first trial in history for crimes against the peace of the world imposes a grave responsibility. The wrongs which we seek to condemn and punish have been so calculated, so malignant, and so devastating, that civilisation cannot tolerate their being ignored, because it cannot survive their being repeated. That four great nations, flushed with victory and stung with injury stay the hand of vengeance and voluntarily submit their captive enemies to the judgment of the law is one of the most significant tributes that Power has ever paid to reason.

This Tribunal, while it is novel and experimental, is not the product of abstract speculations nor is it created to vindicate legalistic theories. This inquest represents the practical effort of four of the most mighty of nations, with the support of seventeen more, to utilise international law to meet the greatest menace of our times – aggressive war. The common sense of mankind demands that law shall not stop with the punishment of petty crimes by little people. It must also reach men who possess themselves of great power and make deliberate and concerted use of it to set in motion evils which leave no home in the world untouched. It is a cause of that magnitude that the United Nations will lay before Your Honours.

In the prisoners' dock sit twenty-odd broken men. Reproached by the humiliation of those they have led almost as bitterly as by the desolation of those they have attacked, their personal capacity for evil is forever past. It is hard now to perceive in these men as captives the power by which as Nazi leaders they once dominated much of the world and terrified most of it. Merely as individuals their fate is of little consequence to the world.

What makes this inquest significant is that these prisoners represent sinister influences that will lurk in the world long after their bodies have returned to dust. We will show them to be living symbols of racial hatreds, of terrorism and violence, and of the arrogance and cruelty of power. They are symbols of fierce nationalisms and of militarism, of intrigue and war-making which have embroiled Europe generation after generation, crushing its manhood, destroying its homes, and impoverishing its life. They have so identified themselves with the philosophies they conceived and with the forces they directed that any tenderness to them is a victory and an encouragement to all the evils which are attached to their names. Civilisation can afford no compromise with the social forces which would gain renewed strength if we deal ambiguously or indecisively with the men in whom those forces now precariously survive.

What these men stand for we will patiently and temperately disclose. We will give you undeniable proofs of incredible events. The catalogue of crimes will omit nothing that could be conceived by a pathological pride, cruelty, and lust for power. These men created in Germany, under the *Führerprinzip,* a National Socialist despotism equalled only by the dynasties of the ancient East. They took from the German people all those dignities and freedoms that we hold natural and inalienable rights in every human being. The people were compensated by inflaming and gratifying hatreds towards those who were marked as 'scapegoats'. Against their opponents, including Jews, Catholics, and free labour, the Nazis directed such a campaign of arrogance, brutality, and annihilation as the world has not witnessed since the pre-Christian ages. They excited the German ambition to be a 'master race', which of course implies serfdom for others. They led their people on a mad gamble for domination. They diverted social energies and resources to the creation of what they thought to be an invincible war machine. They overran their neighbours. To sustain the 'master race' in its war-making, they enslaved millions of human beings and brought them into Germany, where these hapless creatures now wander as 'displaced persons'. At length bestiality and bad faith reached such excess that they aroused the sleeping strength of imperilled Civilisation. Its united efforts have ground the German war machine to fragments. But the struggle has left Europe a liberated yet prostrate land where a demoralised society struggles to survive. These are the fruits of the sinister forces that sit with these defendants in the prisoners' dock.

In justice to the nations and the men associated in this prosecution, I must remind you of certain difficulties which may leave their mark on this case. Never before in legal history has an effort been made to bring within the scope of a single litigation the developments of a decade, covering a whole continent, and involving a score of nations, countless individuals, and innumerable events. Despite the magnitude of the task, the world has demanded immediate action. This demand has had to be met, though perhaps at the cost of finished craftsmanship. To my country, established courts, following familiar procedures, applying well-thumbed precedents, and dealing with the legal consequences of local and limited events, seldom commence a trial within a year of the event in litigation. Yet less than eight months ago today the courtroom in which you sit was an enemy fortress in the hands of German SS troops. Less than eight months ago nearly all our witnesses and documents were in enemy hands. The law had not been codified, no procedures had been established, no Tribunal was in existence, no usable courthouse stood here, none of the hundreds of tons of official German documents had been examined, no prosecuting staff had been assembled, nearly all of the present defendants were at large, and the four prosecuting powers had not yet joined in common cause to try them. I should be the last to deny that the case may well suffer from incomplete researches and quite likely will not be the example of professional work which any of the prosecuting nations would normally wish to sponsor. It is, however, a completely adequate case to the judgment we shall ask you to render, and its full development we shall be obliged to leave to historians . . .

Unfortunately, the nature of these crimes is such that both prosecution and judgment must be by victor nations over vanquished foes. The worldwide scope of the aggressions carried out by these men has left but few real neutrals. Either the victors must judge the vanquished or we must leave the defeated to judge themselves. After the first World War, we learned the futility of the latter course. The former high station of these defendants, the notoriety of their acts, and the adaptability of their conduct to provoke retaliation make it hard to distinguish between the demand for a just and measured retribution, and the unthinking cry for vengeance which arises from the anguish of war. It is our task, so far as humanly possible, to draw the line between the two. We must never forget that the record on which we judge these defendants today is the record on which history will judge us tomorrow. To pass these defendants a poisoned chalice is to put it to our own lips as well. We must summon such detachment and intellectual integrity to our task that this Trial will commend itself to posterity as fulfilling humanity's aspirations to do justice . . .

It may be that these men of troubled conscience, whose only wish is that the world forget them, do not regard a trial as a favour. But they do have a fair opportunity to defend themselves – a favour which these men, when in power, rarely extended to their fellow countrymen. Despite the fact that public opinion already condemns their acts, we agree that here they must be given a presumption of innocence, and we accept the burden of proving criminal acts and the responsibility of these defendants for their commission.

When I say that we do not ask for convictions unless we prove crime, I do not mean mere technical or incidental transgression of international conventions. We charge guilt on planned and intended conduct that involves moral as well as legal wrong. And we do not mean conduct that is a natural and human, even if illegal, cutting of corners, such as many of us might well have committed had we been in the defendants' positions. It is not because they yielded to the normal frailties of human beings that we accuse them. It is their abnormal and inhuman conduct which brings them to this bar.

We will not ask you to convict these men on the testimony of their foes. There is no count in the indictment that cannot be proved by books and records. The Germans were always meticulous record keepers, and these defendants had their share of the Teutonic passion for thoroughness in putting things on paper. Nor were they without vanity. They arranged frequently to be photographed in action. We will show you their own films. You will see their own conduct and hear their own voices as these defendants re-enact for you, from the screen, some of the events in the course of the conspiracy.

We would also make clear that we have no purpose to incriminate the whole German people. We know that the Nazi Party was not put in power by a majority of the German vote . . . The German, no less than the non-German world, has accounts to settle with these defendants . . .

This war did not just happen – it was planned and prepared for over a long period of time and with no small skill and cunning. The world has perhaps never seen such a concentration and stimulation of the energies of any people as that which enabled Germany twenty years after it was defeated, disarmed, and dismembered to come so near carrying out its plan to dominate Europe. Whatever else we may say of those who were the authors of this war, they did achieve a stupendous work in organisation, and our first task is to examine the means by which these defendants and their fellow conspirators prepared and incited Germany to go to war.

In general, our case will disclose these defendants all uniting at some time with the Nazi Party in a plan which they well knew could be accomplished only by an outbreak of war in Europe. Their seizure of the German State, their subjugation of the German people, their terrorism and extermination of dissident elements, their planning and waging of war, their calculated and planned ruthlessness in the conduct of warfare, their deliberate and planned criminality toward conquered peoples – all these are ends for which they acted in concert; and all these are phases of the conspiracy, a conspiracy which reached one goal only to set out for another and more ambitious one . . .

The case as presented by the United States will be concerned with the brains and authority back of all the crimes. These defendants were men of a station and rank which does not soil its own hands with blood. They were men who knew how to use lesser folk as tools. We want to reach the planners and designers, the inciters and leaders without whose evil architecture the world would not have been for so long scourged with the violence and lawlessness, and wracked with the agonies and convulsions, of this terrible war.

22 November–14 December 1945:
The case for the prosecution

The impact of Jackson's opening speech was soon blunted by the ineptness with which the Americans' case was mounted. It was neither well organised nor coherent, and relied overmuch on a mass of documentary evidence that had not been properly digested. On 22 November, they began to outline the material relating to the conspiracy charge, the Common Plan, telling the story of the Nazis' rise to power and their plotting for war. Half a dozen different lawyers rotated places, detailing ever more confusing aspects of the case. Colonel Robert Storey dealt with the processing of evidence; Ralph Albrecht tried to explain the Nazi hierarchy on a cumbersome chart; Major Frank Wallis and Thomas Dodd rattled respectively through the propaganda and economic preparations for war. The impression given was of haste and a lack of attention to specifics – Sidney Alderman even told the court that one document bore initials whose meaning he did not know, and as it was in German he could not read it. The courtroom, already made sleepy by the heat from the lights for the cameras filming the trial, soon acquired an air of barely suppressed boredom, and public interest dwindled.

It was revived when, on 26 November, attention turned to the military and political prelude to the war. Here, Alderman reads from one of the principal pieces of evidence for the conspiracy charge, a memorandum of a meeting in 1937 in which Hitler outlined his future strategy to a group that included three of those now on trial – Goering, Erich Raeder, then Commander-in-Chief of the Navy, and

Constantin von Neurath, Foreign Minister at the time. Since the notes were made some time after the conference, the accuracy of its wording has been questioned, but it nonetheless offers a revealing insight into the Fuehrer's capacities as a strategist, and into his ambitions for Germany.

Trial transcript, 26 November 1945: Sidney Alderman on the Hossbach memorandum

One of the most striking and revealing of all the captured documents which have come to hand is a document which we have come to know as the Hossbach notes of a conference in the Reich Chancellery on 5 November 1937 from 1615 to 2030 hours, in the course of which Hitler outlined to those present the possibilities and necessities of expanding their foreign policy, and requested – I quote: 'That his statements be looked upon in the case of his death as his last will and testament.' . . .

The minutes of this meeting reveal a crystallisation towards the end of 1937 in the policy of the Nazi regime. Austria and Czechoslovakia were to be acquired by force. They would provide *Lebensraum* (living space) and improve Germany's military position for further operations. While it is true that actual events unfolded themselves in a somewhat different manner than that outlined at this meeting, in essence the purposes stated at the meeting were carried out. The document destroys any possible doubt concerning the Nazis' premeditation of their Crimes against Peace. This document is of such tremendous importance that I feel obliged to read it in full into the record:

'Berlin, 10 November 1937. Notes on the conference in the Reichskanzlei on 5 November 1937 from 1615 to 2030 hours. Present: The Fuehrer and Reich Chancellor; the Reich Minister for War, Generalfeldmarschall von Blomberg; the C-in-C Army, Generaloberst Freiherr von Fritsch; the C-in-C Navy, Generaladmiral Dr H.C. Raeder; the C-in-C Luftwaffe, Generaloberst Goering; the Reichsminister for Foreign Affairs, Freiherr von Neurath; Oberst Hossbach [the adjutant who took the minutes].

'The Fuehrer stated . . . The aim of German policy is the security and the preservation of the nation and its propagation. This is consequently a problem of space. The German nation comprises 35 million people, which, because of the number of individuals and the compactness of habitation, form a homogeneous European racial body, the like of which cannot be found in any other country. On the other hand it justifies the demand for larger living space more than for any other nation . . . An arrest of the decrease of the German element in Austria and in Czechoslovakia is just as little possible as the preservation of the present state in Germany itself.

'Instead of growth, sterility will be introduced, and as a consequence, tensions of a social nature will appear after a number of years, because political and philosophical ideas are of a permanent nature only as long as they are able to produce the basis for the realisation of the actual claim of the existence of a nation. The German future is therefore dependent exclusively on the solution of the need for living space.'

Hitler then expounded various economic solutions before ruling them out, declaring: 'The question for Germany is where the greatest possible conquest could be made at lowest cost . . . '

'The German question can be solved only by way of force, and this is never without risk. The battles of Frederick the Great for Silesia, and Bismarck's wars against Austria and France had been a tremendous risk and the speed of Prussian action in 1870 had prevented Austria from participating in the war. If we place the decision to apply force with risk at the head of the following expositions, then we are left to reply to the questions "when" and "how". In this regard we have to decide upon three different cases . . .

'Case 1. Period 1943–45: After this we can only expect a change for the worse. The rearming of the Army, the Navy, and the Air Force, as well as the formation of the Officers' Corps, are practically concluded . . .

'Our material equipment and armaments are modern; with further delay the danger of their becoming out-of-date will increase. In particular, the secrecy of "special weapons" cannot always be safeguarded . . .

'In comparison with the rearmament, which will have been carried out at that time by other nations, we shall decrease in relative power. Should we not act until 1943–45, then, dependent on the absence of reserves, any year could bring about the food crisis, for the countering of which we do not possess the necessary foreign currency. This must be considered a point of weakness in the regime. Over and above that, the world will anticipate our action and will increase counter-measures yearly. Whilst other nations isolate themselves, we should be forced on the offensive.

'What the actual position would be in the years 1943–45, no one knows today. It is certain, however, that we can wait no longer.

'On the one side the large armed forces, with the necessity for securing their upkeep, the aging of the Nazi movement and of its leaders, and on the other side the prospect of a lowering of the standard of living and a drop in the birth rate, leaves us no other choice but to act. If the Fuehrer is still living, then it will be his irrevocable decision to solve the German space problem no later than 1943–45. The necessity for action before 1943–45 will come under consideration in cases 2 and 3.

'Case 2. Should the social tensions in France lead to an internal political crisis of such dimensions that it absorbs the French Army and thus renders it incapable for employment in war against Germany, then the time for action against Czechoslovakia has come.

'Case 3. It would be equally possible to act against Czechoslovakia if France should be so tied up by a war against another state that it cannot proceed against Germany.

'For the improvement of our military political position it must be our first aim, in every case of entanglement by war, to conquer Czechoslovakia and Austria, simultaneously, in order to remove any threat from the flanks in case of a possible advance westwards . . .

'The Fuehrer believes personally, that in all probability England and perhaps also France, have already silently written off Czechoslovakia, and that they have got used to the idea that this question would one day be cleaned up by Germany . . . Although the population of Czechoslovakia in the first place is not a thin one, the embodiment of Czechoslovakia and Austria would nevertheless constitute the conquest of food for 5 to 6 million people, on the basis that a compulsory emigration of 2 million from Czechoslovakia, and of 1 million from Austria could be carried out. The annexation of the two States to Germany, militarily and politically, would constitute a considerable relief . . .

'The Fuehrer sees case 3 looming nearer; it could develop from the existing tensions in the Mediterranean, and should it occur, he has firmly decided to make use of it any time, perhaps even as early as 1938.'

The effective annexation of Austria did indeed take place just four months later, in March 1938, and in October of that year Germany occupied the Sudetenland, the German-speaking border regions of Czechoslovakia. As Hitler had predicted, for fear of provoking a wider conflict the leading powers of Europe, Britain and France, acquiesced to the invasions, ceding the Sudetenland to Germany at the Munich talks, and taking no action when Hitler seized the rest of Czechoslovakia in March 1939.

§

At the time of the trial, the world was still reeling from the war's devastation, and the facts and interpretation provided by journalists were central to its efforts to come to terms with the conflict's legacy. Among those who watched events unfold in court was the British writer Rebecca West. She noted two features of the case that were much remarked on: the surprising mediocrity of the defendants, whose reputations had been built up by propaganda but who in fact were principally of the subservient type with which Hitler surrounded himself; and the sheer tedium of much of the courtroom proceedings.

Rebecca West: Regarding the defendants

It seemed ridiculous for the defendants to make any effort to stave off the end, for they admitted by their appearance that nothing was to go well with them again on the earth. These Nazi leaders, self-dedicated to the breaking of all rules, broke last of all the rule that the verdict of a court must not be foretold. Their appearance announced what they believed. The Russians had asked for the death penalty for all of them, and it was plain that the defendants thought that wish would be granted. Believing that they were to lose everything, they forgot what possession had been. Not the slightest trace of their power and glory remained; none of them looked as if he could have exercised any valid authority. Goering still used imperial gestures, but they were so vulgar that they did not suggest that he had really filled any great position; it merely seemed probable that in certain bars the frequenters had called him by some such nicknames as 'The Emperor'. These people were also surrendering physical characteristics which might have been thought inalienable during life, such as the colour and texture of their skins and the moulding of their features. Most of them, except Schacht, who was white-haired, and Speer, who was black like a monkey, were neither dark nor fair any more; and there was amongst them no leanness that did not sag and no plumpness that seemed more than inflation by some thin gas. So diminished were their personalities that it was hard to keep in mind which was which, even after one had sat and looked at them for days; and those who stood out defined themselves by oddity rather than character.

Hess was noticeable because he was so plainly mad: so plainly mad that it seemed shameful that he should be tried. His skin was ashen, and he had that odd faculty, peculiar to lunatics, of falling into strained positions which no normal person could maintain for more than a few minutes, and staying fixed in contortion for hours. He had the classless air characteristic of asylum inmates; evidently his distracted personality had torn up all clues to his past. He looked as if his mind had no surface, as if every part of it had been blasted away except the depth where the nightmares live. Schacht was as noticeable because he was so far from mad, so completely his ordinary self in these extraordinary circumstances. He sat twisted in his seat so that his tall body, stiff as a plank, was propped against the end of the dock, which ought to have been at his side. Thus he sat at right angles to his fellow defendants and looked past them and over their heads: it was always his argument that he was far superior to Hitler's gang. Thus too, he sat at right angles to the judges on the bench confronting him: it was his argument that he was a leading international banker, a most respectable man, and no court on earth could have the right to try him. He was petrified by rage because his court was pretending to have this right. He might have been a corpse frozen by rigor mortis, a disagreeable corpse who had contrived to aggravate the process so that he could be specially difficult to fit into his coffin.

A few others were still individuals. Streicher was pitiable, because it was plainly the community and not he who was guilty of his sins. He was a dirty old man of the sort that gives trouble in parks, and a sane Germany would have sent him to an asylum long before. Baldur von Schirach, the [Hitler] Youth Leader, startled because he was like a woman in a way not common among men who looked like women. It was as if a neat and mousy governess sat there, not pretty, but with never a hair out of place, and always to be trusted never to intrude when there were visitors: as it might be Jane Eyre. And though one had read surprising news of Goering for years, he still surprised. He was so very soft. Sometimes he wore a German Air Force uniform, and sometimes a light beach suit in the worst of playful taste, and both hung loosely on him, giving him an air of pregnancy. He had thick brown young hair, the coarse bright skin of an actor who has used greasepaint for decades, and the preternaturally deep wrinkles of the drug addict. It added up to something like the head of a ventriloquist's dummy. He looked infinitely corrupt, and acted naively. When the other defendants' lawyers came to the door to receive instructions, he often intervened and insisted on instructing them himself, in spite of the evident fury of the defendants, which, indeed, must have been poignant, since most of them might well have felt that, had it not been for them, they would never have had to employ these lawyers at all. One of these lawyers was a tiny little man of very Jewish appearance, and when he stood in front of the dock, his head hardly reaching to the top of it, and flapped his gown in annoyance because Goering's smiling wooden mask was bearing down between him and his client, it was as if a ventriloquist had staged a quarrel between two dummies.

Goering's appearance made a strong but obscure allusion to sex. It is a matter of history that his love affairs with women played a decisive part in the development of the Nazi party at various stages, but he looked as one who would never lift a hand against a woman save in something much more peculiar than kindness. He did not look like any recognised type of homosexual, yet he was feminine. Sometimes, particularly when his humour was good, he recalled the madam of a brothel. His like are to be seen in the late morning in doorways along the steep streets of Marseille, the professional mask of geniality still hard on their faces though they stand relaxed in leisure, their fat cats rubbing against their spread skirts. Certainly there had been a concentration on appetite, and on elaborate schemes for gratifying it; and yet there was a sense of desert thirst. No matter what aqueducts he had built to bring water to his encampment, some perversity in the architecture had let it run out and spill on the sands long before it reached him. Sometimes even now his wide lips smacked together as if he were a well-fed man who had heard no news as yet that his meals were to stop. He was the only one of the defendants who, if he had the chance, would have walked out the Palace of Justice and taken over Germany again, and turned it into a stage for the enactment of the private fantasy which had brought him into the dock.

As these men gave up the effort to be themselves, they joined to make a common pattern which simply reiterated the plea of not guilty. All the time they had made quite unidiosyncratic gestures expressive of innocence and outraged common sense, and in the intervals they stood up and chatted among themselves, forming little protesting groups, each one of which, painted as a mural, would be instantly recognised as a holy band that had tried to save the world but had been frustrated by mistaken men. But this performance they rendered more weakly every day. They were visibly receding from the field of existence and were, perhaps, no longer conscious of the recession. It is possible that they never thought directly of death or even of imprisonment, and there was nothing positive in them at all except their desire to hold time still. They were all praying with their sharp-set nerves: 'Let this trial never finish, let it go on for ever and ever, without end.'

The nerves of all others present in the Palace of Justice were sending out a counter-prayer: the eight judges on the bench, who were plainly dragging the proceedings over the threshold of their consciousness by sheer force of will; the lawyers and the secretaries who sat sagged in their seats at the tables in the well of the court; the interpreters twittering unhappily in their glass box like cage-birds kept awake by a bright light, feeding the microphones with French and Russian and English versions of the proceedings for the spectators' earphones; the guards who stood with their arms gripping their white truncheons behind their backs, all still and hard as metal save their childish faces, which were puffy with boredom. All these people wanted to leave Nuremberg as urgently as a dental patient wants to up and leave the chair; and they would have had as much difficulty as the dental patient in explaining the cause of that urgency. Modern drills do not inflict real pain, only discomfort. But all the same the patients on whom they are used feel that they will go mad if the grinding does not stop.

The trial was the first occasion on which simultaneous interpretation had been tried on such a scale. The equipment was provided free of charge by IBM. Its success made the company's reputation, and secured it the contract to provide similar facilities for the newly established United Nations.

§

By its eighth day, the prosecution case had forfeited almost all of its momentum, a requirement vital to the team's sense of waging a just war against evil. Sitting side by side in two long rows in the dock, their expressions concealed by the dark glasses they wore because of the bright lights needed by the cameras, many of the defendants grew rather cockier than they had been, until for the first time the court – and most of the accused too – were confronted with hard evidence of the consequences of the Nazis' plans: a film about the concentration camps. The reactions of the defendants were monitored by the prison psychiatrist, Douglas Kelley, and its American psychologist, Gustave Gilbert, who noted his impressions in his diary.

Gustave Gilbert: The accused watch the film of the death camps

Afternoon session: Goering, Ribbentrop, and Hess had a great laugh over the reading of Goering's telephone conversation with Ribbentrop on the day of Hitler's triumphant entry into Vienna, describing the whole thing as a lark, with birds twittering, etc. Then the hilarity in the dock suddenly stopped as Commander Donovan announced the showing of a documentary film on Nazi concentration camps as they were found by American troops.

(Kelley and I were posted at either end of the defendants' dock and observed the prisoners during the showing of this film. Following are my notes jotted down during the showing of the film at about 1–2 minute intervals:)

Schacht objects to being made to look at film as I ask him to move over; turns away, folds arms, gazes into gallery . . . (Film starts). Frank nods at authentication at introduction of film . . . Fritzsche (who had not seen any part of film before) already looks pale and sits aghast as it starts with scenes of prisoners burned alive in a barn . . . Keitel wipes brow, takes off headphones . . . Hess glares at screen, looking like a ghoul with sunken eyes over the footlamp . . . Keitel puts on headphone, glares at screen out of the corner of his eye . . . von Neurath has head bowed, doesn't look . . . Funk covers his eyes, looks as if he is in agony, shakes his head . . . Ribbentrop closes his eyes, looks away . . . Sauckel mops brow . . . Frank swallows hard, blinks eyes, trying to stifle tears . . . Fritzsche watches intensely with knitted brow, cramped at the end of his seat, evidently in agony . . . Goering keeps leaning on balustrade, not watching most of the time, looking droopy . . . Funk mumbles something under his breath . . . Streicher keeps watching, immobile except for an occasional squint . . . Funk now in tears, blows nose, wipes eyes, looks down . . . Frick shakes head at illustration of 'violent death' – Frank mutters 'Horrible!' . . . Rosenberg fidgets, peeks at screen, bows head, looks to see how others are reacting . . . Seyss-Inquart stoic throughout . . . Speer looks very sad, swallows hard . . . Defence attorneys are now muttering, 'for God's sake – terrible.' Raeder watches without budging . . . von Papen sits with hand over brow, looking down, has not looked at screen yet . . . Hess keeps looking bewildered . . . piles of dead are shown in a slave labour camp . . . von Schirach watching intently, gasps, whispers to Sauckel . . . Funk crying now . . . Goering looks sad, leaning on elbow . . . Doenitz has head bowed, no longer watching . . . Sauckel shudders at picture of Buchenwald crematorium oven . . . as human skin lampshade is shown, Streicher says, 'I don't believe that' . . . Goering coughing . . . Attorneys gasping . . . Now Dachau . . . Schacht still not looking . . . Frank nods his head bitterly and says, 'Horrible!' . . . Rosenberg still fidgeting, leans forward, looks around, leans back, hangs head . . . Fritzsche, pale, biting lips, really seems in agony . . . Doenitz has head buried in hands . . . Keitel now hanging head . . . Ribbentrop looks up at screen as British officer starts to speak, saying he has already buried 17,000 corpses . . . Frank biting his nails . . . Frick shakes his head incredulously at speech of female doctor describing treatment and experiments on female prisoners at Belsen . . . As Kramer [Commandant of the Bergen-Belsen camp] is shown, Funk says with choking voice, 'The dirty swine!' . . . Ribbentrop sitting with pursed lips and blinking eyes, not looking at screen . . . Funk crying bitterly, claps hand over mouth as women's naked corpses are thrown into pit . . . Keitel and Ribbentrop look up at mention of tractor clearing corpses, see it, then hang their heads . . . Streicher shows signs of disturbance for first time . . . Film ends.

After showing of the film, Hess remarks, 'I don't believe it.' Goering whispers to him to keep quiet, his own cockiness quite gone. Streicher says something about 'perhaps in the last days.' Fritzsche retorts scornfully. 'Millions? In the last days? – No.' Otherwise there is a gloomy silence as the prisoners file out of the courtroom.

§

Although the prosecution had reached only the Anschluss in their case on conspiracy, the next witness to be called was – much to their irritation – a surprise to the defence, and dealt with the invasion of Poland. Erwin Lahousen had been an officer of the Abwehr, German military intelligence, and had worked for its director, Admiral Wilhelm Canaris. Here he gives evidence about a conference on Hitler's train in September 1939 just before the fall of Warsaw. Among those participating had been von Ribbentrop, Alfred Jodl, chief of the Armed Forces' Operation Staff, and the head of the High Command or OKW, Wilhelm Keitel, all of whom had been indicted. Lahousen was quizzed on the stand by Colonel John Amen, a lawyer who had supervised the interrogations of potential defendants and witnesses before the trial began.

Trial transcript, 30 November 1945: The extermination measures in Poland

ERWIN LAHOUSEN: First of all, Canaris had a short talk with Ribbentrop, in which the latter explained the general political aims with regard to Poland and in connection with the Ukrainian question. The Chief of the OKW took up the Ukrainian question in subsequent discussions which took place in his private carriage. These are recorded in the files which I immediately prepared on Canaris's order. While we were still in the carriage of the Chief of the OKW, Canaris expressed his serious misgivings regarding the proposed bombardment of Warsaw, of which he knew. Canaris stressed the devastating repercussions which this bombardment would have in the foreign political field. The Chief of the OKW, Keitel, replied that these measures had been agreed upon directly by the Fuehrer and Goering, and that he, Keitel, had had no influence on these decisions. I quote Keitel's own words here – naturally only after re-reading my notes. Keitel said: 'The Fuehrer and Goering are in frequent telephone communication; sometimes I also hear something of what was said, but not always.'

Secondly, Canaris very urgently warned against the measures which had come to his knowledge, namely the proposed shootings and extermination measures directed particularly against the Polish intelligentsia, the nobility, the clergy, and in fact all elements which could be regarded as leaders of a national resistance. Canaris said at that time – I am quoting his approximate words: 'One day the world will also hold the Wehrmacht, under whose eyes these events occurred, responsible for such methods.'

The Chief of the OKW replied – and this is also based on my notes, which I re-read a few days ago – that these things had been decided upon by the Fuehrer, and that the Fuehrer, the Commander-in-Chief of the Army, had let it be known that, should the Armed Forces be unwilling to carry through these measures, or should they not agree with them, they would have to accept the presence at their side of the SS, the SIPO and similar units who would carry them through. A civilian official would then be appointed to function with each military commander. This, in outline, was our discussion on the proposed shooting and extermination measures in Poland.

COL. AMEN: Was anything said about a so-called 'political housecleaning'?

LAHOUSEN: Yes, the Chief of the OKW used an expression which was certainly derived from Hitler and which characterised these measures as 'political housecleaning'. I recall this expression very clearly, even without the aid of my notes.

COL. AMEN: In order that the record may be perfectly clear, exactly what measures did Keitel say had already been agreed upon?

LAHOUSEN: According to the Chief of the OKW, the bombardment of Warsaw and the shooting of the categories of people which I mentioned before had been agreed upon already.

COL. AMEN: And what were they?

LAHOUSEN: Mainly the Polish intelligentsia, the nobility, the clergy, and, of course, the Jews.

COL. AMEN: What, if anything, was said about possible co-operation with a Ukrainian group?

LAHOUSEN: Canaris was ordered by the Chief of the OKW, who stated that he was transmitting a directive which he had apparently received from Ribbentrop since he spoke of it in connection with the political plans of the Foreign Minister, to instigate in the Galician Ukraine an uprising aimed at the extermination of Jews and Poles.

COL. AMEN: At what point did Hitler and Jodl enter this meeting?

LAHOUSEN: Hitler and Jodl entered either after the discussions I have just described or towards the conclusion of the whole discussion of this subject, when Canaris had already begun his report on the situation in the West; that is, on the news which had meanwhile come in on the reaction of the French Army at the West Wall.

COL. AMEN: And what further discussions took place then?

LAHOUSEN: After this discussion in the private carriage of the Chief of the OKW, Canaris left the coach and had another short talk with Ribbentrop, who, returning to the subject of the Ukraine, told him once more that the uprising should be so staged that all farms and dwellings of the Poles should go up in flames, and all Jews be killed.

COL. AMEN: Who said that?

LAHOUSEN: The Foreign Minister of that time, Ribbentrop, said that to Canaris. I was standing next to him.

COL. AMEN: Is there any slightest doubt in your mind about that?

LAHOUSEN: No. I have not the slightest doubt about that. I remember with particular clarity the somewhat new phrasing that 'all farms and dwellings should go up in flames'. Previously there had only been talk of 'liquidation' and 'elimination'.

In the summer of 1941, at the start of the invasion of Russia, Lahousen had attended another conference, this time dealing with the treatment of Soviet political commissars, and the Jews.

COL. AMEN: Did you learn from the conversation at this conference what the substance of these orders under discussion was?

LAHOUSEN: These orders dealt with two groups of measures which were to be taken. Firstly, the killing of Russian commissars, and secondly, the killing of all those elements among the Russian prisoners of war who, under a special selection programme of the SD [German State Security Service], could be identified as thoroughly bolshevised or as active representatives of the Bolshevist ideology.

COL. AMEN: Did you also learn from the conversation what the basis for these orders was?

LAHOUSEN: The basis for these orders was explained by General Reinecke in its outlines as follows:

The war between Germany and Russia is not a war between two states or two armies, but between two ideologies – namely, the National Socialist and the Bolshevist ideology. The Red Army soldier must not be looked upon as a soldier in the sense of the word applying to our western opponents, but as an ideological enemy. He must be regarded as the archenemy of National Socialism, and must be treated accordingly . . .

COL. AMEN: Now, will you explain to the Tribunal from what you learned at this conference the exact manner in which the sorting of these prisoners was made and in what way it was determined which of the prisoners should be killed?

LAHOUSEN: The prisoners were sorted out by Kommandos of the SD and according to peculiar and utterly arbitrary ways of procedure. Some of the leaders of these Einsatzkommandos [special mission squads] were guided by racial considerations; particularly, of course, if someone were a Jew or of Jewish type or could otherwise be classified as racially inferior, he was picked for execution. Other leaders of the Einsatzkommando selected people according to their intelligence. Some had views all of their own and usually most peculiar, so that I felt compelled to ask Mueller [chief of the security services], 'Tell me, according to what principles does this selection take place? Do you determine it by the height of a person or the size of his shoes?' . . .

COL. AMEN: You referred to a change in the plans to take the Soviet prisoners back to German territory. Is that correct?

LAHOUSEN: Yes, they were not brought back into Germany.

COL. AMEN: And what was the result of this action, namely of their not being brought back at the direct order of Hitler? . . .

LAHOUSEN: The enormous crowds of prisoners of war remained in the theatre of operation, without proper care – care in the sense of prisoner of war conventions – with regard to housing, food, medical care; and many of them died . . . Epidemics broke out, and cannibalism – human beings driven by hunger devouring one another – manifested itself.

The significance of Lahousen's evidence was that it showed that the murderous policies against the commissars, the Jews and the Polish intelligentsia were widely discussed within both the Nazi leadership and the military High Command.

§

Lahousen had been part of the circle around Canaris that came to plot Hitler's downfall, most of whom were executed after the failed attempt on his life with a bomb on 20 July 1944. Gilbert recorded the reactions of the accused to his unexpected appearance on the stand.

Gustave Gilbert: Defendants' reactions to Lahousen's evidence

Lunch hour: Goering was fuming. 'That traitor! That's one we forgot on the 20th of July. Hitler was right – the Abwehr was a traitor's organisation! How do you like that! No wonder we lost the war – our own Intelligence Service was sold out to the enemy!' He was talking quite loud, half to me but obviously announcing the 'Party line' on Lahousen's testimony.

'Well, opinions may differ on that,' I said, 'but it seems to me it's only a question of whether his testimony was true or not.'

'What good is the testimony of a traitor? He should have been busy giving me accurate reports on our bombing missions instead of sabotaging our war effort. Now I know why I could never depend on him for accurate information. Just wait till I ask him that one question. "Why did you not renounce your position, if you were convinced a German victory would be a tragedy?" Just wait till I get a chance at him.'

Jodl took it all more philosophically. 'If he was convinced of it, all well and good, but then he should have said something, and not betrayed his officer's honour. I know they are always asking me what I would have done if I had known of Hitler's plans. I would have said something, but I wouldn't have acted dishonourably.'

'Well, it seems to me that there was a struggle between conscience and duty, and this man followed his conscience,' I said.

'Oh, but you can't do such things. An officer must either follow orders or resign.'

Keitel agreed, but was evidently disturbed about the damning evidence. 'That man was just reading from a prepared script! I'm going to tell my lawyer!' I told him I didn't think he was reading any prepared script, and anyway, it was a question of the truth of the testimony. He fell back on the 'officer's honour' argument, without making much sense.

I spoke to Lahousen again later, and he remarked, 'Now they talk of honour, after millions have been murdered! No doubt it's unpleasant for them to have someone who can stand up and state these uncomfortable truths to their faces. I've got to speak for those whom they murdered. I am the only one left.'

§

As great as their alleged crimes were, there was a downcast air about the defendants that might almost have evoked sympathy for them. If the trial was a spectacle, it was not the grand one envisaged by Washington, more like a crowd at the zoo poking sticks at a group of shabby hyenas, the most peculiar of which was Rudolf Hess, once Deputy Fuehrer.

Born in Egypt, Hess had fought in the same regiment as Hitler in the First World War and had been imprisoned with him after the failure of the Nazis' attempt to seize power in Bavaria in 1923 – the Munich Putsch. When both were subsequently imprisoned, it was Hess who had taken down the dictation of *Mein Kampf*, Hitler's mix of autobiography and political philosophy. After their release, he had assumed a key role in rebuilding the Party.

Hess's mind had always been a delicate instrument. Aside from mild paranoia about his health and his diet, his predominant characteristic was his loyalty – almost worship – of Hitler. He gained fulfilment largely through a sense of being of use to his Fuehrer. When war came, and Hitler became preoccupied by military matters, Hess felt the purpose drain from his life, and it was probably this feeling of failure that prompted him to try to bring off an astounding diplomatic coup in May 1941.

Knowing that the invasion of Russia was imminent, Hess purloined a Messerschmitt fighter and piloted it to Scotland, parachuting down at night into a field outside Glasgow. He seems to have hoped to have brokered a peace with Britain that would have removed her from the war, allowing the Nazis to concentrate on fighting their ideological enemy, Communism, but though Hess's bravery was not in question, his sanity was already in doubt. Such a peace agreement could never have been more than a private fantasy of his, and he was arrested soon after his arrival, without making contact with Churchill. He spent the remainder of the war in British custody.

There he began to exhibit signs of severe mental disturbance, including loss of memory. Sitting in the dock between Goering and von Ribbentrop, he appeared aloof and introspective, as if he was observing some strange dream in which he was a participant. In the weeks before the court opened, he had been examined by ten psychiatrists, all of whom had concluded that he was not insane but neither fully competent to stand trial. Then, on 30 November, just as the Tribunal was about to make its ruling on this issue, which would have meant Hess being separated from the other defendants and confined to his cell, he made a startling announcement.

Trial transcript, 30 November 1945: Hess confesses the truth about his amnesia

Mr President, I would like to say this. At the beginning of the proceedings this afternoon I gave my defence counsel a note saying that I thought the proceedings could be shortened if I would be allowed to speak. I wish to say the following:

In order to forestall the possibility of my being pronounced incapable of pleading, in spite of my willingness to take part in the proceedings and to hear the verdict alongside my comrades, I would like to make the following declaration before the Tribunal, although, originally, I intended to make it during a later stage of the trial:

Henceforth my memory will again respond to the outside world. The reasons for simulating loss of memory were of a tactical nature. Only my ability to concentrate is, in fact, somewhat reduced. But my capacity to follow the trial, to defend myself, to put questions to witnesses, or to answer questions myself is not affected thereby.

I emphasise that I bear full responsibility for everything that I did, signed or co-signed. My fundamental attitude that the Tribunal is not competent, is not affected by the statement I have just made. I also simulated loss of memory in consultations with my officially appointed defence counsel. He has, therefore, represented it in good faith.

Despite his confession that he had hitherto been shamming, Hess continued to behave oddly throughout the trial, believing for instance that his guards wished to poison his food. No one was ever sure quite what his real state of mind was. It is probable that, though he may have temporarily recovered his memory, he was genuinely afflicted by paranoia and amnesia brought on by the trauma of his break with Hitler, who had repudiated him after his Scottish adventure, and was perhaps suffering from them to a greater extent than he himself realised.

§

The petty regulations that governed the prisoners' life in jail began to get under their skin, relates Hans Fritzsche, as did the psychological abuse handed out by their young American guards, who were stationed outside every cell and ordered to check on the defendants at least once a minute through the small hatch in the door. Some of them were so hypnotised by the pattern of the grille covering the opening that they fainted.

Hans Fritzsche: In the cells at Nuremberg

During my first few weeks in Nuremberg gaol I managed to adjust myself to some extent to this new form of captivity. I cannot say that I got used to it, for that implies a certain resignation and I was never resigned to any loss of liberty.

The most striking innovation in my existence as a prisoner was the constant presence of the guard. The three men assigned the duty of watching me relieved one another every three hours, the first shift of the day coming on duty at 8 am: these guards were mere boys; not one of them appeared older than twenty-one and some of them looked barely nineteen and they were all frisky as colts. In different circumstances the still perceptible signs of boyishness in them would have been amusing, though they lacked something of that which, in the old Europe, would have been regarded not as repression but simply as good breeding. In any event they were definitely not of the right material to make good prison warders.

One morning at the time when the trial was just beginning, I was busy washing when I heard a 'Psst! . . .' 'Psst!' I turned, but saw no one; the peep-hole was empty – or was it? No, there was something framed in the opening. I dried my eyes, put on my spectacles and saw – a model gallows! A thread quivered and a figure bearing my likeness (a photograph cut from an illustrated paper) was drawn up and swung from a little gibbet. When I made a movement to snatch this proof of human tact and sympathy, a soldier who had been hovering outside grabbed the thing and bolted. The next moment my guard approached from the opposite direction with the most innocent expression imaginable and gazed at my wet face in apparent astonishment. Mad with rage I bellowed at him that he was a shining example of gentlemanliness and fair play; first he incited others to play a vile practical joke, and then pretended to know nothing about it! The boy flushed furiously and begged me not to give him away. When the officer came on his rounds I kept silent, plunged my face once again into the cold water and gave no sign of anything being amiss. Gradually, my anger cooled, I realised that it was not a case of deliberate cruelty, but simply the result of the unconscious indoctrination practised by the Allies.

A few days later, however, the whole affair came to light. It appeared that some of the other prisoners had also been victims of similar amiable attentions and the Commandant summoned us all to the courtyard and demanded that, in future, any such occurrence should be reported.

There were several other instances of amazing behaviour on the part of the guards; the day, for instance, when Goering asked for the chair which was brought back from the guard room and replaced in the cell every morning. The guard was sitting on it, playing the fool with his truncheon, and he took not the slightest notice of Goering's question which was made in English; whereupon the Field Marshal leant out of the peep-hole, touched the man on the shoulder and said distinctly: 'Give me the chair, please.'

Instantly, the soldier leapt up, thrust back the bolt of the door, and forcing his way into the cell began to belabour Goering with the truncheon which, only a few minutes before, he had been playing with as though it were a toy. I was afraid that Goering would snatch the weapon from the young fellow's hand and throw him out – judging by their comparative physiques it could easily have happened – with all the risks of misconstructions and unforeseen consequences arising. It was probably only for this very reason that Goering kept perfectly quiet, only raising his arms above his head as protection as each blow from the club jerked them down to shoulder-level. I witnessed every detail of this scene which took place in the doorway of Cell No 5, immediately opposite my own spy-hole.

At length, following my repeated shouts for the officer in charge, the Lieutenant on duty emerged from his office, and seizing the enraged guard by the arm, led him away and sent a relief.

This was the only case of actual violence. All the same, every time the guard was changed I looked anxiously to see who my new Cerberus might be, for it was only too evident that identical orders could be very differently interpreted.

No one can expect a young soldier to stand motionless for hours on end; he must obviously find some sort of occupation, and he is unlikely to mind whether it is a quiet one or not. But it made all the difference to us how our guard employed his spare time. If, for instance, he whistled incessantly outside one's cell it was often enough to upset one's entire day. At night it mattered even more; the spot lamps illuminated our cells all night long and almost everything depended on whether the guard chose to direct the light on to our heads or our bodies as we lay in bed. More disturbing still was the flashing of light over one, a treatment that never failed to wake the soundest sleeper. But worst of all were the night noises; we would imagine that we had endured every conceivable variation of sound but there always seemed to be a fresh one.

No clanking steam-engine can compare with the step of a hobnailed boot on flagstones close to one's ear when one is longing for sleep, though things are not much improved when the rhythm is broken by the rattling of the chain at a spy-hole, the jingling of keys, or the bullfrog-like croaking of guards' voices humming in unison some tune from the previous evening's concert party. Sometimes one youth would make a remark, another would get a bit above himself and a regular competition to see who could make the most din would follow. Each sound in itself was harmless enough; collectively the effort was like that most cruel of Chinese tortures, the continual dropping of water till the victim is driven mad. If a prisoner demanded or begged to be left in peace it had no lasting effect even in the case of the more intelligent guards, and with the ill-natured ones it simply caused more row than ever. Our best course was to keep perfectly quiet until sheer exhaustion got the better of frayed nerves; but it cost something! In the end I used to stuff cotton-wool in my ears and, if possible, take something to make me sleep. Everyone knew that it was no good getting upset; but to practise what one preached was no easy matter.

Like almost everybody else, Jodl, Ribbentrop and Streicher were driven nearly crazy by these disturbances. I, on the other hand, suffered even more from another infliction – the rule that one had invariably to face the warder, which meant that at night I had to lie on my right side. It is possible to go to sleep in a certain position if necessary; but nobody can guarantee that he will not turn over while he is unconscious. Someone had issued an order that anyone with his back to the guard was to be wakened, and, since the guard might not enter the cell, this command was carried out either by shouting at the sleeper or by prodding him with the long pole used for opening windows. On the face of it the regulation seemed harmless enough: in reality it imposed an indescribable strain. Doctors, clergymen and lawyers all pressed for its repeal, but in vain. Where security measures were concerned our captors were masters, and remained adamant, declaring that the rule was an indispensable part of the precautions against suicide, and that anyone revoking it must take responsibility for whatever might follow. Naturally no one was prepared to take such a risk, and as a result, the guards, who were at heart good-natured fellows, became a veritable scourge. Their responsible position went to their heads and as long as the trial lasted they seldom missed a chance of demonstrating their efficiency.

There were none the less quite a few of them who, at a pinch, would be satisfied with a glance at the back of a sleeper's head; but there were others who took their orders quite literally. I remember one night when I was trying to make up for lost sleep with the sleeping-draught which was but seldom allowed. Within a marvellously short time I sank into unconsciousness; but for some reason or other I unwittingly turned over on to my fatal left side. A prod from the stick awoke me; again and again the same thing happened and each time it became harder to overcome the bitterness which is infinitely more destructive of repose than outward disturbance. In addition the effect of the sedative was gradually wearing off; each time I was taking longer and longer to get to sleep.

Then, just as the metallic note of the prison clock struck four and I realised with dismay that in a few hours I should have to face a prosecuting counsel who had enjoyed a good night's rest, just, so it seemed, as I was still wondering how I was going to keep my wits about me when the day came, that stick poked me awake for the twentieth time – and my self-control gave.

Shouting with rage I flung aside the blankets and sprang out of bed. The guard, who now had good reason to keep an eye on my movements, raised the lamp so as to get a better view and flattened his nose against the grille. I seized my washbasin and flung its contents at his face; with a clatter the lamp was extinguished and I heard him curse. As he did so I experienced a deep feeling of relief and satisfaction, even though I was fully aware that I should be punished.

Instead the guards from the neighbouring cells came and congratulated me on my excellent aim. Their comrade was soaked to the skin. Respectfully they offered me cigarettes. I scarcely knew whether to laugh or cry; who could have foreseen such an ending to my act of defiance?

§

The prosecution case continued to proceed on a piecemeal basis. The presentation of the conspiracy charge was interrupted on 4 December by the opening of the case on the waging of aggressive war. This was made by Sir Hartley Shawcross, the chief British prosecutor, and for a week the court heard evidence of Germany's invasions of its European neighbours. Then, once the tale had reached Pearl Harbor in 1941, the Americans abruptly began once more to adduce material on those aspects of War Crimes and Crimes against Humanity that touched on the Common Plan.

As if this was all not confusing enough, Jackson's team prefaced the evidence on atrocities with a seemingly irrelevant news film summarising the Nazis' rise to power. It was intended to depict the Nazis as swaggering bullies, but many of the defendants, including Goering, visibly basked in the reflected light of their former glory. Gilbert visited him in prison that evening.

Gustave Gilbert: Defendants' reactions to the newsreel

Goering's cell: Goering was still in fine fettle when I visited him in his cell this evening with Kelley. 'I could save the prosecution a lot of trouble,' he said. 'They don't have to show films and read documents to prove that we rearmed for war. – Of course, we rearmed! – Why, I rearmed Germany until we bristled! – I'm only sorry we didn't rearm still more. – *Of course*, I considered your treaties (just between us) so much toilet paper. – *Of course*, I wanted to make Germany great! If it could be done peacefully, all well and good; if not, that was fine too! Why, my plans against Britain were bigger than they suspect even now. – Just wait till I get up on the stand and tell them – I'd like to see their faces. I didn't want war against Russia in 1939, but I was certainly anxious to attack them before they attacked us, which would have come in 1943 or 1944 anyway.' He was speaking freely and expansively, enjoying the whole thing immensely.

'When they told me that I was playing with war by building up the Luftwaffe, I just told them that I certainly wasn't running a girls' finishing school. I joined the Party precisely because it *was* revolutionary, not because of the ideological stuff. Other parties had made revolutions, so I figured I could get in one on too. – And the thing that pleased me was that the Nazi Party was the only one that had the guts to say *'To hell with Versailles!'* while the others were crawling and appeasing. – That's what got me. Naturally, Hitler was glad to have me because I had a great reputation among the young officers of the first World War. – After all, I was the last commander of the Flying Circus, and quite a drawing card for the Party. – Sure, I'd tell them I was willing to go to war to restore Germany's power. – But I just want to defend myself on one point where my honour is involved – I never gave commands for the execution of those atrocities.'

Ribbentrop's cell: Still half moved to tears, Ribbentrop asked me if I hadn't felt the terrific power of Hitler's personality emanating from the screen. I confessed I hadn't. Ribbentrop talked as if he were again hypnotised by the Fuehrer's figure. 'Do you know, even with all I know, if Hitler should come to me in this cell now, and say "Do this!" – I would still do it. – Isn't it amazing? Can't you really feel the terrific magnetism of his personality?'

§

In the courtroom, Jackson's policy seemed to be to keep as much of the trial in American hands as possible, and thus inevitably there was to be much overlap between the evidence of War Crimes now being presented to bolster Count One and the cases on Counts Three and Four made out later by the French and the Soviets. Yet the organisational failings of the prosecution could not deprive the testimony of its power to shock, as for the first time the horrors of the concentration camps in all their detail were made public, here by one of the American prosecutors, Thomas Dodd.

Trial transcript, 13 December 1945: Thomas Dodd on the 'death ledger' at Mauthausen

We do not wish to dwell on this pathological phase of the Nazi culture, but we do feel compelled to offer one additional exhibit, which we offer as Exhibit USA 254. This exhibit, which is on the table, is a human head with the skull bone removed, shrunken, stuffed, and preserved. The Nazis had one of their many victims decapitated, after having had him hanged, apparently for fraternising with a German woman, and fashioned this terrible ornament from his head.

The last paragraph of the official United States Army report from which I have just read deals with the manner in which this exhibit was acquired. It reads as follows:–

'There I also saw the shrunken heads of two young Poles who had been hanged for having relations with German girls. The heads were the size of a fist, and the hair and the marks of the rope were still there.' . . .

We have no accurate estimate of how many persons died in these concentration camps and perhaps none will ever be made, though as the evidence already introduced before this Tribunal indicates, the Nazi conspirators were generally meticulous record keepers. But the records which they kept about concentration camps appear to have been quite incomplete. Perhaps the character of the records resulted from the indifference which the Nazis felt for the lives of their victims. But occasionally we find a death book or a set of index cards. For the most part, nevertheless, the victims apparently faded into an unrecorded death. Reference to a set of death books suggests at once the scale of the concentration camp operations, and we refer now and offer Document 493-PS as Exhibit USA 251. This exhibit is a set of seven books, the death ledger of the Mauthausen concentration camp. Each book has on its cover the word *Totenbuch* or 'Death Book' – Mauthausen.

In these books were recorded the names of some of the inmates who died or were murdered in this camp, and the books cover the period from January, 1939 to April, 1945. They give the name, the place of birth, the assigned cause of death, and time of death of each individual recorded. In addition each corpse is assigned a serial number, and adding up the total serial numbers for the five-year period one arrives at the figure of 35,318.

An examination of the books is very revealing in so far as the camp's routine of death is concerned, and I invite the attention of the Tribunal to Volume 5 from Pages 568 to 582, a photostatic copy of which has been passed to the Tribunal. These pages cover death entries made for the 19th March, 1945, between 1.15 in the morning and 2 o'clock in the afternoon. In this space of 12¾ hours, on these records, 203 persons are reported as having died. They were assigned serial numbers running from 8390 to 8592. The names of the dead are listed. And interestingly enough the victims are all recorded as having died of the same ailment – heart trouble. They died at brief intervals. They died in alphabetical order. The first who died was a man named Ackermann, who died at 1.15 a.m., and the last was a man named Zynger, who died at 2 o'clock in the afternoon.

§

In the autumn of 1940, the Governor of Poland, Hans Frank, had authorised the building of a sealed ghetto in Warsaw into which eventually several hundred thousand of Poland's Jews were herded. By the spring of 1943, all but about 50,000 of these had been deported to death camps, notably that at Treblinka. On 19 April, SS troops and other units under the command of Major-General Jurgen Stroop began to obliterate the ghetto block by block in an attempt to eliminate these remnants of Polish Jewry. Many of them offered heroic if vain resistance. Stroop chronicled the success of his action in a handsomely bound report, extracts from which were read to the court by American prosecutor Major William Walsh.

Trial transcript, 14 December 1945: The destruction of the Warsaw ghetto

MAJOR WILLIAM WALSH: According to this report, the ghetto, which was established in Warsaw in November 1940, was inhabited by about 400,000 Jews; and prior to the action for the destruction of this ghetto, some 316,000 had already been deported. The Court will note that this report is approximately 75 pages in length, and the Prosecution believes that the contents are of such striking evidentiary value that no part should be omitted from the permanent records of the Tribunal and that the Tribunal should consider the entire report in judging the guilt of these defendants.

. . . From Page 6 of the translation before the Court of Document 1061-PS I would like to read the boastful but nonetheless vivid account of some of this ruthless action within the Warsaw ghetto. I quote, second paragraph, Page 6:

'The resistance put up by the Jews and bandits could be broken only by the relentless and energetic use of our shocktroops by day and night. On 23 April 1943 the Reichsfuehrer SS issued through the Higher SS and Police Leader East at Krakow his order to complete the combing out of the Warsaw ghetto with the greatest severity and relentless tenacity. I therefore decided to destroy the entire Jewish residential area by setting every block on fire, including the blocks of residential buildings near the armament works. One building after the other was systematically evacuated and subsequently destroyed by fire. The Jews then emerged from their hiding places and dugouts in almost every case. Not infrequently the Jews stayed in the burning buildings until, because of the heat and the fear of being burned alive, they preferred to jump down from the upper floor after having thrown mattresses and other upholstered articles into the street from the burning buildings. With their bones broken they still tried to crawl across the street into blocks of buildings which had not yet been set on fire or were only partially in flames. Often the Jews changed their hiding places during the night by moving into the rooms of burnt-out buildings, taking refuge there until they were found by our patrols. Their stay in the sewers also ceased to be pleasant after the first week. Frequently from the street we could hear loud voices coming through the sewer shafts. Then the men of the Waffen-SS, the Police, or the Wehrmacht Engineers courageously climbed down the shafts to bring out the Jews and not infrequently they then stumbled over Jews already dead or were shot at. It was always necessary to use smoke candles to drive out the Jews. Thus one day we opened 183 sewer entrance holes and at a fixed time lowered smoke candles into them, with the result that the bandits fled from what they believed to be gas into the centre of the former ghetto, where they could then be pulled out of the sewer holes there. A great number of Jews who could not be counted were exterminated by blowing up sewers and dugouts.

'The longer the resistance lasted, the tougher the men of the Waffen-SS, Police, and Wehrmacht became. They fulfilled their duty indefatigably in faithful comradeship and stood together as models and examples of soldiers. Their duty hours often lasted from early morning until late at night. At night search patrols, with rags wound around their feet, remained at the heels of the Jews and gave them no respite. Not infrequently they caught and killed Jews who used the night hours for supplementing their stores from abandoned dugouts and for contacting neighbouring groups or exchanging news with them.

'Considering that the greater part of the men of the Waffen-SS had only been trained for three to four weeks before being assigned to this action, high credit should be given to the pluck, courage, and devotion to duty which they showed. It must be stated that the Wehrmacht Engineers, too, executed the blowing up of dugouts, sewers, and concrete buildings with indefatigability and great devotion to duty. Officers and men of the Police, a large part of whom had already been at the front, again excelled by their dashing spirit.

'Only through the continuous and untiring work of all involved did we succeed in catching a total of 56,065 Jews whose extermination can be proved. To this should be added the number of Jews who lost their lives in explosions or fires but whose number could not be ascertained.'

THE PRESIDENT: Major Walsh, in the section that you are just upon now, ought you not to read the opening paragraphs of this document, which set out the amount of the losses of the German troops?

MAJOR WALSH: I will do so, Sir. On Page 1 of the translation, I quote. The title: 'The Warsaw Ghetto is no more.'

'For the Fuehrer and their country the following fell in the battle for the destruction of Jews and bandits in the former Jewish residential area of Warsaw.

'Fifteen are thereafter listed.

'Furthermore, the Polish Police Sergeant Julian Zielenski, born 13 November 1891, 8th Commissariat, fell on 19 April 1943 while fulfilling his duty. They gave their utmost, their life. We shall never forget them.

'The following were wounded . . .'

Then follow the names of 60 Waffen-SS personnel, 11 watchmen from training camps (probably Lithuanians), 12 Security Police officers in SS units, 5 men of the Polish Police, and 2 soldiers of the Wehrmacht Engineers.

Permit me to read some brief excerpts of the daily teletype reports. Page 13 of the translation, from the teletype message of 22 April 1943, I read:

'Our setting the block on fire achieved the result in the course of the night that those Jews whom we had not been able to find despite all our search operations left their hideouts under the roofs, in the cellars, and elsewhere and appeared on the outside of the building, trying to escape the flames anyhow. Masses of them – entire families – were already aflame and jumped from the windows or endeavoured to let themselves down by means of sheets tied together or the like. Steps had been taken so that these Jews as well as the remaining ones were liquidated at once.'

And from Page 28 of the translation, the last part of the first paragraph, I read:

'When the blocks of buildings mentioned above were destroyed, 120 Jews were caught and numerous Jews were destroyed when they jumped from the attics to the inner courtyards, trying to escape the flames. Many more Jews perished in the flames or were destroyed when the dugouts and sewer entrances were blown up.'

And on Page 30, second half of the second paragraph, I read:

'Not until the blocks of buildings were well aflame and were about to collapse did a considerable number of Jews emerge, forced to do so by the flames and the smoke. Time and again the Jews tried to escape even through burning buildings. Innumerable Jews whom we saw on the roofs during the conflagration perished in the flames. Others emerged from the upper storeys in the last possible moment and were only able to escape death from the flames by jumping down. Today we caught a total of 2,283 Jews of whom 204 were shot; and innumerable Jews were destroyed in dugouts and in the flames.'

And from Page 34, the second paragraph, I read, beginning the second line:

'The Jews testify that they emerge at night to get fresh air, since it is unbearable to stay permanently within the dugouts owing to the long duration of the operation. On the average the raiding parties shoot 30 to 50 Jews each night. From these statements it was to be inferred that a considerable number of Jews are still underground in the ghetto. Today we blew up a concrete building which we had not been able to destroy by fire. In this operation we learned that the blowing up of a building is a very lengthy process and takes an enormous amount of explosives. The best and only method for destroying the Jews therefore still remains the setting of fires.'

And from Page 35, the last part of the second paragraph, I read:

'Some depositions speak of three to four thousand Jews still remaining in underground holes, sewers, and dugouts. The undersigned is resolved not to terminate the large-scale operation until the last Jew has been destroyed.'

And from the teletype message of 15 May 1943 on Page 44, we gather that the operation is in its last stage. I read the end of the first paragraph on Page 44:

'A special unit once more searched the last block of buildings, which was still intact, in the ghetto and subsequently destroyed it. In the evening the chapel, mortuary, and all other buildings in the Jewish cemetery there blown up or destroyed by fire.'

On 24 May 1943 the final figures have been compiled by Major General Stroop. He reports on Page 45, last paragraph:

'Of the total of 56,065 caught, about 7,000 were destroyed in the former Jewish residential area during large-scale operations; 6,929 Jews were destroyed by transporting them to T. II' – which we believe to be Treblinka, Camp Number 2, which will later be referred to – 'the sum total of Jews destroyed is therefore 13,929. Beyond the number of 56,065 an estimated number of 5,000 to 6,000 Jews were destroyed by being blown up or by perishing in the flames.'

Later December 1945:
The case against the organisations

On 17 December, the Americans moved on to the cases against the indicted organisations, including the SS. This had originated as Hitler's personal bodyguard, but had evolved into the Nazi Party's racial and military elite, with its armed units, which were used for much of the genocidal killing in the East, effectively a parallel army alongside the regular Wehrmacht. One of its former members, Alfred Naujocks, testified to the SS's close co-operation with two other arms of repression on trial, the SD (State Security Service) and the Gestapo. Here he reveals how he was ordered to help fabricate the frontier incident that gave Hitler the excuse to order the invasion of Poland.

Trial transcript, 20 December 1945: Alfred Naujocks on Hitler's excuse to invade Poland

On or about 10 August 1939 the Chief of the Sipo and SD, Heydrich, personally ordered me to simulate an attack on the [German] radio station near Gleiwitz, near the Polish border, and to make it appear that the attacking force consisted of Poles. Heydrich said: 'Actual proof of these attacks of the Poles is needed for the foreign press, as well as for German propaganda purposes.' I was directed to go to Gleiwitz with five or six SD men and wait there until I received a code word from Heydrich indicating that the attack should take place. My instructions were to seize the radio station and to hold it long enough to permit a Polish-speaking German, who would be put at my disposal, to broadcast a speech in Polish. Heydrich told me that this speech should state that the time had come for the conflict between the Germans and the Poles and that the Poles should get together and strike down any Germans from whom they met resistance. Heydrich also told me at this time that he expected an attack on Poland by Germany in a few days.

I went to Gleiwitz and waited there a fortnight. Then I requested permission of Heydrich to return to Berlin but was told to stay in Gleiwitz. Between the 25th and 31st of August I went to see Heinrich Mueller, head of the Gestapo, who was then nearby at Oppeln. In my presence Mueller discussed with a man named Mehlhorn plans for another border incident, in which it should be made to appear that Polish soldiers were attacking German troops . . . Mueller stated that he had twelve or thirteen condemned criminals who were to be dressed in Polish uniforms and left dead on the ground at the scene of the incident to show that they had been killed while attacking. For this purpose they were to be given fatal injections by a doctor employed by Heydrich. Then they were also to be given gunshot wounds. After the assault members of the press and other persons were to be taken to the spot of the incident. A police report was subsequently to be prepared.

Mueller told me that he had an order from Heydrich to make one of those criminals available to me for the action at Gleiwitz. The code name by which he referred to these criminals was 'Canned Goods'.

The incident at Gleiwitz in which I participated was carried out on the evening preceding the German attack on Poland. As I recall war broke out on the 1st of September 1939. At noon on the 31st of August I received by telephone from Heydrich the code word for the attack which was to take place at 8 o'clock that evening. Heydrich said, 'In order to carry out this attack, report to Mueller for "Canned Goods".' I did this and gave Mueller instructions to deliver the man near the radio station. I received this man and had him laid down at the entrance to the station. He was alive, but he was completely unconscious. I tried to open his eyes. I could not recognise by his eyes that he was alive, only by his breathing. I did not see the shot wounds, but a lot of blood was smeared across his face. He was in civilian clothes.

We seized the radio station as ordered, broadcast a speech of three to four minutes over an emergency transmitter, fired some pistol shots, and left.

§

Part of the case against the SS consisted of evidence of the involvement of their doctors in experiments on the inmates of concentration camps. Here, another of the American prosecutors, Major Warren Farr, reads to the court from a report on one such perversion of science.

Trial transcript, 20 December 1945: Major Warren Farr on SS doctors' experiments

'On 11 September 1944, in the presence of SS Sturmbannfuehrer Dr Ding, Dr Widmann, and the undersigned, experiments with aconite nitrate bullets were carried out on five persons who had been sentenced to death. The calibre of the bullets used was 7.65 millimetres, and they were filled with poison in crystal form. Each subject of the experiment received one shot in the upper part of the left thigh, while in a horizontal position. In the case of two persons, the bullets passed clean through the upper part of the thigh. Even later no effect from the poison could be seen. These two subjects were therefore rejected.'

I omit the next few sentences and proceed beginning with Paragraph 3 of the report:

'The symptoms shown by the three condemned persons were surprisingly the same. At first, nothing special was noticeable. After 20 to 25 minutes, a disturbance of the motor nerves and a light flow of saliva began, but both stopped again. After 40 to 44 minutes, a strong flow of saliva appeared. The poisoned persons swallowed frequently; later the flow of saliva is so strong that it can no longer be controlled by swallowing. Foamy saliva flows from the mouth. Then a sensation of choking and vomiting starts.'

The next three paragraphs describe in coldly scientific fashion the reactions of the dying persons. The description then continues, and I want to quote the two paragraphs before the conclusion. It is the last paragraph on Page 1 of the translation, the sixth paragraph of the report:

'At the same time there was pronounced nausea. One of the poisoned persons tried in vain to vomit. In order to succeed he put four fingers of his hand, up to the main joint, right into his mouth. In spite of this, no vomiting occurred. His face became quite red.

'The faces of the other two subjects were already pale at an early stage. Other symptoms were the same. Later on the disturbances of the motor nerves increased so much that the persons threw themselves up and down, rolled their eyes, and made aimless movements with their hands and arms. At last the disturbance subsided, the pupils were enlarged to the maximum, the condemned lay still. Rectal cramps and loss of urine was observed in one of them. Death occurred 121, 123, and 129 minutes after they were shot.'

On 20 December the Tribunal adjourned for a ten-day break over Christmas. Many of the prosecution staff took the opportunity to escape the depressing environs of Nuremberg. Jackson made a quick tour of the Holy Land, while Birkett and Biddle spent the holiday together in England, reading poetry to each other. For the defendants, however, it meant a fortnight largely confined to their cells, their boredom and fears relieved only by a church service on Christmas Eve. Goering is said to have wept as he sang 'Silent Night'.

§

Before the trial had even begun, Colonel Andrus, the rather pernickety officer responsible for the prison, had faced a crisis. Among those indicted had been Robert Ley, the former head of the Labour Front, the sole trade union permitted by the Nazis, all others having been amalgamated with it. The Front regulated workers' wages and controlled many other aspects of their lives, such as their recreation, organised by the Strength Through Joy movement. Ley had for many years been an oafish womaniser, but he had been much disturbed by the recent death of his wife, and despair now lent him ingenuity.

The only privacy afforded the prisoners in their small, bare cells was the lavatory, tucked away in a corner by the entrance where only the user's feet could be seen by a guard looking through the small hatch in the door. A few days after being handed the indictment, Ley gagged himself with his underpants, made a noose from the zipper of his jacket, and by attaching it to the water tank let his weight strangle him when he sat down on the lavatory seat.

Anxious that another of his charges should not escape justice in similar fashion, Andrus had their cells searched regularly in the months that followed, as he later related in his memoirs. His efforts were rewarded with a haul that revealed the resourcefulness and desperation of those on trial.

Colonel Burton Andrus: Guarding the prisoners at Nuremberg

We had already lost Dr Ley and Dr Conti [head of the euthanasia programme, held at the prison but not indicted], who had chosen death by their own hands rather than face the possibility of hanging. Who else would try it?

Now that the prisoners had contact with outsiders, the risks were greater. Some fine German counsel represented these men. They were legally and politically respected, most of them, but we had to be suspicious of all. Every document that had to be passed between counsel and accused was examined and passed through a guard. Though the prisoners were watched at every step they made and every sleeping breath they took, they were still finding opportunities to smuggle potential suicide weapons into their cells.

We had taken away all that could be used for suicide – their razors, ties, shoe-laces, and, at night, spectacles. (They could have spectacles and neck-ties in court, for there was no chance of a successful suicide attempt with them there.) When they returned to the prison each day, they were searched. When they bathed, their underclothing and suits were taken away and examined, and they were given fresh laundry. After bathing, their bodies were searched as well. While they were out of their cells, every possible hiding place was dug into.

And still we were finding contraband.

We had raided the cells of Hess, Goering, Jodl, von Ribbentrop, and Keitel the day the trial started. The searchers found:

Ribbentrop had two tablets (one large, one small), three half-tablets, and four larger tablets wrapped in tissue paper concealed in one of his garters, and one sharp piece of metal measuring one and a half by two inches.

Jodl's cell had one nail, one piece of wire six inches long and one-sixteenth of an inch in diameter, tooth powder, nine assorted tablets, and some stringy rags.

Keitel had hidden away one small piece of sheet-metal, one tube of aspirin tablets, one tube of belladonna tablets, one half-inch screw, and two nails. Goering and Hess were 'clean'.

The austere and pompous Doenitz, who had deliberately informed me that he was the man who had taken over as head of the Reich when Hitler had committed suicide (and therefore should warrant 'special treatment'), had secreted during his stay five shoe-laces tied together, part of a bobby-pin, a screw, and some string. We had no idea what he was planning to do with them. Von Neurath during the year had hidden a steel screwdriver sharp enough to cut an artery and large enough to choke him; Jodl had a nail in his tobacco-pouch; Schacht had a yard-long length of cord and ten paper-clips; Sauckel a broken-off, sharp-edged spoon. In other parts of the cell-block we found a piece of razor-blade and a tiny fragment of glass. On the floor of the dock, searching guards discovered two small nails and two small pieces of broken glass.

Keitel was caught smuggling once more during the trial. His guard, watching him through the cell peephole, saw him hide a shining object in his wallet. He entered the cell and then, with another guard, searched the old army man. Keitel innocently turned out his wallet, but he held one corner tightly with his thumb. The wallet was taken away from him, and a worn piece of metal fell out. It was not from Keitel's shoe. Where had it come from? 'I have had it for a long time,' said Keitel stiffly. But he would say no more.

We were examining every object that came into the jail, whether it was food, clothing or equipment. When a large green suitcase arrived it was, of course, opened. It was addressed to a witness we were holding. Out tumbled a black robe, white shirt, various other pieces of clothing, and a small case. The case was prised open to reveal a complete suicide kit: a vial of the Nazis' favourite potassium cyanide, hypodermic needles, a syringe. My inadequate staff was already overburdened with work, so I decided to take the strain off them. I banned further packages of clothing or food being sent to the prisoners from outside.

Early January 1946: The trial reopens after the Christmas break

The court met again at the start of January, with the weather so bitter that when the heating for the courtroom broke down the lawyers took to wearing several pairs of tights under their trousers. As the case against the security forces of the Reich continued to be made, the world was appalled to learn of the meticulous planning, and the sheer scale, of the Holocaust.

By the summer of 1942, 52,000 Slovakian Jews had been rounded up and sent to Poland as 'workers'. When they heard no news of them, their relatives began to wonder what had happened. The Slovakian Government, ignorant of their fate, asked their adviser on the 'Jewish problem', Dieter Wisliceny of the RSHA, the umbrella organisation that oversaw the German security services, to make enquiries. Just as in the dark as they, he was asked by American counsel Lt-Col. Smith Brookhart to tell the court what had happened when he went to see his superior, Adolf Eichmann.

Trial transcript, 3 January 1946: Eichmann and the order for the Final Solution

DIETER WISLICENY: Then at the end of July or the beginning of August, I went to see him in Berlin and implored him once more to grant the request of the Slovakian Government [to send representatives to the workers' supposed lodgings in Poland]. I pointed out to him that abroad there were rumours to the effect that all Jews in Poland were being exterminated. I pointed out to him that the Pope had intervened with the Slovakian Government on their behalf. I advised him that such a proceeding, if really true, would seriously injure our prestige, that is, the prestige of Germany, abroad. For all these reasons I begged him to permit the inspection in question. After a lengthy discussion Eichmann told me that this request to visit the Polish ghettos could not be granted under any circumstances whatsoever. In reply to my question 'Why?' he said that most of these Jews were no longer alive. I asked him who had given such instructions and he referred me to an order of Himmler's. I then begged him to show me this order, because I could not believe that it actually existed in writing . . . Eichmann told me he could show me this order in writing if it would soothe my conscience. He took a small volume of documents from his safe, turned over the pages, and showed me a letter from Himmler to the Chief of the Security Police and the SD. The gist of the letter was roughly as follows:

The Fuehrer had ordered the final solution of the Jewish question; the Chief of the Security Police and the SD and the Inspector of Concentration Camps were entrusted with carrying out this so-called final solution. All Jewish men and women who were able to work were to be temporarily exempted from the so-called final solution and used for work in the concentration camps. This letter was signed by Himmler himself. I could not possibly be mistaken since Himmler's signature was well known to me . . .

LT-COL. BROOKHART: Was any question asked by you as to the meaning of the words 'final solution' as used in the order?

WISLICENY: Eichmann went on to explain to me what was meant by this. He said that the planned biological annihilation of the Jewish race in the Eastern Territories was disguised by the concept and wording 'final solution'. In later discussions on this subject the same words 'final solution' appeared over and over again . . .

LT-COL. BROOKHART: Did you make any comment to Eichmann about his authority?

WISLICENY: Yes. It was perfectly clear to me that this order spelled death to millions of people. I said to Eichmann, 'God grant that our enemies never have the opportunity of doing the same to the German people,' in reply to which Eichmann told me not to be sentimental; it was an order of the Fuehrer's and would have to be carried out . . . This order was in force until October 1944. At that time Himmler gave a counter order which forbade the annihilation of the Jews.

LT-COL. BROOKHART: Who was Chief of the Reichssicherheits-hauptamt (RSHA) at the time the order was first issued?

WISLICENY: That would be Heydrich.

LT-COL. BROOKHART: Did the programme under this order continue with equal force under Kaltenbrunner?

WISLICENY: Yes; there was no diminution or change of any kind . . .

LT-COL. BROOKHART: In your meetings with the other specialists on the Jewish problem and Eichmann did you gain any knowledge or information as to the total number of Jews killed under this programme?

WISLICENY: Eichmann personally always talked about at least 4 million Jews. Sometimes he even mentioned 5 million. According to my own estimate I should say that at least 4 million must have been destined for the so-called final solution. How many of those actually survived, I am not in a position to say.

LT-COL. BROOKHART: When did you last see Eichmann?

WISLICENY: I last saw Eichmann towards the end of February 1945 in Berlin. At that time he said that if the war were lost he would commit suicide.

LT-COL. BROOKHART: Did he say anything at that time as to the number of Jews that had been killed?

WISLICENY: Yes, he expressed this in a particularly cynical manner. He said he would leap laughing into the grave because the feeling that he had 5 million people on his conscience would be for him a source of extraordinary satisfaction.

Though evidence about the Holocaust featured prominently at Nuremberg, to an extent the prosecution failed at the time to appreciate its uniquely genocidal nature. This was in part due to the Soviets' refusal to agree that the murder of the Jews was distinguishable as a programme from the Nazis' treatment of other groups of political and racial undesirables, such as Slavs and commissars, and in part because the Allies had failed to capture Eichmann, whose role was only beginning to be understood and who, far from committing suicide, had fled to Argentina. He was to be finally apprehended by Israeli secret service agents in 1960. So unfocused was much of the case relating to the Jews – the evidence of Hoess, the commandant of Auschwitz, came out in public only because he was called as a defence witness for Kaltenbrunner – that one begins to wonder what part the anti-Semitic tendencies of both the Soviet and French states played in glossing over at times the institutional nature of their persecution.

There has been much debate about whether a written order for the destruction of the Jews was ever given, and if so whether its ultimate origin was Hitler himself rather than, say, Heinrich Himmler, the head of the SS and the Gestapo. There seems no good reason to doubt Wisliceny's evidence, in as far as it goes, just as there seem few grounds to doubt that many of the defendants had known or suspected more at the time than they now admitted. From the earliest, all denied being aware of any plan for the Final Solution, and despite the evidence produced day after day after day, many of them continued to deny that it had happened at all.

§

Following the German invasion of the Soviet Union in 1941, the Nazis began to implement their genocidal policies against its populations of Jews and Gypsies. Rather than being moved to camps, more than a million people in the Baltic, the Ukraine, the Crimea and Belarus were rounded up by special task forces or Einsatzgruppen and shot, hundreds at a time, before being buried in mass graves. Many of the squads' members were SS, and they were controlled by the Reich Security Main Office (RSHA), headed first by Reinhard Heydrich and later by one of the defendants, Ernst Kaltenbrunner.

Otto Ohlendorf had led a mobile Einsatzgruppe in southern Ukraine from 1941 to 1942. Called as a witness on 3 January to establish Kaltenbrunner's place in the chain of command, he told the court that his troops had slaughtered 90,000 people in a year.

Trial transcript, 3 January 1945: Mass murder in the East

OTTO OHLENDORF: I was present at two mass executions for purposes of inspection.

COL. AMEN: Will you explain to the Tribunal in detail how an individual mass execution was carried out?

OHLENDORF: A local Einsatzkommando attempted to collect all the Jews in its area by registering them. This registration was performed by the Jews themselves.

COL. AMEN: On what pretext, if any, were they rounded up?

OHLENDORF: On the pretext that they were to be resettled.

COL. AMEN: Will you continue?

OHLENDORF: After the registration the Jews were collected at one place; and from there they were later transported to the place of execution, which was, as a rule an antitank ditch or a natural excavation. The executions were carried out in a military manner, by firing squads under command.

COL. AMEN: In what way were they transported to the place of execution?

OHLENDORF: They were transported to the place of execution in trucks, always only as many as could be executed immediately. In this way it was attempted to keep the span of time from the moment in which the victims knew what was about to happen to them until the time of their actual execution as short as possible.

COL. AMEN: Was that your idea?

OHLENDORF: Yes.

COL. AMEN: And after they were shot what was done with the bodies?

OHLENDORF: The bodies were buried in the antitank ditch or excavation.

COL. AMEN: What determination, if any, was made as to whether the persons were actually dead?

OHLENDORF: The unit leaders or the firing-squad commanders had orders to see to this and, if need be, finish them off themselves.

COL. AMEN: And who would do that?

OHLENDORF: Either the unit leader himself or somebody designated by him.

COL. AMEN: In what positions were the victims shot?

OHLENDORF: Standing or kneeling.

COL. AMEN: What was done with the personal property and clothing of the persons executed?

OHLENDORF: All valuables were confiscated at the time of the registration or the rounding up and handed over to the Finance Ministry, either through the RSHA or directly . . .

COL. AMEN: All their personal property was registered at the time?

OHLENDORF: No, not all of it, only valuables were registered.

COL. AMEN: What happened to the garments which the victims were wearing when they went to the place of execution?

OHLENDORF: They were obliged to take off their outer garments immediately before the execution.

COL. AMEN: All of them?

OHLENDORF: The outer garments, yes.

COL. AMEN: How about the rest of the garments they were wearing?

OHLENDORF: The other garments remained on the bodies.

COL. AMEN: Was that true of not only your group but of the other Einsatz groups?

OHLENDORF: That was the order in my Einsatzgruppe. I don't know how it was done in other Einsatzgruppen.

COL. AMEN: In what way did they handle it?

OHLENDORF: Some of the unit leaders did not carry out the liquidation in the military manner, but killed the victims singly by shooting them in the back of the neck.

COL. AMEN: And you objected to that procedure?

OHLENDORF: I was against that procedure, yes.

COL. AMEN: For what reason?

OHLENDORF: Because both for the victims and for those who carried out the executions, it was, psychologically, an immense burden to bear.

COL. AMEN: Now, what was done with the property collected by the Einsatzkommandos from these victims?

OHLENDORF: All valuables were sent to Berlin, to the RSHA or to the Reich Ministry of Finance. The articles which could be used in the operational area were disposed of there.

COL. AMEN: For example, what happened to gold and silver taken from the victims?

OHLENDORF: That was, as I have just said, turned over to Berlin, to the Reich Ministry of Finance.

COL. AMEN: How do you know that?

OHLENDORF: I can remember that it was actually handled in that way from Simferopol.

COL. AMEN: How about watches, for example, taken from the victims?

OHLENDORF: At the request of the Army, watches were made available to the forces at the front.

COL. AMEN: Were all victims, including the men, women, and children, executed in the same manner?

OHLENDORF: Until the spring of 1942, yes. Then an order came from Himmler that in the future women and children were to be killed only in gas vans.

COL. AMEN: How had the women and children been killed previously?

OHLENDORF: In the same way as the men – by shooting.

COL. AMEN: What, if anything, was done about burying the victims after they had been executed?

OHLENDORF: The Kommandos filled the graves to efface the signs of the execution, and then labour units of the population levelled them.

COL. AMEN: Referring to the gas vans which you said you received in the spring of 1942, what order did you receive with respect to the use of these vans?

OHLENDORF: These gas vans were in future to be used for the killing of women and children.

COL. AMEN: Will you explain to the Tribunal the construction of these vans and their appearance?

OHLENDORF: The actual purpose of these vans could not be seen from the outside. They looked like closed trucks, and were so constructed that at the start of the motor, gas was conducted into the van causing death in 10 to 15 minutes.

COL. AMEN: Explain in detail just how one of these vans was used for an execution.

OHLENDORF: The vans were loaded with the victims and driven to the place of burial, which was usually the same as that used for the mass executions. The time needed for transportation was sufficient to ensure the death of the victims.

COL. AMEN: How were the victims induced to enter the vans?

OHLENDORF: They were told that they were to be transported to another locality.

COL. AMEN: How was the gas turned on?

OHLENDORF: I am not familiar with the technical details.

COL. AMEN: How long did it take to kill the victims ordinarily?

OHLENDORF About 10 to 15 minutes; the victims were not conscious of what was happening to them.

COL. AMEN: How many persons could be killed simultaneously in one such van?

OHLENDORF: About 15 to 25 persons. The vans varied in size.

COL. AMEN: Did you receive reports from those persons operating these vans from time to time?

OHLENDORF: I didn't understand the question.

COL. AMEN: Did you receive reports from those who were working on the vans?

OHLENDORF: I received the report that the Einsatzkommandos did not willingly use the vans.

COL. AMEN: Why not?

OHLENDORF: Because the burial of the victims was a great ordeal for the members of the Einsatzkommandos . . .

Ohlendorf was then questioned by Ludwig Babel, defending counsel for the SS and SD.

HERR BABEL: You personally were not concerned with the execution of these orders?

OHLENDORF: I led the Einsatzgruppe, and therefore I had the task of seeing how the Einsatzkommandos executed the orders received.

HERR BABEL: But did you have no scruples in regard to the execution of these orders?

OHLENDORF: Yes, of course.

HERR BABEL: And how is it that they were carried out regardless of these scruples?

OHLENDORF: Because to me it is inconceivable that a sub-ordinate leader should not carry out orders given by the leaders of the state.

HERR BABEL: This is your own opinion. But this must have been not only your point of view but also the point of view of the majority of the people involved. Didn't some of the men appointed to execute these orders ask you to be relieved of such tasks?

OHLENDORF: I cannot remember any one concrete case. I excluded some whom I did not consider emotionally suitable for executing these tasks and I sent some of them home.

HERR BABEL: Was the legality of the orders explained to these people under false pretences?

OHLENDORF: I do not understand your question; since the order was issued by the superior authorities, the question of legality could not arise in the minds of these individuals, for they had sworn obedience to the people who had issued the orders.

HERR BABEL: Could any individual expect to succeed in evading the execution of these orders?

OHLENDORF: No, the result would have been a court-martial with a corresponding sentence.

§

Among the indicted organisations was the OKW, the German High Command. The prosecution, here in the form of Colonel Telford Taylor, sought to show that it was implicated, both at staff level and through the actions of the Wehrmacht, in war crimes and crimes against humanity. General Erich von dem Bach-Zelewski – a veteran Nazi – had commanded the SS and the police in the central sector of the Russian Front at the start of the Einsatzgruppen campaign in 1941. He also had charge of anti-partisan operations — often used as cover for racial killings – in the course of which savage reprisals were inflicted on civilian populations that aided those resisting the invaders.

Trial transcript, 7 January 1946: 'A wild state of anarchy'

COL. TAYLOR: In the course of your duties did you confer with the commanders of army groups and armies on the Eastern Front?

ERICH VON DEM BACH-ZELEWSKI: With the commanders of the army groups, not of the armies, and with the district commanders of the Wehrmacht.

COL. TAYLOR: Did you advise these commanders with respect to the methods which should be employed to combat partisans?

VON DEM BACH-ZELEWSKI: Yes . . .

COL. TAYLOR: What proportion of Wehrmacht troops was used in anti-partisan operations as compared to Police and SS troops?

VON DEM BACH-ZELEWSKI: Since the number of Police and SS troops was very small, anti-partisan operations were undertaken mainly by Wehrmacht formations.

COL. TAYLOR: Were the anti-partisan troops usually commanded by Wehrmacht officers or by SS officers?

VON DEM BACH-ZELEWSKI: It varied, depending mostly on the individual area; in the operational areas Wehrmacht officers nearly always commanded, but an order existed to the effect that the formation, be it Wehrmacht, Waffen-SS or Police, which supplied the most troops for a particular operation, had command of it.

COL. TAYLOR: Did the highest military leaders issue instructions that anti-partisan operations were to be conducted with severity?

VON DEM BACH-ZELEWSKI: Yes.

COL. TAYLOR: Did the highest military authorities issue any detailed instructions as to the methods to be used in anti-partisan operations?

VON DEM BACH-ZELEWSKI: No.

COL. TAYLOR: What was the result, in the occupied territories, of this lack of detailed directives from above?

VON DEM BACH-ZELEWSKI: This lack of detailed directives resulted in a wild state of anarchy in all anti-partisan operations.

COL. TAYLOR: In your opinion, were the measures taken in anti-partisan operations far more severe than the circumstances warranted, or were they not?

VON DEM BACH-ZELEWSKI: Since there were no definite orders and the lower commanders were forced to act independently, the operations varied according to the character of the officer in command and the quality of the troops. I am of the opinion that the operations often not only failed in their purpose but even overshot their mark.

COL. TAYLOR: Did these measures result in the unnecessary killing of large numbers of the civilian population?

VON DEM BACH-ZELEWSKI: Yes.

COL. TAYLOR: Did you report these excessive measures to the commanders of the army groups and other Wehrmacht officers with whom you worked?

VON DEM BACH-ZELEWSKI: This state of affairs was generally known. There was no necessity to make a special report about it, since every operation had immediately to be reported in all detail, and was known to every responsible leader . . .

COL. TAYLOR: Was an order ever issued by the highest authorities, that German soldiers who committed offences against the civilian population were not to be punished in the military courts?

VON DEM BACH-ZELEWSKI: Yes, this order was issued.

COL. TAYLOR: Was this order an obstacle to correcting the excesses of the troops?

VON DEM BACH-ZELEWSKI: Yes, in my opinion this order prevented the orderly conduct of operations, since one can train troops only if one has adequate disciplinary powers and jurisdiction over them and is able to check excesses.

Von dem Bach-Zelewski also testified that in 1941 Himmler had made a speech stating that the purpose of invading Russia would be to reduce the Slav population by 30 million. Alfred Thoma was defence counsel for Alfred Rosenberg, the fount of much of the Nazis' thinking on race.

DR THOMA: Do you believe that Himmler's speech, in which he demanded the extermination of 30 million Slavs, expressed only his personal opinion; or do you consider that it corresponded to the National Socialist ideology?

VON DEM BACH-ZELEWSKI: Today I believe that it was the logical consequence of our ideology.

DR THOMA: Today?

VON DEM BACH-ZELEWSKI: Today.

DR THOMA: What was your own opinion at that time?

VON DEM BACH-ZELEWSKI: It is difficult for a German to fight through to this conviction. It took me a long time.

DR THOMA: Then how is it that a few days ago a witness, namely, the witness Ohlendorf, appeared here and admitted that through the Einsatzgruppen he had killed 90,000 people, but told the Tribunal that this did not harmonise with the National Socialist ideology?

VON DEM BACH-ZELEWSKI: I am of a different opinion. If for years, for decades, a doctrine is preached to the effect that the Slav race is an inferior race, that the Jews are not even human beings, then an explosion of this sort is inevitable.

During the next recess, Goering, Keitel and Jodl could be seen raging at Bach-Zelewski's damning testimony. As Goering pointed out, Bach-Zelewski's own hands were not clean of blood. It had been he who had brutally suppressed the Warsaw Rising of the Poles in 1944, and he had been extolled by Hitler as a model soldier.

11 January–27 February 1946: The cases against the individual defendants, on War Crimes and Crimes against Humanity

From 2 January, the prosecution had started to weave in yet another layer of complexity to the presentation, the cases against the individual defendants as they related to the four charges. The first to be heard was that concerning Kaltenbrunner. Thereafter, over the next three weeks, cases were slotted in seemingly at random, with breaks for evidence relating to other counts and, indeed, the opening of the cases on War Crimes and Crimes against Humanity.

At the long table at which sat the eight judges, sighs of exasperation could be heard as yet another mountain of documents was put in evidence, much of it often irrelevant, as the Tribunal frequently commented. Yet the testimony of certain witnesses was so appalling, so revelatory of the casual contempt for life that had been the ethic of Nazi Germany, that it could not but hold the attention. One survivor of the regime's attentions was Franz Blaha, a Czech doctor sent to the Dachau concentration camp in 1941. He told the court how, having found a berth in the autopsy room of its hospital, he had witnessed the price paid by his fellow prisoners in the pursuit of scientific discoveries and material for novelty handbags.

Trial transcript, 11 January 1946: Franz Blaha on the perversion of science in Dachau

In 1942 and 1943 experiments on human beings were conducted by Dr Sigmund Rascher to determine the effects of changing air pressure.

As many as 25 persons were put at one time into a specially constructed van in which pressure could be increased or decreased as required. The purpose was to find out the effects on human beings of high altitude and of rapid descents by parachute. Through a window in the van I have seen the people lying on the floor of the van.

Most of the prisoners used died from these experiments, from internal haemorrhage of the lungs or brain. The survivors coughed blood when taken out. It was my job to take the bodies out and as soon as they were found to be dead to send the internal organs to Munich for study. About 400 to 500 prisoners were experimented on. The survivors were sent to invalid blocks and liquidated shortly afterwards. Only a few escaped.

Rascher also conducted experiments on the effect of cold water on human beings. This was done to find a way for reviving airmen who had fallen into the ocean. The subject was placed in ice cold water and kept there until he was unconscious. Blood was taken from his neck and tested each time his body temperature dropped one degree. This drop was determined by a rectal thermometer. Urine was also periodically tested. Some men stood it as long as 24 to 36 hours. The lowest body temperature reached was 19 degrees centigrade, but most men died at 25 or 26 degrees. When the men were removed from the ice water attempts were made to revive them by artificial sunshine, with hot water, by electro-therapy, or by animal warmth. For this last experiment prostitutes were used and the body of the unconscious man was placed between the bodies of two women. Himmler was present at one such experiment. I could see him from one of the windows in the street between the blocks. I have personally been present at some of these cold water experiments when Rascher was absent, and I have seen notes and diagrams on them in Rascher's laboratory. About 300 persons were used in these experiments. The majority died. Of those who survived, many became mentally deranged. Those who did not die were sent to invalid blocks and were killed just as were the victims of the air pressure experiments. I know only two who survived, a Yugoslav and a Pole, both of whom are mental cases.

Liver puncture experiments were performed by Dr Brachtl on

healthy people and on people who had diseases of the stomach and gall bladder. For this purpose a needle was jabbed into the liver of a person and a small piece of the liver was extracted. No anaesthetic was used. The experiment is very painful and often had serious results, as the stomach or large blood vessels were often punctured, resulting in haemorrhage . . .

It was common practice to remove the skin from dead prisoners. I was commanded to do this on many occasions. Dr Rascher and Dr Wolter in particular asked for this human skin from human backs and chests. It was chemically treated and placed in the sun to dry. After that it was cut into various sizes for use as saddles, riding breeches, gloves, house slippers, and ladies' handbags. Tattooed skin was especially valued by SS men. Russians, Poles, and other inmates were used in this way, but it was forbidden to cut out the skin of a German. This skin had to be from healthy prisoners and free from defects. Sometimes we did not have enough bodies with good skin and Rascher would say, 'All right, you will get the bodies'. The next day we would receive 20 or 30 bodies of young people. They would have been shot in the neck or struck on the head so that the skin would be uninjured. Also we frequently got requests for the skulls or skeletons of prisoners. In those cases we boiled the skull or the body. Then the soft parts were removed and the bones were bleached and dried and reassembled. In the case of skulls it was important to have a good set of teeth. When we got an order for skulls from Oranienburg the SS men would say, 'We will try to get you some with good teeth.' So it was dangerous to have good skin or good teeth.

§

Largely because of what was revealed at Nuremberg, the trials are now most remembered for their associations with war crimes. In the bleak depths of January 1946, however, when François de Menthon came to open the French part of the Allied case on Counts Three and Four, War Crimes and Crimes against Humanity were seen as having less prominence than those charges being prosecuted by the bigger American and British teams of lawyers, the Common Plan and Aggressive

War. De Menthon quickly made the point that all the crimes with which the defendants were charged stemmed in the same fashion from the Nazis' ideology. National Socialism, as he saw it, was, an attempt to return civilisation to barbarism, in that it denied the value of an individual's own worth.

Trial transcript, 17 January 1946: François de Menthon's opening speech on Crimes against Humanity

Crimes committed by the Nazis in the course of the war, like the war of aggression itself, will be, as Mr Justice Jackson has demonstrated to you, the manifestation of a concerted and methodically executed plan.

These crimes flow directly, like the war itself, from the National Socialist doctrine. This doctrine is indifferent to the moral choice of means to attain a final success, and for this doctrine the aim of war is pillage, destruction, and extermination.

Total war, totalitarian war in its methods and its aims, is dictated by the primacy of the German race and the negation of any other value. The Nazi conception maintains selection as a natural principle. The man who does not belong to the superior race counts for nothing. Human life and even less liberty, personality, the dignity of man, have no importance when an adversary of the German community is involved. It is truly 'the return to barbarism' with all its consequences.

Logically consistent, National Socialism goes to the length of assuming the right, either to exterminate totally races judged hostile or decadent, or to subjugate or put to use individuals and groups capable of resistance, in the nations. Does not the idea of totalitarian war imply the annihilation of any eventual resistance? All those who, in any way, may be capable of opposing the New Order and the German hegemony will be liquidated. It will thus become possible to assure an absolute domination over a neighbouring people that has been reduced to impotence and to utilise, for the benefit of the Reich, the resources and the human material of those people reduced to slavery.

All the moral conceptions which tended to make war more humane are obviously outdated, and the more so, all international conventions which had undertaken to bring some extenuation of the evils of war.

The conquered peoples must concur, willingly or by force, in the German victory by their material resources, as well as by their labour potential. Means will be found to subject them.

The treatment to which the occupied countries will be subjected is likewise related to this war aim. One could read in 'Deutsche Volkskraft' of 13 June 1935 that the totalitarian war will end in a totalitarian victory. 'Totalitarian' signifies the entire destruction of the conquered nation and its complete and final disappearance from the historic scene.

Among the conquered peoples distinctions can be made according to whether or not the National Socialists consider them as belonging to the Master Race. For the former, an effort is made to integrate them into the German Reich against their will. For the latter, there is applied a policy of weakening them and bringing about their extinction by every means, from that of appropriation of their property to that of extermination of their persons. In regard to both groups, the Nazi rulers assault not only the property and physical persons, but also the spirits and souls. They seek to align the populations according to the Nazi dogma and behaviour, when they wish to integrate them in the German community; they apply themselves at least to rooting out whatever conceptions are irreconcilable with the Nazi universe; they aim to reduce to a mentality and status of slaves, those men whose nationality they wish to eradicate for the benefit of the German race.

Inspired by these general conceptions as to the conduct to be observed in occupied countries, the defendants gave special orders or general directives or deliberately identified themselves with such. Their responsibility is that of perpetrators, co-perpetrators, or accomplices in the War Crimes systematically committed between 1 September 1939 and 8 May 1945 by Germany at war. They deliberately willed, premeditated, and ordered these crimes, or knowingly associated themselves with this policy of organised criminality.

We shall expose the various aspects of this policy of criminality as it was pursued in the occupied countries of Western Europe, by dealing successively with Forced Labour, Economic Looting, Crimes against Persons, and Crimes against Mankind.

§

The British judge Norman Birkett kept a diary throughout the proceedings in which he recorded his hopes for the trial and his frequent annoyance at the failings of its protagonists. He also sent letters to friends, such as this on 20 January, which is followed by his journal entry of the following day.

Norman Birkett: 'The greatest trial in history'

The thing that sustains me is the knowledge that this trial can be a very great landmark in the history of International Law. There will be a precedent of the highest standing for all successive generations, and aggressor nations great and small will embark on war with the certain knowledge that *if they fail* they will be called to grim account. To make the trial secure against all criticism it must be shown to be fair, convincing and built on evidence that cannot be shaken as the years go past. That is why the trial is taking so much time and why documents are being piled on documents.

There are, in truth, two trials going on at the same time, the trial of the Defendants in the dock and the greater trial of a whole nation and its way of thought. The world must be patient (and so must I!) for what is being done now assuredly belongs to history. But it will be late summer at earliest, I think, before the final acts.

The Court is an interesting place and the moods of the Defendants are full of perpetual speculation. Many of them must know that the sands of life are running out for them, and I watch them sometimes with a fascinated interest and would give much to know the secrecy of their thoughts. And you could certainly never tell from their faces that they have been guilty of the deaths of millions or had reduced millions of men and women to slavery.

21 January 1946 This is supposed to be, and no doubt is, the greatest trial in history. The historian of the future will look back to it with fascinated eyes. It will have a glamour, an intensity, an ever-present sense of tragedy that will enthral the mind engaged upon its consideration.

But to have been present at every moment of it is to occupy a position of advantage given to but few.

If it were possible to capture the moment, and to record in imperishable form the changing moods of the Assembly, a contribution to History would be made of the highest value. But there are but few Gibbons in this world, and they are not usually to be found among His Majesty's Judges! Moreover the documents that have been produced in such profusion are there for all men to read.

What alone is missing is the emotion, the colour, the movement that characterises these days. And how shall that be captured, and when captured, how shall it be recorded?

The Master Race on trial sounds dramatic enough, but the Master Race in the dock seems singularly like the dregs of humanity. Funk, for example, once a dictator in the economic sphere, is here presented as a broken heap of flesh, half-asleep during most of the days, apathetic and listless, and raising blinking eyes to the bright lights installed in the Court for the benefit of cinematograph operators.

§

Nothing stirred the emotions of those in court more than the ever-swelling tide of evidence of German atrocities. As part of the case on crimes against humanity, French prosecutor Charles Dubost asked his fellow countryman Maurice Lampe to recall the hellish conditions he had endured at the Mauthausen concentration camp in Austria, the site of the murder of thousands of Soviet and Allied prisoners of war.

Trial transcript, 25 January 1945: Murder at Mauthasen

MAURICE LAMPE: I was arrested on 8 November 1941. After two years and a half of internment in France, I was deported on

22 March 1944 to Mauthausen in Austria. The journey lasted three days and three nights under particularly vile conditions – 104 deportees in a cattle truck without air. I do not believe that it is necessary to give all the details of this journey, but one can well imagine the state in which we arrived at Mauthausen on the morning of 25 March 1944, in weather 12 degrees below zero. I mention, however, that from the French border we travelled in the trucks, naked.

When we arrived at Mauthausen, the SS officer who received this convoy of about 1,200 Frenchmen informed us in the following words, which I shall quote from memory almost word for word:

'Germany needs your arms. You are, therefore, going to work; but I want to tell you that you will never see your families again. When one enters this camp, one leaves it by the chimney of the crematorium.'

I remained about three weeks in quarantine in an isolated block, and I was then detailed to work with a squad in a stone quarry. The quarry at Mauthausen was in a hollow about 800 metres from the camp proper. There were 186 steps down to it. It was particularly painful torture, because the steps were so rough-hewn that to climb them even without a load was extremely tiring.

One day, 15 April 1944, 1 was detailed to a team of twelve men – all of them French – under the orders of a German *Kapo*, a common criminal, and of an SS man.

We started work at seven o'clock in the morning. By eight o'clock, one hour later, two of my comrades had already been murdered. They were an elderly man, M. Grégoire from Lyons, and a quite young man, Lefèvre from Tours. They were murdered because they had not understood the order, given in German, detailing them for a task. We were very frequently beaten because of our inability to understand the German language.

On the evening of that first day, 15 April 1944, we were told to carry the two corpses to the top, and the one that I, with three of my comrades, carried was that of old Grégoire, a very heavy man; we had to go up 186 steps with a corpse and we all received blows before we reached the top.

Life in Mauthausen – and I shall declare before this Tribunal only what I myself saw and experienced – was a long cycle of torture and of suffering. However, I would like to recall a few scenes which were particularly horrible and have remained more firmly fixed in my memory.

During September, I think it was on the 6th of September 1944, there came to Mauthausen a small convoy of forty-seven British, American, and Dutch officers. They were airmen who had come down by parachute. They had been arrested after having tried to make their way back to their own lines. Because of this they were condemned to death by a German Tribunal. They had been in prison about a year and a half and were brought to Mauthausen for execution.

On their arrival they were transferred to the bunker, the camp prison. They were made to undress and had only their pants and a shirt. They were barefooted. The following morning they were at the roll call at seven o'clock. The work gangs went to their tasks. The forty-seven officers were assembled in front of the office and were told by the commanding officer of the camp that they were all under sentence of death.

I must mention that one of the American officers asked the commander that he should be allowed to meet his death as a soldier. In reply, he was bashed with a whip. The forty-seven were led barefoot to the quarry.

For all the prisoners at Mauthausen the murder of these men has remained in their minds like a scene from Dante's *Inferno*. This is how it was done: At the bottom of the steps they loaded stone on the backs of these poor men and they had to carry them to the top. The first journey was made with stones weighing 25 to 30 kilos and was accompanied by blows. Then they were made to run down. For the second journey the stones were still heavier; and whenever the poor wretches sank under their burden, they were kicked and hit with a bludgeon, even stones were hurled at them.

This went on for several days. In the evening when I returned from the gang with which I was then working, the road which led to the camp was a bath of blood. I almost stepped on the lower jaw of a man. Twenty-one bodies were strewn along the road. Twenty-one had died on the first day. The twenty-six others died the following morning. I have tried to make my account of this horrible episode as short as possible . . .

In September 1944 Himmler visited us. Nothing was changed in the camp routine. The work gangs went to their tasks as usual, and I had – we had – the unhappy opportunity of seeing Himmler close. If I mention Himmler's visit to the camp – after all it was not a great event – it is because that day they presented to Himmler the execution of fifty Soviet officers.

I must tell you that I was then working in a Messerschmitt gang, and that day I was on night shift. The block where I was billeted was just opposite the crematorium; and in the execution room, we saw – I saw – these Soviet officers lined up in rows of five in front of my block. They were called one by one. The way to the execution room was relatively short. It was reached by a stairway. The execution room was under the crematorium.

The execution, which Himmler himself witnessed – at least the beginning of it, because it lasted throughout the afternoon – was another particularly horrible spectacle. I repeat, the Soviet Army officers were called one by one, and there was a sort of human chain between the group which was awaiting its turn and that which was in the stairway listening to the shots which killed their predecessors. They were all killed by a shot in the neck . . .

If you will allow me, I would like to go on with my description of the murder of these 400 people from Sachsenhausen. I said that after selecting the sick, the feeble and the older prisoners, Dachmeier, the camp commander, gave orders that these men should be stripped entirely naked in weather 18 degrees below zero. Several of them rapidly got congestion of the lungs, but that did not seem fast enough for the SS. Three times during the night these men were sent down to the shower-baths; three times they were drenched for half an hour in freezing water and then made to come up without being dried. In the morning when the gangs went to work the corpses were strewn over the ground. I must add that the last of them were finished off with blows from an axe . . .

M. DUBOST: Do you know why this execution was carried out?

LAMPE: Because there were too many people in the camp; because the prisoners coming from all the camps that were falling back could not be drafted into working gangs at a quick enough pace. The blocks were overcrowded. That is the only explanation that was given . . .

The German population, that is, the Austrian population; were perfectly aware of what was going on at Mauthausen. The working squads were nearly all for work outside. I said just now that I was working at Messerschmitt's. The foremen were mobilised German civilians who, in the evening, went home to their families. They knew quite well of our sufferings and privations. They frequently saw men fetched from the shop to be executed, and they could bear witness to most of the massacres I mentioned a little while ago.

I should add that once we received – I am sorry I put it like that – once there arrived in Mauthausen thirty firemen from Vienna. They were imprisoned, I think, for having taken part in some sort of workers' activity. The firemen from Vienna told us that, when one wanted to frighten children in Vienna, one said to them, 'If you are not good, I will send you to Mauthausen.'

Another detail, a more concrete one: Mauthausen Camp is built on a plateau and every night the chimneys of the crematorium would light up the whole district, and everyone knew what the crematorium was for.

Another detail: The town of Mauthausen was situated 5 kilometres from the camp. The convoys of deportees were brought to the station of the town. The whole population could see these convoys pass. The whole population knew in what state these convoys were brought into the camp.

§

It became all too clear that even women and children were not immune from the mass killings carried out by the Nazis. In 1942, 29-year-old Marie Vaillant-Couturier had been arrested because of her work with the French Resistance and sent to Poland, to what is remembered as the most infamous of all the camps – Auschwitz. Her testimony, in which she told in a firm, calm voice of the drowning of babies and the raking of the ashes of the dead in search of gold, made an indelible impression on all who heard it, and forced some of the defendants to remove their headphones rather than endure any more of the horrors of which she spoke.

Trial transcript, 28 January: Auschwitz – 'They had thrown the children into the furnaces alive'

MME MARIE VAILLANT-COUTURIER: It was a terrible journey. We were 60 in a car and we were given no food or drink during the journey. At the various stopping places we asked the Lorraine soldiers of the Wehrmacht who were guarding us whether we would arrive soon; and they replied, 'If you knew where you are going you would not be in a hurry to get there.'

We arrived at Auschwitz at dawn. The seals on our cars were broken, and we were driven out by blows with the butt end of a rifle, and taken to the Birkenau Camp, a section of the Auschwitz Camp. It is situated in the middle of a great plain, which was frozen in the month of January. During this part of the journey we had to drag our luggage. As we passed through the door we knew only too well how slender our chances were that we would come out again, for we had already met columns of living skeletons going to work; and as we entered we sang 'The Marseillaise' to keep up our courage . . .

M. DUBOST: Did you see any pregnant women?

MME VAILLANT-COUTURIER: Yes. The Jewish women, when they arrived in the first months of pregnancy, were subjected to abortion. When their pregnancy was near the end, after confinement, the babies were drowned in a bucket of water. I know that because I worked in the Revier and the woman who was in charge of that task was a German midwife, who was imprisoned for having performed illegal operations. After a while another doctor arrived and for two months they did not kill the Jewish babies. But one day an order came from Berlin saying that again they had to be done away with. Then the mothers and their babies were called to the infirmary. They were put in a lorry and taken away to the gas chamber . . .

M. DUBOST: Were you an eye witness of the selections on the arrival of the convoys?

MME VAILLANT-COUTURIER: Yes, because when we worked at the sewing block in 1944, the block where we lived directly faced the stopping place of the trains. The system had been improved. Instead of making the selection at the place where they arrived, a side line now took the train practically right up to the gas chamber; and the stopping place, about 100 metres from the gas chamber, was right opposite our block though, of course, separated from us by two rows of barbed wire. Consequently, we saw the unsealing of the cars and the soldiers letting men, women, and children out of them. We then witnessed heart-rending scenes; old couples forced to part from each other, mothers made to abandon their young daughters, since the latter were sent to the camp, whereas mothers and children were sent to the gas chambers. All these people were unaware of the fate awaiting them. They were merely upset at being separated, but they did not know that they were going to their death . . .

M. DUBOST: These were not given an identification number?

MME VAILLANT-COUTURIER: No.

M. DUBOST: They were not tattooed?

MME VAILLANT-COUTURIER: No. They were not even counted.

M. DUBOST: You were tattooed?

MME VAILLANT-COUTURIER: Yes, look. [The witness showed her arm.] They were taken to a red brick building, which bore the letters *Baden*, that is to say 'Baths'. There, to begin with, they were made to undress and given a towel before they went into the so-called shower room. Later on, at the time of the large convoys from Hungary, they had no more time left to play-act or to pretend; they were brutally undressed, and I know these details as I knew a little Jewess from France who lived with her family at the République district.

M. DUBOST: In Paris?

MME VAILLANT-COUTURIER: In Paris. She was called 'little Marie' and she was the only one, the sole survivor of a family of nine. Her mother and her seven brothers and sisters had been gassed on arrival. When I met her she was employed to undress the babies before they were taken into the gas chamber. Once the people were undressed they took them into a room which was somewhat like a shower room, and gas capsules were thrown through an opening in the ceiling. An SS man would watch the effect produced through a porthole. At the end of five or seven minutes, when the gas had completed its work, he gave the signal to open the doors; and men with gas masks – they too were internees – went into the room and removed the corpses. They told us that the internees must have suffered before dying, because they were closely clinging to one another and it was very difficult to separate them.

After that a special squad would come to pull out gold teeth and dentures; and again, when the bodies had been reduced to ashes, they would sift them in an attempt to recover the gold.

At Auschwitz there were eight crematories but, as from 1944, these proved insufficient. The SS had large pits dug by the internees, where they put branches, sprinkled with gasoline, which they set on fire. Then they threw the corpses into the pits. From our block we could see after about three-quarters of an hour or an hour after the arrival of a convoy, large flames coming from the crematory, and the sky was lighted up by the burning pits.

One night we were awakened by terrifying cries. And we discovered, on the following day, from the men working in the *Sonderkommando* – the 'Gas Kommando' – that on the preceding day, the gas supply having run out, they had thrown the children into the furnaces alive . . .

So vivid was her testimony, and so damningly well delivered had it been, that one of the German lawyers, Hans Marx, put it to her in cross-examination that in civilian life she must have been a lecturer or teacher. The implication was that she had shaped her words for effect. No, she replied, I was a newspaper photographer. Her trained eye had recorded everything just as she had seen it.

§

Though the Tribunal heard of many instances where German troops had broken the Geneva Convention in their treatment of Soviet prisoners, who were regarded as almost subhuman by their captors, rarer were instances of its breach when Allied troops surrendered. One grave exception was a massacre of 129 Americans at Baignes, Belgium, during the Battle of the Bulge in December 1944, a report on which was read to the court by Dubost.

Trial transcript, 31 January 1945: Charles Dubost on the slaughter of American prisoners at Baignes

The author of this report summarises the facts. The American prisoners were brought together near the crossroad. A few soldiers, whose names are indicated, rushed across the field toward the west, hid among the trees in the high grass, in thickets, and ditches, and thus escaped the massacre of their companions. A few others who, at the moment when this massacre began, were in the proximity of a barn, were able to hide in it. They also are survivors.

'... the artillery and machine gun fire on the column of American vehicles continued for about 10 to 15 minutes, and then two German tanks and some armoured cars came down the road from the direction of Weismes. Upon reaching the intersection, these vehicles turned south on the road toward St Vith. The tanks directed machine gun fire into the ditch along the side of the road in which the American soldiers were crouching; and upon seeing this, the other American soldiers dropped their weapons and raised their hands over their heads. The surrendered American soldiers were then made to march back to the crossroad, and as they passed by some of the German vehicles on highway N-23, German soldiers on these vehicles took from the American prisoners of war such personal belongings as wrist watches, rings, and gloves. The American soldiers were then assembled on the St Vith road in front of a house standing on the southwest corner of the crossroad. Other German soldiers, in tanks and armoured cars, halted at the crossroad and also searched some of the captured Americans and took valuables from them ...

'... an American prisoner was questioned and taken with his other comrades to the crossroads just referred to.

' . . . at about this same time a German light tank attempted to manoeuvre itself into position on the road so that its cannon would be directed at the group of American prisoners gathered in the field approximately 20 to 25 yards from the road . . . '

I again skip four lines.

' . . . some of these tanks stopped when they came opposite the field in which the unarmed American prisoners were standing in a group, with their hands up or clasped behind their heads. A German soldier, either an officer or a non-commissioned officer, in one of these vehicles which had stopped, got up, drew his revolver, took deliberate aim and fired into the group of American prisoners. One of the American soldiers fell. This was repeated a second time and another American soldier in the group fell to the ground. At about the same time, from two of the vehicles on the road, fire was opened on the group of American prisoners in the field. All, or most, of the American soldiers dropped to the ground and stayed there while the firing continued, for 2 or 3 minutes. Most of the soldiers in the field were hit by this machine gun fire. The German vehicles then moved off toward the south and were followed by more vehicles which also came from the direction of Weismes. As these latter vehicles came opposite the field in which the American soldiers were lying, they also fired with small arms from the moving vehicles at the prostrate bodies in the field.

' . . . some German soldiers, evidently from the group of those who were on guard at the crossroad, then walked to the group of the wounded American prisoners who were still lying on the ground in the field . . . and shot with pistol or rifle, or clubbed with a rifle butt or other heavy object, any of the American soldiers who still showed any sign of life. In some instances, American prisoners were evidently shot at close range, squarely between the eyes, in the temple, or the back of the head . . .

This deed constitutes an act of pure terrorism, the shame of which will remain on the German Army, for nothing justified this. These prisoners were unarmed and had surrendered.'

§

On 1 February, Dubost concluded his argument that the defendants should be found guilty of having participated in or connived at the exploitation of forced labour and the atrocities in the camps. Unlike Jackson, who had insisted that the Allies bore no grudge against the German people, Dubost refused to absolve them of responsibility. Unlike the United States, France had been occupied by the Nazis.

Trial transcript, 1 February 1946: Charles Dubost – The Germans have retrogressed more than twelve centuries

The German people whose military virtue we recognise, whose poets and musicians we love, whose application to work we admire, and who did not fail to give examples of probity in the most noble works of the spirit; this German people, which came rather late to civilisation, beginning only with the eighth century, had slowly raised itself to the ranks of nations possessing the oldest culture. The contribution to modern or contemporary thought seemed to prove that this conquest of the spirit was final; Kant, Goethe, Johann Sebastian Bach belong to humanity just as much as Calvin, Dante, or Shakespeare; nevertheless, we behold the fact that millions of innocent men have been exterminated on the very soil of this people, by men of this people, in execution of a common plan conceived by their leaders, and this people made not a single effort to revolt.

This is what has become of it because it has scorned the virtues of political freedom, of civic equality, of human fraternity. This is what has become of it, because it forgot that all men are born free and equal before the law, that the essential action of a state has for its purpose the deeper and deeper penetration of a respect for spiritual liberty and fraternal solidarity in social relations and in international institutions.

It allowed itself to be robbed of its conscience and its very soul. Evil masters came who awakened its primitive passions and made possible the atrocities which I have described to you. In truth, the crime of these men is that they caused the German people to retrogress more than twelve centuries.

Their crime is that they conceived and achieved, as an instrument of government, a policy of terrorism toward the whole of the subjugated nations and toward their own people; their crime is that they pursued, as an end in itself, a policy of extermination of entire categories of innocent citizens. That alone would suffice to determine capital punishment.

§

The burden of establishing the cases on Counts Three and Four had been divided between the French, who covered crimes committed in Western Europe, and the Soviets, who took the East. Their chief prosecutor was a Ukrainian, General Roman Rudenko. His powerfully expressed opening speech, which glossed over the fact that the USSR had been allied with the Nazis until 1941, and had divided Poland with it, gave an insight both into the Soviet mindset and into the extraordinary scale of losses they had suffered at the hands of the Germans.

Trial transcript, 8 February 1946: Roman Rudenko's opening speech on War Crimes in the East

On 22 June 1941 the Hitlerite conspirators, having perfidiously violated the pact of non-aggression between the USSR and Germany without any declaration of war, started an attack against Soviet territory, initiating thereby an aggressive war against the USSR without the slightest provocation on the part of the Soviet Union. Enormous masses of German troops, secretly concentrated on the borders beforehand, were thrown against the USSR . . .

In its attempt to conceal its imperialistic aims the Hitlerite clique hysterically shrieked, as usual, about a danger alleged to be forthcoming from the USSR and proclaimed that the predatory war which it started against the Soviet Union with aggressive purposes was a 'preventive' war.

A pitiful effort!

What 'preventive' war can we speak of, when documents prove that long in advance Germany worked out and prepared a plan for an attack on the USSR, formulated the predatory aims of this attack, earmarked the territories of the Soviet Union which she intended to seize, established the methods for pillaging of these territories and for the extermination of their population, mobilised her army in good time, and moved to the borders of the USSR 170 fully equipped divisions only waiting for the signal to advance?

The fact of aggression committed by fascist Germany against the USSR, as well as the original documents of the Hitlerite Government which now have been made public, definitely show to the whole world and to history how untrue and laughable was the assertion of the Hitlerite propaganda about the 'preventive' character of the war against the USSR.

Much as the fascist wolf might disguise himself in a sheep's skin, he cannot hide his teeth!

Having committed the perfidious attack on the USSR, the Hitlerite Government calculated that lengthy preparation for this attack, the concentration of all the armed forces of Germany for this thrust, the participation of Romanian and Finnish armies, as well as of Italian and Hungarian units in this operation, and, finally, the advantage of surprise would assure a rapid defeat of the USSR.

However, all these calculations of the aggressors were frustrated by the heroic resistance of the Red Army, which with self-denial defended the honour and the independence of its country. The German plans of attack were broken up one after another. I shall not describe all the phases of the patriotic war of the Soviet People against the German fascist invaders and the great and courageous struggle of the Red Army with German, Romanian, Finnish, and other armies that invaded the soil of the Soviet. The whole world watched this struggle with admiration, and it will never be forgotten by history.

The Soviet people, in battles the scale and ferocity of which were unmatched in history, steadfastly defended and saved the freedom and independence of their country and, together with the Allied armies, liberated the freedom-loving nations throughout the whole world from the terrible menace of Nazi enslavement.

Having prepared and carried out the perfidious assault against the freedom-loving nations, fascist Germany turned the war into a system of militarised banditry. The murder of war prisoners, extermination of civilian populations, plunder of occupied territories, and other war crimes were committed as part of a totalitarian lightning war programme projected by the fascists. In particular the terrorism practised by the fascists on the temporarily occupied Soviet territories reached fabulous proportions and was carried out with an outspoken cruelty . . .

The German fascist invaders completely or partially destroyed or burned 1,710 cities and more than 70,000 villages and hamlets; they burned or destroyed over 6 million buildings and rendered some 25 million persons homeless . . .

The Germans destroyed 65,000 kilometres of railway tracks, 4,100 railway stations, 36,000 post and telegraph offices, telephone exchanges, and other installations for communications. The Germans destroyed or devastated 40,000 hospitals and other medical institutions, 84,000 schools, technical colleges, universities, institutes for scientific research, and 43,000 public libraries.

The Hitlerites destroyed and looted 98,000 collective farms, 1,876 state farms, and 2,890 machine and tractor stations; they slaughtered, seized or drove into Germany 7 million horses, 17 million head of horned cattle, 20 million pigs, 27 million sheep and goats, and 110 million head of poultry.

§

Much of Nuremberg had been reduced to rubble by aerial attack during the war. Here and there stumps of houses stuck up like rotten teeth, but the greater part of the historic city centre had been obliterated. Those attending the trial were mostly housed in the suburbs and in country villas confiscated from wealthy Germans. For many of the Russian staff, their time at Nuremberg represented a taste of a more liberal way of life. But, recalled Biddle, not for long.

Francis Biddle: Under Soviet eyes – a brief taste of liberal ways

Judge Parker had selected as his aide Major Robert Stewart, the son of an old friend from Charlotte, fresh from active service in the

Battle of the Bulge. He had that essential quality of a capable officer, the ability to handle men without friction, not uncommon among Southerners. He was young, attractive, unattached; and it was pleasantly appropriate that he should have, in a very short time, found it unreasonable to resist the charms of Tania, one of the best of the Russian interpreters, the very young, very pretty wife of an absent Russian brigadier. She spoke slangy American, read *Life* and *Newsweek*, adored American movies – *Gone with the Wind*, *The Great Waltz*, *For Whom the Bell Tolls*; and dressed and danced to perfection. After a few months she departed suddenly to rejoin her brigadier in Moscow. Doubtless she was having too good a time, and had been so reported by the representative of the NKVD [secret police] at Nuremberg, who stalked joylessly about the corridors in ill-fitting incognito, his dour eye on citizens of the Union of Soviet Socialist Republics, or in and out of the Grand Hotel, the former Reichsparteitag Goestahus (Guest House for the Nazi Party Conventions), where members of all nations went to relax and eat passable food, and drink, and flirt, and witness vaudeville performances of tumblers and jugglers and thin, overpainted half-starved German girls, not very young any longer, who danced . . . The Soviet secret agent touched everything, enjoying with a fixed and frowning solemnity the pleasures of the flesh, a little violent when touched with drunkenness, relaxing now and then at one of the Russian parties, which were always informal, after the first hour of slow unbending; or singing a gypsy song to his own piano accompaniment, the others joining in the choruses under his beacon eye, then all of them letting go in the final burst.

The best translator for the Russians was young O.A. Troyanovski, son of a former ambassador to the United States, who had been at school and college in America, and spoke fluent English. He had picked up American idioms, turns of humour, and ways of thinking and seemed like an American boy, friendly and easy. We all liked him. I suppose it was conceived that he might be contaminated, for I can remember one evening, when three or four of us were lounging in a corner, laughing and gossiping, seeing him leap to his feet and leave the room as if he had suddenly remembered an engagement, when the NKVD man stalked by, pausing to frown for a split second. Troyanovski left for a conference of ministers in Paris shortly afterwards.

§

After surrendering to the Germans, much of Poland had been incorporated directly into the Reich. What remained of it was ruled with brutality by Frank. As Lahousen had earlier testified, the Nazis' plan was to eliminate all potential leaders of Polish resistance to the Occupation – lawyers, teachers, the aristocracy and civil service – and in May 1940 Frank gave a chillingly matter-of-fact speech to police about the forthcoming 'pacification action'. It was read to the court by Soviet prosecutor Lev Smirnov.

Trial transcript, 15 February 1946: Lev Smirnov quoting Hans Frank's speech on 'pacification action' in Poland

'I frankly admit that it will cost the lives of some thousands of Poles and that these will be taken mainly from leading members of the Polish intelligentsia. In these times we, as National Socialists, are bound to ensure that no further resistance is offered by the Polish people . . . Furthermore, SS-Obergruppenfuehrer Kruger and I have decided that appeasement measures should be speeded up. I pray you, gentlemen, to take the most rigorous measures possible to help us in this task. For my own part, I will do everything in my power in order to facilitate its execution. I appeal to you as the champions of National Socialism, and I need surely say nothing further. We will carry out this measure and I may tell you in confidence that we shall be acting on the Fuehrer's orders. The Fuehrer said to me, "The handling of German policy in the Government General and its establishment on a firm basis is a matter which devolves personally on the responsible men in the Government General."

'He expressed himself in this way: The men capable of leadership whom we have found to exist in Poland must be liquidated. Those following men must . . . be eliminated in their turn. There is no need to burden the Reich and the Reich police organisation with this. There is no need to send these elements to Reich concentration camps, and by so doing involve ourselves in disputes and unnecessary correspondence with their relations. We will liquidate our difficulties in the country itself, and we will do it in the simplest way possible.'

Frank had been so zealous in his duties that he had once boasted: 'In Prague, for instance, there were hung up red posters announcing that seven Czechs had been shot that day. I then said to myself: If I wished to order that one should hang up posters about every seven Poles shot, there would not be enough forests in Poland with which to make the paper for these posters. Indeed, we must act cruelly.'

§

Gustave Gilbert, the psychologist stationed in the prison, saw the prisoners on an almost daily basis. He checked up on their well-being, asked them about their attitudes to the trial, and questioned them about their feelings of guilt. So detailed were his notes of his examinations that the suspicion must be that he always intended to publish them; there was money to be made from the notoriety of those in his care. Yet even if some of the conversations he recorded appear exaggerated for effect, they do provide a vivid portrait of the defendants' personalities, and reveal a side of them not seen by the court.

Hjalmar Schacht was one of those accused who believed firmly that he should not be on trial. For much of the 1920s, Schacht had been President of the Reichsbank – Germany's central bank – trying vainly to stem the hyper-inflation that had gripped the economy. Convinced that the huge reparations demanded by the Allies as punishment for the First World War were the root of the problem, Schacht made common cause with the nationalist Hitler when he came to power, and having taken charge of the economy dedicated himself to reviving it by finding ways of financing the rebuilding of the armed forces.

Schacht claimed that his aim had only ever been to restore Germany's self-respect. He resigned as Minister of Economics in 1937 after, he said, realising the aggressive intent behind Hitler's policies. He remained a Minister Without Portfolio until 1943, but the following year was imprisoned on suspicion of working against the regime. His admirers thought him a high-minded financial genius, while his critics thought him the epitome of the haughty, unprincipled banker. He regarded himself as a cut above most of the other defendants, and sat rigidly upright in court, keeping a little distance from his co-accused. Normally he was every inch the fastidious financier. Not on this occasion, however.

Gustave Gilbert: True confessions – the rage of Hjalmar Schacht

Schacht's cell: Schacht was furious over the new ruling [banning communication between the prisoners]. He actually screamed as he worked himself into a frenzy over his treatment in prison: 'It is disgraceful! – *shabby!!* – The colonel can do with us what he likes, but I do not envy him his power! . . . This shows treatment by people who have no tradition and no culture – it is *contemptible!!*' His contemptuous reference to the Americans was the Goering line probably transmitted by his table companion Raeder. His fury disclosed a good deal of feeling concealed under a shell of hurt innocence. 'I assure you I don't *want* to talk to most of those people! – criminals like Goering, Rosenberg, Ribbentrop, Streicher, Frank – but there are a few gentlemen I *do* enjoy talking to: – decent people like von Papen, von Neurath. – But how dare they treat us in such a high-handed manner! – Don't forget what desperate straits the Allies drove us into. They hemmed us in from every side – they fairly strangled us! Just try to imagine what a cultured people like the German people has to go through to fall for a demagogue like Hitler. – Just try to imagine: a people that led the culture of Europe ever since the Dark Ages, with great figures like Goethe, Schiller, Kant, Beethoven – the most outstanding figures in every field – music, literature, art, philosophy –'

'Didn't the French have a fairly respectable culture too?' I put in edgewise.

'Oh, the French!' he retorted with chauvinistic contempt. 'In a small court circle perhaps – but even that was the influence of the Germans. – Just imagine what a cultured people like ours has to go through to be dragged to such desperation. – And think of what a demon it was who seized upon the desperate plight of the German people to abuse their faith in such a criminal way. – Don't worry, I'll have plenty to say about that. – And the German people were so willing to do anything for peace. – We were so modest in our demands. – All we wanted was some possibility for export, for trade, to live somehow –'

'You mean the Weimar Republic?'

'Yes, of course. – And to every little suggestion the Allies said NO! We asked for a colony or two – anything for trading possibilities – out of the question! We asked for a trade union with Austria and Czechoslovakia, and they said NO! We pointed out that Austria had voted 90 per cent for union with Germany. – They said nothing doing. – But when a gangster like Hitler comes to power – oh, my, take all of Austria, remilitarise the Rhineland, take the Sudetenland, take all of Czechoslovakia, take everything – we won't say a word. – Why, before the Munich Pact Hitler didn't even dare dream of getting the Sudetenland incorporated into the Reich. – All he thought he *might* get was a measure of autonomy for the Sudetenland. – And then those fools Daladier [the French premier] and Chamberlain drop the whole thing in his lap. –Why didn't they give the Weimar Republic *one-tenth* that much support? They wouldn't give us one damn little crumb!! – And because I finally tried to build up some economic security without the Versailles Treaty to *avoid* a catastrophe, and sabotaged the war measures and finally tried to kill that maniac – they threw me in jail like a CRIMINAL!!' He screamed so that the whole jail must have heard it. '– With the most *disgraceful*, *undignified*, SHAMELESS treatment!! Even in concentration camp I didn't have to sweep out my own cell and be forced to face this way or that way so that I couldn't sleep!' He sat biting his lips and quivering with emotion, his face flushed. After a while he said apologetically. 'Well, I am sorry, but if you want to know my reaction, there it is. – I will have nothing more to do with any American institutions. I will not even attend chapel any more.'

§

Day after day, the Soviet prosecutors continued to make out their case on Counts Three and Four, piling ever more evidence in front of the Tribunal. Perhaps it was the only way to convey some idea of the monumental scale of the Russians' losses during the war – as many as 20 million dead – yet the avalanche of documents diluted the effectiveness of their presentation and tried the patience of the judges. Though, as Smirnov demonstrates here, numbed as the courtroom was by all they had heard, some things still retained the power to shock.

Trial transcript, 19 February 1946: Lev Smirnov on soap made from corpses

I submit to the Tribunal, as Exhibit Number USSR-197 (Document Number USSR-197), the testimony of one of the direct participants in the production of soap from human fat. It is the testimony of Sigmund Mazur, who was a laboratory assistant at the Danzig Anatomic Institute . . .

'In February 1944 Professor Spanner gave me the recipe for the preparation of soap from human fat. According to this recipe 5 kilos of human fat are mixed with 10 litres of water and 500 or 1,000 grams of caustic soda. All this is boiled 2 or 3 hours and then cooled. The soap floats to the surface while the water and other sediment remain at the bottom. A bit of salt and soda is added to this mixture. Then fresh water is added, and the mixture again boiled 2 or 3 hours. After having cooled the soap is poured into moulds.'

I will present to the Tribunal these moulds into which the soap was poured. Further I shall prove that this half-finished sample of human soap was really found in Danzig.

'The soap had an unpleasant odour. In order to destroy this disagreeable odour, Benzolaldehyde was added. The fat of the human bodies was collected by Borkmann and Reichert. I boiled the soap out of the bodies of women and men. The process of boiling alone took several days – from 3 to 7. During two manufacturing processes, in which I directly participated, more than 25 kilograms of soap were produced. The amount of human fat necessary for these two processes was 70 to 80 kilograms collected from some 40 bodies. The finished soap then went to Professor Spanner, who kept it personally. I used this human soap for my personal needs, for toilet and for laundering. For myself I took 4 kilograms of this soap.'

§

In the summer of 1943, as the Soviet forces began to retake territory in the East, Himmler became concerned that they might stumble upon evidence of the Einsatzgruppen's murderous work. He therefore ordered that the remains of tens of thousands of bodies should be exhumed and destroyed – by Jewish work parties. The statement of one of their guards, Gerhard Adametz, was read to the court.

Trial transcript, 19 February 1946: Gerhard Adametz on covering the traces of the Einsatzgruppen's work

'The place smelled of corpses. We felt faint, stopped our noses, and tried not to breathe. Oberleutnant Hanisch addressed us. I remember the following excerpts: "You have come to the place where you are to serve and support your comrades. You already smell an odour coming from the church behind us. We must all get used to this, and you must all do your duties. We will have to guard internees and do so very strictly. Everything that takes place here is the secret affair of the Reich. Everyone of you answers with his head if ever an internee under his guard succeeds in escaping; besides this, he will be subjected to a special regime. The same fate awaits anyone who lets out anything or is careless in his correspondence . . . "

'After this speech of Oberleutnant Hanisch, we were led out so as to acquaint ourselves with the place where we were to serve. We left the cemetery and were brought to an adjoining field. The road which crossed this field was guarded on both sides by policemen, who chased away all those who tried to approach it. In the field we saw about 100 internees resting from work. The legs of each internee were in chains of about 75 centimetres long. The internees were dressed in civilian clothes . . .

'The work of the internees consisted, as we found out later, of exhuming corpses which were buried here in two common graves, transporting them, piling them up in two enormous piles, and burning them. It is difficult to estimate; however, I believe that on this spot were buried from 40,000 to 45,000 corpses. One antitank ditch served as a grave and was partially filled with corpses. This ditch was 100 metres long, 10 metres wide, and 4 to 5 metres deep . . .

'On the day of our arrival, about 10 September 1943, there were three or four small piles of corpses on the field . . . Every such pile consisted of about 700 corpses. It was about 7 metres long, 4 metres wide, and 2 metres high . . . Here and in other places I observed the following methods which were employed (burning of corpses): with the aid of iron hooks, the corpses were dragged to certain spots and then piled on a wooden platform. Then the whole pile of corpses was surrounded with logs, petroleum was poured on and ignited.

'We, the policemen of detachment 1005-B, were then led back to the cemetery to the church. However, not one of us could eat because of the terrible smell and because of all we had seen.'

Smirnov claimed that the concealment pointed, because of the similarity of method used, to the guilt of the German army in another, much-disputed, allegation against them. This was that in 1941 they had massacred more than 10,000 Polish officer prisoners in the forest of Katyn near Smolensk. The Russians had insisted on including this charge in the indictment, though the truth was, as many already believed, that it was they who had committed the murders, in 1940.

When the circumstances came to be examined by the Tribunal in July 1946, it rapidly became apparent that the Soviets could not prove at all satisfactorily that the culprits had been a German unit. It was not the court's function to inquire further into the matter, but their finding that the Wehrmacht was not guilty of the killings left little doubt as to who had been responsible for one of the worst crimes of the war.

§

The conquest of new territories was intended not only to supply more room for the German population to expand, but also to provide the Reich with additional

The artist Laura Knight drew the defendants in the dock. Those shown are: *(centre row, from top)* Goering, the balding Hess, Von Ribbentrop, Keitel in uniform, Kaltenbrunner, Rosenberg, Frank, Frick, Streicher (turning away); *(back row)* Doenitz, Raeder, Von Schirach, Sauckel, the uniformed Jodl, Von Papen, Seyss-Inquart, Speer, Von Neurath. *[Rex Features]*

Hitler greets Goering at the 1938 Nuremberg Nazi Party Congress, watched by Streicher *(right)* and Von Ribbentrop *(far right)*. *[Getty Images]*

The crowd, including some of the 50,000 children present, acclaim Hitler's speech at the 1937 Party rally. *[Getty Images]*

A pile of corpses heaped in a room at the Dachau concentration camp and found by American troops in 1945. The prisoners had been gassed and were awaiting cremation. *[Time Life Pictures/Getty Images]*

Female German guards move bodies into a mass grave at the Bergen-Belsen concentration camp in 1945 under the gaze of appalled British soldiers who had just liberated it. *[Getty Images]*

Speer (in the raincoat), Doenitz and Jodl under arrest at Flensburg, the final seat of the government of the Third Reich, in May 1945. *[Getty Images]*

The ruins of Nuremberg in 1945: more than half of the city had been destroyed by Allied bombing, but the survival of its courthouse and prison determined the trial's venue.

[Getty Images]

Kaltenbrunner, who had controlled the regime's instruments of repression, including the concentration camps, arrives at Nuremberg supported by military policemen after attempting to commit suicide.
[IWM DEU 503578]

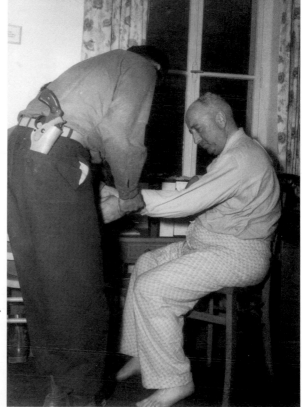

A dazed-looking Ley, head of the Labour Front, the sole trade union permitted by the Nazis, is handcuffed after being arrested while in hiding in 1945.
[Getty Images]

Jackson in 1940, when nominated to the Supreme Court. His opening speech at the trial made a strong impression, but his failure to cross-examine Goering effectively embarrassed the prosecution.
[Time Life Pictures/Getty Images]

American troops guard the approaches to the court buildings at the start of the trial in case of attack by Nazi sympathisers. *[Popperfoto]*

Birkett *(left)* served as the alternate British judge to the president of the court, Lawrence *(right)*, and recorded his caustic impressions of the trial in his diary. *[Getty Images]*

Shawcross *(seated left)* was the chief British prosecutor, but it was his deputy Maxwell Fyfe *(right)* who undertook the bulk of the work, and forced Goering into damaging admissions. *[Getty Images]*

Gang of Four: *(left to right)* Speer, the wartime Minister of Production, Funk, the former Economics Minister *(foreground)*, Von Neurath, once Foreign Minister, and broadcaster Fritzsche confer in the dock. *[Time Life Pictures/Getty Images]*

resources plundered from the subjugated peoples. Everything from food to oil to art was dispatched to Germany, regardless of the implications of such asset-stripping for the needs of the local population. Much of this callous campaign of freebooting, said Smirnov, was overseen by Goering.

Trial transcript, 20 February 1946: Lev Smirnov on Goering's plunder of Europe – 'Until the pips squeak'

As the documents which I have just presented show, the Defendant Goering, on account of his position in Hitler's Government as Reich Marshal and Plenipotentiary for the Four Year Plan and as head of the whole criminal system for the plundering of the occupied territories, was guilty of these crimes.

For this reason the stenographic record of a secret conference of German administrative leaders (Reich Commissioners) for the occupied countries, which took place on 6 August 1942, is of particular interest. Goering presided over the meeting. This document, like many other original documents which I had the honour of presenting today to the Tribunal, was found by Soviet military authorities in September 1945 in one of the municipal buildings of the town of Jena, in Thuringia.

This extraordinary document contains a long speech by Goering and the replies of the Hitlerite rulers of the occupied countries. And, Your Honours, many of the people who are sitting in the dock now took part in this conference. The contents of this document are such that any comment on my part is unnecessary. Therefore, if it pleases the Tribunal, I shall proceed to read from this document.

'Stenographic notes; Thursday, 6 August 1942, 4 p.m., in the Hermann Goering Hall in the Air Ministry.

Reich Marshal Goering: 'The Gauleiter stated their views here yesterday. Although they may have differed in tone and manner, it was evident that they all feel that the German people have too little to eat. Gentlemen, the Fuehrer has given me general powers exceeding any hitherto granted within the Four Year Plan.

'At this moment Germany commands the richest granaries that

ever existed in the European area, stretching from the Atlantic to the Volga and the Caucasus, lands more highly developed and fruitful than ever before, even if a few of them cannot be described as granaries. I need only remind you of the fabulous fertility of the Netherlands, the unique paradise that is France. Belgium too is extraordinarily fruitful, and so is the province of Posen. Then above all, the Government General has to a great extent the rye and wheat granary of Europe, and along with it the amazingly fertile districts of Lemberg (Lvov) and Galicia, where the harvest is exceptionally good. Then there comes Russia, the black earth of the Ukraine on both shores of the Dnieper, the Don region, with its remarkably fertile districts which have scarcely been destroyed. Our troops have now occupied, or are in process of occupying, the excessively fertile districts between the Don and the Caucasus.'

Goering then goes on to say:

'God knows, you are not sent out there to work for the welfare of the people in your charge but to squeeze the utmost out of them, so that the German people may live. That is what I expect of your exertions. This everlasting concern about foreign peoples must cease now, once and for all.

'I have here before me reports on what you expect to be able to deliver. It is nothing at all when I consider your territories. It makes no difference to me if you say that your people are starving.

'One thing I shall certainly do. I will make you deliver the quantities asked of you; and if you cannot do so, I will set forces to work that will force you to do so whether you want to or not.

'The wealth of Holland lies close to the Ruhr. It could send a much greater quantity of vegetables into this stricken area now than it has done so far. What do I care what the Dutchmen think of it.

'The only people in whom I am interested in the occupied territories are those who work to provide armaments and food supplies. They must receive just enough to enable them to continue working. It is all one to me whether Dutchmen are Germanic or not. They are only all the greater blockheads if they are; and more important persons than they have shown in the past how Germanic numbskulls sometimes have to be treated. Even if you receive abuses from every quarter, you will have acted rightly, for it is the Reich alone that counts.'

And now I come to the next excerpt:

'I am still discussing the western territories. Belgium has taken care of herself extraordinarily well. That was very sensible of Belgium. But there, too, gentlemen, rage incarnate could seize me. If every plot of ground in Belgium is planted with vegetables, then they must surely have had vegetable seed. When Germany wanted to start a big campaign last year for utilising uncultivated land, we did not have nearly as much seed as we needed. Neither Holland nor Belgium nor France have delivered it, although I myself was able to count 170 sacks of vegetable seed on a single street in Paris. It is all very well for the French to plant vegetables for themselves. They are accustomed to doing this. But, gentlemen, these people are all our enemies and you will not win over any of them by humane measures. The people are polite to us now because they have to be polite. But let the English once force their way in and then you will see the real face of the Frenchman. The same Frenchman who dines with you and in turn invites you to dine with him will at once make it plain to you that the Frenchman is a German-hater. That is the situation, and we do not want to see it any other way than it is.

'It is a matter of indifference to me how many courses are served every day at the table of the Belgian king. The king is a prisoner of war; and if he is not treated as such, I will see to it that he is taken to some other place where this can be made clear to him. I am really fed up with the business.

'I have forgotten one country because nothing is to be had there except fish; that is Norway . . .

'All that interests me is what we can squeeze out of the territory now under our control with the utmost application and by straining every nerve; and how much of that can be diverted to Germany. I don't give a damn about import and export statistics of former years.

'Now, regarding shipments to the Reich. Last year France shipped 550,000 tons of grain, and now I demand 1.2 million tons. Two weeks from now a plan will be submitted for handling it. There will be no more discussion about it. What happens to the Frenchmen is of no importance. One million two hundred thousand tons will be delivered.'

§

In July 1942, as the Holocaust started in earnest, the inhabitants of the Warsaw Ghetto began to be deported to the newly constructed site at Treblinka, 70 miles away, which they were assured was a labour camp but which had in fact been erected for their extermination. By the end of September, more than 400,000 men, women and children had been sent to Treblinka, among them Samuel Rajzman. Later convoys bore Jews from other countries in Europe. Rajzman told the court in unsparing detail of the fate that awaited the new arrivals, including his own wife and child.

Trial transcript, 27 February 1946: Enduring Treblinka – 'A photograph is all I have left'

SAMUEL RAJZMAN: Transports arrived there every day; their number depended on the number of trains arriving; sometimes three, four, or five trains filled exclusively with Jews – from Czechoslovakia, Germany, Greece, and Poland. Immediately after their arrival, the people had to leave the trains in five minutes and line up on the platform. All those who were driven from the cars were divided into groups – men, children, and women, all separate. They were all forced to strip immediately, and this procedure continued under the lashes of the German guards' whips. Workers who were employed in this operation immediately picked up all the clothes and carried them away to barracks. Then the people were obliged to walk naked through the street to the gas chambers.

MR COUNSELLOR SMIRNOV: I would like you to tell the Tribunal what the Germans called the street to the gas chambers.

RAJZMAN: It was named Himmelfahrt Street.

MR COUNSELLOR SMIRNOV: That is to say, the 'street to heaven'? . . . Please tell us, how long did a person live after he had arrived in the Treblinka Camp?

RAJZMAN: The whole process of undressing and the walk down to the gas chambers lasted, for the men 8 or 10 minutes, and for the women some 15 minutes. The women took 15 minutes because they had to have their hair shaved off before they went to the gas chambers.

MR COUNSELLOR SMIRNOV: Why was their hair cut off?

RAJZMAN: According to the ideas of the masters, this hair was to be used in the manufacture of mattresses for German women.

THE PRESIDENT: Do you mean that there was only 10 minutes between the time when they were taken out of the trucks and the time when they were put into the gas chambers?

RAJZMAN: As far as men were concerned, I am sure it did not last longer than 10 minutes.

MR COUNSELLOR SMIRNOV: Including the undressing?

RAJZMAN: Yes, including the undressing . . .

MR COUNSELLOR SMIRNOV: Please tell us, what was the subsequent aspect of the station at Treblinka?

RAJZMAN: At first there were no signboards whatsoever at the station, but a few months later the commander of the camp, one Kurt Franz, built a first-class railroad station with signboards. The barracks where the clothing was stored had signs reading 'restaurant', 'ticket office', 'telegraph', 'telephone', and so forth. There were even train schedules for the departure and the arrival of trains to and from Grodno, Suwalki, Vienna, and Berlin.

MR COUNSELLOR SMIRNOV: Did I rightly understand you, Witness, that a kind of make-believe station was built with signboards and train schedules, with indications of platforms for train departures to Suwalki, and so forth?

RAJZMAN: When the persons descended from the trains, they really had the impression that they were at a very good station from where they could go to Suwalki, Vienna, Grodno, or other cities.

MR COUNSELLOR SMIRNOV: And what happened later on to these people?

RAJZMAN: These people were taken directly along the Himmelfahrtstrasse to the gas chambers.

MR COUNSELLOR SMIRNOV: And tell us, please, how did the

Germans behave while killing their victims in Treblinka?

RAJZMAN: If you mean the actual executions, every German guard had his special job. I shall cite only one example. We had a ScharFuehrer Menz, whose special job was to guard the so-called *Lazarett*. In this *Lazarett* all weak women and little children were exterminated who had not the strength to go themselves to the gas chambers.

MR COUNSELLOR SMIRNOV: Perhaps, Witness, you can describe this *Lazarett* to the Tribunal?

RAJZMAN: This was part of a square which was closed in with a wooden fence. All women, aged persons, and sick children were driven there. At the gates of this *Lazarett*, there was a large Red Cross flag. Menz, who specialised in the murder of all persons brought to this *Lazarett*, would not let anybody else do this job. There might have been hundreds of persons who wanted to see and know what was in store for them, but he insisted on carrying out this work by himself.

Here is just one example of what was the fate of the children there. A ten-year-old girl was brought to this building from the train with her two-year-old sister. When the elder girl saw that Menz had taken out a revolver to shoot her two-year-old sister, she threw herself upon him, crying out, and asking why he wanted to kill her. He did not kill the little sister; he threw her alive into the oven and then killed the elder sister.

Another example: They brought an aged woman with her daughter to this building. The latter was in the last stage of pregnancy. She was brought to the *Lazarett*, was put on a grass plot, and several Germans came to watch the delivery. This spectacle lasted two hours. When the child was born, Menz asked the grandmother – that is the mother of this woman – whom she preferred to see killed first. The grandmother begged to be killed. But, of course, they did the opposite; the newborn baby was killed first, then the child's mother, and finally the grandmother.

MR COUNSELLOR SMIRNOV: Please tell us, Witness, does the name Kurt Franz mean anything to you?

RAJZMAN: This man was deputy of the camp commander, Stengel, the biggest murderer in the camp. Kurt Franz was known for having published in January 1943, a report to the effect that a million Jews had been killed in Treblinka – a report which had procured for him a promotion from the rank of SturmbannFuehrer to that of ObersturmbannFuehrer.

MR COUNSELLOR SMIRNOV: Witness, will you please tell how Kurt Franz killed a woman who claimed to be the sister of Sigmund Freud. Do you remember this incident?

RAJZMAN: A train arrived from Vienna. I was standing on the platform when the passengers left the cars. An elderly woman came up to Kurt Franz, took out a document, and said that she was the sister of Sigmund Freud. She begged him to give her light work in an office. Franz read this document through very seriously and said that there must be a mistake here; he led her up to the train schedule and said that in two hours a train would leave again for Vienna. She should leave all her documents and valuables and then go to a bathhouse; after the bath she would have her documents and a ticket to Vienna. Of course, the woman went to the bathhouse and never returned.

MR COUNSELLOR SMIRNOV: Please tell us, Witness, why was it that you yourself remained alive in Treblinka?

RAJZMAN: I was already quite undressed, and had to pass through this Himmelfahrtstrasse to the gas chambers. Some 8,000 Jews had arrived with my transport from Warsaw. At the last minute before we moved toward the street an engineer, Galevski, an old friend of mine, whom I had known in Warsaw for many years, caught sight of me. He was overseer of workers among the Jews. He told me that I should turn back from the street; and as they needed an interpreter for Hebrew, French, Russian, Polish, and German, he managed to obtain permission to liberate me.

MR COUNSELLOR SMIRNOV: You were therefore a member of the labour unit of the camp?

RAJZMAN: At first my work was to load the clothes of the murdered persons on the trains. When I had been in the camp two days, my mother, my sister, and two brothers were brought to the camp from the town of Vinegrova. I had to watch them being led away to the gas chambers. Several days later, when I was loading clothes on the freight cars, my comrades found my wife's documents and a photograph of my wife and child. That is all I have left of my family, only a photograph.

MR COUNSELLOR SMIRNOV: Tell us, Witness, how many persons were brought daily to the Treblinka Camp?

RAJZMAN: Between July and December 1942 an average of three transports of 60 cars each arrived every day. In 1943 the transport arrived more rarely.

MR COUNSELLOR SMIRNOV: Tell us, Witness, how many persons were exterminated in the camp, on an average, daily?

RAJZMAN: On an average, I believe they killed in Treblinka from ten to twelve thousand persons daily.

March–June 1946:
The case for the defendants

At the start of March, the prosecution had concluded its case against the accused. Now it was the turn of those in the dock to be heard. The first to give evidence, reflecting his unchallenged primacy among the defendants, was Hermann Goering. There was an air of expectation as he took his seat in the witness box, and at first he appeared nervous, wetting his lips and grasping tightly at the sides of the stand. Yet, weaned of his dependency on medication, he had regained his mental agility and physical presence and in response to the questions of his counsel, Otto Stahmer, soon began to cut an impressive and unrepentant figure; one barrister later recalled that Goering grew so bold as to pinch the bottom of a secretary passing the dock. Speaking with confidence, at length and largely without notes, he described how the Nazis' policy towards the Jews was merely of a part with their wider nationalist values.

Trial transcript, 14 March 1946: Goering gives evidence about the plans for the Jews

DR STAHMER: The Party programme included two points, I believe, dealing with the question of the Jews. What was your basic attitude towards this question?

GOERING: This question, which has been so strongly emphasised in the indictment, forces me under all circumstances to interpose certain statements.

After Germany's collapse in 1918 Jewry became very powerful in Germany in all spheres of life, especially in the political, general intellectual and cultural, and, most particularly, the economic spheres. The men came back from the front, had nothing to look forward to, and found a large number of Jews who had come in during the war from Poland and the East, holding positions, particularly economic positions. It is known that, under the influence of the war and business concerned with it – demobilisation, which offered great possibilities for doing business, inflation, deflation – enormous shifts and transfers took place in the propertied classes.

There were many Jews who did not show the necessary restraint and who stood out more and more in public life, so that they actually invited certain comparisons because of their numbers and the position they controlled in contrast to the German people. In addition there was the fact that particularly those parties which were avoided by nationally minded people also had Jewish leadership out of proportion to the total number of Jews . . .

At that time, there thus ensued a continuous uninterrupted attack on everything national, national concepts and national ideals. I draw attention to all the magazines and articles which dragged through the mud things which were holy to us. I likewise call attention to the distortion which was practised in the field of art in this direction, to plays which dragged the fighting at the front through the mud and befouled the ideal of the brave soldier. In fact I could submit an enormous pile of such articles, books, plays, and so forth; but this would lead too far afield and I am actually not too well informed on the subject. Because of all this, a defence movement arose which was by no means created by National Socialism but which had existed before, which was already strong during the war and which came even more strongly to the fore after the war, when the influence of Jewry had such effects . . .

Everywhere Jewry was in the lead in the fight against National Socialism, whether in the press, in politics, in cultural life by making National Socialism contemptible and ridiculous, or in the economic sphere. Whoever was a National Socialist could not get a position;

the National Socialist businessman could not get supplies or space for advertisements, and so on. All this naturally resulted in a strong defensive attitude on the part of the Party and led from the very beginning to an intensification of the fight, such as had not originally been the intention of the programme. For the programme aimed very definitely at one thing above all – that Germany should be led by Germans. And it was desired that the leadership, especially the political shaping of the fate of the German people, should be in the hands of German persons who could raise up the spirit of the German people again in a way that people of a different kind could not. Therefore the main point was at first merely to exclude Jewry from politics, from the leadership of the State. Later on, the cultural field was also included because of the very strong fight which had developed, particularly in this sphere, between Jewry on the one side and National Socialism on the other . . .

The Nuremberg Laws were intended to bring about a clear separation of races and, in particular, to do away with the notion of persons of mixed blood in the future, as the term of half Jew or quarter Jew led to continuous distinctions and confusion as far as their position was concerned . . .

The extraordinary intensification which set in later did not really start in until after the events of 1933, and then to a still greater extent in the war years. But here, again, there was naturally one more radical group for whom the Jewish question was more significantly in the foreground than it was for other groups of the Movement; just as, as I should like to emphasise at this point, the idea of National Socialism as a philosophy was understood in various ways – by one person more philosophically, by another mystically, by a third in a practical and political sense. This was also true of the different points of the programme. For one person certain points were more important, for another person less so. One person would see in the point of the programme which was directed against Versailles and toward a free and strong Germany the main point of the programme; another person, perhaps, would consider the Jewish question the main point . . .

DR STAHMER: In the indictment it says that the destruction of the Jewish race was part of the planning of aggressive wars.

GOERING: That has nothing to do with the planning of aggressive wars; also, the destruction of the Jewish race was not planned in advance.

§

By choosing to give evidence in person, Goering also exposed himself to cross-examination by the prosecution, which had long been aware that this would be the crux of the trial. His multiple roles within the Nazi regime, notably as overseer in the late 1930s of the Four Year Plan that had put the economy on a war footing, as well as head of the Air Force, meant that he was implicated in all the political and military aspects of the Allies' case. He was accused, too, of personal responsibility for a number of war crimes and those against humanity.

As the most prominent of the defendants – for many years he had been Hitler's designated successor – it was vital that Jackson mastered him in the witness box, both to set the tone for the other examinations to come and to destroy Goering's representation of the Nazis as a government that, like those of every other country, was motivated solely by pardonable national interest.

For the first time, the prosecution was able to attack in person a key symbol of the Nazis' rule. Yet, fatally, from the beginning Jackson's line of questioning was too vague and too passive, seemingly seeking to engage Goering in elevated moral debate rather than to pin down his involvement in specific crimes. Perhaps expecting the judges to confine Goering to 'yes or no' answers, Jackson, rather than framing his questions so as to give the Reichsmarschall no latitude, allowed him to justify his actions in long replies that often bore little relevance to what he had been asked. All the while, Goering displayed a breezy confidence, and Jackson became increasingly testy.

Trial transcript, 18 March 1946: Jackson begins his cross-examination of Goering

MR JUSTICE JACKSON: You are perhaps aware that you are the only living man who can expound to us the true purposes of the Nazi Party and the inner workings of its leadership?

GOERING: I am perfectly aware of that.

MR JUSTICE JACKSON: You, from the very beginning, together with those who were associated with you, intended to overthrow and later did overthrow, the Weimar Republic?

GOERING: That was, as far as I am concerned, my firm intention.

MR JUSTICE JACKSON: And, upon coming to power, you immediately abolished parliamentary government in Germany?

GOERING: We found it to be no longer necessary. Also I should like to emphasise the fact that we were moreover the strongest parliamentary party, and had the majority. But you are correct, when you say that parliamentary procedure was done away with, because the various parties were disbanded and forbidden.

MR JUSTICE JACKSON: You established the Leadership Principle, which you have described as a system under which authority existed only at the top, and is passed downwards and is imposed on the people below; is that correct?

GOERING: In order to avoid any misunderstanding, I should like once more to explain the idea briefly, as I understand it. In German parliamentary procedure in the past responsibility rested with the highest officials, who were responsible for carrying out the anonymous wishes of the majorities, and it was they who exercised the authority. In the Leadership Principle we sought to reverse the direction, that is, the authority existed at the top and passed downwards, while the responsibility began at the bottom and passed upwards.

MR JUSTICE JACKSON: In other words, you did not believe in and did not permit government, as we call it, by consent of the governed, in which the people, through their representatives, were the source of power and authority?

GOERING: That is not entirely correct. We repeatedly called on the people to express unequivocally and clearly what they thought of our system, only it was in a different way from that previously adopted and from the system in practice in other countries. We chose the way of a so-called plebiscite. We also took the point of view that even a government founded on the Leadership Principle could maintain itself only if it was based in some way on the confidence of the people. If it no longer had such confidence, then it would have to rule with bayonets, and the Fuehrer was always of the opinion that that was impossible in the long run to rule against the will of the people.

MR JUSTICE JACKSON: But you did not permit the election of those who should act with authority by the people, but they were designated from the top downward continuously, were they not?

GOERING: Quite right. The people were merely to acknowledge the authority of the Fuehrer, or, let us say, to declare themselves in agreement with the Fuehrer. If they gave the Fuehrer their confidence, then it was their concern to exercise the other functions. Thus, not the individual persons were to be selected according to the will of the people, but solely the leadership itself.

MR JUSTICE JACKSON: Now, was this Leadership Principle supported and adopted by you in Germany because you believed that no people are capable of self-government, or because you believed that some may be, not the German people; or that no matter whether some of us are capable of using our own system, it should not be allowed in Germany?

GOERING: I beg your pardon, I did not quite understand the question, but I could perhaps answer it as follows: I consider the Leadership Principle necessary because the system which previously existed, and which we called parliamentary or democratic, had brought Germany to the verge of ruin. I might perhaps in this connection remind you that your own President Roosevelt, as far as I can recall – I do not want to quote it word for word – declared, 'Certain peoples in Europe have forsaken democracy, not because they did not wish for democracy as such, but because democracy had brought forth men who were too weak to give their people work and bread, and to satisfy them. For this reason the peoples have abandoned this system and the men belonging to it.' There is much truth in that statement. This system had brought ruin by mismanagement and according to my own opinion, only an organisation made up of a strong, clearly defined leadership hierarchy could restore order again. But, let it be understood, not against the will of the people, but only when the people, having in the course of time, and by means of a series of elections, grown stronger and stronger, had expressed their wish to entrust their destiny to the National Socialist leadership.

MR JUSTICE JACKSON: The principles of the authoritarian

government which you set up required, as I understand you, that there be tolerated no opposition by political parties which might defeat or obstruct the policy of the Nazi Party?

GOERING: You have understood this quite correctly. By that time we had lived long enough with opposition and we had had enough of it. Through opposition we had been completely ruined. It was now time to have done with it and to start building up.

MR JUSTICE JACKSON: After you came to power, you regarded it necessary, in order to maintain power, to suppress all opposition parties?

GOERING: We found it necessary not to permit any more opposition, yes.

MR JUSTICE JACKSON: And you also held it necessary that you should suppress all individual opposition lest it should develop into a party of opposition?

GOERING: Insofar as opposition seriously hampered our work of building up, this opposition of individual persons was, of course, not tolerated. Insofar as it was simply a matter of harmless talk, it was considered to be of no consequence.

MR JUSTICE JACKSON: Now, in order to make sure that you suppressed the parties, and individuals also, you found it necessary to have a secret political police to detect opposition?

GOERING: I have already stated that I considered that necessary, just as previously the political police had existed, but on a firmer basis and larger scale.

MR JUSTICE JACKSON: And upon coming to power you also considered it immediately necessary to establish concentration camps to take care of your incorrigible opponents?

GOERING: I have already stated that the reason for the concentration camps was not because it could be said, 'Here are a number of people who are opposed to us and they must be taken into protective custody.' Rather they were set up as a lightning measure against the functionaries of the Communist Party who were attacking us in the thousands, and who, since they were taken into protective custody, were not put in prison. But it was necessary, as I said, to erect a camp for them – one, two, or three camps.

MR JUSTICE JACKSON: But you are explaining, as the high
authority of this system, to men who do not understand it very well,
and I want to know what was necessary to run the kind of system that
you set up in Germany. The concentration camp was one of the things
you found immediately necessary upon coming into power, was it
not? And you set them up as a matter of necessity, as you saw it?

GOERING: That was faultily translated – it went too fast. But I
believe I have understood the sense of your remarks. You asked me
if I considered it necessary to establish concentration camps
immediately in order to eliminate opposition. Is that correct?

MR JUSTICE JACKSON: Your answer is 'yes', I take it?

GOERING: Yes.

MR JUSTICE JACKSON: Was it also necessary, in operating this
system, that you must not have persons entitled to public trials in
independent courts? And you immediately issued an order that your
political police would not be subject to court review or to court
orders, did you not?

GOERING: You must differentiate between the two categories;
those who had committed some act of treason against the new state,
or those who might be proved to have committed such an act, were
naturally turned over to the courts. The others, however, of whom
one might expect such acts, but who had not yet committed them,
were taken into protective custody, and these were the people who
were taken to concentration camps. I am now speaking of what
happened at the beginning. Later things changed a great deal.
Likewise, if for political reasons – to answer your question – someone
was taken into protective custody, that is, purely for reasons of state,
this could not be reviewed or stopped by any court. Later, when
some people were also taken into protective custody for non-political
reasons, people who had opposed the system in some other way, I
once, as Prussian Prime Minister and Reich Minister of the Interior,
I remember . . .

MR JUSTICE JACKSON: Let's omit that. I have not asked for
that. If you will just answer my question, we shall save a great deal
of time. Your counsel will be permitted to bring out any explanations
you want to make. You did prohibit all court review and considered

it necessary to prohibit court review of the causes for taking people into what you called protective custody?

GOERING: That I answered very clearly, but I should like to make an explanation in connection with my answer.

MR JUSTICE JACKSON: Your counsel will see to that. Now, the concentration camps and the protective custody . . .

THE PRESIDENT: Mr Justice Jackson, the Tribunal thinks the witness ought to be allowed to make what explanation he thinks right in answer to this question.

The atmosphere grew even more heated in the courtroom as Jackson then endeavoured to show Goering's part in the decisions to attack the USSR and to continue the war long after the German position had become hopeless. Goering had the advantage of understanding English, and thus as the questions were translated into German he had time in which to ready well-prepared answers that evaded the thrust of Jackson's attacks. The Tribunal, too, refused to intervene. It was for Jackson, not them, to challenge Goering's answers.

His evidence cast light on the workings of the highest echelons of the regime, which were then little understood, and Jackson's probing certainly underlined Hitler's responsibility for the central events of the war. Yet it was not Hitler who was on trial.

Trial transcript, 18 March 1946: Goering is questioned about the invasion of Russia

MR JUSTICE JACKSON: Did you at that time see any military necessity for an attack by Germany on Soviet Russia?

GOERING: I personally believed that at that time the danger had not yet reached its climax, and therefore the attack might not yet be necessary. But that was my personal view.

MR JUSTICE JACKSON: And you were the Number 2 man at that time in all Germany?

GOERING: It has nothing to do with my being second in importance. There were two conflicting points of view as regards strategy.

The Fuehrer, the Number 1 man, saw one danger, and I, as the Number 2 man, if you wish to express it so, wanted to carry out another strategic measure. If I had imposed my will every time, then

I would probably have become the Number 1 man. But since the Number 1 man was of a different opinion, and I was only the Number 2 man, his opinion naturally prevailed.

MR JUSTICE JACKSON: I have understood from your testimony – and I think you can answer this 'yes' or 'no', and I would greatly appreciate it if you would – I have understood from your testimony that you were opposed, and told the Fuehrer that you were opposed, to an attack upon Russia at that time. Am I right or wrong?

GOERING: That is correct . . .

MR JUSTICE JACKSON: And yet, because of the Fuehrer system, as I understand you, you could give no warning to the German people; you could bring no pressure of any kind to bear to prevent that step, and you could not even resign to protect your own place in history.

GOERING: These are several questions at once. I should like to answer the first one.

MR JUSTICE JACKSON: Separate them, if you wish.

GOERING: The first question was, I believe, whether I took the opportunity to tell the German people about this danger. I had no occasion to do this. We were at war, and such differences of opinion, as far as strategy was concerned, could not be brought before the public forum during war. I believe that never has happened in world history.

Secondly, as far as my resignation is concerned, I do not wish even to discuss that, for during the war I was an officer, a soldier, and I was not concerned with whether I shared an opinion or not. I had merely to serve my country as a soldier.

Thirdly, I was not the man to forsake someone, to whom I had given my oath of loyalty, every time he was not of my way of thinking. If that had been the case there would have been no need to bind myself to him from the beginning. It never occurred to me to leave the Fuehrer.

MR JUSTICE JACKSON: Insofar as you know, the German people were led into the war, attacking Soviet Russia under the belief that you favoured it?

GOERING: The German people did not know about the declaration of war against Russia until after the war with Russia had started. The German people, therefore, had nothing to do with this. The

German people were not asked; they were told of the fact and of the necessity for it.

MR JUSTICE JACKSON: At what time did you know that the war, as regards achieving the objectives that you had in mind, was a lost war?

GOERING: It is extremely difficult to say. At any rate, according to my conviction, relatively late – I mean, it was only towards the end that I became convinced that the war was lost. Up till then I had always thought and hoped that it would come to a stalemate . . .

MR JUSTICE JACKSON: You said, 'relatively late'. The expression that you used does not tell me anything, because I do not know what you regard as relatively late. Will you fix in terms, either of events or time, when it was that the conviction came to you that the war was lost?

GOERING: When, after 12 January 1945, the Russian offensive pushed forward to the Oder and at the same time the Ardennes offensive had not penetrated, it was then that I was forced to realise that defeat would probably set in slowly. Up to that time I had always hoped that, on the one side, the position at the Vistula toward the East and, on the other side, the position at the West Wall towards the West, could be held until the flow of the new mass-produced weapons should bring about a slackening of the Anglo-American air war . . .

MR JUSTICE JACKSON: Do you want it understood that, as a military man, you did not realise until January of 1945 that Germany could not be successful in the war?

GOERING: As I have already said, we must draw a sharp distinction between two possibilities: First, the successful conclusion of a war, and second, a war which ends by neither side being the victor. As regards a successful outcome, the moment when it was realised that that was no longer possible was much earlier, whereas the realisation of the fact that defeat would set in did not come until the time I have just mentioned.

MR JUSTICE JACKSON: For some period before that, you knew that a successful termination of the war could only be accomplished if you could come to some kind of terms with the enemy; was that not true?

GOERING: Of course, a successful termination of a war can only be considered successful if I either conquer the enemy or, through negotiations with the enemy, come to a conclusion which guarantees me success. That is what I call a successful termination. I call it a draw, when I come to terms with the enemy. This does not bring me the success which victory would have brought but, on the other hand, it precludes a defeat. This is a conclusion without victors or vanquished.

MR JUSTICE JACKSON: But you knew that it was Hitler's policy never to negotiate and you knew that as long as he was the head of the Government the enemy would not negotiate with Germany, did you not?

GOERING: I knew that enemy propaganda emphasised that under no circumstances would there be negotiations with Hitler. That Hitler did not want to negotiate under any circumstances, I also knew, but not in this connection. Hitler wanted to negotiate if there were some prospect of results; but he was absolutely opposed to hopeless and futile negotiations. Because of the declaration of the enemy in the West after the landing in Africa, as far as I remember, that under no circumstances would they negotiate with Germany but would force on her unconditional surrender, Germany's resistance was stiffened to the utmost and measures had to be taken accordingly. If I have no chance of concluding a war through negotiations, then it is useless to negotiate, and I must strain every nerve to bring about a change by a call to arms.

MR JUSTICE JACKSON: By the time of January 1945 you also knew that you were unable to defend the German cities against the air attacks of the Allies, did you not?

GOERING: Concerning the defence of German cities against Allied air attacks, I should like to describe the possibility of doing this as follows: Of itself . . .

MR JUSTICE JACKSON: Can you answer my question? Time may not mean quite as much to you as it does to the rest of us. Can you not answer 'yes' or 'no'? Did you then know, at the same time that you knew that the war was lost, that the German cities could not successfully be defended against air attack by the enemy? Can you not tell us 'yes' or 'no'?

GOERING: I can say that I knew that, at that time, it was not possible.

MR JUSTICE JACKSON: And after that time it was well known to you that the air attacks which were continued against England could not turn the tide of war, and were designed solely to effect a prolongation of what you then knew was a hopeless conflict?

GOERING: I believe you are mistaken. After January 1945 there were no more attacks on England, except perhaps a few single planes, because at that time I needed all my petrol for the fighter planes for defence. If I had had bombers and oil at my disposal, then, of course, I should have continued such attacks up to the last minute as retaliation for the attacks which were being carried out on German cities, whatever our chances might have been.

MR JUSTICE JACKSON: What about robot attacks? Were there any robot attacks after January 1945?

GOERING: Thank God, we still had one weapon that we could use. I have just said that, as long as the fight was on, we had to hit back; and as a soldier I can only regret that we did not have enough of these V-1 and V-2 bombs, for an easing of the attacks on German cities could be brought about only if we could inflict equally heavy losses on the enemy.

MR JUSTICE JACKSON: And there was no way to prevent the war going on as long as Hitler was the head of the German Government, was there?

GOERING: As long as Hitler was the Fuehrer of the German people, he alone decided whether the war was to go on. As long as my enemy threatens me and demands absolutely unconditional surrender, I fight to my last breath, because there is nothing left for me except perhaps a chance that in some way fate may change, even though it seems hopeless.

MR JUSTICE JACKSON: Well, the people of Germany who thought it was time that the slaughter should stop had no means to stop it except revolution or assassination of Hitler, had they?

GOERING: A revolution always changes a situation, if it succeeds. That is a foregone conclusion. The murder of Hitler at this time, say January 1945, would have brought about my succession. If the enemy had given me the same answer, that is unconditional surrender, and had held out those terrible conditions which had been intimated, I would have continued fighting whatever the circumstances.

Jackson now moved on to deal with Goering's role in the Anschluss. In the run-up to the annexation in March 1938, the Nazis' inside man in the Austrian Government had been Arthur Seyss-Inquart. Goering and Hitler had bullied the Austrian president into naming him Chancellor, so paving the way for German soldiers to cross the frontier unopposed. Later Seyss-Inquart had become Frank's deputy in Poland and Governor of Holland, and was now also on trial at Nuremberg.

Due to his political and judicial career, it had been some years since Jackson had had to examine a witness, and now that lack of practice was exposed. Standing at a lectern, he doggedly continued to put questions across the room to Goering, who was looking full of fight. Try as he might, Jackson could not get Goering to give a straight answer.

Trial transcript, 18 March 1946: Goering is asked about his role in the Anschluss

MR JUSTICE JACKSON: Now, did Seyss-Inquart become Chancellor of Austria with the understanding that he was to surrender his country to Germany, or did you lead him to believe that he would be independent, have an independent country?

GOERING: I explained the other day that even at the time when he left by plane the next morning, the Fuehrer himself had still not made up his mind as to whether the union with Austria should not be brought about by means of a joint head of state. I also said that I personally did not consider this solution far-reaching enough and that I was for an absolute, direct, and total Anschluss.

I did not know exactly what Seyss-Inquart's attitude was at this time. Nevertheless I feared that his attitude was rather in the direction of continued separation with co-operation, and did not go as far as my attitude in the direction of a total Anschluss. Therefore I was very satisfied when this total Anschluss crystallised in the course of the day.

MR JUSTICE JACKSON: I respectfully submit that the answers are not responsive, and I repeat the question. Did Seyss-Inquart become Chancellor of Austria with an understanding that he would call in the German troops and surrender Austria to Germany, or did you lead him to believe that he could continue an independent Austria?

GOERING: Excuse me, but that is a number of questions which I cannot answer simply with 'yes' or 'no'.

If you ask me, 'Did Seyss-Inquart become Chancellor according to Hitler's wishes and yours?' – yes.

If you then ask me, 'Did he become Chancellor with the understanding that he should send a telegram for troops to march in?' – I say, 'No,' because at the time of the Chancellorship there was no question of his sending us a telegram.

If you ask me, thirdly, 'Did he become Chancellor on the understanding that he would be able to maintain an independent Austria?' – then I have to say again that the final turn of events was not clear in the Fuehrer's mind on that evening.

That is what I tried to explain . . .

Even on the rare occasion when Jackson appeared to catch out Goering, fate seemed to conspire against him. By the terms of the Versailles Treaty that concluded the First World War, the Rhineland had become a demilitarised zone. Goering now testified that the movement of troops into the area in 1936, in breach of the treaty, had not been planned in advance. Jackson triumphantly flourished the minutes of a conference in June 1935 of the Reich Defence Council that seemed to indicate the contrary, but a poor piece of translation in the English version of the document allowed Goering to humiliate him, and to sidestep the evidence that pointed to the planning of the zone's remilitarisation. To the embarrassment of all in the hushed courtroom, it also caused Jackson to lose his temper.

Trial transcript, 19 March 1946: Jackson loses his temper over the Rhineland

MR JUSTICE JACKSON: Do you find this: 'The demilitarised

zone requires special treatment. In his speech of 21 May 1935 and in other statements, the Fuehrer and Reich Chancellor declared that the stipulations of the Versailles Treaty and the Locarno Pact regarding the demilitarised zone would be observed.' Do you find this?

GOERING: Yes.

MR JUSTICE JACKSON: And do you find the next paragraph, 'Since at present international entanglements must be avoided under all circumstances, all urgently needed preparations may be made. The preparations as such, or their planning, must be kept in strictest secrecy in the zone itself as well as in the rest of the Reich.' Do you find this?

GOERING: Yes.

MR JUSTICE JACKSON: And you also find, 'These preparations include in particular'– a) and b) are not important to my present question – 'c) Preparation for the liberation of the Rhine.'

GOERING: Oh, no, here you have made a great mistake. The original phrase – and this alone is the point in question – is: 'c) Preparation for the clearing of the Rhine.' It is a purely technical preparation that has nothing at all to do with the liberation of the Rhineland. Here it says, first, mobilisation measures for transportation and communications, then 'c) Preparation for the clearing of the Rhine', that is, in case of mobilisation preparations the Rhine is not to be overburdened with freighters, tugboats, et cetera, but the river has to be clear for military measures. Then it continues: 'd) Preparation for local defence', et cetera. Thus you see, it figures among small quite general, ordinary and usual preparations for mobilisation. The phrase used by the Prosecution . . .

MR JUSTICE JACKSON: Mobilisation, exactly.

GOERING: That, if you remember, I stressed clearly in my statement, that in the demilitarised zone general preparations for mobilisation were made. I mentioned the purchase of horses, et cetera. I wanted only to point out the mistake regarding 'clearing of the Rhine', which has nothing to do with the Rhineland, but only with the river.

MR JUSTICE JACKSON: Well, those preparations were preparations for armed occupation of the Rhineland, were they not?

GOERING: No, that is altogether wrong. If Germany had become involved in a war, no matter from which side, let us assume from the East, then mobilisation measures would have had to be carried out for security reasons throughout the Reich, in this event even in the demilitarised Rhineland; but not for the purpose of occupation, of liberating the Rhineland.

MR JUSTICE JACKSON: You mean the preparations were not military preparations?

GOERING: Those were general preparations for mobilisation, such as every country makes, and not for the purpose of the occupation of the Rhineland.

MR JUSTICE JACKSON: But were of a character which had to be kept entirely secret from foreign powers?

GOERING: I do not think I can recall reading beforehand the publication of the mobilisation preparations of the United States.

MR JUSTICE JACKSON: Well, I respectfully submit to the Tribunal that this witness is not being responsive, and has not been in his examination, and that it is . . .

[The defendant interposed a few words which were not recorded.]

It is perfectly futile to spend our time if we cannot have responsive answers to our questions.

[The defendant interposed a few words which were not recorded.]

We can strike these things out. I do not want to spend time doing that, but this witness, it seems to me, is adopting, and has adopted, in the witness box and in the dock, an arrogant and contemptuous attitude toward the Tribunal which is giving him the trial which he never gave a living soul, nor dead ones either.

I respectfully submit that the witness be instructed to make notes, if he wishes, of his explanations, but that he be required to answer my questions and reserve his explanations for his counsel to bring out.

THE PRESIDENT: I have already laid down the general rule, which is binding upon this defendant as upon other witnesses.

Perhaps we had better adjourn now . . .

Lawrence had hoped that a night's rest would give Jackson the chance to recover his composure, but the next morning he straightaway staked the remaining vestiges of his authority on getting the Tribunal's backing on the pettiest of points. His stance, which presumed too much that the prosecution and the judges were on the same side, baffled Lawrence and lost Jackson much respect.

Trial transcript, 20 March 1946: The Tribunal declines to back Jackson against Goering

MR JUSTICE JACKSON: If the Tribunal please, the last question which I asked last night referring to mobilisation preparations in the Rhineland, as shown in the official transcript, was this: 'But of a character which had to be kept entirely secret from foreign powers?' The answer was: 'I do not believe I can recall the publication of the preparations of the United States for mobilisation.'

Now, representing the United States of America, I am confronted with these choices – to ignore that remark and allow it to stand for people who do not understand our system; or to develop, at considerable expense of time, its falsity; or to answer it in rebuttal. The difficulty arises from this, Your Honour, that if the witness is permitted to volunteer statements in cross-examination there is no opportunity to make objection until they are placed on the record. Of course, if such an answer had been indicated by a question of counsel, as I respectfully submit would be the orderly procedure, there would have been objection; the Tribunal would have been in a position to discharge its duty under the Charter and I would have been in a position to have shortened the case by not having that remark placed.

The Charter in Article 18 provides that the Tribunal shall rule out irrelevant issues and statements of any kind whatsoever. We are squarely confronted with that question; we cannot discharge those duties if the defendant is to volunteer these statements without questions which bring them up. I respectfully submit that, if the ruling of the Tribunal that the defendant may volunteer questions of this kind is to prevail, the control of these proceedings is put in the hands of this defendant, and the United States has been substantially denied its right of cross-examination under the Charter, because cross-examination cannot be effective under this kind of procedure. Since we cannot anticipate, we cannot meet . . .

THE PRESIDENT: I quite agree with you that any reference to the United States' secrecy with reference to mobilisation is entirely irrelevant, and that the answer ought not to have been made, but the only rule which the Tribunal can lay down as a general rule is the rule – already laid down – that the witness must answer if possible 'yes' or 'no', and that he may make such explanations as may be necessary after answering questions directly in that way, and that such explanations must be brief and not be speeches. As far as this particular answer goes, I think it is entirely irrelevant.

MR JUSTICE JACKSON: I must, of course, bow to the ruling of the Tribunal, but it is to the second part, I quite recall the admonition of the Court that there shall be answers 'yes' or 'no'. This witness, of course, pays not the slightest attention to that, and I must say I cannot blame him; he is pursuing his interests. But we have no way of anticipating, and here we are confronted with this statement in the record, because when these statements are volunteered they are in the record before the Tribunal can rule upon them and I have no opportunity to make objections, and the Tribunal has no opportunity to rule. And it puts, as I said before, the control of these proceedings in the hands of the defendant, if he first makes the charges and then puts it up to us to ignore them or answer them by long cross-examination in rebuttal; and I think the specific charge made against the United States of America from the witness stand presents that. Your Honour now advises the United States that it is an improper answer, but it is in the record and we must deal with it. I respectfully submit that unless we have . . .

THE PRESIDENT: What exactly is the motion you are making? Are you asking the Tribunal to strike the answer out of the record?

MR JUSTICE JACKSON: Well, no; in a Trial of this kind, where propaganda is one of the purposes of the defendant, striking out does no good after the answer is made, and Goering knows that as well as I. The charge has been made against the United States and it is in the record. I am now moving that this witness be instructed that he must answer my questions 'yes' or 'no' if they permit an answer, and that the explanation be brought out by his counsel in a fashion that will permit us to make objections, if they are irrelevant, and to obtain rulings of the Tribunal, so that the Tribunal can discharge its functions of ruling out irrelevant issues and statements of any kind whatsoever. We must not let the Trial degenerate into a bickering contest between counsel and the witness. That is not what the United States would expect me to participate in. I respectfully suggest that if he can draw any kind of challenge . . .

THE PRESIDENT: Are you submitting to the Tribunal that the witness has to answer every question 'yes' or 'no' and wait until he is re-examined for the purpose of making any explanations at all?

MR JUSTICE JACKSON: I think that is the rule of cross-examination under ordinary circumstances. The witness, if the question permits it, must answer, and if there are relevant explanations they should be reserved until later . . .

THE PRESIDENT: Surely it is making too much of a sentence the witness has said, whether the United States makes its orders for mobilisation public or not. Surely that is not a matter of very great importance. Every country keeps certain things secret. Certainly it would be much wiser to ignore a statement of that sort. But as to the general rule, the Tribunal will now consider the matter. I have already laid down what I believe to be the rule, and I think with the assent of the Tribunal, but I will ascertain . . .

MR JUSTICE JACKSON: Let me say that I agree with Your Honour that as far as the United States is concerned we are not worried by anything the witness can say about it – and we expected plenty. The point is, do we answer these things or leave them, apart from the control of the Trial? And it does seem to me that this is the beginning of this Trial's getting out of hand, if I may say so, if we do not have control of this situation. I trust the Tribunal will pardon my earnestness in presenting this. I think it is a very vital thing.

THE PRESIDENT: I have never heard it suggested that the Counsel for the Prosecution have to answer every irrelevant observation made in cross-examination.

MR JUSTICE JACKSON: That would be true in a private litigation, but I trust the Court is not unaware that outside of this courtroom is a great social question of the revival of Nazism and that one of the purposes of the Defendant Goering – I think he would be the first to admit – is to revive and perpetuate it by propaganda from this trial now in process . . .

THE PRESIDENT: Mr Justice Jackson, the Tribunal considers that the rule which it has laid down is the only possible rule and that the witness must be confined strictly to answering the question directly where the question admits of a direct answer, and that he must not make his explanation before he gives a direct answer; but, after having given a direct answer to any question which admits of a direct answer, he may make a short explanation; and that he is not to be confined simply to making direct answers 'yes' or 'no' and leaving the explanation until his counsel puts it to him in his re-examination.

As to this particular observation of the defendant, the defendant ought not to have referred to the United States, but it is a matter which I think you might well ignore.

MR JUSTICE JACKSON: I shall bow to the ruling, of course.

Aside from Jackson's lack of skill in cross-examination, he was handicapped by his lofty aspirations for the trial, which he hoped would demonstrate the moral superiority of democratic government and, on a personal level, might cap his legal career with a world-resounding success.

A few weeks after his exchanges with Goering, the leadership of the Supreme Court fell vacant when Chief Justice Harlan Stone died. Jackson had long been mooted as a potential successor, but in the event he was not chosen. Might things have gone differently had he fared better with Goering? He, at any event, remained bitter afterwards at the lack of support he felt he had had from the Tribunal – especially the other Americans – in corralling the Reichsmarschall. Yet ultimately, in the context of the trial, his failure was to make little difference to the verdict.

§

Downcast as he was by his rebuff by the Tribunal, Jackson still had a number of incriminating documents to put to Goering, notably on his involvement in the Nazis' plans for the Jews. Among these were the notes of a high-level meeting that, as the economy's supremo, he had chaired in November 1938 after the Kristallnacht riots, which had targeted Jewish shops and synagogues. Those present included the regime's chief propagandist, Joseph Goebbels, a fervent anti-Semite, who unveiled his plans to further humiliate the Jews through a system of apartheid.

Trial transcript, 20 March 1946: Goering and Goebbels' schemes for Jewish apartheid

MR JUSTICE JACKSON: You opened the meeting: 'Gentlemen, today's meeting is of a decisive nature. I have received a letter written on the Fuehrer's orders by the Stabsleiter of the Fuehrer's Deputy, Bormann, requesting that the Jewish question be now, once and for all, co-ordinated and solved one way or another.' Is that correct?
GOERING: Yes, that is correct.
MR JUSTICE JACKSON: Further down, I find this: 'Gentlemen, I have had enough of these demonstrations. They do not harm the Jews, but finally devolve on me, the highest authority for the German economy. If today a Jewish shop is destroyed, if goods are thrown into the street, the insurance company will pay the Jew for the damages so that he does not suffer any damage at all. Furthermore, consumer goods, goods belonging to the people, are destroyed. If, in the future, demonstrations occur – and on occasion they may be necessary – then I ask that they be so directed that we do not cut our own throats.'
   Am I correct?
GOERING: Yes, quite correct . . .
MR JUSTICE JACKSON: 'I do not want to leave any doubt, gentlemen, as to the purpose of today's meeting. We have not come together merely to talk again, but to make decisions; and I earnestly ask the competent departments to take trenchant measures for the Aryanising of the German economy and to submit them to me as far as is necessary.'
GOERING: That is correct . . .
MR JUSTICE JACKSON: Well, then Dr Goebbels interposed, 'I am of the opinion that this is our chance to dissolve the synagogues.'

And then you have a discussion about the dissolving of the synagogues, have you not?

GOERING: By Dr Goebbels, yes.

MR JUSTICE JACKSON: Then, Dr Goebbels raised the question of Jews travelling in railway trains?

GOERING: Yes.

MR JUSTICE JACKSON: Let me know if I quote correctly the dialogue between you and Dr Goebbels on that subject. Dr Goebbels said: 'Furthermore, I advocate that Jews be banned from all public places where they might cause provocation. It is still possible for a Jew to share a sleeper with a German. Therefore, the Reich Ministry of Transport must issue a decree ordering that there shall be separate compartments for Jews. If this compartment is full, then the Jews cannot claim a seat. They can only be given separate compartments after all Germans have secured seats. They must not mix with the Germans; if there is no more room, they will have to stand in the corridor.'

Is that right?

GOERING: Yes, that is correct.

MR JUSTICE JACKSON: '*Goering:* I think it would be more sensible to give them separate compartments.

'*Goebbels:* Not if the train is overcrowded.

'*Goering:* Just a moment. There will be only one Jewish coach. If that is filled up the other Jews will have to stay at home.

'*Goebbels:* But suppose there are not many Jews going, let us say, on the long-distance express train to Munich. Suppose there are two Jews on the train, and the other compartments are overcrowded; these two Jews would then have a compartment to themselves. Therefore, the decree must state, Jews may claim a seat only after all Germans have secured a seat.

'*Goering:* I would give the Jews one coach or one compartment, and should a case such as you mention arise, and the train be overcrowded, believe me, we will not need a law. He will be kicked out all right, and will have to sit alone in the toilet all the way.'

Is that correct?

GOERING: Yes. I was getting irritated when Goebbels came with his small details when important laws were being discussed. I refused to do anything. I issued no decrees or laws in this connection. Of course, today, it is very pleasant for the Prosecution to bring it up, but I wish to state that it was a very lively meeting at which Goebbels made demands which were quite outside the economic sphere, and I used these expressions to give vent to my feelings.

MR JUSTICE JACKSON: Then Goebbels, who felt very strongly about these things, said that Jews should stand in the corridor, and you said that they would have to sit in the toilet. That is the way you said it?

GOERING: No, it is not. I said that they should have a special compartment; and when Goebbels still was not satisfied, and harped on it, I finally told him, 'I do not need a law. He can either sit in the toilet or leave the train.' These are utterances made in this connection which, however, have nothing to do with the world-wide importance of the great conflict.

MR JUSTICE JACKSON: Let us go down to where Goebbels brings up the subject of the German forests.

GOERING: Just a moment. Yes. It starts where Goebbels asked for a decree which would prevent Jews from going to German holiday resorts. To which I replied 'Give them their own.' And then he suggested that it would have to be considered whether we should give them their own resorts, or place some German bathing places at their disposal, but not the best ones so that people might say: 'You allow the Jews to get fit by using our bathing resorts.' The question must also be considered whether it was necessary to forbid the Jews to go into the German forests. Herds of Jews are today running around in Grünewald; that is a constant provocation – and so on. Then when he broke in again, I replied very sharply, 'It would be better to put a certain part of the forest at the disposal of the Jews,' as he wanted them out of the whole of the forests. Then I made the remark which seems to be of so much interest.

MR JUSTICE JACKSON: Let us have that remark. Is it not correct, you did state: 'We will give the Jews a certain part of the forest, and Alpers [foresters] will see to it that the various animals, which are damnably like the Jews – the Elk too has a hooked nose – go into the Jewish enclosure and settle down among them.'

Is that what you said?

GOERING: Yes, I said it, but it should be linked up with the whole atmosphere of the meeting . . .

MR JUSTICE JACKSON: Now, I call your attention to the following conversation . . .

'One question has still to be discussed. Most of the goods in the stores were not the property of the shopkeepers but were on consignment from other firms which had supplied them. Now the unpaid invoices are being sent in by these firms, which are certainly not all Jewish, but Aryan, in respect to these goods on consignment. '*Hilgard:* We will have to pay for them too.

'*Goering:* I wish you had killed 200 Jews instead of destroying such valuables.

'*Heydrich:* There were 35 killed.'

Do I read that correctly?

GOERING: Yes, this was said in a moment of bad temper and excitement.

MR JUSTICE JACKSON: Spontaneously sincere, wasn't it?

GOERING: As I said, it was not meant seriously. It was the expression of spontaneous excitement caused by the events, and by the destruction of valuables, and by the difficulties which arose. Of course, if you are going to bring up every word I said in the course of 25 years in these circles, I myself could give you instances of even stronger remarks . . .

MR JUSTICE JACKSON: Pass on a little further. Heydrich is making suggestions and says:

'As for the isolating, I would like to make a few proposals regarding police measures, which are important also because of their psychological effect on public opinion. For example, anybody who is Jewish according to the Nuremberg Laws will have to wear a certain badge. That is a possibility which will facilitate many other things. I see no danger of excesses, and it will make our relationship with the foreign Jews easier.

'*Goering:* A uniform?

'*Heydrich:* A badge. In this way we could put an end to foreign Jews being molested who do not look different from ours.
'*Goering:* But my dear Heydrich, you will not be able to avoid the creation of ghettos on a very large scale in all the cities. They will have to be created.' . . .
Toward the close of that meeting you said the following, didn't you? 'I demand that German Jewry as a whole shall, as a punishment for the abominable crimes, et cetera, make a contribution of 1,000,000,000 marks. That will work. The pigs will not commit a second murder [the assassination of a German diplomat which was the excuse for the riots] so quickly. Incidentally, I would like to say again that I would not like to be a Jew in Germany.'
GOERING: That was correct, yes.

The Nazis' measures against the Jews drew support from the perception that they exerted a dominant and disproportionate influence in business, the professions, the arts and politics. In fact, less than 1 per cent of the German population was Jewish.

§

Jackson now turned to the collection of looted art that Goering had amassed during the war. A special snatch squad, the Einsatzstab Rosenberg, had been set up to seize the cultural treasures of those countries occupied by the Germans. Their work was in part born of the Nazis' imperial conceptions of themselves, and in part was simply an opportunity for the top ranks of the Party to indulge their taste for plunder. Citing a statement given by one of Rosenberg's officials, Dr Bunjes, Jackson reminded Goering of the brazen and acquisitive mood he had been in when making a tour of Paris's museums.

Trial transcript, 20 March 1946: Jackson quotes Bunjes on Goering as 'art collector'

'On Wednesday, 5 February 1941, I was ordered to the Jeu de Paume by the Reich Marshal. At 1500 o'clock, the Reich Marshal, accompanied by General Hanesse, Herr Angerer, and Herr Hofer, visited the exhibition of Jewish art treasures newly set up there . . .

Then, with me as his guide, the Reich Marshal inspected the exhibited art treasures and made a selection of those works of art which were to go to the Fuehrer, and those which were to be placed in his own collection.

'During this confidential conversation, I again called the Reich Marshal's attention to the fact that a note of protest had been received from the French Government against the activity of the Einsatzstab Rosenberg, with reference to the Hague Rules on Land Warfare recognised by Germany at the Armistice of Compiègne and I pointed out that General von Stulpnagel's interpretation of the manner in which the confiscated Jewish art treasures are to be treated was apparently contrary to the Reich Marshal's interpretation. Thereupon, the Reich Marshal asked for a detailed explanation and gave the following orders:

'"First, it is my orders that you have to follow. You will act directly according to my orders. The art objects collected in the Jeu de Paume are to be loaded on a special train immediately and taken to Germany by order of the Reich Marshal. These art objects which are to go into the Fuehrer's possession, and those art objects which the Reich Marshal claims for himself, will be loaded on two railroad cars which will be attached to the Reich Marshal's special train, and upon his departure for Germany, at the beginning of next week, will be taken along to Berlin. FeldFuehrer von Behr will accompany the Reich Marshal in his special train on the journey to Berlin."

'When I made the objection that the jurists would probably be of a different opinion and that protests would most likely be made by the military commander in France, the Reich Marshal answered, saying verbatim as follows, "Dear Bunjes, let me worry about that; I am the highest jurist in the State."'

§

Jackson's failure to force admissions from Goering now threatened to derail the entire prosecution case against the leading defendant. The chief British prosecutor, Sir David Maxwell Fyfe, had expected to have to cross-examine Goering on just that part of the case that was the responsibility of his team, Count Two. Now, suddenly, as if there was not enough pressure already on him, it seemed as if any conviction might depend on what Maxwell Fyfe could make of what had been seen as more minor charges. Yet, unlike Jackson, the Scotsman was a seasoned courtroom advocate, well capable of confining a witness to the matters in hand, and one focused on winning the case. He began by quizzing Goering about his knowledge of what became known as 'The Great Escape' from a Luftwaffe-run prisoner-of-war-camp in 1944, following which fifty recaptured British servicemen had been executed.

Trial transcript, 20 March 1946: Goering and 'The Great Escape' – Maxwell Fyfe takes the offensive

SIR DAVID MAXWELL FYFE: I want to ask you first some questions about the matter of the British Air Force officers who escaped from Stalag Luft III. Do you remember that you said in giving your evidence that you knew this incident very completely and very minutely? Do you remember saying that?

GOERING: No – that I had received accurate knowledge; not that I had accurate knowledge – but that I received it.

SIR DAVID MAXWELL FYFE: Let me quote your own words, as they were taken down, 'I know this incident very completely, very minutely, but it came to my attention, unfortunately, at a later period of time.' That is what you said the other day, is that right?

GOERING: Yes, that is what I meant; that I know about the incident exactly, but only heard of it two days later.

SIR DAVID MAXWELL FYFE: You told the Tribunal that you were on leave at this time, in the last period of March 1944, is that right?

GOERING: Yes, as far as I remember I was on leave in March until a few days before Easter.

SIR DAVID MAXWELL FYFE: And you said, 'As I can prove.' I want you to tell the Tribunal the dates of your leave.

GOERING: I say again, that this refers to the whole of March – I remember it well – and for proof I would like to mention the people who were with me on this leave . . .

SIR DAVID MAXWELL FYFE: I want you to help me with regard to one or two other dates of which you have spoken. You say: 'I heard one or two days later about this escape.' Do you understand, Witness, that it is about the escape I am asking you, not about the shooting, for the moment; I want to make it quite clear.

GOERING: It is clear to me.

SIR DAVID MAXWELL FYFE: Did you mean by that, that you heard about the actual escape one or two days after it happened?

GOERING: Yes . . .

SIR DAVID MAXWELL FYFE: I want you to tell the Tribunal another date: You say that on your return from leave your chief of staff made a communication to you. Who was your chief of staff?

GOERING: General Korten was chief of staff at that time.

SIR DAVID MAXWELL FYFE: Can you tell us the date at which he made this communication to you?

GOERING: No, I cannot tell you that exactly. I believe I discussed this incident with my chief of staff later, telling him what I had already heard about it from other sources . . .

SIR DAVID MAXWELL FYFE: What was the date that you talked about it with your chief of staff?

GOERING: I cannot tell you the date exactly from memory, but it must have been around Easter.

SIR DAVID MAXWELL FYFE: That would be just about the end of March, wouldn't it?

GOERING: No. It might have been at the beginning of April, the first half of April . . .

SIR DAVID MAXWELL FYFE: You said the other day that you could prove when you were on leave. Am I to take it that you haven't taken the trouble to look up what your leave dates were?

GOERING: I have already said that I was on leave during March. Whether I returned on the 26th or the 28th or the 29th of March I cannot tell you. For proof of that you would have to ask the people who accompanied me, who perhaps can fix this date more definitely. I know only that I was there in March.

SIR DAVID MAXWELL FYFE: Witness, will it be perfectly fair to you if I take the latest of your dates, the 29th of March, to work on?

GOERING: It would be more expedient if you would tell me when Easter was that year, because I do not recall it . . .

SIR DAVID MAXWELL FYFE: Well, I can't give you Easter offhand, but I happen to remember Whitsuntide was the 28th of May, so that Easter would be early, somewhere about the 5th of April. So that your leave would finish somewhere about the end of March, maybe the 26th or the 29th; that is right, isn't it?

Now, these shootings of these officers went on from the 25th of March to the 13th of April; do you know that?

GOERING: I do not know that exactly.

SIR DAVID MAXWELL FYFE: You may take that from me, because there is an official report of the shooting, and I want to be quite fair with you. Only 49 of these officers were shot on the 6th of April, as far as we can be sure, and one was shot either on the 13th of April or later. But the critical period is the end of March, and we may take it that you were back from leave by about the 29th of March.

I just want you to tell the Tribunal this was a matter of great importance, wasn't it? Considered a matter of great importance?

GOERING: It was a very important matter.

SIR DAVID MAXWELL FYFE: General Milch – I beg pardon – Field Marshal Milch has said that it was a matter which would require the highest authority, and I think you have said that you know it was Hitler's decision that these officers should be shot; is that so?

GOERING: The question did not come through clearly.

SIR DAVID MAXWELL FYFE: It was Hitler's decision that these officers should be shot?

GOERING: That is correct; and I was later notified that it was Hitler's decree . . .

Having secured the admissions he wanted, Maxwell Fyfe allowed Goering to believe the moment of danger had passed and moved on to a separate though related matter.

SIR DAVID MAXWELL FYFE: You knew about the general plan for treatment of prisoners of war, which we have had in evidence as the 'Aktion Kugel' plan, didn't you?

GOERING: No. I knew nothing of this action. I was not advised of it.

SIR DAVID MAXWELL FYFE: You were never advised of Aktion Kugel?

GOERING: I first heard of Aktion Kugel here; saw the document and heard the expression for the first time. Moreover no officer of the Luftwaffe ever informed me of such a thing; and I do not believe that a single officer was ever taken away from the Luftwaffe camps. A report to this effect was never presented to me, in any case.

SIR DAVID MAXWELL FYFE: You know what Aktion Kugel was: That escaped officers and noncommissioned officers, other than British and American, were to be handed over to the police and taken to Mauthausen, where they were shot by the device of having a gun concealed in the measuring equipment when they thought they were getting their prison clothes. You know what Aktion Kugel is, don't you?

GOERING: I heard of it here.

SIR DAVID MAXWELL FYFE: Are you telling the Tribunal that you did not know that escaped prisoners of war who were picked up by the police were retained by the police and taken to Mauthausen?

GOERING: No, I did not know that. On the contrary, various prisoners who escaped from my camps were caught again by the police; and they were all brought back to the camps; this was the first case where this to some extent did not take place.

SIR DAVID MAXWELL FYFE: But didn't you know that Colonel Walde, as second in command of your ministry's inspectorate, issued a written order a month before this, in February 1944, that prisoners of war picked up by the Luftwaffe should be delivered back to their camp, and prisoners of war picked up by the police should be held by them and no longer counted as being under the protection of the Luftwaffe; didn't you know that?

GOERING: No. Please summon this colonel to testify if he ever made a report of that nature to me, or addressed such a letter to me . . .

SIR DAVID MAXWELL FYFE: I see. So you say that you had never heard – this was 3½ years after the beginning of the war – and you had never heard that any escaped prisoners of war were to be handed over to the police. Is that what you ask the Tribunal to believe?

GOERING: To the extent that escaped prisoners of war committed any offences or crimes, they were of course turned over to the police, I believe. But I wish to testify before the Court that I never gave any order that they should be handed over to the police or sent to concentration camps merely because they had attempted to break out or escape, nor did I ever know that such measures were taken.

The court adjourned for the day, and first thing next morning Maxwell Fyfe sought to undermine Goering's assertion that his evidence was truthful, before returning to the more potentially damning matter of what he had known about the reprisals for the escape.

Trial transcript, 21 March 1946: Goering admits to knowing about the reprisals for the escape

SIR DAVID MAXWELL FYFE: Witness, do you remember telling me last night that the only prisoners of war handed over to the police were those guilty of crimes or misdemeanours?

GOERING: I did not express myself that way. I said if the police apprehended prisoners of war, those who had committed a crime during the escape, as far as I know, were detained by the police and were not returned to the camp. To what extent the police kept prisoners of war, without returning them to a camp, I was able to gather from interrogations and explanations here.

SIR DAVID MAXWELL FYFE: Would you look at Document D-569? Would you look first at the top left-hand corner, which shows that it is a document published by the Oberkommando der Wehrmacht? . . . Now, look at the left-hand bottom corner, as to distribution. The second person to whom it is distributed is the Air Ministry and Commander-in-Chief of the Air Force on 22 November 1941. That would be you.

GOERING: That's correct. I would like to make the following statement in connection with this . . .

SIR DAVID MAXWELL FYFE: Just for a moment. I would like you to appreciate the document and then make your statement upon it. I shall not stop you. I want you to look at the third sentence in Paragraph 1. This deals with Soviet prisoners of war, you understand. The third sentence says:

'If escaped Soviet prisoners of war are returned to the camp in accordance with this order, they have to be handed over to the nearest post of the Secret State Police, in any case.' . . . Do I understand this document to say that a man who escapes will be handed over to the Security Police? You understand this document says a man who escapes will be handed over to the Secret Police . . .

This order would be dealt by your prisoner-of-war department in your ministry, wouldn't it?

GOERING: This department, according to the procedure adopted for these orders, received the order, but no other department received it.

SIR DAVID MAXWELL FYFE: I think the answer to my question must be 'yes'. It would be dealt with by the prisoner-of-war department – your ministry. Isn't that so?

GOERING: I would say yes.

SIR DAVID MAXWELL FYFE: It is quicker, you see, if you say 'yes' in the beginning; do you understand?

GOERING: No; it depends upon whether I personally have read the order or not, and I will then determine as to my responsibility.

SIR DAVID MAXWELL FYFE: Well now, the escape . . .

THE PRESIDENT: You were not asked about responsibility, you were asked whether it would be dealt with by your prisoner-of-war department.

SIR DAVID MAXWELL FYFE: Now, the escape about which I am asking you took place on the night of the 24th to the 25th March. I want you to have that date in mind. The decision to murder these young officers must have been taken very quickly because the first murder which actually took place was on the 26th of March. Do you agree with that? It must have been taken quickly?

GOERING: I assume that this order, as I was informed later, was given immediately, but it had no connection with this document.

SIR DAVID MAXWELL FYFE: No, no; we are finished with that document; we are going into the murder of these young men. The *Grossfahndung* – a general hue and cry, I think, would be the British translation – was also issued at once in order that these men should be arrested; isn't that so?

GOERING: That is correct. Whenever there was an escape, and such a large number of prisoners escaped, automatically in the whole Reich a hue and cry was raised, that is all authorities had to be on the lookout to recapture the prisoners.

SIR DAVID MAXWELL FYFE: So that in order to give this order to murder these men, and for the *Grossfahndung,* there must have been a meeting of Hitler, at any rate with Himmler or Kaltenbrunner, in order that that order would be put into effect; isn't that so?

GOERING: That is correct. According to what I heard, Himmler was the first to report this escape to the Fuehrer.

SIR DAVID MAXWELL FYFE: Now, General Westhoff, who was in Defendant Keitel's *Kriegsgefangenenwesen*, in his prisoner-of-war set-up, says this, that 'On a date, which I think was the 26th, Keitel said to him, "This morning Goering reproached me in the presence of Himmler for having let some more prisoners of war escape. It was unheard of."'

   Do you say that General Westhoff is wrong?

GOERING: Yes. This is not in accordance with the facts. General Westhoff is referring to a statement of Field Marshal Keitel. This utterance in itself is illogical, for I could not accuse Keitel because he would not draw my attention to it, as the guarding was his responsibility and not mine.

SIR DAVID MAXWELL FYFE: One of the Defendant Keitel's officers dealing with this matter was a general inspector, General Rottich. I do not know if you know him.

GOERING: No.

SIR DAVID MAXWELL FYFE: Well, General Westhoff, as one could understand, is very anxious to assure everyone that his senior officer had nothing to do with it, and he goes on to say this about General Rottich: 'He was completely excluded from it by the fact that these matters were taken out of his hands. Apparently at that conference with the Fuehrer in the morning, that is to say, the conference between Himmler, Field Marshal Keitel, and Goering, which took place in the Fuehrer's presence, the Fuehrer himself always took a hand in these affairs when officers escaped.'

You say that is wrong? You were at no such conference?
GOERING: I was not present at this conference, neither was General Westhoff; he is giving a purely subjective view, not the facts of the case.

Although Goering was clearly discomfited by Maxwell Fyfe's line of questioning, he continued to claim that he had not learned of the execution order until some days after it had been given by Hitler, and thus had been unable to intervene. In what had become a game of cat and mouse, Maxwell Fyfe increased the tension in the courtroom by producing documents that told another story. One affidavit was from Lt-Gen. Grosch, the Luftwaffe's chief prison inspector.

'Colonel Walde informed me . . . that there was a decision by the Fuehrer to the effect that, on recapture, the escaped British airmen were not to be handed back to the Luftwaffe but were to be shot . . . I asked Colonel Walde whether such a far-reaching decision would be notified in writing to the High Command of the Luftwaffe or the Reich Air Ministry or whether he had been given anything in writing. Colonel Walde gave me to understand that the assembly were told by the spokesman of the OKW that they would receive nothing in writing, nor was there to be any correspondence on this subject. The circle of those in the know was to be kept as small as possible. I asked Colonel Walde whether the spokesman of the OKW had said anything to the effect that the Reich Marshal or the High Command of the Luftwaffe had been informed about the matter. Colonel Walde assured me that the OKW spokesman had told them that the Reich Marshal was informed.'
SIR DAVID MAXWELL FYFE [*Turning to the witness*]: You understand, what I am suggesting to you is that here was a matter which was not only known in the OKW, not only known in the Gestapo and the Kripo, but was known to your own director of operations, General Forster, who told General Grosch that he had informed Field Marshal Milch. I am suggesting to you that it is

absolutely impossible and untrue that in these circumstances you knew nothing about it . . .

GOERING: . . . The important factor is – and I want to maintain it – that I was not present at the time when the command was given by the Fuehrer. When I heard about it, I vehemently opposed it. But at the time I heard of it, it was already too late. That a few were shot later, was not yet known at the time, neither was the exact time of the event. Most of them had been shot already . . . I personally pointed out to the Fuehrer repeatedly that it is the duty of these officers to escape, and that on their return after the war, they would have to give an account of such attempts, which as far as I can remember should be repeated three times, according to English rules . . .

SIR DAVID MAXWELL FYFE: And according to your evidence in chief, what you did was to turn to Himmler, asking him if he had received the order, and then you said, 'I told him what excitement would result in my branch, because we could not understand such measures; and if he had received such orders, he would please inform me before carrying them through so that I would have the possibility to prevent such orders from being carried out, if possible' – and then you said that you – 'talked to the Fuehrer and that he confirmed that he had given the order and told me why.'

You, according to that evidence, still had enough influence in Germany, in your opinion, to stop even Himmler issuing such orders or carrying – I am sorry, I said 'issuing' – carrying out such orders.

GOERING: You are giving my statement a completely wrong meaning. I told Himmler plainly that it was his duty to telephone me before the execution of this matter, to give me the possibility, even at this period of my much diminished influence, to prevent the Fuehrer from carrying out this decree. I did not mean to say that I would have been completely successful, but it was a matter of course that I, as Chief of the Luftwaffe, should make it clear to Himmler that it was his duty to telephone me first of all, because it was I who was most concerned with this matter. I told the Fuehrer in very clear terms just how I felt, and I saw from his answers that, even if I had known of it before, I could not have prevented this decree, and we must keep in mind that two different methods of procedure are in question. The order was not given to the Luftwaffe, that these people were to be shot by the Luftwaffe personnel, but to the police. If the Fuehrer had said to me, 'I will persist in this decree which I gave the police,' I would not have been able to order the police not to carry through the Fuehrer's decree. Only if this decree had had to be carried out by my men, would it have been possible for me perhaps to circumvent the decree, and I would like to emphasise this point strongly.

SIR DAVID MAXWELL FYFE: Well, that may be your view that you could not have got anywhere with the Fuehrer; but I suggested to you that when all these officers that I mentioned knew about it, you knew about it, and that you did nothing to prevent these men from being shot, but co-operated in this foul series of murders.

THE PRESIDENT: Sir David, are you passing from that now? . . . Should you not refer perhaps to the second paragraph in 731? . . . It shows that apparently, in the early hours of the 25th of March the matter was communicated to the office of the adjutant of the Reich Marshal – the second paragraph beginning with 'the escape'.

SIR DAVID MAXWELL FYFE: Yes. 'The escape of about 30 to 40 prisoners, the exact number having to be ascertained by roll call, was reported by telephone from the Sagan Camp to the inspectorate in the early hours of the 25th of March, Saturday morning, and duly passed on in the same way by this office to the higher authorities which were to be informed in case of mass escapes. These were: 1.) the Office of the Adjutant of the Reich Marshal; 2.) the OKW, for directors of these prisoners of war; 3.) the Inspector General of Prisoners of War; and 4.) Director of Operations, Air Ministry.'

I am much obliged. You must remember that the witness did not admit yesterday afternoon that the news of the escape had been given to the office of his adjutant.

THE PRESIDENT: Yes.

Maxwell Fyfe had manoeuvred Goering away from his evasive claim that he had been on leave at the time of the shootings and had not known of Hitler's order. Now he stated that he had known of it before all the executions had been carried out, but had realised that it would be futile to argue the matter with the Fuehrer.

Despite the large claims made for the effectiveness of Maxwell Fyfe's cross-examination – journalists wrote that Goering was visibly shaken by it – he had not really forced any incriminating admissions from him. Yet Maxwell Fyfe had certainly rattled Goering and, with a barrister's skill, had made him seem untrustworthy over the rather irrelevant question of the Aktion Kugel document, a policy generally applied to Soviet rather than British escaped prisoners and which Goering may well not have read. Indeed, it is likely that, as Goering maintained, he would not have been able to change Hitler's mind regarding the shooting of the escapers. In the final reckoning, however, he and his officers had gone along with it, and by the standards of the trial his failure to act made him an accessory to murder.

§

Using all his experience, Maxwell Fyfe had skilfully made the most of what had been previously thought of as a side issue. Returning to the main thrust of the British case, Goering's role in planning and waging the wars of aggression, Maxwell Fyfe showed that he had plenty of other material to draw on as well. Here, he deals with the assurances of goodwill given by Hitler to Germany's neighbours shortly before they were invaded, beginning with the Low Countries.

Trial transcript, 21 March 1946: Hitler's false assurances of goodwill to Germany's neighbours

SIR DAVID MAXWELL FYFE: And on the 6th of October, 1939, he [Hitler] gave a further assurance, and on the 7th of October, the day after that last assurance, the order, which is Document Number 2329-PS, Exhibit GB-105, was issued. 'Army Group B has to make all preparations according to special orders for immediate invasion of Dutch and Belgian territory, if the political situation so demands.'

And on the 9th of October, there is a directive from Hitler: 'Preparations should be made for offensive action on the northern flank of the Western Front crossing the area of Luxembourg, Belgium, and Holland. This attack must be carried out as soon and as forcibly as possible.'

Isn't it quite clear from that, that all along you knew, as Hitler stated on the 22nd of August, that England and France would not violate the neutrality of the Low Countries, and you were prepared to violate them whenever it suited your strategical and tactical interests? Isn't that quite clear?

GOERING: Not entirely. Only if the political situation made it necessary. And in the meantime the British air penetration of the neutrality of Holland and Belgium had taken place, up to October.

SIR DAVID MAXWELL FYFE: You say not entirely. That is as near agreement with me as you are probably prepared to go.

Now I want to ask you quite shortly again about Yugoslavia. You remember that you have told us in your evidence in chief that Germany before the war, before the beginning of the war, had the very best relations with the Yugoslav people, and that you yourself had contributed to it. I am putting it quite shortly.

GOERING: That is correct.

SIR DAVID MAXWELL FYFE: And that was emphasised, if you will remember, on the 1st of June 1939 by a speech of Hitler at a dinner with Prince Paul [the Regent of Yugoslavia].

GOERING: Yes.

SIR DAVID MAXWELL FYFE: Now, 80 days after that, on the 12th of August 1939, the Defendant Ribbentrop, Hitler, and Ciano [the Italian Foreign Minister] had a meeting, and just let me recall to you what Hitler said at that meeting to Count Ciano . . . This is the official report. 'Generally speaking, the best thing to happen would be for uncertain neutrals to be liquidated one after the other. This process could be carried out more easily if on every occasion one partner of the Axis covered the other while it was dealing with an uncertain neutral. Italy might well regard Yugoslavia as a neutral of this kind.'

That was rather inconsistent with your statement as to the good intentions towards Yugoslavia, and the Fuehrer's statement to Prince Paul, wasn't it?

GOERING: I should like to read that through carefully once more and see in what connection that statement was made. As it is presented now it certainly would not fit in with that.

SIR DAVID MAXWELL FYFE: You know I do not want to stop

you unnecessarily in any way, but that document has been read at least twice during the Trial and any further matter perhaps you will consider. But you will agree, unless I have wrenched it out of its context – and I hope I have not – that is quite inconsistent with friendly intentions, is it not?

GOERING: As I said, it does not fit in with that.

At a conference with his military leaders on 23 November 1939, Hitler had said: 'I shall attack France and England at the most favourable and earliest moment. Breach of the neutrality of Belgium and Holland is meaningless. No one will question that when we have won . . . If we do not break the neutrality England and France will. Without attack the war is not to be ended victoriously.'

There is no doubt that the Nazis' intentions were expansionist rather than defensive, and that success prompted them to continue their invasions. Nonetheless, the opportunistic nature of the Nazis' later conquests bore out Goering's contention that the prosecution had exaggerated the degree of ambition of any prior conspiracy to wage war on Europe.

§

The Russians now took their turn to cross-examine Goering. The antipathy between the representatives in court of the National Socialist and Communist doctrines was marked. Goering saw his time on the stand as an opportunity to justify the actions of the Nazis, and remained largely unrepentant of the suffering they had caused, which infuriated the Russians. Nonetheless, his desire to set the record straight meant that he did not always glorify his former colleagues, including Hitler. He told the court that he had initially opposed the Fuehrer's decision to attack the USSR and, being more cautious than him, had felt that conquest of its regions and plans for their administration should proceed piecemeal. As Soviet prosecutor Rudenko sought in his heavy-handed fashion to emphasise the extent of Goering's culpability, the latter made little attempt to hide his contempt.

Trial transcript, 21 March 1946: 'Shooting the bear' – Rudenko cross-examines Goering on the invasion

GEN. RUDENKO: . . . However, the objection you just gave does not mean that you objected to the annexation of the Crimea or the annexation of other regions, is that not correct?

GOERING: If you spoke German, then, from the sentence which says, 'opposing that, the Reich Marshal emphasised . . . ' you would understand everything that is implied. In other words, I did not say here, 'I protest against the annexation of the Crimea', or, 'I protest against the annexation of the Baltic States.' I had no reason to do so. Had we been victorious, then after the signing of peace we would in any case have decided how far annexation would serve our purpose. At the moment we had not finished the war, we had not won the war yet, and consequently I personally confined myself to practical problems.

GEN. RUDENKO: I understand you. In that case, you considered the annexation of these regions a step to come later. As you said yourself, after the war was won you would have seized these provinces and annexed them. In principle you have not protested.

GOERING: Not in principle. As an old hunter, I acted according to the principle of not dividing the bear's skin before the bear was shot.

GEN. RUDENKO: I understand. And the bear's skin should be divided only when the territories were seized completely, is that correct?

GOERING: Just what to do with the skin could be decided definitely only after the bear was shot.

GEN. RUDENKO: Luckily, this did not happen.

GOERING: Luckily for you.

§

The prosecution may have weakened their case by their lack of organisation, but the defence counsel, all of whom were German, also laboured under handicaps. They found it harder than the prosecution to adapt to the mixed systems of law that governed proceedings, especially the adversarial nature of the examination of witnesses, the purpose of which tends to be to discredit what is being said rather than attempting to establish where the truth lies. They had limited time with their clients, had to cope single-handedly with a mass of documents (many of which they received late in the day), had to notify the prosecution in advance of the evidence they intended to call, and had to be constantly reassured that the defendants would be given adequate opportunity to make out their cases.

Moreover, the lawyers could not present a united front, for the acquittal of their individual clients often depended on passing responsibility for their actions on to their co-accused. Above all, the defence team was limited by the fact that it was the victorious nations who had made the rules of the trial, and while the other judges had vetoed the Soviet argument that the accused should not be allowed to give evidence at all, they were firm in not allowing the German advocates to raise the defence of justification - that crimes had been committed by both sides during the war and that such provocation should be taken into account when considering the motives for their behaviour. Following Goering's cross-examination, his barrister took up the matter with the Tribunal in the face of Soviet objections.

Trial transcript, 22 March 1946: The Tribunal refuses to allow Goering's lawyer to introduce evidence of Allied war crimes

DR STAHMER: . . . The German Wehrmacht entered the war fully respecting the international conventions. No large-scale excesses by German soldiers were noted. Individual offences were severely punished. However, immediately after the beginning of hostilities there appeared reports and descriptions of atrocities committed against German soldiers. These reports were carefully investigated. The result was recorded by the German Foreign Office in White Papers, which were sent to Geneva. In this way the White Book came into being which deals with the crimes against the laws of war and humanity committed by the Russian soldiers.

GEN. RUDENKO: Your Honours, Defence Counsel for Goering, Dr Stahmer, intends to submit to the Tribunal and to read into the record excerpts from the so-called White Book which was published by the Hitler Government in 1941 in connection with some of the violations which supposedly took place concerning German prisoners of war. I consider that these excerpts cannot be submitted and read into the record here because of the following reasons:

There can be put in evidence only facts which refer to this case;

there can be submitted to the Tribunal only documents which refer to the crimes which were perpetrated by the German major war criminals.

The White Book is a series of documents of invented data regarding violations which were perpetrated not by the fascist Germans but by other countries. Therefore the data contained in the White Book cannot serve as evidence in this case. This conclusion is all the more justified in that the White Book is a publication which served the purpose of fascist propaganda, and which tried by inventions and forged documents to justify or hide crimes which were perpetrated by the fascists. Therefore I request the Tribunal to refuse the reading into the record, or submitting to the Tribunal, excerpts from the so-called White Book.

THE PRESIDENT: On what theory do you justify the presentation of this evidence, Dr Stahmer?

DR STAHMER: The question whether it is possible and permissible to refer to these White Papers during this trial as a means of evidence, has been discussed repeatedly. In particular it was the subject of debate when we were concerned with the question of whether I should be allowed to refer to this White Book as evidence. So far as I know, it has been admitted as evidence for the time being. It was already pointed out, during the debate which arose in regard to this subject, that, as far as evidence is concerned, it is relevant for the evaluation of the motives.

At the time I already pointed out that the crimes committed against German prisoners of war are of importance in order to understand the measures taken on the part of Germany. One cannot evaluate the underlying motives of the men who committed these offences, or gave orders to commit them, if one fails to consider the background against which these deeds were enacted, or investigate the motives which caused them to commit these acts. And because of the importance of the motive, in order to know about the accusations raised by the Germans, it seems to me that this reference to this document is absolutely necessary.

THE PRESIDENT: Have you finished?

DR STAHMER: Yes.

THE PRESIDENT: Well, we are here to try major war criminals; we are not here to try any of the signatory powers. Therefore you must justify the introduction of evidence against the signatory powers in some legal way.

DR STAHMER: The presentation, if I may repeat, is made for the following reasons: the defendants here are accused that under their leadership crimes and offences against members of foreign armed forces were committed which are not in accordance with the Geneva Convention. On our part we plead that if harsh treatment and excesses occurred on the German side, they were caused by the fact that similar violations occurred also on the other side, and that consequently these offences must be judged differently and not be considered as grave as would be the case if the opposite side had conducted itself correctly. Anyway, these facts are relevant for the evaluation of the motive . . .

THE PRESIDENT: You are asking us to admit a document, a German governmental document. Now, under the Charter we are bound to admit documents, governmental documents, and reports of the United Nations, but it is nowhere said that we are bound to admit or are at liberty to admit documents issued by the German Government. We cannot tell whether those documents contained facts truly stated or not . . . The question is, how can you justify in a trial of the major war criminals of Germany, evidence against Great Britain, or against the United States of America or against the USSR or against France? If you are going to try the actions of all those four signatory powers, apart from other considerations, there would be no end to the trial at all, and their conduct has no relevance to the guilt of the major war criminals of Germany, unless it can be justified by reference to the doctrine of reprisal, and this cannot be justified in that way. And therefore the Tribunal considers the document is irrelevant.

The defence counsel had the great advantage of working with documents in their own language and with clients who, unlike the prosecutors, understood exactly how the various departments of government had functioned and co-operated. As it was, they erred in concentrating too much on the Germans' sense of injustice stemming from the terms imposed on them in 1919, rather than focusing on the charges pertaining to the war of 1939–45. Yet they were still entitled to feel that the trial smacked – more than must inevitably have been the case – of victors' justice.

§

Life in Nuremberg could be claustrophobic. Entertainment was hard to come by, and what nightlife there was revolved in rather frenetic fashion around the Grand Hotel, once the official guest house during the Party rallies. Drink was a refuge from the horrors and boredom of the courtroom, although, recalled Ron Chapman, a clerk working on the trial and stationed just outside the city, sometimes things got out of hand.

Ron Chapman: An evening at the Grand Hotel

While we were at Zirndorf we used occasionally to have a truck take us into Nuremberg for the evening. A friend and I went in one night, and we went to the ice-skating rink. Our driver had arranged to pick us up at the Grand Hotel, which is a really luscious hotel now, and in those days was used purely for high-ranking officers of the Allied troops, a lot of whom were working on the trials. We'd arranged to meet him there at about ten o'clock. It was snowing, a cold night. When we got to the Grand Hotel he hadn't turned up, and we were standing outside, and there were two Americans always on guard there, two military police with their armbands, restricting whoever went into the hotel. These two Americans saw us standing outside waiting in the snow, and said, 'You can come in and stand in here.' So we went into the foyer, and they got talking to us, and we were still waiting for the truck. Then suddenly, without any warning at all, the two glass doors flung open, and a little Russian in uniform – he must have been forty-five at least – came staggering in, holding his throat and making a horrible gurgling noise. He just collapsed at our feet, and these two American military police were looking absolutely flabbergasted. One of them bent down over this chap who was gurgling, and said, 'This guy's been shot!' And we could see blood coming out of his chest. So the other American went flying into the hotel to call an officer, and an American medical officer came out, and he and a Russian civilian came out who was something to do with the trial. And *he* got down on the floor, putting his ear right against this Russian's mouth and asking questions, trying to hear what the poor chap was saying. The medical officer was down on the other side, saying 'Get this guy to hospital, quick!' This officer asked us what we'd seen, and luckily the two military police said, 'They don't know anything – they were standing with us when he came in.' That let us off the hook. Next thing we knew our truck arrived, and we crept in the back and went to Zirndorf.

A few days later, in the American *Stars and Stripes*, which was their army paper, there was a report of this. Apparently they'd arrested an American soldier for shooting him. The story went that this Russian was a chauffeur driving for one of the high-ranking Russian officers who stayed at the hotel, and he was just around the corner with his car, waiting, when this American came along and asked him for a lift. I don't think the Russian understood him, and he said no, and the American just shot him. Pulled out a gun and shot him. He died in hospital; he was dead in about twelve hours. I said to my friend Smith, 'I'm glad we weren't outside!' Whether the American was drunk or went berserk . . .

Though international observers such as journalist Seaghan Maynes were absorbed in the trial, the local population, he afterwards recalled, had more pressing concerns on their mind.

Seaghan Maynes: The hardships of life in post-war Germany

The conditions we lived in were palatial compared with those of the Germans. We were living in a big castle, with all our food laid on and German cooks to cook it for us. We had transport if we needed it. We had no expenses. But the Germans were experiencing a lot of deprivation. After the trial I spent some time in Hamburg and Cologne, and there was real hunger there – in fact their ration limit was, I would say, below that of any international standard nowadays. The Germans used to go out and ambush coal trains coming from the Ruhr. They would wait for them to pull up at a siding, and then youngsters would jump up on them and throw down bits of coal which their mothers and fathers would collect. They had no heat. All over the British zone this happened. They would go out from the towns into the country, and work for farmers to get a bag of potatoes or some cabbage.

In Hamburg in my office – I set up a Reuters bureau there – I had a German secretary. She was impeccable in appearance: spotless dress, and so on. One time I had been out on a story about Jewish refugees being brought back to Hamburg on a ship, working very late, and this girl was staying on at the office till all hours. She had no transport, of course – no German had any transport, they had to walk – and Hamburg was devastated. We had launched tremendous air raids on the place. So I told her I would run her home. We got into the car and drove off to the district which had been flattened. It was a mass of rubble, and a bulldozer had cleared tracks through it where we could drive. I wondered, 'Where the devil is she going?' Then she said, 'Here.' I said, 'Well, look, I'll bring you home! I can't leave you here.' And she said, 'No, this is it.' And I saw where she went: she went into a hole in the ground. Her mother and two other youngsters were living there, living in this hole which had been the cellar of a house. And yet this girl appeared as though she had come out of a very nice home where the laundry had taken care of her clothes. How the devil they did it I just don't know. A packet of cigarettes was of more value to her than her weekly wage in Deutschmarks. This was the way they lived, bartering. Of course, some of the German girls, young girls with children, just had to become prostitutes, or not exactly prostitutes but 'mistresses' to put it more politely. They would shack up with a soldier to get things from army supplies – cigarettes, bars of soap, silk stockings – for barter, in order to keep their children. These were decent girls from decent families.

§

The defendants were due to give evidence in the order in which they were seated in the dock. Hess, placed next to Goering, should have followed him into the witness box, but decided after all that his memory was not up to dealing with the prosecution's questions. Accordingly, the next to be heard was Joachim von Ribbentrop, the Nazis' Foreign Minister from 1938 until the end of the war.

Von Ribbentrop had been a wine merchant who had married into a wealthy champagne-producing family, and was always regarded by other prominent Nazis as rather lightweight, not least because he had dubiously added an aristocratic 'von' to his surname. Much of his ambition was stoked by his manipulative and pushy wife, Annelies. An ardent flatterer of Hitler, von Ribbentrop became the Fuehrer's adviser on foreign policy from 1933, and steadily built up a parallel organisation, the Ribbentrop Bureau, to rival the German Foreign Office, then run by another of the accused, Constantin von Neurath. In this unofficial capacity, von Ribbentrop conducted negotiations for the Anti-Comintern Pact of 1936, which allied Germany with Japan and Italy against Communism.

Yet his role was more that of an intermediary than a principal, and his limitations as a diplomat were revealed in his two years as ambassador in London from 1936, where his attempts to bully the British Government into an alliance met with scorn, as did his efforts to integrate himself into high society. He brought off the Nazi–Soviet Pact shortly before the war began, but in the ensuing years there was little call for diplomacy and his status within the regime declined.

By the time of the trial he was a nervous wreck, his once smart appearance displaced by slovenly habits. He failed to shave for days at a time, and piled his cell high with documents, through which he searched frantically for proof of his peaceful intentions in the 1930s before taking to his bed in despair. In January, he had sacked his lawyer and replaced him with Martin Horn. One of the witnesses called on his behalf was Paul Schmidt, a former interpreter at the German Foreign Office. His evidence cast an intriguing light on the events leading up to the outbreak of war in September 1939.

Trial transcript, 28 March 1946: Paul Schmidt gives Hitler the news of Britain's declaration of war

SCHMIDT: On the morning of the 3rd, at about 2 or 3 o'clock, the British Embassy telephoned the Reich Chancellery, where I was still present with the Foreign Minister in order to be available for possible conferences, to give the information that the British Ambassador had received instructions from his Government, according to which, at exactly 9 o'clock, he was to make an important announcement on behalf of the British Government to the Foreign Minister. He therefore asked to be received by Herr von Ribbentrop at that time. He was given the reply that Ribbentrop himself would not be available but that a member of the Foreign Office, namely I, would be authorised to receive the British Government's announcement from the British Ambassador on his behalf. Thus it happened that at 9 o'clock in the morning I received the British Ambassador in Ribbentrop's office. When I asked him to be seated Henderson refused and while still standing he read to me the well-known ultimatum of the British Government to the German Government, according to which, unless certain conditions were fulfilled by Germany, the British Government would consider themselves at war with Germany at 11 o'clock that morning.

After we had exchanged a few words of farewell, I took the document to the Reich Chancellery.

DR HORN: To whom did you submit this document there?

SCHMIDT: In the Reich Chancellery I gave it to Hitler, that is to say, I found Hitler in his office in conference with the Foreign Minister and I translated the document into German for him. When I had completed my translation, there was at first silence.

DR HORN: Was Hitler alone in the room?

SCHMIDT: No as I said before, he was in his office with the Foreign Minister. And when I had completed my translation, both gentlemen were absolutely silent for about a minute. I could clearly see that this development did not suit them at all. For a while Hitler sat in his chair deep in thought and stared somewhat worriedly into space. Then he broke the silence with a rather abrupt question to the Foreign Minister, saying, 'What shall we do now?' Thereupon they began to discuss the next diplomatic steps to be taken, whether this or that ambassador should be called, et cetera. I, of course, left the room since I had nothing more to do. When I entered the anteroom, I found assembled there – or rather I had already seen on my way in – some Cabinet members and higher officials, to whose questioning looks – they knew I had seen the British Ambassador – I had said only that there would be no second Munich. When I came out again, I saw by their anxious faces that my remark had been correctly interpreted. When I then told them that I had just handed a British ultimatum to Hitler, a heavy silence fell on the room. The faces suddenly grew rather serious. I still remember that Goering, for instance, who was standing in front of me, turned round to me and said, 'If we lose this war, then God help us.' Goebbels was standing in a corner by himself and had a very serious, not to say depressed, expression. This depressing atmosphere prevailed over all those present, and it naturally lives in my memory as something most remarkable for the frame of mind prevailing in the anteroom of the Reich Chancellery on the first day of the war.

DR HORN: So you did not have the impression, then, that these men expected a declaration of war?

SCHMIDT: No, I did not have that impression.

Although Schmidt was notionally a defence witness, everything he said confirmed the prosecution's allegations about the Nazis, on to each of whose bandwagons the sycophantic von Ribbentrop had leapt. The following assessment by Schmidt of the Party's aims and strategy is seen by historians as being broadly accurate, and is consistent with his testimony that Hitler and von Ribbentrop had not expected the British and French to call their bluff over the invasion of Poland.

The general objectives of the Nazi leadership were apparent from the start, namely, the domination of the European Continent, to be achieved, first, by the incorporation of all German-speaking groups in the Reich, and secondly, by territorial expansion under the slogan of *Lebensraum* [living space]. The execution of these basic objectives, however, seemed to be characterised by improvisation. Each succeeding step apparently was carried out as each new situation arose, but all consistent with the ultimate objectives mentioned above.

§

Those in the dock frequently found the trial a frustrating business. Reminiscing later on, Hans Fritzsche told how he had felt that so much of the trial was beyond his control, with aspects of it vital to his defence – such as the rules for examining witnesses – determined by the Allies. Like his co-defendants, Fritzsche thought it a manifestly unfair procedure, and hour by hour believed his chances of acquittal to be slipping away.

Hans Fritzsche: Thoughts on the adversarial system

Some of us tried to grasp the system of cross-examination by means of various illustrations and comparisons. The most apt simile seemed to me to be a duel between two unequally matched opponents; one of whom – the accused – has both his feet and one of his arms shackled while the other – the prosecutor – is free and unfettered and can make full use of his weapons. It was only by degrees that we realised that the very purpose of the English and American system of cross-examination is not to establish a fact objectively, but to destroy confidence in the witness and his evidence – the means employed to this end being of no great consequence. The rules are extraordinarily elastic for it is also permissible, on the flimsiest pretext, to drag in some remote subject which has no connection whatever with the charge before the court.

Added to this, we were compelled to answer every question allowed by the court, even in instances where German law grants the right to refuse evidence. This obligation grants the right to refuse evidence. This obligation to answer meant that misleading questions could give rise to misleading impressions entirely against the witness's will, for he was not always clever enough to round off the sharp corners of the fragments of knowledge which his opponent prised out of him.

It was still possible to rectify such errors in the re-examination which followed the Prosecution's questioning. This was conducted by counsel for the Defence who had the right to offer his client the chance of retrieving previously missed opportunities: but in this re-examination he was obliged to confine himself to points which had arisen during the cross-examination.

In this method of enquiry the British proved themselves in every respect superior to the French and Russians – let alone the Germans. We had no experience whatever of such contests and, furthermore, were handicapped by nervousness, which is the last attribute useful in this type of procedure. Our German lawyers, too, were often under the impression that an attack on a prosecutor implied an attack on the Bench; they failed to realise that such an attack was considered perfectly legitimate, since it was not aimed at the court as a whole but only at their opponent in this species of legal duel. A few made up for their lack of experience by hard work and eventually became good seconds to their clients.

On the other side, cross-examining counsel were by no means exempt from all restraint. They were limited to the substance of the reply given under oath; and it was only when a prosecutor had succeeded in clearly disproving such evidence that he was free to draw whatever conclusions he pleased.

During the spring and summer of 1946 I listened to the public examination of eighteen of my fellow-prisoners, in the course of which it seemed to me that many facts were obscured rather than cleared up. Prisoners who only a few seconds before had ready a regular stack of arguments, were completely dumb when they went on the witness stand; they just could not think of anything to say. We saw the most disastrous instance of complete mental inadequacy to deal with a situation of this kind, and had to watch men deliberately shirk the attempt to defend themselves. Though there were, on the other hand, prisoners who refused to own themselves beaten when they had been driven into the furthest corner of some logical blind alley.

But no matter how inadequate the results of these examinations may have been from an objective standpoint, they undoubtedly showed up a prisoner's character in the most uncanny fashion. Isolated issues might be distorted during this play and counterplay of question and answer; the individuality of the man behind stood out crystal clear.

§

In his evidence, Schmidt had said further that Hitler had dominated the conferences at which government policy was decided and that von Ribbentrop, in common with the others, had given his tacit approval to the Fuehrer's plans. Once in the box, the former Foreign Minister struck a rather pathetic figure, confiding in Gilbert that he felt his tie oddly tight in recent days. His evasions were obvious, as here when cross-examined by French prosecutor Edgar Faure about a meeting in April 1943 (at which Schmidt had taken notes) between himself, Hitler and Admiral Horthy, the ruler of Germany's ally Hungary, regarding the fate of the Jews of Budapest.

Trial transcript, 2 April 1946: 'There was no other solution' – von Ribbentrop and the Jewish question

M. FAURE: ... During the interrogation of your witness, Schmidt, the British prosecutor asked this witness if he admitted having compiled this account, and this was confirmed by Schmidt. This note bears the following remark at the bottom of the first paragraph: 'The Foreign Minister declared that the Jews were either to be exterminated or sent to concentration camps. There was no other solution.'

You did say that, did you not?

VON RIBBENTROP: I definitely did not say it in those words ... The remark mentioned was definitely not made in this way. M. Horthy had apparently said that he could not, after all, beat the Jews to death. It is possible, since there would have been no question of that in any case, that in this connection I did endeavour to persuade Horthy to do something or other at once about the Jewish question in Budapest, namely, that he should undertake now the centralisation which the Fuehrer had already wished to carry out for a long time. My objection or my interpolation may have referred to this question.

I must add that the situation, at that time, was as follows: We had been receiving repeated indications from Himmler, to the effect that Himmler wished to handle the Jewish situation in Hungary himself. I did not want this, since, one way or another, it would probably have created political difficulties abroad.

Consequently, acting on the wish of the Fuehrer, who was

extremely obstinate on this subject, I, as is known, repeatedly attempted to smooth matters over and, at the same time, pin the Hungarians down to do something about it in any case. Therefore, if, from a long conversation, some remark has been extracted and summarised in brief, and contains some such statement, it certainly does not mean that I wished the Jews to be beaten to death. It was 100 per cent contrary to my personal convictions.

M. FAURE: I do not understand whether you answered my question or not. I will have to ask you again. Is the report correct, or is it not correct?

VON RIBBENTROP: No, in this form it cannot be correct. These are notes. I personally have never seen these notes before; otherwise I should have said at once that this is nonsense and liable to misconstruction. I did not see these notes before; I saw them for the first time in Nuremberg.

I can say only one thing which may possibly have occurred. I might have said . . . well yes, 'the Jews cannot be exterminated or beaten to death, so, please do something in order that the Fuehrer will be satisfied at long last, and centralise the Jews.' . . .

THE PRESIDENT: Well, Defendant, the Tribunal would like to know whether you did say to the Regent Horthy that Jews ought to be taken to concentration camps.

VON RIBBENTROP: I consider it possible that such may have been the case, for we had, at that time, received an order that a concentration camp was to be installed near Budapest or else that the Jews should be centralised there, and the Fuehrer had instructed me a long time before to discuss with the Hungarians a possible solution of the Jewish question. This solution should consist of two points. One was the removal of the Jews from important government positions and two, since there were so many Jews in Budapest, to centralise the Jews in certain quarters of Budapest.

THE PRESIDENT: . . . What I wanted to ask you was this: Are you suggesting that Schmidt, who drew up this memorandum, invented the last few sentences, beginning with the words: 'If the Jews there did not want to work they would be shot. If they could not work they would have to perish. They had to be treated like tuberculosis bacilli with which a healthy body may become infected. This was not cruel if one remembered that innocent creatures of nature, such as hares or deer, have to be killed so that no harm is caused by them. Why should the beasts who wanted to bring us Bolshevism be shown more leniency? Nations which did not rid themselves of Jews perished. One of the most famous examples of this was the downfall of a people who once were so proud, the Persians, who now lead a pitiful existence as Armenians [a wholly inaccurate assertion].'

Are you suggesting that Schmidt invented those sentences or imagined them?

VON RIBBENTROP: Mr President, I should like to add that I myself was very grieved by these words of the Fuehrer, and I did not quite understand them. But perhaps this attitude can be understood only if we remember that the Fuehrer believed that the Jews had caused this war, and that he had gradually developed a very fanatical hatred for them . . . The Fuehrer did express himself in some such way at that time. That is true.

THE PRESIDENT: Yes, M. Faure.

M. FAURE: It appears from his document that you thought there were concentration camps in Hungary and yet you said yesterday that you did not know there were any in Germany. Is that not so?

VON RIBBENTROP: I did not know that there were any concentration camps in Hungary, but I did say that the Fuehrer had instructed me to ask Horthy to ask the Hungarian Government to concentrate the Jews in Budapest, in certain parts of the city of Budapest. As to concentration camps in Germany, I already spoke yesterday about my knowledge of that subject.

M. FAURE: You admitted that you knew Hitler's policy to deport all Jews and you admitted that insofar as you were competent as Minister for Foreign Affairs, you assisted this policy, did you not? That is right, is it not?

VON RIBBENTROP: As his faithful follower I adhered to the Fuehrer's orders even in this field, but I always did my utmost to alleviate the situation as far as possible. This can be stated and proved by many witnesses. Even in 1943 I submitted a comprehensive memorandum to the Fuehrer in which I urged him to alter the Jewish policy completely. I could also quote many other examples.

M. FAURE: If I understand your testimony rightly, you were morally opposed to this persecution of Jews, but you did help to carry them out, is that not so?

VON RIBBENTROP: I repeatedly said at the very beginning of my examination, that in that sense I have never been anti-Semitic. But I was a faithful follower of Adolf Hitler.

Although Horthy had, under German pressure, passed some anti-Jewish measures before the war, he was largely able to resist being drawn into the Holocaust until the Nazis occupied Hungary in March 1944. Thereafter, some two-thirds of Hungary's 825,000 Jews were deported and murdered, but the survival of the remainder, principally in Budapest itself, owed much to Horthy's earlier stance.

Von Ribbentrop's remarks to him were evidence, too, of one of the main motives for the genocide. The Nazis believed that the Jews were inherently well disposed towards Communism, and were thus an ideological as well as a racial enemy.

§

A key part of the prosecution's strategy was to show that the German armed forces had been fully complicit in the Nazis' aggressive schemes. To that end they had indicted Field Marshal Wilhelm Keitel, who had been chief of staff of the High Command since 1938, when Hitler had forced the last Minister of War to resign and had assumed command of the military himself. In theory, Keitel was responsible for effecting Hitler's instructions to the armed forces. In practice, he was a figurehead, so subservient that, punning on his name, other officers called him 'lackey'. For his part, Keitel not only argued that he had simply been carrying out orders but, as he showed here when examined by his counsel Otto Nelte, he was positively proud of the loyalty he had shown his Fuehrer, in the best traditions of the Prussian soldier.

Trial transcript, 3 April 1946: 'A soldier by inclination and conviction' – Wilhelm Keitel takes the stand

DR NELTE: Field Marshal Keitel, beginning with essential matters, I would like to put the following basic questions to you: What basic attitude did you, as a soldier, an officer, and a general, have toward the problems with which you had to deal in your profession?

KEITEL: I can say that I was a soldier by inclination and conviction. For more than 44 years without interruption I served my country and my people as a soldier, and I tried to do my best in the service of my profession. I believed that I should do this as a matter of duty, labouring unceasingly and giving myself completely to those tasks which fell to me in my many and diverse positions. I did this with the same devotion under the Kaiser, under President Ebert, under Field Marshal von Hindenburg, and under the Fuehrer, Adolf Hitler.

DR NELTE: What is your attitude today?

KEITEL: As a German officer, I naturally consider it my duty to answer for what I have done, even if it should have been wrong. I am grateful that I am being given the opportunity to give an account here and before the German people of what I was and my participation in the events which have taken place. It will not always be possible to separate clearly guilt and entanglement in the threads of destiny. But I do consider one thing impossible, that the men in the front lines and the leaders and the subleaders at the front should be charged with the guilt, while the highest leaders reject responsibility. That, in my opinion, is wrong, and I consider it unworthy. I am convinced that the large mass of our brave soldiers were really decent, and that wherever they overstepped the bounds of acceptable behaviour, our soldiers acted in good faith, believing in military necessity, and the orders which they received . . .

DR NELTE: I now come to the question of rearmament, and the various cases of Austria, Czechoslovakia, et cetera. I would like to ask you about the accusation of the Prosecution that you participated in the planning and preparation of wars of aggression. So that we can understand each other, and that you can give your answers correctly, we must be quite clear as to what is meant by war of aggression. Will you tell us your views on that subject?

KEITEL: As a soldier, I must say that the term 'war of aggression' as used here is meaningless as far as I am concerned; we learned how to conduct actions of attack, actions of defence, and actions of retreat. However, according to my own personal feelings as a military man, the concept 'war of aggression' is a purely political concept and not a military one. I mean that if the Wehrmacht and the soldier are a tool of the politicians, they are not qualified in my opinion to decide or to judge whether these military operations did or did not constitute a war of aggression. I think I can summarise my views by saying that military officers should not have authority to decide this question and are not in a position to do so; and that these decisions are not the task of the soldier, but solely that of the statesman.

DR NELTE: Then you mean to say, and this applies also to all commanders and officers involved, that the question of whether or not a war is a war of aggression, or whether it has to be conducted for the defence of a country, in other words, whether a war is a just war or not, was not in the field of your professional deliberations and decisions?

KEITEL: No; that is what I wish to express, since . . .

DR NELTE: What you are giving is an explanation. But you are not only a soldier, you are also an individual with a life of your own. When facts brought to your notice in your professional capacity seemed to reveal that a projected operation was unjust, did you not give it consideration?

KEITEL: I believe I can truthfully say that throughout the whole of my military career I was brought up, so to speak, in the old traditional concept that one never discussed this question. Naturally, one has one's own opinion and a life of one's own, but in the exercise of one's professional functions as a soldier and an officer, one has given this life away, yielded it up. Therefore I could not say either at that time or later that I had misgivings about questions of a purely political discretion, for I took the stand that a soldier has a right to have confidence in his state leadership, and accordingly he is obliged to do his duty and to obey.

§

Keitel had countersigned a number of orders that were the basis of the prosecution's case on war crimes committed by the military, among them reprisals against civilians for actions by partisans and the Nacht und Nebel ('Night and Fog') decree, which authorised the summary arrest and spiriting away to prison or execution of opponents of the regime.

As the Charter had made clear, Keitel's defence that he was only obeying orders was a false one, for dutifulness could not absolve him of his higher responsibility to obey the law. The Field Marshal claimed that he had tried to sway Hitler when he felt that he was going too far, but accepted that ultimately he had carried out his commands.

Trial transcript, 6 April 1946: '100 lives for every German soldier' – Rudenko cross-examines Keitel

GEN. RUDENKO: Defendant Keitel, I am asking you about the directive concerning the so-called communist insurrectionary movement in the occupied territories. Yesterday your counsel showed you this directive. It is an order of 16 September 1941, Number R-98. I shall remind you of one passage from this order. It states: 'In order to nip in the bud any conspiracy, the strongest measures should be taken at the first sign of trouble in order to maintain the authority of the occupying power and to prevent the conspiracy from spreading . . .'; and furthermore: '. . . one must bear in mind that in the countries affected human life has absolutely no value and that a deterrent effect can be achieved only through the application of extraordinarily harsh measures.'

You remember this basic idea of the order, that human life absolutely does not amount to anything. Do you remember this statement, the basic statement of the order, that 'human life has absolutely no value'? Do you remember this sentence?
KEITEL: Yes.
GEN. RUDENKO: You signed the order containing this statement?
KEITEL: Yes.
GEN. RUDENKO: Do you consider that necessity demanded this extremely evil order?
KEITEL: I explained some of the reasons for this order yesterday and I pointed out that these instructions were addressed in the first place to the Commander-in-Chief of the Wehrmacht offices in the Southeast; that is, the Balkan regions, where extensive partisan

warfare and a war between the leaders had assumed enormous proportions, and secondly, because the same phenomena had been observed and established on the same or similar scale in certain defined areas of the occupied Soviet territory.

GEN. RUDENKO: Does this mean that you consider this order to have been entirely correct?

KEITEL: I have already explained in detail, in replying to questions, my fundamental standpoint with regard to all orders concerning the treatment of the population. I signed the order and by doing so I assumed responsibility within the scope of my official jurisdiction.

THE PRESIDENT: The Tribunal considers that you are not answering the question. The question was perfectly capable of an answer 'yes' or 'no' and an explanation afterwards. It is not an answer to the question to say that you have already explained to your counsel.

GEN. RUDENKO: I ask you once more, do you consider this order, this particular order – and I emphasise, in which it is stated that 'human life has absolutely no value' – do you consider this order correct?

KEITEL: It does not contain these words; but I knew from years of experience that in the Southeastern territories and in certain parts of the Soviet territory, human life was not respected to the same degree.

GEN. RUDENKO: You say that these words do not exist in the order? . . .

KEITEL: The text in the German language says that 'in the countries affected human life frequently has no value . . .'

GEN. RUDENKO: And further?

KEITEL: Yes, ' . . . and a deterrent effect can be obtained only by extreme harshness. To atone for the life of a German soldier . . .'

GEN. RUDENKO: Quite clear. And in this same order, in this same Subparagraph 'b', it is stated that: 'To atone for the life of one German soldier, 50 to 100 Communists must, as a rule, be sentenced to death. The method of execution should strengthen the measure of determent.' Is that correct?

KEITEL: The German text is slightly different. It says: 'In such cases in general, the death penalty for 50 to 100 Communists may be considered adequate.' That is the German wording.

GEN. RUDENKO: For one German soldier?

KEITEL: Yes. I know that and I see it here.

GEN. RUDENKO: That is what I was asking you about. So now I ask you once more . . .

KEITEL: Do you want an explanation of that or am I not to say any more?

GEN. RUDENKO: I shall now interrogate you on this matter. I ask you whether, when signing this order you thereby expressed your personal opinion on these cruel measures? In other words, were you in agreement with Hitler?

KEITEL: I signed the order but the figures contained in it are alterations made personally by Hitler himself.

GEN. RUDENKO: And what figures did you present to Hitler?

KEITEL: The figures in the original were 5 to 10.

GEN. RUDENKO: In other words, the divergence between you and Hitler consisted merely in the figures and not in the spirit of the document?

KEITEL: The idea was that the only way of deterring them was to demand several sacrifices for the life of one soldier, as is stated here.

GEN. RUDENKO: You . . .

THE PRESIDENT: That was not an answer to the question. The question was whether the only difference between you and Hitler on this document was a question of figures. That admits of the answer 'yes' or 'no'. Was the only difference between you and Hitler a question of figures?

KEITEL: Then I must say that with reference to the underlying principle there was a difference of opinion, the final results of which I no longer feel myself in a position to justify, since I added my signature on behalf of my department. There was a fundamental difference of opinion on the entire question . . .

GEN. RUDENKO [*Handing a document to the defendant*]: I shall interrogate you, Defendant Keitel, only on one question in connection with this order. In Subparagraph 1 of this order, Paragraph 3, it is stated, and I would draw your attention to the following sentence: 'The troops are therefore authorised and ordered in this struggle to take any measures without restriction even against women and children, if that is necessary to achieve success.' Have you found this passage?

KEITEL: Yes.

GEN. RUDENKO: Have you found the order calling for the application of any kind of measures you like without restriction, also against women and children?

KEITEL: 'To employ without restriction any means, even against women and children, if it is necessary.' I have found that.

GEN. RUDENKO: That is exactly what I am asking you about. I ask you, Defendant Keitel, Field Marshal of the former German Army, do you consider that this order is a just one, that measures may be employed at will against women and children?

KEITEL: Measures, insofar as it means that women and children were also to be removed from territories where there was partisan warfare, never atrocities or the murder of women or children. Never!

GEN. RUDENKO: To remove – a German term – means to kill?

KEITEL: No. I do not think it would ever have been necessary to tell German soldiers that they could not and must not kill women and children.

GEN.RUDENKO: You did not answer my question. Do you consider this order a just one in regard to measures against women and children or do you consider it unjust? Answer 'yes' or 'no'. Is it just or unjust? Explain the matter later.

KEITEL: I considered these measures to be right and as such I admit them; but not measures to kill. That was a crime.

GEN. RUDENKO: 'Any kind of measures' includes murder.

KEITEL: Yes, but not of women and children.

GEN. RUDENKO: Yes, but it says here 'Any kind of measures against women and children.'

KEITEL: No, it does not say 'any measures'. It says ' . . . and not to shrink from taking measures against women and children.' That is what it says. No German soldier or German officer ever thought of killing women and children.

GEN. RUDENKO: And in reality . . . ?

KEITEL: I cannot say in every individual case, since I do not know and I could not be everywhere and since I received no reports about it.

GEN. RUDENKO: But there were millions of such cases?

KEITEL: I have no knowledge of that and I do not believe that it happened in millions of cases.

GEN. RUDENKO: You do not believe it?

KEITEL: No . . .

GEN. RUDENKO: I am not going to argue with you since this means arguing against documents; and documents speak for themselves . . . You stated here that in 1944, after the law [forbidding soldiers to be members of the Party] had been amended, you received an offer to join the Nazi Party.

You accepted this offer, presented your personal credentials to the leadership of the Party, and paid your membership fees. Tell us, did not your acceptance to join the membership of the Nazi Party signify that you were in agreement with the programme, objectives, and methods of the Party?

KEITEL: As I had already been in possession of the Golden Party Badge for three or four years, I thought that this request for my personal particulars was only a formal registration; and I paid the required Party membership subscription. I did both these things and have admitted doing them.

GEN. RUDENKO: In other words, before this formal offer was ever made, you already, de facto, considered yourself a member of the Nazi Party?

KEITEL: I have always thought of myself as a soldier; not as a political soldier or politician.

GEN. RUDENKO: Should we not conclude, after all that has been said here, that you were a Hitler General, not because duty called you but on account of your own convictions?

KEITEL: I have stated here that I was a loyal and obedient soldier of my Fuehrer. And I do not think that there are generals in Russia who do not give Marshal Stalin implicit obedience.

§

Not all of the evidence collected by the various commissions investigating war crimes committed by the German military was used at Nuremberg, although some of it was published in supplementary volumes to the transcript detailing Nazi aggression, or called on at later trials. This affidavit details the atrocities carried out by troops commanded by Erich von dem Bach-Zelewski, including Soviet POWs known as the Vlassov forces, during the Warsaw Rising by the Polish Resistance against the German Occupation in the summer and autumn of 1944. The revolt was ultimately put down by the Germans, who indiscriminately massacred as many as 200,000 civilians in the course of its repression, deliberately using terror in an attempt to crush the Poles' fighting spirit.

6 April 1946: Affidavit of a war crime – the suppression of the Warsaw Uprising

My husband was absent, taking an active part in the Rising, and I was alone with my three children, aged four, six and twelve, and in the last month of pregnancy. I delayed my departure, hoping they would allow me to remain, and left the cellar at the very last moment. All the inhabitants of our house had already been escorted to the 'Ursus' works in Wolska Street at the corner of Skierniewicka Street, and I too was ordered to go there. I went alone, accompanied only by my three children. It was difficult to pass, the road being full of wire, cable, remains of barricades, corpses, and rubble. Houses were burning on both sides of the street; I reached the 'Ursus' works with great difficulty. Shots, cries, supplications and groans could be heard from the factory yard. We had no doubt that this was a place for mass executions. The people who stood at the entrance were led, no, pushed in, not all at once but in groups of twenty. A boy of twelve, seeing the bodies of his parents and of his little brother through the half-open entrance door, fell in a fit and began to shriek. The Germans and Vlassov's men beat him and pushed him back, while he was endeavouring to get inside. He called for his father and his mother. We all knew what awaited us here; there was no possibility of escape or of buying one's life; there was a crowd of Germans, Ukrainians (Vlassov's men), and cars. I came last and kept in the background, continuing to let the others pass, in the hope that they would not kill a pregnant woman, but I was driven in with the last lot. In the yard I saw heaps of corpses three feet high, in several places. The whole right and left side of the big yard (the first yard) was strewn with bodies. [A sketch of the yard was made by the deponent.] We were led through the second. There were about twenty people in our group, mostly children of ten to twelve. There were children without parents, and also a paralysed old woman whose son-in-law had been carrying her all the time on his back. At her side was her daughter with two children of four and seven. They were all killed. The old woman was literally killed on her son-in-law's back, and he along with her. We were called out in groups of four and led to the end of the second yard to a pile of bodies. When the four reached this point, the Germans shot them through the backs of their heads with revolvers. The victims fell on the heap, and others came. Seeing what was to be their fate, some attempted to escape; they cried, begged, and prayed for mercy. I was in the last group of four. I begged the Vlassov's men around me to save me and the children, and they asked if I had anything with which to buy my life. I had a large amount of gold with me and gave it them. They took it all and wanted to lead me away, but the German supervising the execution would not allow them to do so, and when I begged him to let me go he pushed me off, shouting 'Quicker!' I fell when he pushed me. He also hit and pushed my elder boy, shouting 'Hurry up, you Polish bandit'. Thus I came to the place of execution, in the last group of four, with my three children. I held my two younger children by one hand, and my elder boy by the other. The children were crying and praying. The elder boy, seeing the mass of bodies, cried out: 'They are going to kill us' and called for his father. The first shot hit him, the second me; the next two killed the two younger children. I fell on my right side. The shot was not fatal. The bullet penetrated the back of my head from the right side and went out through my cheek. I spat out several teeth; I felt the left side of my body growing numb, but I was still conscious and saw everything that was going on around me. I witnessed other executions, lying there among the dead. More groups of men were led in. I heard cries, supplications, moaning, and shots. The bodies of these men fell on me. I was covered by four bodies. Then I again saw a group of women and children; thus it went on with group after group until late in the evening. It was already quite, quite dark when the executions stopped. In the intervals between the shootings the murderers walked on the corpses, kicked them, and turned them over, finishing off those who still gave any sign of life and stealing valuables. (They took a watch from my wrist, but I did not give any sign of life.) They did not touch the bodies with their bare hands, but put rags round them. During these dreadful doings they sang and drank vodka. Near me, there lay a big, tall man of middle age in a brown leather coat. He was alive, I heard his death-rattle; they fired five shots at him before they killed him. During this shooting some shots wounded my feet. I lay quite numb for a long time in a pool of blood, the dead weighing on me. I was, however, conscious all the time and fully realised what was happening to me. Towards evening I succeeded in pushing away the corpses which lay over me. It is impossible to imagine how much blood there was all round. Next day the executions ceased. The Germans broke in two or three times during the day. Now they had dogs with them. They walked and jumped on the corpses to see if any of the supposed dead were still alive. On the third day I felt the child move in my womb. The thought that I dare not kill this child made me look round to examine the situation and the possibilities of escape.

§

The defendants, including Fritzsche, came to prize their time in court as a break from the routine of the prison, among the deprivations of which was the absence of women.

Hans Fritzsche: A vision from another world

Their presence seemed to stress the fact that in that hall the boundaries of two worlds – the world of captivity and the world of freedom – overlapped and that the road from one to the other passed close beside us. I had already had one opportunity of learning how a woman's presence can help to moderate the conduct even of the most blustering cross-examiner, At a Russian interrogation, when excitement over the conquest of Berlin was at its height, a pistol was pointed at my head because, it was averred, I was hiding something. A glance at the woman stenographer standing by was sufficient to calm my fears; her horrified eyes revealed that she was not accustomed to seeing men shot dead in her presence. I experienced no surprise, when a few hours later, the same trick was repeated – this time in a gloomy wood.

Here in court there was naturally no question of anybody putting a pistol to one's head; but if Death was not actually present on the stage, he hovered always in the wings. It was, in fact, though it had little of the appearance of one, a life-and-death struggle and the combatants were not squeamish in their use of the weapons at their disposal; indeed, some of the methods employed against us often reminded me strongly of all-in wrestling. In this singular atmosphere of outwardly civilised but inwardly unbridled conflict, the feminine element was the one neutral influence. Every man in that vast room could be immediately labelled as either friend or enemy; but the women were first and foremost human beings, and only secondly members of the opposite side. I have never seen them blindly swayed by blind prejudice, as was frequently the case with many of the masculine actors on what was, after all, a political stage.

The women members of the staff, on the other hand, represented to us not persons but an abstraction, an idea. Now and again we caught a whiff of some delicious perfume, an intoxicating change from the stuffy atmosphere of the prison to which we had become accustomed; but we did not attach any great significance to it. We soon learned to distinguish between the various groups of women assistants. The healthy, full-figured Russians carried themselves proudly and, old or young, dressed plainly; the Frenchwomen were deliberately inconspicuous (perhaps because of their part, small though it was, in the grim drama that was being played); while the Englishwomen, efficient and well-bred, were entirely outshone by their transatlantic sisters, who alone infused any real life and colour into their surroundings. Naturally attractive, the Americans had an almost sublime self-possession, a thorough understanding of the art of make-up, and no wish to remain unnoticed. Even we, the living dead, could not begrudge them their vitality. Some time later I came across a number of pictures of wives of prominent American functionaries and smiled when I recognised among them former members of the IMT staff. One young lady, it is true, learned when her husband died that he had another 'wife' besides herself; but such misfortunes are, after all, one of the inevitable hazards of war service.

§

His great height, lean figure and scarred face soon made the relatively unknown Austrian Ernst Kaltenbrunner one of the most recognisable of the defendants. Trained as a lawyer, he been appointed Austria's Minister of Security after the Anschluss, and following the assassination of Heydrich in Prague in 1943 had succeeded him as head of the RSHA, which controlled the Gestapo, various police and security agencies, and the administration of the concentration camps.

Like many of those in the dock, he claimed that his post was in fact without real power or responsibility, and that he had not been told of the darkest aspects of Nazi rule, which had been planned and executed by Himmler and the Gestapo chief Heinrich Mueller, neither of whom were present in court. When confronted by documents linking him to the murder of prisoners or to the use of slave labour, Kaltenbrunner argued repeatedly that his signature had been forged. American prosecutor John Amen then showed him yet another letter.

Trial transcript, 12 April 1946: Ernst Kaltenbrunner of the RSHA claims his signature was forged

COL. AMEN: Well, you have already testified that you had nothing to do with participating in this forced labour programme; is that not correct?

KALTENBRUNNER: Yes.

COL. AMEN: All right. I ask to have the defendant shown Document 3803-PS, Exhibit Number USA-802. You will note that the letter comes from yourself, and reads as follows:

'To the Burgermeister of the city of Vienna, SS Brigadefuehrer Blaschke.

'Subject: Assignment of labour to essential war work in the city of Vienna.

'Re: Your letter of 7 June 1944.

'Dear Blaschke: For the special reasons cited by you I have in the meantime given orders to direct several evacuation transports to Vienna-Strasshof. SS Brigadefuehrer Dr Dellbruegge had, as a matter of fact, already written to me concerning the same matter. At the moment it is a question of four transports with approximately 12,000 Jews. They will reach Vienna within the next few days.

'According to previous experience it is estimated that 30 per cent of the transport will consist of Jews able to work, approximately 3,600 in this case, who can be utilised for the work in question, it being understood that they are subject to removal at any time. It is obvious that these people must be assigned to work in large, well-guarded groups, and accommodated in secured camps, and this is an absolute prerequisite for making these Jews available.

'The women and children of these Jews who were unable to work, and who are all being kept in readiness for a special action and therefore one day will be removed again, must stay in the guarded camp also during the day . . . I hope these transports will be of help to you in carrying out the urgent work you have in view.

'Heil Hitler. Yours, Kaltenbrunner.'

Now do you recall that communication?

KALTENBRUNNER: No.

COL. AMEN: Do you deny having written that letter?

KALTENBRUNNER: Yes . . .

COL. AMEN: Is that not your signature?

KALTENBRUNNER: No, that is not my signature. It is a signature either in ink or it is a facsimile, but it is not mine . . .

COL. AMEN: Will you look at the signature and tell me whether you do not find, written by hand just above the signature, the letters *Dein*?

KALTENBRUNNER: Yes.

COL. AMEN: And as I understand it, that word means 'yours'; in other words, it is an intimate expression used only between close personal friends, is that not correct?

KALTENBRUNNER: In German there are only two forms of concluding a letter: either *Ihr* or *Dein*. We use the latter, *Dein*, if we are on close terms, friendly terms. Blaschke, the Mayor of Vienna, is a friend of mine and apparently . . .

COL. AMEN: Now, would it not be an absolutely ridiculous and unthinkable thing that a stamp or facsimile would be made up which contained not only a signature but the expression *Dein* above the signature?

KALTENBRUNNER: That would be nonsensical, I wholly agree with that; but I did not say that it must be a facsimile signature. I just said that it is not my signature.

It is either a facsimile or it has been put underneath with another signature. The author of this letter – you did not allow me to finish before – as it can be seen from the code in the upper left-hand corner, is to be found in Section IV A and B. Everyone in the department and the entire German Reich knew that the Mayor of Vienna, Blaschke, and myself had been close personal friends since our common political activity in Vienna, that is for about ten years, and had used the familiar form of address, *Du*. Therefore, if, for instance, I had been absent from Berlin, and the letter was urgent – as I assume to be the case from the contents – the official might have considered it justifiable to write in this form. I did not authorise him and, of course, it is quite impossible, but that is the only way I can explain it . . .

COL. AMEN: Is it not a fact that you are simply lying about your signature on this letter, in the same way that you are lying to this Tribunal about almost everything else you have given testimony about? Is not that a fact?

KALTENBRUNNER: Mr Prosecutor, for a whole year I have had to submit to this insult of being called a liar. For a whole year I have been interrogated hundreds of times both here and in London, and I have been insulted in this way and even much worse. My mother, who died in 1943, was called a whore, and many other similar things were hurled at me. This term is not new to me but I should like to state that in a matter of this kind I certainly would not tell an untruth, when I claim to be believed by this Tribunal in far more important matters.

COL. AMEN: I am suggesting, Defendant, that when your testimony is so directly contrary to that of 20 or 30 other witnesses and even more documents, it is almost an incredible thing you should be telling the truth and that every witness and every document should be false.

§

In an effort to prove Kaltenbrunner's lack of involvement in the Holocaust, his lawyer, Kurt Kauffmann, called a witness. Rudolf Hoess was then revealed to the world at Nuremberg as the former commandant of Auschwitz.

The site, including the neighbouring camp at Birkenau where the great bulk of the gassings were carried out, was constructed in 1940 and 1941. Hoess was a former SS camp guard with experience of prison himself, having served five years in the 1920s for a political murder he had carried out with Martin Bormann. He supervised Auschwitz's operations until 1943, returning the following year to organise the extermination of the Hungarian Jews. His evidence was to prove among the most dramatic and, in the detached tone of its delivery, the most chilling of the trial.

Trial transcript, 15 April 1946: 'We knew when the people were dead because their screaming stopped' – Rudolf Hoess, commandant of Auschwitz

DR KAUFFMANN: Witness, your statements will have far-reaching significance. You are perhaps the only one who can throw some light upon certain hidden aspects, and who can tell which people gave the orders for the destruction of European Jewry, and can further state how this order was carried out and to what degree the execution was kept a secret . . . *[Turning to the witness]* From 1940 to 1943, you were the Commander of the camp at Auschwitz. Is that true?
HOESS: Yes.
DR KAUFFMANN: And during that time, hundreds of thousands of human beings were sent to their death there. Is that correct?
HOESS: Yes.
DR KAUFFMANN: Is it true that you, yourself, have made no

exact notes regarding the figures of the number of those victims because you were forbidden to make them?

HOESS: Yes, that is correct.

DR KAUFFMANN: Is it furthermore correct that exclusively one man by the name of Eichmann had notes about this, the man who had the task of organising and assembling these people?

HOESS: Yes.

DR KAUFFMANN: Is it furthermore true that Eichmann stated to you that in Auschwitz a total sum of more than 2 million Jews had been destroyed?

HOESS: Yes.

DR KAUFFMANN: Men, women, and children?

HOESS: Yes . . .

DR KAUFFMANN: Is it true that in 1941 you were ordered to Berlin to see Himmler? Please state briefly what was discussed.

HOESS: Yes. In the summer of 1941 I was summoned to Berlin to Reichsfuehrer SS Himmler to receive personal orders. He told me something to the effect – I do not remember the exact words – that the Fuehrer had given the order for a final solution of the Jewish question. We, the SS, must carry out that order. If it is not carried out now then the Jews will later on destroy the German people. He had chosen Auschwitz on account of its easy access by rail and also because the extensive site offered space for measures ensuring isolation.

DR KAUFFMANN: During that conference did Himmler tell you that this planned action had to be treated as a secret Reich matter?

HOESS: Yes. He stressed that point. He told me that I was not even allowed to say anything about it to my immediate superior Gruppenfuehrer Glucks. This conference concerned the two of us only and I was to observe the strictest secrecy . . .

DR KAUFFMANN: Does the expression 'secret Reich matter' mean that no one was permitted to make even the slightest allusion to outsiders without endangering his own life?

HOESS: Yes, 'secret Reich matter' means that no one was allowed to speak about these matters with any person and that everyone promised upon his life to keep the utmost secrecy.

DR KAUFFMANN: Did you happen to break that promise?

HOESS: No, not until the end of 1942.

DR KAUFFMANN: Why do you mention that date? Did you talk to outsiders after that date?

HOESS: At the end of 1942 my wife's curiosity was aroused by remarks made by the then Gauleiter of Upper Silesia, regarding happenings in my camp. She asked me whether this was the truth and I admitted that it was. That was my only breach of the promise I had given to the Reichsfuehrer. Otherwise I have never talked about it to anyone else.

DR KAUFFMANN: When did you meet Eichmann?

HOESS: I met Eichmann about four weeks after having received that order from the Reichsfuehrer. He came to Auschwitz to discuss the details with me on the carrying out of the given order. As the Reichsfuehrer had told me during our discussion, he had instructed Eichmann to discuss the carrying out of the order with me and I was to receive all further instructions from him.

DR KAUFFMANN: Will you briefly tell whether it is correct that the camp of Auschwitz was completely isolated, describing the measures taken to ensure as far as possible the secrecy of carrying out of the task given to you.

HOESS: The Auschwitz camp as such was about three kilometres away from the town. About 20,000 acres of the surrounding country had been cleared of all former inhabitants, and the entire area could be entered only by SS men or civilian employees who had special passes. The actual compound called 'Birkenau', where later on the extermination camp was constructed, was situated two kilometres from the Auschwitz camp. The camp installations themselves, that is to say, the provisional installations used at first were deep in the woods and could from nowhere be detected by the eye. In addition to that, this area had been declared a prohibited area and even members of the SS who did not have a special pass could not enter it. Thus, as far as one could judge, it was impossible for anyone except authorised persons to enter that area.

DR KAUFFMANN: And then the railway transports arrived. During what period did these transports arrive and about how many people, roughly, were in such a transport?

HOESS: During the whole period up until 1944 certain operations were carried out at irregular intervals in the different countries, so that one cannot speak of a continuous flow of incoming transports.

It was always a matter of four to six weeks. During those four to six weeks two to three trains, containing about 2,000 persons each, arrived daily. These trains were first of all shunted to a siding in the Birkenau region and the locomotives then went back. The guards who had accompanied the transport had to leave the area at once and the persons who had been brought in were taken over by guards belonging to the camp.

They were there examined by two SS medical officers as to their fitness for work. The internees capable of work at once marched to Auschwitz or to the camp at Birkenau and those incapable of work were at first taken to the provisional installations, then later to the newly constructed crematoria . . .

DR KAUFFMANN: And after the arrival of the transports were the victims stripped of everything they had? Did they have to undress completely; did they have to surrender their valuables? Is that true?

HOESS: Yes.

DR KAUFFMANN: And then they immediately went to their death?

HOESS: Yes.

DR KAUFFMANN: I ask you, according to your knowledge, did these people know what was in store for them?

HOESS: The majority of them did not, for steps were taken to keep them in doubt about it and suspicion would not arise that they were to go to their death. For instance, all doors and all walls bore inscriptions to the effect that they were going to undergo a delousing operation or take a shower. This was made known in several languages to the internees by other internees who had come in with earlier transports and who were being used as auxiliary crews during the whole action.

DR KAUFFMANN: And then, you told me the other day, that death by gassing set in within a period of three to fifteen minutes. Is that correct?

HOESS: Yes.

DR KAUFFMANN: You also told me that even before death finally set in, the victims fell into a state of unconsciousness?

HOESS: Yes. From what I was able to find out myself or from what was told me by medical officers, the time necessary for reaching unconsciousness or death varied according to the temperature and the number of people present in the chambers. Loss of consciousness took place within a few seconds or a few minutes.

DR KAUFFMANN: Did you yourself ever feel pity with the victims, thinking of your own family and children?

HOESS: Yes.

DR KAUFFMANN: How was it possible for you to carry out these actions in spite of this?

HOESS: In view of all these doubts which I had, the only one and decisive argument was the strict order and the reason given for it by the Reichsfuehrer Himmler.

DR KAUFFMANN: I ask you whether Himmler inspected the camp and convinced himself, too, of the process of annihilation?

HOESS: Yes. Himmler visited the camp in 1942 and he watched in detail one processing from beginning to end.

DR KAUFFMANN: Does the same apply to Eichmann?

HOESS: Eichmann came repeatedly to Auschwitz and was intimately acquainted with the proceedings.

DR KAUFFMANN: Did the Defendant Kaltenbrunner ever inspect the camp?

HOESS: No.

DR KAUFFMANN: Did you ever talk with Kaltenbrunner with reference to your task?

HOESS: No, never.

Hoess had supplied further details of the horror he had supervised in an earlier affidavit which was now put to him in court. Like others intimately involved in the genocide of the Jews, he had endeavoured to maintain an inner distance from his task. It was thus not the deaths themselves that were a heavy load to bear, but being asked to execute such an order, and one could always take pride in the efficiency of one's work.

COL. AMEN: I will omit the first paragraph and start with Paragraph 2 . . . 'I commanded Auschwitz until 1 December 1943, and estimate that at least 2,500,000 victims were executed and exterminated there by gassing and burning, and at least another half million succumbed to starvation and disease making a total dead of about 3,000,000. This figure represents about 70 or 80 per cent of all persons sent to Auschwitz as prisoners, the remainder having been selected and used for slave labour in the concentration camp industries; included among the executed and burned were approximately 20,000 Russian prisoners of war (previously screened out of prisoner-of-war cages by the Gestapo) who were delivered at Auschwitz in Wehrmacht transports operated by regular Wehrmacht officers and men. The remainder of the total number of victims included about 100,000 German Jews, and great numbers of citizens, mostly Jewish, from Holland, France, Belgium, Poland, Hungary, Czechoslovakia, Greece, or other countries. We executed about 400,000 Hungarian Jews alone at Auschwitz in the summer of 1944.'

That is all true, Witness?

HOESS: Yes, it is.

COL. AMEN: Now I omit the first few lines of Paragraph 3 and start in the middle of Paragraph 3:

'While Kaltenbrunner was Chief of RSHA orders for protective custody, commitments, punishment, and individual executions were signed by Kaltenbrunner or by Mueller, Chief of the Gestapo, as Kaltenbrunner's deputy.' . . .

'4. Mass executions by gassing commenced during the summer of 1941 and continued until fall 1944. I personally supervised executions at Auschwitz until 1st December 1943 and know by reason of my continued duties in the Inspectorate of Concentration Camps, WVHA, that these mass executions continued as stated above. All mass executions by gassing took place under the direct order, supervision, and responsibility of RSHA. I received all orders for carrying out these mass executions directly from RSHA.' Are those statements true and correct, Witness?

HOESS: Yes, they are.

COL. AMEN: '5. On 1 December 1943 I became Chief of Amt I

in Amt Group D of the WVHA, and in that office was responsible for co-ordinating all matters arising between RSHA and concentration camps under the administration of WVHA. I held this position until the end of the war. Pohl, as Chief of WVHA, and Kaltenbrunner, as Chief of RSHA, often conferred personally and frequently communicated orally and in writing concerning concentration camps.

'6. The "final solution" of the Jewish question meant the complete extermination of all Jews in Europe. I was ordered to establish extermination facilities at Auschwitz in June 1941. At that time, there were already in the General Government [of Poland] three other extermination camps: Belzek, Treblinka, and Wolzek. These camps were under the Einsatzkommando of the Security Police and SD. I visited Treblinka to find out how they carried out their exterminations. The camp commandant at Treblinka told me that he had liquidated 80,000 in the course of one half year. He was principally concerned with liquidating all the Jews from the Warsaw Ghetto. I Ie used monoxide gas, and I did not think that his methods were very efficient. So when I set up the extermination building at Auschwitz, I used Cyklon B which was a crystallised prussic acid which we dropped into the death chamber from a small opening. It took from three to fifteen minutes to kill the people in the death chamber, depending upon climatic conditions. We knew when the people were dead because their screaming stopped. We usually waited about one half hour before we opened the doors and removed the bodies. After the bodies were removed our special Kommandos took off the rings and extracted the gold from the teeth of the corpses.' Is that all true and correct, Witness?

HOESS: Yes.

COL. AMEN: Incidentally, what was done with the gold which was taken from the teeth of the corpses, do you know?

HOESS: Yes.

COL. AMEN: Will you tell the Tribunal?

HOESS: This gold was melted down and brought to the Chief Medical Office of the SS at Berlin.

COL. AMEN: '7. Another improvement we made over Treblinka

was that we built our gas chamber to accommodate 2,000 people at one time whereas at Treblinka their ten gas chambers only accommodated 200 people each. The way we selected our victims was as follows: We had two SS doctors on duty at Auschwitz to examine the incoming transports of prisoners. The prisoners would be marched by one of the doctors who would make spot decisions as they walked by. Those who were fit for work were sent into the camp. Others were sent immediately to the extermination plants. Children of tender years were invariably exterminated since by reason of their youth they were unable to work. Still another improvement we made over Treblinka was that at Treblinka the victims almost always knew that they were to be exterminated and at Auschwitz we endeavoured to fool the victims into thinking that they were to go through a delousing process. Of course, frequently they realised our true intentions and we sometimes had riots and difficulties due to that fact. Very frequently women would hide their children under the clothes, but of course when we found them we would send the children in to be exterminated. We were required to carry out these exterminations in secrecy but of course the foul and nauseating stench from the continuous burning of bodies permeated the entire area and all of the people living in the surrounding communities knew that exterminations were going on at Auschwitz.'

Is that all true and correct, Witness?

HOESS: Yes.

The number of those killed at Auschwitz has been the subject of much debate and Hoess's memory of dates and figures has since been shown to be unreliable. Many historians now believe that approximately 1 million Jews perished there, and perhaps 300,000 other people, mainly Poles and Gypsies. Hoess was subsequently tried by the Polish Government and hanged at Auschwitz in 1947.

§

The court's attention now turned to the defendant whose ideas had underpinned much of Nazi ideology, including the persecution of the Jews. Alfred Rosenberg had been born to German parents in Estonia, then part of Russia, and had embraced nationalism after witnessing the upheaval of the Revolution in 1917. He moved to Germany, joined the Nazi Party, and was appointed its leader by Hitler while he was in prison after the failure of the Munich Putsch. Rosenberg had few inspirational qualities, and the Party fell into factionalism until Hitler's release.

His influence on the Nazis was as a philosopher, specifically of racial theory based on the notion of Aryan supremacy and Jewish worthlessness. These ideas, which provided quasi-scientific backing for Hitler's own beliefs, were embodied in his widely read, if little understood, text *The Myth of the Twentieth Century*, which itself built on the works of the British writer Houston Stewart Chamberlain. (One of Chamberlain's convictions was that Christ was not ethnically Jewish, which led some Nazis to claim Aryan ancestry for him.) After the invasion of Russia, Rosenberg became Minister for the Occupied Eastern Territories, into which the highest example of the Aryan race, the German people, were to expand. He was seen by the prosecution as having been a driving force behind the Holocaust and the ethnic and political cleansing of Russia. In fact, he had been deeply shocked when he had learned of the killings by the Einsatzgruppen of Slavs, although his conscience was easier about the fate of the Jews. Nonetheless, in court he denied having argued for their extermination.

Trial transcript, 17 April 1946: The difference between Jewry and the Jews – Alfred Rosenberg is cross-examined

MR DODD: Now, in your Party Day speech to which you made reference yesterday, you said you used harsh language about the Jews. In those days you were objecting to the fact that they were in certain professions, I suppose, and things of that character. Is that a fair statement?

ROSENBERG: I said yesterday that in two speeches I demanded a chivalrous solution and equal treatment, and I said the foreign nations might not accuse us of discriminating against the Jewish people, so long as these foreign nations discriminate against our nation . . .

MR DODD: Yes, very well. Did you ever talk about the extermination of the Jews?

ROSENBERG: I have not in general spoken about the extermination of the Jews in the sense of this term. One has to consider the words here. The term 'extermination' has been used by the British Prime Minister . . .

MR DODD: You will get around to the words. You just tell me now whether you ever said it or not? You said that, did you not?

ROSENBERG: Not in a single speech in that sense . . .

MR DODD: I understand the sense. Did you ever talk about it with anybody as a matter of State policy or Party policy, about the extermination of the Jews?

ROSENBERG: In a conference with the Fuehrer there was once an open discussion on this question about an intended speech which was not delivered. The sense of it was that now a war was going on and that this threat which had been made should not be mentioned again. That whole speech was also not delivered.

MR DODD: When was it you were going to deliver that speech? Approximately what was the date?

ROSENBERG: In December 1941.

MR DODD: Then you have written into your speech remarks about the extermination of Jews, haven't you? Answer that 'yes' or 'no'.

ROSENBERG: I have said already that that word does not have the sense which you attribute to it.

MR DODD: I will get around to the word and the meaning of it. I am asking you, did you not use the word or the term 'extermination of the Jews' in the speech which you were prepared to make in the Sportpalast in December of 1941? Now, you can answer that pretty simply.

ROSENBERG: That may be, but I do not remember. I myself did not read the phrasing of the draft any further. In which form it was expressed I can no longer say.

MR DODD: Well then, perhaps we can help you on that. I will ask you be shown Document 1517-PS. It becomes Exhibit USA-824.

Now, this is also a memorandum of yours written by you about a discussion you had with Hitler on the 14th of December 1941, and it is quite clear from the first paragraph that you and Hitler were discussing a speech which you were to deliver in the Sportpalast in Berlin, and if you will look at the second paragraph, you will find these words . . . 'I took the standpoint not to speak of the extermination (*Ausrottung*) of Jewry. The Fuehrer affirmed this view and said that they had laid the burden of war on us and that they had brought the destruction; it is no wonder if the results would strike them first.'

Now, you have indicated that you have some difficulty with the meaning of that word, and I am going to ask you about the word *Ausrottung*. I am going to ask that you be shown – you are familiar with the standard German–English dictionary, Cassell's, I suppose, are you? Do you know this word, ever heard of it?

ROSENBERG: No.

MR DODD: This is something you will be interested in. Will you look up and read out to the Tribunal what the definition of *Ausrottung* is?

ROSENBERG: I do not need a foreign dictionary in order to explain the various meanings *Ausrottung* may have in the German language. One can exterminate an idea, an economic system, a social order, and as a final consequence, also a group of human beings, certainly. Those are the many possibilities which are contained in that word. For that I do not need an English–German dictionary. Translations from German into English are so often wrong – and just as in that last document you have submitted to me, I heard again the translation of *Herrenrasse*. In the document itself *Herrenrasse* is not even mentioned; however, there is the term '*ein falsches Herrenmenschentum*' (a false master mankind). Apparently everything is translated here in another sense.

MR DODD: All right, I am not interested in that. Let us stay on this term of *Ausrottung*. I take it then that you agree it does mean to 'wipe out' or to 'kill off', as it is understood, and that you did use the term in speaking to Hitler.

ROSENBERG: Here I heard again a different translation, which again used new German words, so I cannot determine what you wanted to express in English.

MR DODD: Are you very serious in pressing this apparent inability of yours to agree with me about this word or are you trying to kill time? Don't you know that there are plenty of people in this courtroom who speak German and who agree that that word does mean to 'wipe out', to 'extirpate'?

ROSENBERG: It means 'to overcome' on one side and then it is to be used not with respect to individuals but rather to juridical entities, to certain historical traditions. On the other side this word has been used with respect to the German people and we have also not believed that in consequence thereof 60 millions of Germans would be shot.

MR DODD: I want to remind you that this speech of yours in which you use the term *Ausrottung* was made about six months after Himmler told Hoess, whom you heard on this witness stand, to start exterminating the Jews. That is a fact, is it not?

ROSENBERG: No, that is not correct, for Adolf Hitler said in his declaration before the Reichstag: 'Should a new world war be started by these attacks of the emigrants and their backers, then as a consequence there would be an extermination and an extirpation.' That has been understood as a result and as a political threat. Apparently, a similar political threat was also used by me before the war against America broke out. And, when the war had already broken out, I have apparently said that, since it has come to this, there is no use to speak of it at all.

MR DODD: Well, actually, the Jews were being exterminated in the Eastern Occupied Territories at that time and thereafter, weren't they?

ROSENBERG: Then, may I perhaps say something about the use of the words here? We are speaking here of extermination of Jewry; there is also still a difference between 'Jewry' and 'the Jews'.

§

When the court rose for the morning, the other defendants discussed Rosenberg's evidence with Gilbert.

Gustave Gilbert: 'Rosenberg wrote too much' – the accused appraise his evidence

Lunch hour: At lunch von Papen commented, 'Dodd asked him if he knew that Hoess, Commandant of Auschwitz, had read his works. That was, of course, the crux of the whole thing. Rosenberg just gave an evasive answer.'

'Yes,' said Schacht, 'Rosenberg wrote too much.'

In the Youth lunchroom [Gilbert's name for the group of younger defendants who ate together] that question was also commented upon and a lively argument was started on the psychological aspects of the trial. Fritzsche was most emphatic in criticising the failure of the trial to recognise that the German people should also be represented among those sitting in judgment on their leaders, and assured me again that the judgment would be even more harsh than that of foreigners who are interested only in the crimes against their own nations. There was general agreement among the four that Hitler betrayed Germany, but there was some disagreement as to whether this would have been realised and would have created a revolution in case of victory. Fritzsche was of the opinion that millions of betrayed Germans would have revolted at the end of the war, but von Schirach commented that a victorious country never revolts against its victorious leaders.

Frank was overheard preparing his audience for his defence. 'No matter what you admit or deny on the stand, if they have got a document with your signature on it, it goes down as evidence against you. All we can do when we get up there is our best, and let things work out as they may. We can knock our heads against the wall but it doesn't change the facts. Our lawyers have to do the talking for us but there is no use our trying to deny what all of the world knows . . . *Ja*, it was a great Reich while it lasted.'

§

Douglas Kelley, the American psychiatrist working at the jail, was treated to some more of Rosenberg's ponderings on what to do with the Jews.

Douglas Kelley: Deport the Jews to Madagascar – Rosenberg's brainwave

Another example of Rosenberg's superficiality was given in a discussion in which he outlined his recommended solutions for America's 'problems'. He was certain that the only way out is by transplanting each racial group to an area where it can develop by itself and without contamination of the Nordic group by others.

Rosenberg explained that he had always held the idea that the Jews should be transported, and he suggested Madagascar – a French possession, incidentally – as a likely resettlement area for American Jews. He excused the Germans for not transporting their Jews by saying that this was made impossible by outside pressure, so they simply had to exterminate them. He paid Americans the compliment of considering us less likely to carry out such direct and 'efficient' measures, and he said that, for us, deportations of the Jews would probably be more feasible than extermination.

I discussed this hare-brained project solemnly with him for a time until I professed to have struck on a grave difficulty. Suppose, I said, the Jews, who tend to live in towns, simply moved into the Madagascarean cities, leaving no one to do the rural work.

Rosenberg, who told me he had been mulling over this deportation idea for twenty years, was extremely surprised and said that at no time had he ever thought of this. Then as if to give double proof of his tendency to 'solve' a problem by glossing it over, he was struck by inspiration. A beatific grin spread across his face. 'But, of course,' he said, 'how simple! You only need deport your Negroes to Madagascar, too. The Jews can then congregate in the cities, the Negroes can be settled on the land, and all will be well.'

§

As the trial progressed, the prison psychologists noted the various strategies employed by the defendants to disassociate themselves from what was being revealed day after day in court. Some smuggled in reading material – *Three Men in a Boat* in Hess's case – while Schacht wrote poetry, Streicher played with matchsticks and Speer drew pictures in crayon.

Hans Frank turned to God. Almost uniquely among those indicted, the former Governor of Poland admitted to feelings of guilt and responsibility, an awareness that he had helped administer a system of government that had inevitably brought misery to millions. Having started his career in the Party as the Nazis' legal adviser, he was made Minister of Justice in 1933. His complaints about the killings during Hitler's purge of the SA damaged his standing, and he was given a chance to redeem himself by being given charge of the suppression of Poland. It was a task he took to with relish, intending to reduce the Poles to a race of serfs. Both the Warsaw Ghetto and Auschwitz were built during his governorship, and he also presided over the extermination of the Polish intelligentsia. More than three million Jews died during his administration. Among the information contained in the diaries that he turned over to the Allies was the information that Hitler's grandfather may have been Jewish.

Though his sense of contrition drove him first to attempt suicide and then to rediscover the consolations of Roman Catholicism, Frank, like many of the other defendants, claimed that repression had never been his original intention. Like most of his co-accused, he continued to revere Hitler, and simply could not accept that it had been the Fuehrer who was the ultimate source of the evil that the Nazis had unleashed on the world. Instead, Frank preferred to blame Himmler, who had commanded the security apparatus and overseen the Final Solution, for distorting the Nazis' aims. His counsel was Alfred Seidl.

Trial transcript, 18 April 1946: 'Possessed by a deep sense of guilt' – Frank's testimony

DR SEIDL: Did you, as a Reich Minister or in any other State or Party post, want this war, or did you desire a war in violation of treaties entered into?

FRANK: War is not a thing one wants. War is terrible. We have lived through it; we did not want the war. We wanted a great Germany and the restoration of the freedom and welfare, the health and happiness of our people. It was my dream, and probably the dream of every one of us, to bring about a revision of the Versailles Treaty by peaceful means, which was provided for in that very treaty. But as in the world of treaties, between nations also, it is only the one who is strong who is listened to; Germany had to become strong first before we could negotiate. This is how I saw the development as a whole: the strengthening of the Reich, reinstatement of its sovereignty in all spheres, and by these means to free ourselves of the intolerable shackles which had been imposed upon our people. I was happy, therefore, when Adolf Hitler, in a most wonderful rise to power, unparalleled in the history of mankind, succeeded by the end of 1938 in achieving most of these aims; and I was equally unhappy when in 1939, to my dismay, I realised more and more that Adolf Hitler appeared to be departing from that course and to be following other methods.

DR SEIDL: . . . Witness, what was your share in the events of Poland after 1939?

FRANK: I bear the responsibility; and when, on 30 April 1945, Adolf Hitler ended his life, I resolved to reveal that responsibility of mine to the world as clearly as possible.

I did not destroy the forty-three volumes of my diary, which report on all these events and the share I had in them; but of my own accord I handed them voluntarily to the officers of the American Army who arrested me.

DR SEIDL: Witness, do you feel guilty of having committed crimes in violation of international conventions or crimes against humanity?

THE PRESIDENT: That is a question that the Tribunal has got to decide.

DR SEIDL: Then I shall drop the question. Witness, what do you have to say regarding the accusations which have been brought against you in the indictment?

FRANK: To these accusations I can only say that I ask the Tribunal to decide upon the degree of my guilt at the end of my case.

I myself, speaking from the very depths of my feelings and having lived through the five months of this trial, want to say that now after I have gained a full insight into all the horrible atrocities which have been committed, I am possessed by a deep sense of guilt . . .

DR SEIDL: Did you ever participate in the annihilation of Jews?

FRANK: I say 'yes'; and the reason why I say 'yes' is because, having lived through the five months of this trial, and particularly after having heard the testimony of the witness Hoess, my conscience does not allow me to throw the responsibility solely on these minor people. I myself have never installed an extermination camp for Jews, or promoted the existence of such camps; but if Adolf Hitler personally has laid that dreadful responsibility on his people, then it is mine too, for we have fought against Jewry for years; and we have indulged in the most horrible utterances – my own diary bears witness against me. Therefore, it is no more than my duty to answer your question in this connection with 'yes'. A thousand years will pass and still this guilt of Germany will not have been erased . . .

DR SEIDL: Did Adolf Hitler support you in your work as Governor General?

FRANK: All my complaints, everything I reported to him, were unfortunately dropped into the wastepaper basket by him. I did not send in my resignation fourteen times for nothing. It was not for nothing that I tried to join my brave troops as an officer. In his heart he was always opposed to lawyers, and that was one of the most serious shortcomings of this outstandingly great man. He did not want to admit formal responsibility, and that, unfortunately, applied to his policy too, as I have found out now. Every lawyer [Frank's profession] to him was a disturbing element working against his power. All I can say, therefore, is that, by supporting Himmler's and Bormann's aims to the utmost, he permanently jeopardised any attempt to find a form of government worthy of the German name . . .

In answer to my repeated questions as to what happened to the Jews who were deported, I was always told they were to be sent to the East, to be assembled, and put to work there. But, the stench seemed to penetrate the walls, and therefore I persisted in my investigations as to what was going on. Once a report came to me that there was something going on near Belcec. I went to Belcec the next day. Globocznik showed me an enormous ditch which he was having made as a protective wall and on which many thousands of workers, apparently Jews, were engaged. I spoke to some of them, asked them where they came from, how long they had been there, and he told me, that is, Globocznik, 'They are working here now, and when they are through – they come from the Reich, or some from France – they will be sent further east.' I did not make any further inquiries in that same area.

The rumour, however, that the Jews were being killed in the manner which is now known to the entire world would not be silenced. When I expressed the wish to visit the SS workshop near Lublin, in order to get some idea of the value of the work that was being done, I was told that special permission from Heinrich Himmler was required.

I asked Heinrich Himmler for this special permission. He said that he would urge me not to go to the camp. Again some time passed. On 7 February 1944 I succeeded in being received by Adolf Hitler personally – I might add that throughout the war he received me three times only. In the presence of Bormann I put the question to him: 'My Fuehrer, rumours about the extermination of the Jews will not be silenced. They are heard everywhere. No one is allowed in anywhere. Once I paid a surprise visit to Auschwitz in order to see the camp, but I was told that there was an epidemic in the camp and my car was diverted before I got there. Tell me, my Fuehrer, is there anything in it?' The Fuehrer said, 'You can very well imagine that there are executions going on – of insurgents. Apart from that I do not know anything. Why don't you speak to Heinrich Himmler about it?'

And I said, 'Well, Himmler made a speech to us in Krakow and declared in front of all the people whom I had officially called to the meeting that these rumours about the systematic extermination of the Jews were false; the Jews were merely being brought to the East.'

Thereupon the Fuehrer said, 'Then you must believe that.'

§

The next to give evidence was Julius Streicher, whose personality was, for many, the most repulsive of the defendants. A former schoolteacher, he had taken part in the Munich Putsch, and had become Gauleiter of Franconia (which included Nuremberg) in 1925. He was best known, however, as the former editor of *Der Stuermer*, an anti-Semitic weekly that consisted largely of salacious warnings about the lecherous tendencies of Jewish men towards German schoolgirls. Streicher himself gave off the whiff of an elderly satyr, and he had a reputation for sexual excess. While in prison he exercised in the nude, and the others gave him a wide berth.

Der Stuermer had never been taken very seriously by most adult Germans, although it had achieved a circulation of more than half a million, many of its readers being impressionable schoolchildren. As a public speaker, however, Streicher had been one of the Nazis' most effective rabble-rousers, consistently urging segregation and discrimination against the Jews. Yet he had held no senior government post, and for most of the war had been under house arrest on corruption charges.

The case against him, the British prosecutor explained, was less that he had been directly involved in the regime's crimes than that in the 1930s he had helped create the moral climate that had allowed them to happen. He had poisoned 'millions and millions of young boys and girls with hate . . . Without him, the Kaltenbrunners, the Himmlers, the General Stroops would have had nobody to carry out their orders.' Cross-examined by British prosecutor Mervyn Griffith-Jones, Streicher insisted that he had tried not to inflame but to enlighten. For him, all he had done was to speak the truth.

Trial transcript, 24 April 1946: 'We educated no murderers' – the influence of Julius Streicher

LT-COL. GRIFFITH-JONES: I want to turn now to the question of the Jews. May I remind you of the speech that you made on 1 April 1933 . . . 'For fourteen years we have been crying to the German nation, "German people, learn to recognise your true enemy", and fourteen years ago the German Philistines listened and then declared that we preached religious hatred. Today German people have awakened; even all over the world there is talk of the eternal Jews. Never since the beginning of the world and the creation of man has there been a nation which dared to fight against the nation of blood-suckers and extortioners who, for a thousand years, have spread all over the world.'

And then I go down to the last line of the next paragraph: 'It was left to our Movement to expose the eternal Jew as a mass murderer.' Is it right that for fourteen years you had been repeating in Germany, 'German people, learn to recognise your true enemy'?

STREICHER: I state first of all that what you have given me here has nothing to do with that. You have given me an article . . .

THE PRESIDENT: You are asked a question. You are asked whether it is true that for fourteen years you had been repeating to Germany, 'Learn to recognise your true enemy'. Is that true?

STREICHER: Yes.

LT-COL. GRIFFITH-JONES: And in doing so, is it true that you had been preaching religious hatred?

STREICHER: No.

LT-COL. GRIFFITH-JONES: Will you look at . . .

STREICHER: May I be permitted to make a statement concerning this answer? In my weekly, *Der Stuermer*, I repeatedly stated that for me the Jews are not a religious group but a race, a people.

LT-COL. GRIFFITH-JONES: And do you think to call them 'blood-suckers', 'a nation of blood-suckers and extortioners' – do you think that's preaching hatred?

STREICHER: I beg your pardon. I have not understood you?

LT-COL. GRIFFITH-JONES: You may call them a race or a nation, whichever you like, now; but you were saying, on 1 April 1933, that they were a 'nation of blood-suckers and extortioners'. Do you call that preaching hatred?

STREICHER: That is a statement, the expression of a conviction which can be proved on the basis of historical facts.

LT-COL. GRIFFITH-JONES: Understand me. I did not ask you whether it was a fact or not. I am asking whether you called it preaching hatred. Your answer is 'yes' or 'no'.

STREICHER: No, it is not preaching hatred; it is just a statement of facts.

LT-COL. GRIFFITH-JONES: Will you look two pages further on in that last document, M-33, and do you see the fourth paragraph from the end of the extract? That is Page 17 of the document book: 'As long as I stand at the head of the struggle, this struggle will be conducted so honestly that the eternal Jew will derive no joy from it.'

STREICHER: That I wrote; that was right.

LT-COL. GRIFFITH-JONES: And you were, were you not, one of those who did stand and continue to stand at the head of that struggle?

STREICHER: Did I stand at the head? I am too modest a man for that. But I do claim to have declared my conviction and my knowledge clearly and unmistakably.

LT-COL. GRIFFITH-JONES: Why did you say that so long as you were at the head of it, the Jew would derive no joy from it?

STREICHER: Because I considered myself a man whom destiny had placed in a position to enlighten people on the Jewish question.

LT-COL. GRIFFITH-JONES: And 'enlightenment' – is that another word for persecution? Do you mean by 'enlightenment', 'persecution'?

STREICHER: I did not understand that.

LT-COL. GRIFFITH-JONES: Do you mean by 'enlightenment' the word 'persecution'? Is that why the Jew was to have no joy from it, from your enlightenment?

STREICHER: I ask to have the question repeated.

LT-COL. GRIFFITH-JONES: I can show it to you and we will repeat the question as loud as you want it. Do you mean by 'enlightenment' the word 'persecution'? Do you hear that?

STREICHER: I hear 'enlightenment' and 'production'. I mean by 'enlightenment' telling another person something which he does not yet know.

LT-COL. GRIFFITH-JONES: We won't go on with that. You know, do you not, that starting with the boycott which you led yourself in 1933, the Jews thereafter were, during the course of the years, deprived of the right to vote, deprived of holding any public office, excluded from the professions; demonstrations were conducted against them in 1938, they were fined a billion marks after that, they were forced to wear a yellow star, they had their own separate seats to sit on, and they had their houses and their businesses taken away from them. Do you call that 'enlightenment'?

STREICHER: That has nothing to do with what I wrote, nothing to do with it. I did not issue the orders. I did not make the laws. I was not asked when laws were prepared. I had nothing to do with these laws and orders.

LT-COL. GRIFFITH-JONES: But as those laws and orders were passed you were applauding them, and you were going on abusing the Jews and asking for more and more orders to be passed; isn't that a fact?

STREICHER: I ask to have put to me which law I applauded.

LT-COL. GRIFFITH-JONES: Now, you told the Tribunal yesterday, did you not: that you were responsible, you thought, for the Nuremberg Decrees, which you had been advocating for years before they came into force; isn't that a fact?

STREICHER: The Nuremberg Decrees? I did not make them. I was not asked beforehand, and I did not sign them either. But I state here that these laws are the same laws which the Jewish people have as their own. It is the greatest and most important act of legislation which a modern nation has at any time made for its protection . . .

LT-COL. GRIFFITH-JONES: Do you think that it would have been possible to carry out the extermination of six million Jews in 1921? Do you think the German people would have stood for it? Do you think it would have been possible under any regime in 1921 to have carried out the murder of 6 million men, women, and children of the Jewish race?

STREICHER: Whether that would have been possible with the knowledge of the people – no, it would not have been possible. The prosecutor himself has said here that since 1937 the Party had full control over the people. Now even if the people had known this, according to the opinion of the Prosecution, they could not have done anything against that dictatorship because of that control. But the people did not know it. That is my belief, my conviction, and my knowledge.

LT-COL. GRIFFITH-JONES: Was it possible to exterminate people in that way only after some twenty years of incitement and propaganda by you and other Nazis? Is that what made that possible?

STREICHER: I deny that the population was incited. It was enlightened, and sometimes a harsh word may have been directed against the other side as an answer. It was enlightenment, not incitement. And if we want to keep our place before history I have to state again and again that the German people did not want any killings, whether individually or *en masse*.

Streicher was so obsessed with the Jews that he believed Jackson's real name must be Jacobson. He admitted that during the war he had read reports in the Swiss press of the disappearance of large numbers of Jews but had thought them exaggerated. Though he exasperated the court – at one point Griffith-Jones cut him off by remarking, 'We really don't want another long speech about the Fuehrer' – the question of his direct involvement in the crimes with which he was charged was one that would trouble both the judges and observers.

§

Hjalmar Schacht, the former Minister of Economics, had been an admirer of Hitler, he said, until about 1937, when he had resigned his meaningful posts, realising that the Fuehrer intended war. In court, he sought to explain Hitler's personal magnetism, all the while taking care to distance himself from the accusation that he had been under his spell.

Trial transcript, 2 May 1946: 'Hitler deceived us' – Schacht's defence

SCHACHT: In former statements which I have made here, I have spoken of Hitler as a semi-educated man. I still maintain that. He did not have sufficient school education, but he read an enormous amount later, and acquired a wide knowledge. He juggled with that knowledge in a masterly manner in all debates, discussions, and speeches.

No doubt he was a man of genius in certain respects. He had sudden ideas of which nobody else had thought and which were at times useful in solving great difficulties, sometimes with astounding simplicity, sometimes, however, with equally astounding brutality.

He was a mass psychologist of really diabolical genius. While I myself and several others – for instance, General von Witzleben told me so once – while we were never captivated in personal conversations, still he had a very peculiar influence on other people, and particularly he was able – in spite of his screeching and occasionally breaking voice – to stir up the utmost overwhelming enthusiasm of large masses in a filled auditorium.

I believe that originally he was not filled only with evil desires;

originally, no doubt, he believed he was aiming at good, but gradually he himself fell victim to the same spell which he exercised over the masses; because whoever ventures to seduce the masses is finally led and seduced by them, and so this reciprocal relation between leader and those led, in my opinion, contributed to ensnaring him in the evil ways of mass instincts, which every political leader should avoid.

One more thing was to be admired in Hitler. He was a man of unbending energy, of a will power which overcame all obstacles, and in my estimate only those two characteristics – mass psychology and his energy and will power – explain that Hitler was able to rally up to 40 per cent, and later almost 50 per cent, of the German people behind him . . .

He was asked by his lawyer, Rudolf Dix, about the part that Goering and Hitler had played in 1938 in concocting scandals to remove from office two senior generals who had opposed their plans for war. Schacht adopted the tone of a man hurt by the lies that had been told to him.

DR DIX: Were you only disappointed by Hitler, or did you consider yourself deceived by Hitler at that time? Will you answer that?
SCHACHT: The answer is that I have never felt disappointed by Hitler, because I had not expected more of him than my appraisal of his personality allowed me. But I certainly consider myself deceived, swindled, and cheated by him to the highest degree, because whatever he had previously promised to the German people and thereby to me, he did not keep afterwards.

He promised equal rights for all citizens, but his adherents, regardless of their capabilities, enjoyed privileges before all other citizens. He promised to put the Jews under the same protection which foreigners enjoyed, yet he deprived them of every legal protection. He had promised to fight against political lies, but together with his Minister Goebbels he cultivated nothing but political lies and political fraud. He promised the German people to maintain the principles of positive Christianity yet he tolerated and sponsored measures by which institutions of the Church were abused, reviled, and damaged. Also, in the foreign political field he always spoke against a war on two fronts – and then later undertook it himself. He despised and disregarded all laws of the Weimar Republic, to which he had taken the oath when he became Chancellor. He mobilised the Gestapo against personal liberty. He gagged and bound all free exchange of ideas and information. He pardoned criminals and enlisted them in his service. He did everything to break his promises. He lied to and deceived the world, Germany, and me.

§

In his diary, Birkett had privately been highly critical of Jackson's cross-examination of Goering. He had written that he was 'overwhelmed by his documents, and there was no chance of the lightning question . . . and above all no clear over-riding conception of the great issues'. When Jackson came to question Schacht, Birkett – who had been a renowned inquisitor in his days as a barrister – remained unimpressed.

Norman Birkett: The weakness of Jackson as a cross-examiner

1 May Jackson has come to the microphone twice this morning to protest against some of the questions [by the defence]. He has done this in a most petulant and aggressive manner, and is obviously suffering from frayed nerves. This is the result of his failure against Goering, and he seems to fear a similar failure against Schacht and he is anxious to prepare the way.

Despite the extremely flattering press notices of some of the cross-examination by the British, it yet remains true that a true cross-examination has not yet been given. It is cross-examination in name only, which consists of putting incriminating documents [to the witness]. The true art of cross-examination is something in a different plane altogether; and it has not yet been seen at Nuremberg in any shape or form.

2 May Today at 3pm Jackson began his cross-examination of Schacht. With the memory of his failure to crush Goering, some considerable interest was aroused in this second attempt. Schacht, of course, was an extremely able witness with great knowledge, complete self-control and mastery of the details of this long and complicated history. But again quite soon the reasons for Jackson's weakness and, indeed, failure were made manifest. It may be of some slight interest to set them, or some of them, down.

1. Jackson has no real knowledge of the art of cross-examination. Almost the chief quality of a cross-examiner is to have a complete grasp of the case he proposes to make, so that he may attack the witness whenever a weak place appears, with the knowledge he carries in his head. If he is unsure of his case or his facts, so he stumbles or delays, the richest opportunity of the cross-examiner is lost. This is one of the first and main weaknesses of Jackson . . .

Schacht said that he had hoped to use limited rearmament as a way of expanding the economy and had believed that Germany could develop an armed neutrality similar to that of Switzerland. His conscience was easy. The prosecution, however, characterised him as having always sat on the fence, and though Jackson again failed to ask sufficiently precise questions, it was clear that while the self-satisfied but shrewd Schacht wished to give the appearance of frankness, he was in fact dissembling.

Trial transcript, 2 May 1946: Jackson's examination of Schacht

MR JUSTICE JACKSON: Now, you also testified yesterday that you were never told about the extent, the type, and the speed of rearmament. Do you recall that?

SCHACHT: Yes.

MR JUSTICE JACKSON: But although you had no such information, you said it was too much?

SCHACHT: I had the feeling that one ought to go slowly.

MR JUSTICE JACKSON: Now, let me remind you of certain statements made by General von Blomberg concerning 1937.

'Answer: "At that time, the organisation of the planned Wehrmacht was about complete."

'Question: "When? 1937?"

'Answer: "I believe it was 1937."

'Question: "Was that a plan that had been discussed with Doctor Schacht in connection with the financing, as to how big the Wehrmacht would be?"

'Answer: "Yes. Schacht knew the plan for the formation of the Wehrmacht very well, since we informed him every year about the creation of new formations for which we had been expending money. I remember that in the year 1937 we discussed what the Wehrmacht would need for current expenses after a large amount had been spent for creating it."

'Question: ". . . When you say that Schacht was familiar with those figures, how were they brought to his attention?"

'Answer: "The demands for the money needed were handed to Schacht in writing."

'Question: "That means that in connection with the money which Schacht was raising for the rearmament programme, he was informed of how many divisions and how many tanks and so forth would be procured through these means?"

'Answer: "I don't think we put down the amount of money we would need for every tank and so forth, but we would put down how much every branch of the Wehrmacht, like the Navy or Air Force, needed, and then we would state how much was required for activating and how much for operating."

'Question: "That is, Doctor Schacht could see each year how much of an increase there would be in the size of the Armed Forces as a result of the money he was procuring?"

'Answer: "That is certain."'

I ask whether you deny the statements made by von Blomberg as I have put them to you?

SCHACHT: Yes, unfortunately, I must say that I know nothing about this . . .

MR JUSTICE JACKSON: Now, I understood you to say in your testimony that you really didn't have anything to do socially with Hitler or with the other Nazis and that you refused their invitation to lunch at the Reich Chancellery; and one of the chief reasons was that those present showed such abject humility to Hitler. Did you say that?

SCHACHT: Yes.

MR JUSTICE JACKSON: Now, I want to read to you from your speech, Document Number EC-501, your inaugural speech on the occasion of the Fuehrer's birthday. This was a public speech, by the way, wasn't it?

SCHACHT: I do not know. I do not remember.

MR JUSTICE JACKSON: You made a speech on the Fuehrer's birthday on the 21st of April 1937, carried in the newspapers?

SCHACHT: Maybe.

MR JUSTICE JACKSON: 'We are meeting together here to remember with respect and love the man to whom the German people entrusted the control of its destiny more than four years ago.' And then, after some other remarks, you say, 'With the limitless passion of a glowing heart and the infallible instinct of a born statesman, Adolf Hitler, in a struggle which he led for fourteen years with calm logic, has won for himself the soul of the German people.' . . .

SCHACHT: I assume that you have quoted it quite correctly. I do not believe that anyone, on the occasion of the birthday celebration of the head of a state, could say anything very different . . .

MR JUSTICE JACKSON: For upwards of ten years, not quite ten years, you accepted and held office of one kind or another under this regime, did you not?

SCHACHT: From 17 March 1933 to 21 January 1943.

MR JUSTICE JACKSON: And as I understand you, that during this time, at least a part of the time, Hitler deceived you, and all the time you deceived Hitler.

SCHACHT: No, oh no.

MR JUSTICE JACKSON: I have misunderstood you?

SCHACHT: Yes.

MR JUSTICE JACKSON: Well now . . .

SCHACHT: I believe that in the first years, at least, I did not deceive Hitler. I not only believe so, I know it. I only started to deceive him in 1938. Until then, I always told him my honest opinion. I did not cheat him at all, on the contrary . . .

MR JUSTICE JACKSON: What becomes, then, of your explanation

that you entered his government in order to put brakes on his programme? Did you tell him that?

SCHACHT: Oh, no. I should hardly have done that or he would never have admitted me into the government. But I did not deceive him about it.

MR JUSTICE JACKSON: Did he know your purpose in joining his government was to defeat his programme by sabotage?

SCHACHT: I did not say that I wanted to defeat his programme. I said that I wanted to direct it into orderly channels.

MR JUSTICE JACKSON: Well, you have said that you wanted to put brakes on it. You used that expression.

SCHACHT: Yes.

MR JUSTICE JACKSON: Which meant slow down? Didn't it?

SCHACHT: Yes.

MR JUSTICE JACKSON: And he wanted to speed it up, isn't that right?

SCHACHT: Yes, perhaps.

MR JUSTICE JACKSON: You never allowed him to know that you had entered his government for the purpose of slowing down his rearmament programme, did you?

SCHACHT: It was not necessary to tell him what I was thinking. I did not deceive him. I made no false statements, but I would hardly tell him what I actually thought and wanted. He did not tell me his innermost thoughts either, and you do not tell them to your political opponents either. I never deceived Hitler except after 1938 . . .

MR JUSTICE JACKSON: Now, meanwhile, while you were remaining as Minister without Portfolio because you thought it might be dangerous to resign, you were encouraging the generals in the army to commit treason against the head of the State, were you not?

SCHACHT: Yes, and I should like now to make an additional statement to this. It was not because of threatening danger to my life that I could not resign earlier. For I was not afraid of endangering my life because I was used to that ever since 1937, having constantly been exposed to the arbitrariness of the Party and its heads.

Your question as to whether I tried to turn a number of generals to high treason, I answer in the affirmative.

MR JUSTICE JACKSON: And you also tried to get assassins to assassinate Hitler, did you not?

SCHACHT: In 1938 when I made my first attempt, I was not thinking as yet of an assassination of Hitler. However, I must admit that later I said if it could not be done any other way, we would have to kill the man, if possible . . .

MR JUSTICE JACKSON: And the Gestapo, with all its searching of you, never was in a position to put you under arrest until after the 20 July attack on Hitler's life?

SCHACHT: They could have put me under arrest much earlier than that if they had been a little smarter; but that seems to be a strange attribute of any police force.

MR JUSTICE JACKSON: And it was not until 1943 that the Hitler regime dismissed you? Until that time apparently they believed that you were doing them more good than harm?

SCHACHT: I do not know what they believed at that time, hence I ask you not to question me about that. You will have to ask somebody from the regime; you still have enough people here.

§

The tubby, flaccid Walther Funk had entered Hitler's circle as an adviser on industrial policy, using his knowledge as a financial journalist to help the Nazis gain support from business leaders in the 1930s. He had succeeded Schacht as head of the central bank and as Minister for Economics in 1937, albeit that all real authority in that sphere now resided with Goering and later with Speer. A sensitive man, troubled by his homosexuality and possibly by venereal disease, Funk was shattered by his arrest and under interrogation constantly dissolved into tears. The revelations of the extent of the Holocaust brought him to the verge of a nervous breakdown. He claimed that he had done his best to help the Jews, especially musicians he had known and admired, but had, he said, been compelled to place the will of the State above his conscience. The prosecution alleged that they had striking evidence that he had known all along of the fate of European Jewry.

Trial transcript, 7 May 1946: Blood on the Reichsbank's gold – Walther Funk and the teeth in the vaults

MR DODD: Now, I want to talk a little bit about the gold in the Reichsbank. How much gold did you have on hand at the end of the year 1941, roughly? Do not give me a long story about it, because I am not too much interested. I am merely trying to find out if you were short on gold in 1941.

FUNK: The gold reserve which I took over amounted to about 500 million Reichsmark when I received the post of Schacht.

MR DODD: Well, all right.

FUNK: It was increased in any substantial manner only by the Belgian gold, as far as I know.

MR DODD: That is really – it is interesting to hear all about it, but I have another purpose in mind. From whence did you obtain gold after you took over? Where did you get any new gold reserves from?

FUNK: Only by changing foreign currency into gold, and then, after I took over the post, we got in addition the gold reserve of the Czech National Bank. But we mainly increased our reserve through the Belgian gold.

MR DODD: All right. Now, of course, gold became very important to you as a matter of payment in foreign exchange. You had to pay off in gold along in 1942 and 1943, did you not? Is that so?

FUNK: It was very difficult to pay in gold.

MR DODD: I know it was.

FUNK: Because the countries with which we still had business relations introduced gold embargoes. Sweden refused to accept gold at all. Only in Switzerland could we still do business through changing gold into foreign currency.

MR DODD: I think you have established that you had to use gold as foreign exchange in 1942 and 1943 and that is all I wanted to know. When did you start to do business with the SS, Mr Funk?

FUNK: Business with the SS? I have never done that.

MR DODD: Yes, sir, business with the SS. Are you sure about that? I want you to take this very seriously. It is about the end of your examination, and it is very important to you. I ask you again, when did you start to do business with the SS?

FUNK: I never started business with the SS. I can only repeat what I said in the preliminary interrogation. Puhl [his deputy] one day informed me that a deposit had been received from the SS. First I assumed that it was a regular deposit, that is, a deposit which remained locked and which was of no further concern to us, but then Puhl told me later that these deposits of the SS should be used by the Reichsbank. I assumed they consisted of gold coins and foreign currency, but principally gold coins, which every German citizen had had to turn in as it was, and which were taken from inmates of concentration camps and turned over to the Reichsbank . . .

MR DODD: Just a minute. Were you in the habit of having gold teeth deposited in the Reichsbank?

FUNK: No.

MR DODD: But you did have it from the SS, did you not?

FUNK: I do not know.

MR DODD: You do not know? Well, now, if Your Honour please, we have a very brief film, and I think we can show it before we adjourn, and I would like to show it to the witness before I examine him further on this gold business in the Reichsbank. It is a picture that was taken by the Allied Forces when they entered the Reichsbank, and it will show gold teeth and bridges and so on in their vaults.

FUNK: I know nothing about it.

MR DODD: Well now, let us see. You were not ordinarily in the habit, in the Reichsbank, of accepting jewels, monocles, spectacles, watches, cigarette cases, pearls, diamonds, gold dentures, were you? You ordinarily accepted that sort of material for deposit in your bank?

FUNK: No; there could be no question, in my opinion, that the bank had no right to do that, because these things were supposed to be delivered to an entirely different place. If I am correctly informed about the legal position, these things were supposed to be delivered to the Reich Office for Precious Metals and not to the Reichsbank. Diamonds, jewels, and precious stones were not the concern of the Reichsbank because it was not a place of sale for these things. And in my opinion, if the Reichsbank did that, then it was unlawful . . . [The film was shown. Numerous gold objects, including dental plates and bridgework, had been found in the bank's vaults.]

MR DODD: Well, do you recall the testimony of the witness Hoess in this courtroom not so long ago? You remember the man? He sat where you are sitting now. He said that he exterminated between 2½ and 3 million Jews and other people at Auschwitz. Now, before I ask you the next question I want you to recall that testimony and I will point something out for you about it that may help you. You recall that he said that Himmler sent for him in June 1941, and that Himmler told him that the final solution of the Jewish problem was at hand, and that he was to conduct these exterminations. Do you recall that he went back and looked over the facilities in one camp in Poland and found it was not big enough to kill the number of people involved and he had to construct gas chambers that would hold 2,000 people at a time, and so his extermination programme could not have got under way until pretty late in 1941, and you observe that your assistant and credible friend Puhl says it was in 1942 that these shipments began to arrive from the SS?

FUNK: No, I know nothing about the date. I do not know when these things happened. I had nothing to do with them. It is all news to me that the Reichsbank was concerned with these things to this extent.

MR DODD: Then I take it you want to stand on an absolute denial that at any time you had any knowledge of any kind about these transactions with the SS or their relationship to the victims of the concentration camps. After seeing this film, after hearing Puhl's affidavit, you absolutely deny any knowledge at all?

FUNK: Only as far as I have mentioned it here . . .

MR DODD: All right. You know you did on one occasion at least, and possibly two, break down and weep when you were being interrogated, you recall, and you did say you were a guilty man and you gave an explanation of that yesterday. You remember those tears. I am just asking you now; I am sure you do. I am just trying to establish the basis here for another question. You remember that happened?

FUNK: Yes.

MR DODD: And you said, 'I am a guilty man'. You told us yesterday it was because you were upset a little bit in the general situation. I am suggesting to you that is it not a fact that this matter that we have been talking about since yesterday has been on your conscience all the time and that was really what is on your mind, and it has been a shadow on you ever since you have been in custody? And is it not about time that you told the whole story?

FUNK: I cannot tell more to the Tribunal than I have already said, that is the truth. Let Herr Puhl be responsible before God for what he put in the affidavit; I am responsible for what I state here. It is absolutely clear that Herr Puhl is now trying to put the blame on me and to exculpate himself. If he has done these things for years with the SS, it is his guilt and his responsibility. I have only spoken to him two or three times about these things, that is, about the things I have mentioned here.

MR DODD: You are trying to put the blame on Puhl, are you not?

FUNK: No. He is blaming me and I repudiate that.

MR DODD: The trouble is, there was blood on this gold, was there not, and you knew this since 1942 . . .

Funk had said that it was not his job to inspect vaults, but when Emil Puhl testified he claimed that Funk had told him to accept deposits from the SS and to keep them secret. Puhl said he had assumed the material had merely been confiscated. There was no definite proof that the items had come from the camps, but the impression given was that both men had at least suspected rather more than they were now prepared to admit.

§

From 1935 to 1943, Admiral Karl Doenitz had been the first commander of Germany's formidable submarine fleet, which had come close to choking Britain's supply line in the early years of the war. He had succeeded his co-defendant, Admiral Raeder, as head of the Navy and then, in May 1945, much to his surprise, had learned that Hitler's will named him the next President of the Reich, in which capacity he surrendered Germany to the Allies.

During the First World War, Doenitz was taken prisoner off Malta by the British while serving in submarines. Throughout the 1920s, notwithstanding that U-boats had been forbidden to the German Navy by the Treaty of Versailles, he was actively planning their development. Training of crews commenced as soon as the restrictions were lifted in 1935. Though he had only twenty-two U-boats ready at the start of the war, by March 1943 there were more than 100 and Doenitz was winning the Battle of the Atlantic against Allied shipping.

Hitler replaced Raeder – who had long advocated concentrating instead on capital ships – with Doenitz at the start of 1943, but by the summer the Allies' development of the convoy system, their invention of radar and their code-breaking successes had decisively turned the tide against the U-boats. Nonetheless, Doenitz remained in favour with Hitler, not least because of his aggressive outlook.

Despite being nominated his successor by Hitler, Doenitz maintained, in common with Keitel and Jodl, that he had never been anything other than a loyal, dutiful, professional officer. His lawyer, a good-looking naval advocate named Otto Kranzbuehler, proved to be the equal of any that appeared before the court.

Trial transcript, 9 May 1946: Serving Hitler as 'the first soldier of the Navy' – Karl Doenitz

FLOTTENRICHTER KRANZBUEHLER: In your eyes was the position of Commander-in-Chief, which was offered to you, a political or a military position?

DOENITZ: It was self-evidently a purely military position, namely, that of the first soldier at the head of the Navy. My appointment to this position also came about because of purely military reasons which motivated Grossadmiral Raeder to propose my name for this position. Purely military considerations were the decisive ones in respect to this appointment.

FLOTTENRICHTER KRANZBUEHLER: You know, Admiral, that the Prosecution draws very far-reaching conclusions from your acceptance of this appointment as Commander-in-Chief of the Navy, especially with reference to the conspiracy. The Prosecution contends that through your acceptance of this position you ratified the previous happenings, all the endeavours of the Party since 1920 or 1922, and the entire German policy, domestic and foreign, at least since 1933. Were you aware of the significance of this foreign policy? Did you take this into consideration at all?

DOENITZ: The idea never entered my head. Nor do I believe that there is a soldier who, when he receives a military command, would entertain such thoughts or be conscious of such considerations. My appointment as Commander-in-Chief of the Navy represented for me an order which I of course had to obey, just as I had to obey every other military order, unless for reasons of health I was not able to do so. Since I was in good health and believed that I could be of use to the Navy, I naturally also accepted this command with inner conviction. Anything else would have been desertion or disobedience.

FLOTTENRICHTER KRANZBUEHLER: Then as Commander-in-Chief of the Navy you came into very close contact with Adolf Hitler. You also know just what conclusions the Prosecution draws from this relationship. Please tell me just what this relationship was and on what it was based?

DOENITZ: In order to be brief, I might perhaps explain the matter as follows: This relationship was based on three ties. First of all, I accepted and agreed to the national and social ideas of National Socialism: the national ideas which found expression in the honour and dignity of the nation, its freedom, and its equality among nations and its security; and the social tenets which had perhaps as their basis: no class struggle, but human and social respect of each person regardless of his class, profession, or economic position, and on the other hand, subordination of each and every one to the interests of the common weal. Naturally I regarded Adolf Hitler's high authority with admiration and joyfully acknowledged it, when in times of peace he succeeded so quickly and without bloodshed in realising his national and social objectives.

My second tie was my oath. Adolf Hitler had, in a legal and lawful way, become the Supreme Commander of the Wehrmacht, to whom the Wehrmacht had sworn its oath of allegiance. That this oath was sacred to me is self-evident and I believe that decency in this world will everywhere be on the side of him who keeps his oath.

The third tie was my personal relationship. Before I became Commander-in-Chief of the Navy, I believe Hitler had no definite conception of me and my person. He had seen me too few times and always in large circles. How my relationship to him would shape itself was therefore a completely open question when I became Commander-in-Chief of the Navy. My start in this connection was very unfavourable. It was made difficult, first, by the imminent and then the actual collapse of U-boat warfare and, secondly, by my refusal, just as Grossadmiral Raeder had already refused, to scrap the large ships, which in Hitler's opinion had no fighting value in view of the oppressive superiority of the foe. I, like Grossadmiral Raeder, had opposed the scrapping of these ships, and only after a quarrel did he finally agree. But, despite that, I noticed very soon that in Navy matters he had confidence in me and in other respects as well treated me with decided respect.

Adolf Hitler always saw in me only the first soldier of the Navy. He never asked for my advice in military matters which did not concern the Navy, either in regard to the Army or the Air Force; nor did I ever express my opinion about matters concerning the Army or the Air Force, because basically I did not have sufficient knowledge of these matters. Of course, he never consulted me on political matters of a domestic or foreign nature . . .

I never received from the Fuehrer an order which in any way violated the ethics of war. Neither I nor anyone in the Navy – and this is my conviction – knew anything about the mass extermination of people, which I learned about here from the indictment, or, as far as the concentration camps are concerned, after the capitulation in May 1945.

In Hitler I saw a powerful personality who had extraordinary intelligence and energy and a practically universal knowledge, from whom power seemed to emanate and who was possessed of a remarkable power of suggestion. On the other hand, I purposely very seldom went to his headquarters, for I had the feeling that I would best preserve my power of initiative that way and, secondly, because after several days, say two or three days at his headquarters, I had the feeling that I had to disengage myself from his power of suggestion. I am telling you this because in this connection I was doubtless more fortunate than his staff who were constantly exposed to his powerful personality with its power of suggestion . . .

FLOTTENRICHTER KRANZBUEHLER: . . . I should like to ask you, did you not in your position as Commander-in-Chief, and during your visits to the Fuehrer's headquarters, have experiences which made you consider disassociating yourself from Adolf Hitler?

DOENITZ: I have already stated that as far as my activity was concerned, even at headquarters, I was strictly limited to my own department, since it was a peculiarity of the Fuehrer's to listen to a person only about matters which were that person's express concern. It was also self-evident that at the discussions of the military situation only purely military matters were discussed, that is, no problems of domestic policy, of the SD, or the SS, unless it was a question of SS divisions in military service under one of the army commanders. Therefore I had no knowledge of all these things. As I have already said, I never received an order from the Fuehrer which in any way violated military ethics. Thus I firmly believe that in every respect I kept the Navy unsullied down to the last man until the end. In naval warfare my attention was focused on the sea; and the Navy, small as it was, tried to fulfil its duty according to its tasks. Therefore I had no reason at all to break with the Fuehrer.

FLOTTENRICHTER KRANZBUEHLER: Such a reason would not necessarily refer to a crime; it could also have been for political considerations, having nothing to do with crimes. You have heard the question broached repeatedly as to whether there should have been a Putsch. Did you enter into contact with such a movement and did you yourself consider or attempt a Putsch?

DOENITZ: No. The word 'Putsch' has been used frequently in this courtroom by a wide variety of people. It is easy to say so, but I believe that one would have had to realise the tremendous significance of such an activity.

The German nation was involved in a struggle of life and death. It was surrounded by enemies almost like a fortress. And it is clear, to keep to the simile of the fortress, that every disturbance from within would without doubt perforce have affected our military might and fighting power. Anyone, therefore, who violates his loyalty and his oath to plan and try to bring about an overthrow during such a struggle for survival must be most deeply convinced that the nation needs such an overthrow at all costs and must be aware of his responsibility.

Despite this, every nation will judge such a man to be a traitor, and history will not vindicate him unless the success of the overthrow actually contributes to the welfare and prosperity of his people. This, however, would not have been the case in Germany.

If, for instance, the Putsch of 20 July had been successful, then a dissolution, if only a gradual one, would have resulted inside Germany – a fight against the bearers of weapons, here the SS, there another group, complete chaos inside Germany – for the firm structure of the State would gradually have been destroyed and disintegration and a reduction of our fighting power at the front would have inevitably resulted.

The heart of the case against Doenitz concerned orders that he had given to his U-boat crews early in the war that survivors of ships they had destroyed should not be assisted, lest by lingering at the scene the submarine's own safety was endangered. Despite widespread and almost wholly unfounded rumours of lifeboats being machine-gunned by U-boats, their captains had in fact frequently ignored Doenitz's command in the first years of the war and had rescued survivors.

Then in 1942, a U-boat that had sunk the British transport vessel Laconia was attacked by American aircraft while attempting to aid 1,400 people who had been aboard the ship. Doenitz had consequently taken the opportunity to reiterate his order. The prosecution claimed that the decree contravened international maritime practice agreed before the war, while Kranzbuehler argued that the law had evolved during it in response to changed conditions. He had also to contend, however, with the charge that the strong wording of Doenitz's proclamation had led some commanders to believe that he was actively sanctioning the murder of survivors.

Trial transcript, 9 May 1946: 'Pick up no survivors' – Doenitz and the Laconia order

FLOTTENRICHTER KRANZBUEHLER: Admiral, now I turn to a document which is really the nucleus of the accusation against you. It is Document GB-199, Page 36 of the British document book. This is your radio message of 17 September [1942], and the Prosecution asserts that it is an order for the destruction of the shipwrecked. It is of such importance that I will read it to you again.

'To all Commanding Officers:

'1. No attempt of any kind must be made to rescue members of ships sunk, and this includes picking up persons in the water and putting them in lifeboats, righting capsized lifeboats, and handing over food and water. Rescue runs counter to the most elementary demands of warfare for the destruction of enemy ships and crews. 2. Orders for bringing back captains and chief engineers still apply. 3. Rescue the shipwrecked only if their statements will be of importance for your boat. 4. Be harsh. Bear in mind that the enemy takes no regard of women and children in his bombing attacks on German cities.' . . .

In the opinion of the Prosecution, Admiral, you used that incident [the *Laconia*] to carry out in practice an idea which you had already cherished for a long time, namely, in the future to kill the shipwrecked. Please state your view on this.

DOENITZ: Actually, I cannot say anything in the face of such an accusation. The whole question concerned rescue or nonrescue; the entire development leading up to that order speaks clearly against such an accusation. It was a fact that we rescued with devotion and were bombed while doing so; it was also a fact that the U-boat Command and I were faced with a serious decision and we acted in a humane way, which from a military point of view was wrong. I think, therefore, that no more words need be lost in rebuttal of this charge.

FLOTTENRICHTER KRANZBUEHLER: Admiral, I must put to you now the wording of that order from which the Prosecution draws its conclusions. I have read it before; in the second paragraph it says. 'Rescue is contrary to the most primitive laws of warfare for the destruction of enemy ships and crews.'

What does that sentence mean?

DOENITZ: That sentence is, of course, in a sense intended to be a justification. Now the Prosecution says I could quite simply have ordered that safety did not permit it, that the predominance of the enemy's air force did not permit it – and as we have seen in the case of the *Laconia*, I did order that four times. But that reasoning had been worn out. It was a much-played record, if I may use the expression, and I was now anxious to state to the commanders of the submarines a reason which would exclude all discretion and all independent decisions of the commanders. For again and again I had the experience that, for the reasons mentioned before, a clear sky was judged too favourably by the U-boats and then the submarine was lost; or that a commander, in the role of rescuer, was in time no longer master of his own decisions, as the *Laconia* case showed; therefore under no circumstances – under no circumstances whatsoever – did I want to repeat the old reason which again would give the U-boat commander the opportunity to say, 'Well, at the moment there is no danger of an air attack'; that is, I did not want to give him a chance to act independently, to make his own decision, for instance, to say to himself, 'Since the danger of air attack no longer permits.' That is just what I did not want. I did not want an argument to arise in the mind of one of the 200 U-boat commanders. Nor did I want to say, 'If somebody with great self-sacrifice rescues the enemy and in that process is killed by him, then that is a contradiction of the most elementary laws of warfare.' I could have said that too. But I did not want to put it in that way, and therefore I worded the sentence as it now stands.

FLOTTENRICHTER KRANZBUEHLER: What do you mean by the last sentence in the order, 'Be harsh'?

DOENITZ: I had preached to my U-boat commanders for 5½ years, that they should be hard towards themselves. And when giving this order I again felt that I had to emphasise to my commanders in a very drastic way my whole concern and my grave responsibility for the submarines, and thus the necessity of prohibiting rescue activities in view of the overwhelming power of the enemy air force. After all it is very definite that on one side there is the harshness of war, the necessity of saving one's own submarine, and on the other the traditional sentiment of the sailor.

FLOTTENRICHTER KRANZBUEHLER: You heard the witness Korvettenkapitan Mohle state in this Court that he misunderstood the order in the sense that survivors should be killed, and in several cases he instructed submarine commanders in that sense.

DOENITZ: Mohle is . . .

FLOTTENRICHTER KRANZBUEHLER: One moment, Admiral. I want to put a question first. As commanding officer, do you not have to assume responsibility for a misunderstanding of your order?

DOENITZ: Of course, I am responsible for all orders, for their form and their contents. Mohle, however, is the only person who had doubts about the meaning of that order. I regret that Mohle did not find occasion to clarify these doubts immediately, either through me, to whom everybody had access at all times, or through the numerous staff officers who, as members of my staff, were either also partly responsible or participated in the drafting of these orders; or, as another alternative, through his immediate superior in Kiel. I am convinced that the few U-boat commanders to whom he communicated his doubts remained quite unaffected by them. If there were any consequences I would of course assume responsibility for them.

FLOTTENRICHTER KRANZBUEHLER: You are acquainted with the case of Kapitanleutnant Eck, who after sinking the Greek steamer *Peleus* in the spring of 1944 actually fired on lifeboats. What is your view of this incident?

DOENITZ: Eck knew nothing about the interpretation or the doubts of the Mohle order, nor of this affair. He acted on his own decision, and his aim was not to kill survivors but to remove the wreckage; because he was certain that otherwise this wreckage would on the following day give a clue to Anglo-American planes and that they would spot and destroy him. His purpose, therefore, was entirely different from the one stated in the Mohle interpretation . . .

FLOTTENRICHTER KRANZBUEHLER: Do you approve of his actions, now that you know of them?

DOENITZ: I do not approve his actions because, as I said before, in this respect one must not deviate from military ethics under any circumstances. However, I want to say that Kapitanleutnant Eck was faced with a very grave decision. He had to bear responsibility for his boat and his crew, and that responsibility is a serious one in time of war. Therefore, if for the reason that he believed he would otherwise be spotted and destroyed – and that reason was not unfounded, because in the same operational area and during the same time four submarines, I think, had been bombed – if he came to his decision for that reason, then a German court-martial would undoubtedly have taken it into consideration.

I believe that after the war one views events differently, and one does not fully realise the great responsibility which an unfortunate commander carries.

FLOTTENRICHTER KRANZBUEHLER: Apart from the Eck case did you, during the war, or after, hear of any other instance in which a U-boat commander fired on shipwrecked people or life rafts?

DOENITZ: Not a single one.

FLOTTENRICHTER KRANZBUEHLER: You know, do you not, the documents of the Prosecution which describe the sinking of the ships *Noreen Mary* and *Antonico*? Do you or do you not recognise the soundness of these documents as evidence according to your experience in these matters?

DOENITZ: No. I believe that they cannot stand the test of an impartial examination. We have a large number of similar reports about the other side, and we were always of the opinion, and also stated that opinion in writing to the Fuehrer and the OKW, that one must view these cases with a good deal of scepticism, because a shipwrecked person can easily believe that he is being fired on, whereas the shots may not be aimed at him at all, but at the ship, that is, misses of some sort.

The fact that the Prosecution gives just these two examples proves to me that my conviction is correct, that apart from the Eck case no further instances of this kind occurred during those long years in the ranks of the large German U-boat force.

Uniquely among the defending counsel, Kranzbuehler was able to persuade the Tribunal to admit what is known as *tu quoque* evidence, proof that the other side – in this case the American Navy in the Pacific – had practised similarly unrestricted warfare, thus adding strength to his argument that Doenitz had acted within the rules of a changing body of law. Nonetheless, the Admiral was now perceived as a considerably more ruthless adversary than had hitherto been his reputation.

A year on from the surrender he had negotiated in May 1945, Doenitz gave evidence about the last days of the Third Reich.

Trial transcript, 9 May 1946: Doenitz on the last days of the war

FLOTTENRICHTER KRANZBUEHLER: The Prosecution has submitted a document in which you exhorted the war leaders in the spring of 1945 to carry on tenaciously to the end. It is Exhibit GB-212. You are accused in this connection of being a fanatical Nazi who was ready to carry on a hopeless war at the expense of the women and children of your people. Please define your position in respect to this particularly grave accusation.

DOENITZ: In this connection I can say the following: In the spring of 1945 I was not head of the State; I was a soldier. To continue the fight or not to continue the fight was a political decision. The head of the State wanted to continue the fight. I as a soldier had to obey. It is an impossibility that in a state one soldier should declare, 'I shall continue to fight,' while another declares, 'I shall not continue the fight.' I could not have given any other advice, the way I saw things; and for the following reasons:

First: In the East the collapse of our front at one point meant the extermination of the people living behind that front. We knew that because of practical experiences and because of all the reports which we had about this. It was the belief of all the people that the soldier in the East had to do his military duty in these hard months of the war, these last hard months of the war. This was especially important because otherwise German women and children would have perished.

The Navy was involved to a considerable extent in the East. It had about 100,000 men on land, and the entire surface craft were concentrated in the Baltic for the transport of troops, weapons, wounded, and above all, refugees. Therefore the very existence of the German people in this last hard period depended above all on the soldiers carrying on tenaciously to the end.

Secondly: If we had capitulated in the first few months of the spring or in the winter of 1945, then from everything we knew about the enemy's intentions the country would, according to the Yalta Agreement, have been ruinously torn asunder and partitioned and the German land occupied in the same way as it is today.

Thirdly: Capitulation means that the army, the soldiers, stay where they are and become prisoners. That means that if we had capitulated in January or February 1945, 2 million soldiers in the East, for example, would have fallen into the hands of the Russians. That these millions could not possibly have been cared for during the cold winter is obvious; and we would have lost men on a very large scale, for even at the time of the capitulation in May 1945 – that is, in the late spring – it was not possible in the West to take care of the large masses of prisoners according to the Geneva Convention. Then, as I have already said, since the Yalta Agreement would have been put into effect, we would have lost in the East a much larger number of people who had not yet fled from there.

When on 1 May I became head of the State, circumstances were different. By that time the fronts, the Eastern and Western fronts, had come so close to each other that in a few days people, troops, soldiers, armies, and the great masses of refugees could be transported, from the East to the West. When I became head of the State on 1 May, I therefore strove to make peace as quickly as possible and to capitulate, thus saving German blood and bringing German people from the East to the West; and I acted accordingly, already on 2 May, by making overtures to General Montgomery to capitulate for the territory facing his army, and for Holland and Denmark which we still held firmly; and immediately following that I opened negotiations with General Eisenhower.

The same basic principle – to save and preserve the German population – motivated me in the winter to face bitter necessity and keep on fighting. It was very painful that our cities were still being bombed to pieces and that through these bombing attacks and the continued fight more lives were lost. The number of these people is about 300,000 to 400,000, the majority of whom perished in the bombing attack of Dresden, which cannot be understood from a military point of view and which could not have been predicted. Nevertheless, this figure is relatively small compared with the millions of German people, soldiers and civilian population, we would have lost in the East if we had capitulated in the winter.

Therefore, in my opinion, it was necessary to act as I did: First while I was still a soldier, to call on my troops to keep up the fight, and afterwards, when I became head of the State in May, to capitulate at once. Thereby no German lives were lost; rather were they saved.

Doenitz's determination to salvage what he could from the advancing Russians was understandable, albeit the number of those killed at Dresden is now thought to be much lower than he believed. Perhaps 35,000 people died in firestorms that night in February 1945. As for the other charges against him, the admiral denied having known of the fate of Allied commandos who had been shot in Norway by the SD after being captured by the Navy. More damning was a speech he had made excoriating 'the spreading poison of Jewry', but though he admitted having known that labour for the shipyards was being supplied from the concentration camps, there was no proof that he had been aware of the ultimate purpose of these.

§

Grand Admiral Erich Raeder, Doenitz's predecessor as commander-in-chief of the Navy and another veteran of the First World War, had overseen the build-up of the German fleet in the 1930s. He had been the leading proponent of the plan to build the pocket battleships and convoy raiders that were initially of such concern to the British Admiralty when war began, but the High Seas Fleet's inability to stem the flow of Allied merchant shipping had brought down Hitler's anger on him. He insisted in court that rearmament had been undertaken solely for defensive reasons, much as he claimed that the invasion of Norway, which he was alleged to have urged on Hitler, had been pre-emptive since the British were also contemplating its occupation. His lawyer was Walter Siemers.

Trial transcript, 17 May 1946: Erich Raeder and the decision to invade Norway

DR SIEMERS: The British prosecutor, Major Elwyn Jones, considers the attack against Norway a special case in the series of aggressive wars waged by the Nazi conspirators. In this connection he pointed out that, in this case, Hitler did not think of this himself but rather was persuaded by you. Since his point is very important, I should like to ask you to describe this event exactly, and therefore I ask you first of all: When was the first conversation about this matter between you and Hitler?

RAEDER: The first conversation between Hitler and myself concerning the question of Norway was on 10 October 1939, and that was at my request. The reason for this was that we had received reports at various times during the last week of September through our intelligence service of the offices of Admiral Canaris that the British intended to occupy bases in Norway.

I recall that after reports to this effect had reached me several times Admiral Canaris visited me himself on one occasion – something he did in very important cases only. And, in the presence of my chief of staff, he gave me a coherent explanation concerning the intelligence reports which had been received. In this connection air bases were constantly mentioned, as well as bases in the south of Norway. Stavanger was mentioned constantly with the airport Sola, and Trondheim was usually mentioned and occasionally Christiansand.

During the last days of September I had a telephone conversation with Admiral Carls who was the commander of Navy Group North and was therefore in charge of operations in the Skagerrak, the Kattegat and in the North Sea. This man had obviously received similar reports. He informed me that he had composed a private letter addressed to me, in which he dealt with the question of the danger of Norway's being occupied by British forces and in which he was in a general way dealing with the question as to what disadvantages such a step would have for us, and whether we should have to forestall such an attempt, and also what advantages or disadvantages the occupation of Norway – that is, of the Norwegian coast and the Norwegian bases – by our forces would have.

Up until that point I had not concerned myself with the Norwegian question at all, except for the fact I had received these reports. The arrival of this letter at the end of September or the beginning of October, it must have been about then, impelled me to show it to the Chief of Staff of the SKL [Naval Operations Staff] and to instruct him to deal with all dispatch with the question of the occupation of Norwegian bases by England, and the other questions which Admiral Carls had dealt with, and to have the questions discussed in the SKL. The advantages and disadvantages of an expansion of the war towards the North had to be considered, not only of an expansion on our part but, above all, an expansion on the part of England; what value, what advantage would accrue to us if we acted first; what disadvantages would result if we had to defend the Norwegian coast? . . .

I would like to say, by way of introduction, that it was entirely clear to me that if we undertook to occupy these bases we would violate neutrality. But I also knew of the agreement which existed between the German and Norwegian Governments of 2 September regarding neutrality . . .

DR SIEMERS: . . . You have that document before you?

RAEDER: Yes, I have it before me, and I would like to quote the concluding sentence . . .

'Should the attitude of the Royal Norwegian Government change so that any such breach of neutrality by a third party recurs, the Reich Government would then obviously be compelled to safeguard the interests of the Reich in such a way as would be forced upon the Reich Cabinet by the resulting situation.' . . .

I maintained this point of view [upholding Norway's neutrality] when reporting to Hitler. In that report I first mentioned the intelligence reports which we had at hand. Then I described the dangers which might result to us from a British occupation of bases on the Norwegian coast and might affect our entire warfare, dangers which I considered tremendous. I had the feeling that such an occupation would gravely prejudice and imperil the whole conduct of our war.

If the British occupied bases in Norway, especially in the South of Norway, they would be able to dominate the entrance to the Baltic Sea from those points, and also flank our naval operations from the Heligoland Bight and from the Elbe, Jade and Weser. The second outlet which we had was also gravely imperilled, affecting the operations of battleships as well as the courses of our merchantmen.

In addition to that, from their air bases in Norway, they might endanger our air operations, the operations of our pilots for reconnaissance in the North Sea or for attacks against England.

Furthermore, from Norway they could exert strong pressure on Sweden, and that pressure would have been felt in this respect, that the supplies of ore from Sweden would have been hindered or stopped by purely political pressure. Finally, the export of ore from Narvik to Germany could have been stopped entirely, and it is known how much Germany depended on supplies of ore from Sweden and Norway. They might even have gone so far – and we learned about this subsequently that such plans were discussed – as to attack and destroy the ore deposits at Lulea, or to seize them.

All of these dangers might become decisive factors in the outcome of the war. Aside from the fact that I told Hitler that the best thing for us would be to have strict neutrality on the part of Norway, I also called his attention to the dangers which would result to us from an occupation of the Norwegian coast and Norwegian bases, for there would have been lively naval operations near the Norwegian coast in which the British, even after our occupation of bases, would try to hamper our ore traffic from Narvik. A struggle might ensue which we, with our inadequate supply of surface vessels, would be unable to cope with in the long run.

Therefore, at that time I did not make any proposal that we should occupy Norway or that we should obtain bases in Norway. I only did my duty in telling the Supreme Commander of the Wehrmacht about this grave danger which was threatening us, and against which we might have to use emergency measures for our defence. I also pointed out to him that possible operations for the occupation of Norwegian bases might be very expensive for us. In the course of later discussions I told him that we might even lose our entire fleet. I would consider it a favourable case if we were to lose only one-third, something which actually did happen later on . . .

DR SIEMERS: I believe you said already that the reports increased considerably in the month of March [1940]. When did Hitler give the final order for the occupation?

RAEDER: At the end of March or beginning of April. I cannot recall the exact date.

DR SIEMERS: I believe that is sufficient.

RAEDER: May I also mention a particularly important report which I remember now. Quisling [the pro-German Norwegian politician] reported in February that Lord Halifax had told the Norwegian Ambassador in London that an operation on the part of the British for the acquisition of bases in Norway was planned for the near future. That report also reached us at that time. I should like to add, as I emphasised before, that being fully conscious of my responsibility I always tried to show the Fuehrer both sides of the picture and that the Fuehrer would have to be guided by my documentary proof when deciding, to take or refrain from taking that tremendous step. But that does not mean to say that because I pointed out to my Supreme Commander of the Armed Forces that particular danger, I in any way decline to accept responsibility. Of course, I am in some measure responsible for the whole thing. Moreover, I have been accused because in a letter submitted here under C–155 I had told my officers' corps that I was proud of the way in which this extraordinarily dangerous enterprise had been executed. I should like to confirm this, because I believe I was entitled to be proud that the Navy had carried out that operation with such limited means and in the face of the entire British fleet; I still stick to that.

Although not revealed at the time, or indeed during the trial, in April 1940 the British Government had decided to mine Norwegian waters, in violation of its neutrality, with the intention of damaging German shipping. Unlike the Nazis, however, they had never contemplated invading, and by the time the order had been given to lay mines, the Germans were already approaching the Norwegian coast.

§

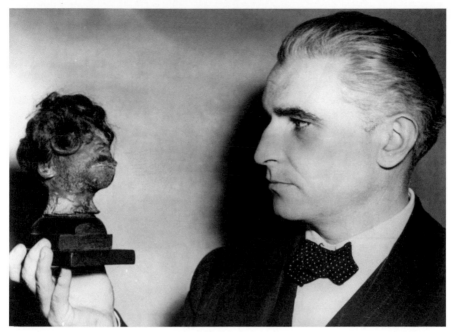

American prosecutor Dodd holds up the shrunken head of a Polish prisoner, used as a paperweight. It formed part of the evidence on Crimes Against Humanity committed by the accused. *[Zuma/Keystone Press]*

Goering grips the sides of the witness box while being questioned by Jackson. He proved to be much the most formidable, and charismatic, of the defendants. *[Getty Images]*

Following several suicides in Nuremberg's jail, guards were stationed permanently outside each of the cells and instructed to observe the prisoners at least once a minute. *[Getty Images]*

Frick, the former Interior Minister, here standing in the dock, had been responsible for instituting many of the measures of control used against the Nazis' political opponents and the Jews. *[Time Life Pictures/Getty Images]*

Hess *(left)* and Von Ribbentrop eat a spartan lunch together during the trial. Both men had had mental breakdowns, with Hess suffering from amnesia and Von Ribbentrop from sheer despair. *[Getty Images]*

As the commandant of Auschwitz, Hoess boasted at Nuremberg of being responsible for the deaths of millions of Jews. He was hanged at his former camp in 1947. *[Corbis]*

The Butcher of Warsaw: under Frank's rule, both the Warsaw Ghetto and Auschwitz were built, and the intelligentsia of Poland ruthlessly eliminated. *[Getty Images]*

Von Papen on the cover of *Time* when Chancellor of Germany in 1932. He had not opposed Hitler's rise, hoping to use him as a tool for controlling the masses. *[Time Life Pictures/Getty Images]*

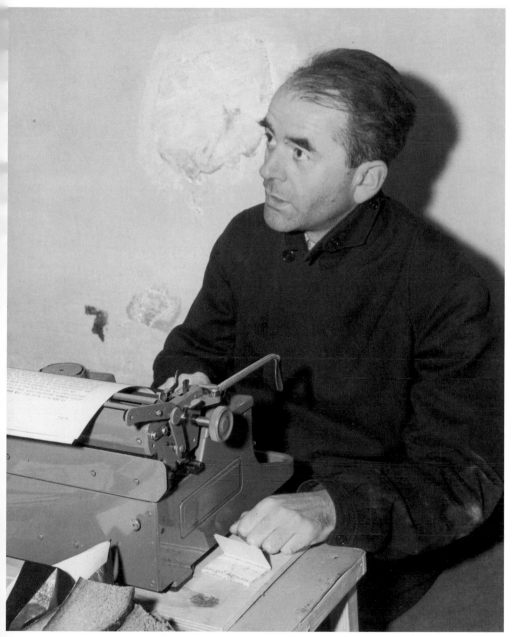

Speer in his cell: his willingness to accept responsibility for the regime swayed the judges, but he had closed his eyes to the maltreatment of those in his munitions programmes. *[Getty Images]*

The Evening News

NO. 20,173   LONDON, TUESDAY, OCTOBER 1, 1946   ONE PENNY

LATE EXTRA

LATEST WEATHER FORECAST

CLOSING PRICES PAGE 6

TWELVE EVIL MEN TO HANG

Goering and von Ribbentrop for the Gallows
Hess Jailed For Life—Three Are Acquitted

Arthur Seyss-Inquart.   Fritz Sauckel.   Ernst Kaltenbrunner.   Julius Streicher.   Hans Frank.   Alfred Jodl.   Alfred Rosenberg.   Wilhelm Frick.   Martin Bormann.   Wilhelm Keitel.

Twelve of the 22 men of Nuremberg were condemned to death by hanging this afternoon. Three were acquitted and the remainder were sentenced to imprisonment for terms ranging from ten years to life. If no appeals within four days succeed the executions are expected to be carried out at Nuremberg. The Russian judge dissented from the acquittals and the fact that Hess is not to die.

Here are the sentences passed, with details of the counts on which they were found guilty. The counts are set out below in Column Five.

Sentenced to Death by Hanging

GOERING, Herman, Wilhelm, 52, Luftwaffe chief and Hitler's chief lieutenant. All counts.

RIBBENTROP, Joachim, 53, Hitler's Foreign Minister and former London Ambassador. All counts.

KEITEL, Wilhelm, 63, former chief of the German High Command. All counts.

ROSENBERG, Alfred, 53, author of the Nazi Herrenvolk creed, former chief of the administration of the invaded countries in the East. All counts.

JODL, Alfred, 56, former Nazi Chief of Staff. All counts.

FRICK, Wilhelm, 69, "protector" of Bohemia-Moravia, once a member of Hitler's Cabinet. Counts 2, 3 and 4.

SEYSS-INQUART, Arthur, 54, the man who betrayed Austria to the Nazis after Hitler's overlord in occupied

STREICHER, Julius, 61, the Jew-baiter. No. 1: man who organised the pogroms and persecutions. Count 4.

Sentenced to Imprisonment

HESS, Rudolf, 52, Hitler's former deputy, who flew to Britain on the eve of the attack on Russia, to try to persuade Britain to make peace. Counts 1 and 2. JAIL FOR LIFE.

FUNK, Walter, 56, the man who succeeded Schacht as head of the Reichsbank, and who organised the financing of Hitler's war. Counts 2, 3 and 4. LIFE.

RAEDER, Erich, 70, chief of Hitler's navy till 1943. Counts 1, 2 and 3. LIFE.

SCHIRACH, Baldur von, 39, Hitler Youth leader. Count 4. 20 YEARS.

SPEER, Albert, 40, Hitler's armaments minister. Counts 3 and 4. 20 YEARS.

NEURATH, Constantin von, 72, Ribbentrop's predecessor as Foreign Minister, former London envoy, and later "protector" of Bohemia-Moravia. 15 YEARS.

DOENITZ, Karl, 54, U-boat chief till 1943, succeeded Hitler as Fuehrer and signed the unconditional surrender.

HIGH-LIGHTS FROM JUDGES' FINAL WORDS

Von R. Behind Attack On Jews

HERE are some of the high lights from what the judges said of the guilty and the innocent—men:

Ribbentrop: He played an important part in Hitler's "diplomacy" which led up to the war.

Goering: The record discloses no excuse for this man.

Hess: Hitler's closest confidant until his flight to Britain. No evidence to overcome the presumption of his sanity at the time of his crimes.

Keitel: Orders issued under his signature and over his name.

Bormann: No conclusive evidence of his death.

THE SHADOW OF DEATH . . . .
. . . on the face of Hermann Goering, Hitler, the most dominant man in the Nazi regime.

GUILTY MEN WILL ALL APPEAL

Sentenced Nazis counsel announced all to appeal to Allied Control Council.

ACQUITTED NAZIS MAY BE TRIED BY GERMANS

SOVIET JUDGE PROTESTS

A delighted Schacht celebrates his release by signing autographs. Although he had financed Hitler's rearmament plans, he claimed not to have realised their aggressive intent.
[Getty Images]

Andrus, a stickler for discipline, was in charge of the prisoners' safety and security, but here is forced to announce that Goering has managed to cheat the gallows.
[Time Life Pictures/Getty Images]

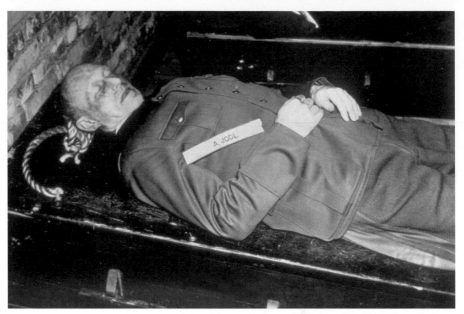

The body of Jodl, chief of military operations, after his execution. The bodies were photographed to prevent later rumours that leading figures in the regime had survived. *[Getty Images]*

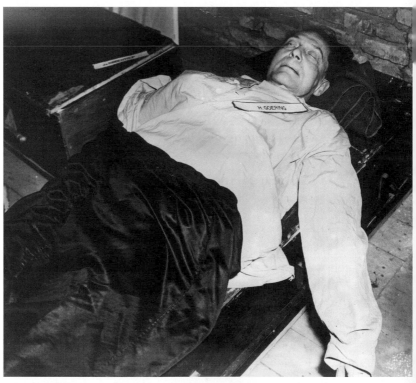

The last victory of Goering: the second man in the Nazi state managed to commit suicide by swallowing poison hours before he was due to be hanged in October 1946. *[Getty Images]*

After serving the indictments, Airey Neave had taken charge of the arrangements for acquiring and sifting evidence from thousands of members of the seven organisations that were also to be tried by the court. In what were trying and often harrowing circumstances in which to be working, his sense of humour endeared him to Biddle.

Francis Biddle: A little light relief

Lieutenant-Colonel A.M.S. Neave was in charge of applications and motions. He was one of those extraordinary Englishmen who were always getting into breathless adventures during the war and wriggling out of them. Dropped here and there in Germany for espionage work, he was constantly being arrested and escaping from prison. Once, he told me one night at dinner, he was incarcerated in an ancient schloss not far from Nuremberg. They tried tunnelling out. After two weeks they broke into an excellently stocked wine cellar. That delayed progress. For two weeks they drank their host's admirable Rhine wines – there was a particularly good Liebfraumilch. The excellent morale of the English prisoners became the subject of comment. He paused.

'And what,' I said in answer to the pause, 'did you do with the empty bottles?'

He grinned. 'We filled them with an unmentionable liquid . . . the Camp Commander was a rather fastidious chap – old school, monocle – you know – pretended to be a connoisseur of wine. We used to picture him holding a bottle up to the light saying it looked a bit cloudy . . .'

§

The trial had now entered its sixth month, and still the evidence continued to pile up, each fresh document providing an insight into the moral corruption of the regime that had governed Germany for twelve years. One piece of evidence, however, demonstrated the double standards of a member of the Allied nations.

When von Ribbentrop had been on the stand in April, Hess's lawyer, Alfred Seidl, had managed briefly to bring to light evidence of a secret addendum to the Russo-

German alliance forged just before the invasion of Poland. Von Ribbentrop had said that Stalin and Hitler had agreed to partition Polish territory between them if there was a war, a statement which if true disproved the Russians' claim that they had signed the treaty as a purely defensive measure. The Soviet legal team had striven to stop Seidl saying any more, and at the time he had lacked a copy of the secret deal to show to the court. By mid-May, however, when Ernst von Weizsaecker, the former head of the German Foreign Office, appeared as a witness for Raeder, Seidl had got his hands on the protocol, and chanced his arm again.

Trial transcript, 21 May 1946: Dividing the Polish spoils – the secret protocol to the Nazi–Soviet pact

THE PRESIDENT: Do any of the Defence Counsel want to ask any questions of this witness?

DR ALFRED SEIDL (Counsel for Defendant Hess): Witness, on 23 August 1939, a nonaggression pact was concluded between Germany and the Soviet Union. Were any other agreements concluded on that day by the two governments, outside of this pact of nonaggression?

GENERAL R. A. RUDENKO (Chief Prosecutor for the USSR): Mr President, the witness is called upon to answer certain definite questions which are set forth in the application of counsel for the defendant, Dr Siemers. I consider that the question which is being put to him at this moment by the defence counsel Seidl has no connection with the examination of the case in hand and should be ruled out.

THE PRESIDENT: You may ask the question, Dr Seidl, that you were going to ask.

DR SEIDL: I ask you again, Herr von Weizsaecker, whether on 23 August 1939, other agreements had been reached between the two governments, which were not contained in the nonaggression pact?

VON WEIZSAECKER: Yes.

DR SEIDL: Where were these agreements contained?

VON WEIZSAECKER: These agreements were contained in a secret protocol.

DR SEIDL: Did you yourself read this secret protocol in your capacity of State Secretary in the Ministry of Foreign Affairs?

VON WEIZSAECKER: Yes.

DR SEIDL: I have before me a text and Ambassador Gaus harbours no doubt at all that the agreements in question are correctly set out in this text. I shall have it put to you.

THE PRESIDENT: One moment, what document are you putting to him?

DR SEIDL: The secret addenda to the protocol of 23 August 1939.

THE PRESIDENT: Is that not the document – what is this document that you are presenting to the witness? There is a document which you have already presented to the Tribunal and which has been ruled out. Is that the same document?

DR SEIDL: It is the document which I submitted to the Tribunal in my documentary evidence and which was refused by the Tribunal, presumably because I refused to divulge the origin and source of this document. But the Tribunal granted me permission to produce a new sworn affidavit by Ambassador Gaus on the subject in question.

THE PRESIDENT: You have not done it? You have not done it?

DR SEIDL: No, but I should, Your Honour, like to read this text in order to stimulate the memory of the witness, and to ask him whether in connection therewith, as far as he can remember, the secret agreements are correctly reproduced in this document.

GEN. RUDENKO: Your Honours! I would like to protest against these questions for two reasons.

First of all, we are examining the matter of the crimes of the major German war criminals. We are not investigating the foreign policies of other states. Secondly, the document which defence counsel Seidl is attempting to put to the witness has been rejected by the Tribunal, since it is – in substance – a forged document and cannot have any probative value whatsoever.

DR SEIDL: May I in this connection say the following, Mr. President. This document is an essential component of the nonaggression pact, submitted by the Prosecution in evidence as GB-145. If I now submit the text to the witness . . .

THE PRESIDENT: The only question is whether it is the document which has been rejected by the Tribunal. Is it the document which has been rejected by the Tribunal?

DR SEIDL: It was rebutted as documentary evidence per se.

THE PRESIDENT: Well, then the answer is 'yes'.

DR SEIDL: But it seems to me that there is a difference as to whether this document may be put to the witness during the hearing of his testimony. I should like to answer this question in the affirmative since the Prosecution when cross-examining can put the document in their possession to the witness, and on the basis of his testimony we should then see which is the correct text or whether these two texts harmonise at all.

THE PRESIDENT: Where does the document which you are presenting come from?

DR SEIDL: I received this document a few weeks ago from a man on the Allied side who appeared absolutely reliable. I received it only on condition that I would not divulge its origin, a condition which seemed to me perfectly reasonable.

THE PRESIDENT: Do you say that you received it a few moments ago?

DR SEIDL: Weeks ago.

THE PRESIDENT: It is the same document that you say just now that you presented to the Tribunal and the Tribunal rejected?

DR SEIDL: Yes, but the Tribunal also decided that I might submit another sworn affidavit from Ambassador Gaus on this subject, and this decision only makes sense . . .

MR DODD: Mr President, I certainly join General Rudenko in objecting to the use of this document. We now know that it comes from some anonymous source. We do not know the source at all, and anyway it is not established that this witness does not remember himself what this purported agreement amounted to. I do not know why he cannot ask him, if that is what he wants to do.

THE PRESIDENT: Dr Seidl, you may ask the witness what his recollection is of the treaty without putting the document to him. Ask him what he remembers of the treaty, or the protocol.

DR SEIDL: Witness, please describe the contents of the agreement insofar as you can remember them.

VON WEIZSAECKER: It is about a very incisive, a very far-reaching secret addendum to the nonaggression pact concluded at that time.

The scope of this document was very extensive since it concerned the partition of the spheres of influence and drew a demarcation line between areas which, under given conditions, belonged to the sphere of Soviet Russia and those which would fall in the German sphere of interest. Finland, Estonia, Latvia, Eastern Poland and, as far as I can remember, certain areas of Romania were to be included in the sphere of the Soviet Union. Anything west of this area fell into the German sphere of interest. It is true that this secret agreement did not maintain its original form. Later on, either in September or October of the same year, a certain change, an amendment was made. As far as I can recall the essential difference in the two documents consisted in the fact that Lithuania, or – at least – the greater part of Lithuania, fell into the sphere of interest of the Soviet Union, while in the Polish territory the line of demarcation between the two spheres of interest was moved very considerably westwards.

I believe that I have herewith given you the gist of the secret agreement and of the subsequent addendum.

DR SEIDL: Is it true that in case of a subsequent territorial reorganisation, a line of demarcation was agreed upon in the territory of the Polish State?

VON WEIZSAECKER: I cannot tell you exactly whether the expression 'line of demarcation' was contained in this protocol or whether 'line of separation of spheres of interest' was the actual term.

DR SEIDL: But a line was drawn.

VON WEIZSAECKER: Precisely the line which I have just mentioned, and I believe I can recall that this line, once the agreement became effective, was adhered to as a general rule with possible slight fluctuations.

DR SEIDL: Can you recall – this is my last question – if this secret addendum of 23 August 1939 also contained an agreement on the future destiny of Poland?

VON WEIZSAECKER: This secret agreement included a complete redirection of Poland's destiny. It may very well have been that explicitly or implicitly such a redirection had been provided for in the agreement. I would not, however, like to commit myself as to the exact wording.

DR SEIDL: Mr President, I have no further questions.

The leniency showed by Lawrence, which meant that the contents of the pact were now out in the open, came amid a change of mood at the trial. A couple of months before, Churchill had made his 'Iron Curtain' speech, and their former allies were now keenly aware of the Soviets' ambitions in Europe. Many of the defendants, meanwhile, felt that their anti-Communist stance of the 1930s had been vindicated.

Weizsaecker was later sentenced to seven years in prison at one of the dozen trials of leading figures in the regime that took place at Nuremberg after that of the principal war criminals. Conducted solely by the United States, each case concentrated on a distinct group, such as the industrialists of the firms of Krupp and I.G. Farben or the doctors who had conducted experiments in the camps. Prominent among those convicted were several who had participated in the first trial, including Otto Ohlendorf, the Einsatzgruppe leader, and Emil Puhl, Funk's vice-president at the Reichsbank.

§

Baldur von Schirach was, at thirty-eight, the youngest of those indicted. He had joined the Nazis as a student and from 1931 was the Party's youth leader, and from 1933 head of the Hitler Youth. By the start of the war, the organisation – the only permitted young people's group – was almost eight million strong. Boys might join its junior branch at six, girls at ten. Its emphasis was on physical exercise and political indoctrination.

In 1940, von Schirach became Gauleiter of Vienna, where he consented to the transport of Jews to concentration camps. He did complain about their mistreatment, and tried to promote the city as an artistic rival to Berlin, neither of which initiatives endeared him to Hitler, who, according to gossip, had once been the lover of von Schirach's wife. He was captured in 1945 while hiding out in the Austrian Tyrol in the guise of a reclusive writer.

Von Schirach was three-quarters American: his grandfather had carried Lincoln's coffin, while his mother, who was from New York, had been killed in Germany by an Allied air raid. Prompted by Albert Speer, von Schirach had latterly discovered his conscience, a point emphasised by his counsel, Fritz Sauter.

Trial transcript, 24 May 1946: 'The youth of Germany is guiltless' – Baldur von Schirach, Hitler Youth leader

DR SAUTER: Witness, I should in this connection like to ask you a question of principle. You admitted yesterday that you had become an anti-Semite – and that is according to your conception – in your very early youth. You have, in the interim, heard the testimony of Hoess, the Auschwitz commander, who informed us that in that camp alone, I believe, 2,500,000 to 3,000,000 innocent people, mostly Jews, had been done to death. What, today, does the name of Auschwitz convey to you?

VON SCHIRACH: It is the greatest, the most devilish mass murder known to history. But that murder was not committed by Hoess; Hoess was merely the executioner. The murder was ordered by Adolf Hitler, as is obvious from his last will and testament . . . The youth of Germany is guiltless. Our youth was anti-Semitically inclined, but it did not call for the extermination of Jewry. It neither realised nor imagined that Hitler had carried out this extermination by the daily murder of thousands of innocent people. The youth of Germany who, today, stand perplexed among the ruins of their native land, knew nothing of these crimes, nor did they desire them. They are innocent of all that Hitler has done to the Jewish and to the German people.

I should like to say the following in connection with Hoess's case. I have educated this generation in faith and loyalty to Hitler. The Youth Organisation which I built up bore his name. I believed that I was serving a leader who would make our people and the youth of our country great and happy and free. Millions of young people believed this, together with me, and saw their ultimate ideal in National Socialism. Many died for it. Before God, before the German nation, and before my German people I alone bear the guilt of having trained our young people for a man whom I for many long years had considered unimpeachable, both as a leader and as the head of the State, of creating for him a generation who saw him as I did. The guilt is mine in that I educated the youth of Germany for a man who murdered by the millions. I believed in this man, that is all I can say for my excuse and for the characterisation of my attitude. This is my own – my own personal guilt. I was responsible for the youth of the country. I was placed in authority over the young people, and the guilt is mine alone. The younger generation is guiltless. It grew up in an anti-Semitic state, ruled by anti-Semitic laws. Our youth was bound by these laws and saw nothing criminal in racial politics.

§

Outside the courtroom, Goering was willing to reveal much of his past and, indeed, present ambitions to those who would listen. The most acute of these was the new prison psychiatrist, Leon Goldensohn, whose records of his conversations with the defendants has only recently been discovered. Goering told him of his misgivings about the selection of those to be tried, and revealed that he had known of the Holocaust but had not attempted to stop it.

Leon Goldensohn: 'It is my intention to make this trial a mockery' – Goering on the couch

I said that there were many things about his world view that I did not really understand. In the first place, what about the concept of the importance of the oath of loyalty and the matter of the all-importance of orders? 'That is another thing I am glad that you asked me about. We Germans consider an oath of fealty more important than anything else. This Tribunal fails to realise that accepting orders is a legitimate excuse for doing almost anything. The Tribunal is wrong. Mind you, I said almost anything. I don't consider the extermination of women and children as proper even if an oath were taken. I myself can hardly believe that women and children were exterminated. It must have been that criminal Goebbels, or Himmler, who influenced Hitler to do such a dastardly thing. I am very cynical about these trials. The trials are being fought in the courtroom by the world press. Everyone knows that the Frenchmen and the Russians who are judges here have made up their minds that we are all guilty and they had their instructions from Paris and Moscow long before the trial even started to condemn us. It's all but planned and the trial is a farce. Maybe the American and English judges are trying to conduct a legitimate trial. But even in their case I have my doubts.'

I asked him to give me further reflections or impressions about the Tribunal as far as his opinion was concerned. Goering seemed wary and not too inclined to speak at length. He did say, however, 'Frankly, it is my intention to make this trial a mockery. I feel that a foreign country has no right to try the government of a sovereign state. I have desisted from making any critical remarks about my co-defendants. Yet they are a mixed-up, unrepresentative group. Some of them are so unimportant, I never even heard of them. I'll admit they are right in including me among the big Nazis who ran Germany. But why include Fritzsche? He was one of many section chiefs in the Propaganda Ministry. And then try a man like Funk, who is guilty of nothing. He followed orders, and they were my orders. And they try a fellow like Keitel, who, although he was called a field marshal, was a small person who did whatever Hitler instructed. Of all the defendants, the only ones who are big enough to merit being tried are me, Schacht, Ribbentrop perhaps, although he was a weak echo of Hitler, Frick, who proposed the Nuremberg Laws, and maybe a few others, like Rosenberg and Seyss-Inquart. The rest of them were followers and showed little initiative.

'Then there is the farce of the case against the general staff. These military men were not a part of any conspiracy to wage war but simply accepted orders and obeyed them as any German soldier or officer would do. If there was a conspiracy, it lay among those who are dead or missing – I mean Himmler, Goebbels, Bormann, and naturally Hitler. I always felt that Bormann was a primitive criminal type and I never trusted Himmler. I would have dismissed them.' Goering smiled knowingly and added, 'You know, you can get rid of a man in many subtle ways. For example, you can dismiss a man suddenly, but that is less effective if that individual has some power and backing than by slowly diminishing his power by giving him more and more meaningless titles. In the case of Himmler, I would have promoted him on paper and made him chief of this and chief of that, but in the end his power would be gone. I would have taken away from him the police power first, and later I would have assumed control of the SS myself. In this way there would have been no such thing as mass murders. For all that Hitler was a genius and a strong character, he nevertheless was suggestible, and Himmler and Goebbels or both must have influenced him to go ahead with such an idiotic scheme as gas chambers and crematoriums to eliminate millions of people.

'Even if one has no compunction about exterminating a race, common sense dictates that in our civilisation this is barbaric and would be subject to so much criticism from abroad and within, that it would be condemned as the greatest criminal act in history. Understand that I am not a moralist, although I have my chivalric code. If I really felt that the killing of the Jews meant anything, such as that it meant the winning of the war, I would not be too bothered by it. But it was so meaningless and did nobody any good whatever except to give Germany a bad name. I have a conscience and I feel that killing women and children simply because they happen to be victims of Goebbels's hysterical propaganda is not the way of a gentleman. I don't believe that I will go to either heaven or hell when I die. I don't believe in the Bible or in a lot of things which religious people think. But I revere women and I think it unsportsmanlike to kill children. That is the main thing that bothers me about the extermination of the Jews. The second thing which I disapprove of is the unfavourable reaction politically which such a meaningless programme of extermination of necessity brings with it. For myself I feel quite free of responsibility for the mass murders. Certainly as second man in the state under Hitler, I heard rumours of mass killings of Jews, but I could do nothing about it and I knew that it was useless to investigate these rumours and to find out about them accurately, which would not have been too hard, but I was busy with other things, and if I had found out what was going on regarding the mass murders, it would simply have made me feel bad and I could do very little to prevent it anyway.'

§

Alfred Jodl had been the head of the Operations Staff of the High Command of the Armed Forces, or OKW, for almost the whole of the war. Though not in agreement with all of the Nazis' ideas, Jodl had like many in the High Command strong nationalist sympathies, and such was his conditioning that he found little difficulty at first in carrying out the orders given him by his immediate superiors Keitel and Hitler, the supreme commander. These included decrees authorising the summary execution of captured Allied commandos and undercover operatives working in Occupied Europe, as well as that of Soviet commissars.

By the middle of the war, he had come to doubt publicly the sense of many of the Fuehrer's strategic decisions, but, though Hitler contemplated replacing him, in the event he retained his post until the end of the war, despite often requesting to be transferred to the front line. In May 1945, as Doenitz's representative, he had signed Germany's surrender to Montgomery.

Though he could be a correct, guarded man, he was respected by his fellow defendants, not least because of the wounds he had suffered during the assassination attempt on Hitler's life in July 1944, when a bomb concealed in a briefcase by a group of officers opposed to continuing the war had exploded at his headquarters in Prussia. When questioned by his lawyer, Franz Exner, to whom Jodl's wife was acting as assistant, he stated that his relations with Hitler always been professional rather than amicable. His evidence provided an insight into life in the rather isolated command posts in which the Fuehrer had spent much of the war.

Trial transcript, 3 June 1946: Obeying the Fuehrer – Alfred Jodl testifies

DR EXNER: The Prosecution speak of your close relationship with Hitler. When did you learn to know Adolf Hitler personally?

JODL: I was presented to the Fuehrer by Field Marshal Keitel in the command train on 3 September 1939 when we were going to the Polish Eastern Front. At any rate that was the day I first exchanged words with him.

DR EXNER: Two days after the outbreak of war?

JODL: Two days after the beginning of the war.

DR EXNER: Did the Fuehrer have confidence in you?

JODL That came about very gradually. The Fuehrer had a certain distrust of all General Staff officers, especially of the Army, as at that time he was still very sceptical toward the Wehrmacht as a whole.

I may, perhaps, quote a statement of his which was often heard: 'I have a reactionary Army, a Christian' – sometimes he said too – 'an imperial Navy, and a National Socialist Air Force.'

The relations between us varied a great deal. At first, until about the end of the campaign in the West, there was considerable reserve. Then his confidence in me increased more and more until August 1942. Then the great crisis arose, and his attitude to me was severely caustic and unfriendly. That lasted until 30 January 1943. Then relations improved and were particularly good, sincere, after the Italian betrayal in 1943 had been warded off. The last year was characterised by numerous sharp altercations.

DR EXNER: To what extent did the Fuehrer confide in you regarding his political intentions?

JODL: Only as far as we needed to know them for our military work. Of course, for the Chief of the Armed Forces Operations Staff political plans are somewhat more necessary than for a battalion commander, for politics is part of strategy.

DR EXNER: Did he permit discussions of political questions between himself and you?

JODL: Discussion of political questions was generally not admissible for us soldiers. One example is especially characteristic. When I reported to the Fuehrer in September 1943 that Fascism was dead in Italy, for party emblems were scattered all over, this is what he said: 'Such nonsense could only be reported by an officer. Once again it is obvious that generals do not understand politics.'

It can be easily understood that after such remarks the desire for any political discussions was slight.

DR EXNER: Were political and military questions therefore kept strictly separate?

JODL: Yes, they were strictly separated.

DR EXNER: Was it possible for you to consult him on military matters or not?

JODL: Consultation on military questions depended entirely on the circumstances of the moment. At a time when he himself was filled with doubts, he often discussed military problems for weeks or months, but if things were clear in his own mind, or if he had formed a spontaneous decision, all discussion came to an end.

DR EXNER: The system of maintaining secrecy has often been discussed here. Were you also subject to this secrecy?

JODL: Yes, and to an extent which I really first realised during this Trial. The Fuehrer informed us of events and occurrences at the beginning of the war – that is, the efforts of other countries to prevent this war, and even to put an end to it after it had already begun – only to the extent that these events were published in the press. He spoke to the politicians and to the Party quite otherwise than to the Wehrmacht; and to the SS differently again.

The secrecy concerning the annihilation of the Jews, and the events in the concentration camps, was a masterpiece of secrecy. It was also a masterpiece of deception by Himmler, who showed us soldiers faked photographs about these things in particular, and told us stories about the gardens and plantations in Dachau, about the ghettos in Warsaw and Theresienstadt, which gave us the impression that they were highly humane establishments.

DR EXNER: Did not news reach the Fuehrer's headquarters from the outside?

JODL: The Fuehrer's headquarters was a cross between a cloister and a concentration camp. There were numerous wire fences and much barbed wire surrounding it. There were outposts on the roads leading to it to safeguard it. In the middle was the so-called Security Ring Number 1. Permanent passes to enter this security ring were not given even to my staff, only to General Warlimont [Jodl's deputy]. Every guard had to check on each officer whom he did not know. Apart from reports on the situation, only very little news from the outer world penetrated into this holy of holies . . .

DR EXNER: It has often been stated here that it was impossible to contradict the Fuehrer. Did you have any success with remonstrances?

JODL: One cannot say it was really impossible to contradict the

Fuehrer. Very many times I contradicted him most emphatically, but there were moments when one actually could not answer a word. Also by my objections I induced the Fuehrer to desist from many things.

DR EXNER: Can you give an example?

JODL: There were a great number of operational questions which do not interest the Court; but in the sphere of interest to the Court, there was, for example, Hitler's intention to renounce the Geneva Convention. I prevented that because I objected.

DR EXNER: Were there other possibilities of influencing Hitler?

JODL: If it was not possible by open contradiction to prevent something which according to my innermost convictions I should prevent, there was still the means I often employed of using delaying tactics, a kind of passive resistance. I delayed work on the matter and waited for a psychologically favourable moment to bring the question up again.

This procedure, too, was occasionally successful, for example, in the case of the intention to turn certain low-level fliers over to lynch justice. It had no success in the case of the Commando Order.

DR EXNER: We will speak about that later.

Jodl's principal line of defence was that he had only carried out his sworn duty and that, insofar as his opinion was of relevance, he considered that Germany had fought a series of wars into which it had largely been forced against its will. Birkett thought him a shrewd witness, well aware of the answers that best served him.

Trial transcript, 5 June 1946: 'A purely preventive war' – Jodl on the invasion of Russia

DR EXNER: You have been accused by the Prosecution of first deceiving these countries and then invading them. Please tell us what you have to say on that subject.

JODL: The same applies here as I said before. I was neither a politician, nor was I the military Commander-in-Chief of the Wehrmacht . . . And as for the ethical code of my action, I must say that it was obedience – for obedience is really the ethical basis of the military profession. That I was far from extending this code of obedience to the blind code of obedience imposed on the slave has, I consider, been proved beyond all manner of doubt by my previous testimony. Nevertheless, you cannot get around the fact that, especially in operational matters of this particular kind, there can be no other course for the soldier but obedience . . .

DR EXNER: We now come back to the Balkan question again. It says in your so-called diary, 'The Balkans should and must remain quiet.' What was meant by that?

JODL: That was a brief note on the statement by the Fuehrer – namely, that he was in perfect agreement with Mussolini that the Balkans must be kept quiet.

DR EXNER: And did we not actually try to keep the Balkan states as quiet as possible?

JODL: Yes. We made unremitting endeavours for that. Our attitude toward Yugoslavia was as considerate as if we were dealing with a prima donna. Matters went so far that when we had to prepare the Greek campaign the Fuehrer even refused a proposal from the Quartermaster General of the Army that sealed trains – the supply trains – should be sent through Yugoslavia, which would have been permissible according to international law. Moreover, we brought pressure to bear on Bulgaria so that she should not participate in the impending campaign against Greece, above all so as not to alarm Turkey. And even after the Greco-Italian campaign, the Fuehrer still hoped that a conflict, an actual war, between Germany and Greece could be avoided.

DR EXNER: . . . Well, what forced us to give up this programme?

JODL: That programme was completely wrecked by Italy's arbitrary act [declaring war on Greece], about which the Reich Marshal and the Grossadmiral have already made statements. I have only a brief addition to make. Italy was beaten, as usual, and sent the Chief of the Operational Staff of the Supreme Command to me crying for help. But in spite of this calamity the Fuehrer did not intervene in the war in Albania. He did not send a single German soldier there, although the matter had been under consideration. He ordered only an operation against Greece, starting from Bulgaria, to be prepared for the following

spring. Even that was for the primary purpose of occupying the Salonika
Basin, thereby giving direct relief to the Italians and only in the event,
which to be sure was feared, of English divisions now landing in the
Balkans as the result of Italy's madness . . .

DR EXNER: Now, when did you first hear of the Fuehrer's fears
that Russia might prove hostile to us?

JODL: For the first time, on 29 July 1940, at the Berghof near
Berchtesgaden.

DR EXNER: In what connection?

JODL: The Fuehrer kept me back alone after a discussion on the
situation and said to me, most unexpectedly, that he was worried
that Russia might occupy still more territory in Romania before the
winter and that the Romanian oil region, which was the *conditio sine
qua non* for our war strategy, would thus be taken from us. He asked
me whether we could not deploy our troops immediately, so that
we would be ready by autumn to oppose with strong forces any
such Russian intention. These are almost the exact words which he
used, and all other versions are false . . .

DR EXNER: Tell me, in these statements, which Hitler made to
you, was there ever any mention made of such things as the extension
of the 'Lebensraum', and of the food basis as a reason for a war of
conquest, and so on?

JODL: In my presence the Fuehrer never even hinted at any other
reason than a purely strategic and operational one. For months on end,
one might say, he incessantly repeated: 'No further doubt is possible.
England is hoping for this final sword-thrust against us on the continent,
else she would have stopped the war after Dunkirk. Private or secret
agreements have certainly already been made. The Russian deployment
is unmistakable. One day we shall suddenly become the victim of
cold-blooded political extortion, or we shall be attacked.'

But otherwise, though one might talk about it for weeks on end,
no word was mentioned to me of any other than purely strategical
reasons of this kind . . .

DR EXNER: Did the reports which you received contain indications
of military reinforcements for the Red Army?

JODL: From maps which were submitted every few days, which were based on intelligence reports and information from the radio interception section, the following picture was formed: In the summer of 1940 there were about 100 Russian divisions along the border. In January 1941, there were already 150 divisions; and these were indicated by number, consequently the reports were reliable. In comparison with this strength, I may add that the English–American–French forces operating from France against Germany never, to my knowledge, amounted to 100 divisions.

DR EXNER: Did Hitler attempt to clear up the political situation by diplomatic means?

JODL: He attempted to do so by the well-known conference with Molotov; and I must say that I placed great hopes on this conference, for the military situation for us soldiers was as follows: With a definitely neutral Russia in our rear – a Russia which in addition sent us supplies – we could not lose the war. An invasion, such as took place on 6 June 1944, would have been entirely out of the question if we had had at our disposal all the forces we had used and lost in this immense struggle in Russia. And it never for a single moment entered my mind that a statesman, who after all was also a strategist, would needlessly let such an opportunity go. And it is a fact that he struggled for months with himself about this decision, being certainly influenced by the many contrary ideas suggested to him by the Reich Marshal, the Commander-in-Chief of the Navy, as well as the Minister for Foreign Affairs . . .

DR EXNER: Then, in your opinion, the Fuehrer waged a preventive war. Did later experiences prove that this was a military necessity?

JODL: It was undeniably a purely preventive war. What we found out later on was the certainty of enormous Russian military preparations opposite our frontiers. I will dispense with details, but I can only say that although we succeeded in a tactical surprise as to the day and the hour, it was no strategic surprise. Russia was fully prepared for war.

Jodl's wife left a note on the witness stand each morning urging him to keep his brisk temper in check. His resolve was tried most sorely during cross-examination by G.D. 'Khaki' Roberts, an England rugby international and rather blustering prosecutor whose questioning was coloured by his memories of Roger Bushell, the executed leader of 'The Great Escape', who had been a barrister in his chambers. He concentrated on the weakest part of Jodl's defence, the fact that he had countersigned Hitler's orders to shoot out of hand captured Commandos and had authorised reprisals for attacks by partisans in Eastern Europe. Jodl argued that he had frequently disagreed with the Fuehrer's directives and had tried his best to make him see reason.

Trial transcript, 6 June 1946: Jodl is cross-examined on Hitler's Commando order

MR ROBERTS: Now, this is another Keitel order. It comes from Wehrmachtfahrungsstab, L; then, in brackets, 'I Op'. Is that your department?

JODL: That is the section which worked with me on all operational questions.

MR ROBERTS: Do you remember that order?

JODL: Yes, I remember the order.

MR ROBERTS: Now – I think you took part in drafting it; did you not?

JODL: Certainly, because it is an operational order which supplements a directive.

MR ROBERTS: Yes, well, will you look at Paragraphs 6 and 7? Paragraph 6: 'In view of the vast size of the occupied areas in the East, forces available for establishing security will be sufficient only if all resistance is punished not by legal prosecution of the guilty, but by the occupation forces spreading such terror as is alone appropriate to eradicate every inclination to resist.

'The respective commanders, together with the troops at their disposal, are to be held responsible for maintaining peace in their respective areas. The commanders must find the means of keeping order within the regions where security is their responsibility, not by demanding more forces, but by applying suitable draconian measures.'

That is a terrible order, is it not?

JODL: No, it is not at all terrible for it is established by international law that the inhabitants of an occupied territory must follow the orders and instructions of the occupying power, and any uprising, any resistance against the army occupying the country is forbidden; it is, in fact, partisan warfare, and international law does not lay down means of combating partisans. The principle of such warfare is an eye for an eye and a tooth for a tooth, and this is not even a German principle.

MR ROBERTS: Is it not the tooth and the eye of the innocent?

JODL: It is not a question of the innocent. It expressly states, 'to eradicate every inclination to resist'. It is a question of those who resist, that is, by partisan warfare.

MR ROBERTS: I will not argue about it, Witness. I gather you approve of the order.

JODL: I approve it as a justified measure conforming to international law and directed against a widespread resistance movement which employed unscrupulous methods. Of that we had evidence.

MR ROBERTS: Very good. Now I want to come to something quite different. I want to come to the Commando Order . . . 'The Fuehrer wishes an order to be issued laying down the proper behaviour of the Armed Forces . . . Members of terror and sabotage detachments of the British Armed Forces who demonstrably break the rules of an honourable way of fighting will be treated as bandits: To be exterminated mercilessly in battle or in flight. If in case of military necessity they should be temporarily arrested, or if they fall into German hands outside combat actions, they are to be brought before an officer immediately for interrogation and are then to be handed over to the SD.

Holding them in a prisoner-of-war camp is forbidden. This order may be distributed only down to armies. From there to the front it must be transmitted only verbally.' . . .

Do you draw any distinction between a British airman who bombs a power station from the air and a British parachutist in uniform who is landed and blows it up with an explosive? Do you draw any distinction in international law?

JODL: No. As such, the destruction of an objective by a demolition troop I consider completely admissible under international law; but I do not consider it admissible during such an operation for civilian clothes to be worn under the uniform and armpit pistols to be carried which start firing as soon as the arms are raised in the act of surrender.

MR ROBERTS: Well, there are two things there, you see, and one answer and I am not going to argue at all with you; but when you consider the case you will find many, many cases where these persons were executed and there is no suggestion they had anything but a uniform at all.

JODL: I believe that these cases were quite rare, that at least these people were mixed with those who wore civilian clothes.

MR ROBERTS: Well, I am not going to argue with you because there are other documents and they will have to be, perhaps, summarised some time. But would you agree that a parachutist in uniform, with no civilian clothes, acting like that, if he is killed, shot by the SD, would you agree that that would be murder? Or would you rather not answer that?

JODL: I have already said that if a soldier in full uniform only blows up or destroys an objective, I do not consider it an action contrary to international law; and for that reason I opposed the Commando Order in this form almost to the last moment . . .

MR ROBERTS: You have said, I think, that part of the Fuehrer's order [summary execution] disgusted you?

JODL: Yes.

MR ROBERTS: And you have said in your interrogation that circulating this order was one of the things which went against your inner conscience – one of the few things. 'Your inner convictions' – to use your actual words.

JODL: In the preliminary interrogation I said that it was one of the few – or the only – order I received from the Fuehrer which I, in my own mind, completely rejected.

MR ROBERTS: You rejected it, but these young men went on being shot, did they not?

JODL: I have already described exactly how the commanding

generals at the front, vigorously supported by me, interpreted this order in the mildest imaginable way in practice; actually, only very few such incidents occurred, and I believe that most – at any rate, nearly all that came to my knowledge – were highly justified, because the fighting methods of those people were not methods of honest soldiers.

MR ROBERTS: You see, you talk about your 'inner convictions'. I think Keitel spoke about his 'inner conscience'. But should we have heard anything about these convictions and this conscience if Germany had not lost the war? . . . Why do you say that you had to circulate this order? No man can compel another to circulate an order for murder, unless he does it.

JODL: I have explained at length that this order could not simply be interpreted as an order to murder, but that very serious and justified doubts and considerations could arise with regard to international law and with regard to the justness of this order. In any case, you should have complete appreciation of such a delicate situation, because even now, in my position here, I cannot say or do as I like, and that exactly is what I experienced during these last 5½ years.

MR ROBERTS: You could have refused. You could have said, and the other generals could have said, could you not: 'We are all honourable soldiers. We will not publish and issue those orders'?

JODL: Certainly under other circumstances it might have been possible, first, if at the time I had not had that conflict with the Fuehrer, and secondly, if the British Ministry of War had made my task a little easier . . .

MR ROBERTS: I am now going to put to you your own Document D-606 . . . Now that is signed by you, is it not? It deals with the subject of the breach of the Geneva Convention. If you would say first if it is signed by you? Is it signed by you? Please answer my question: Is it signed by you?

JODL: Yes; my signature is at the end.

MR ROBERTS: Well, that is where one usually finds the signature. Now, it is dated 21 February 1945, and it is written on your letterhead notepaper . . . Well, now, I want to read the last paragraph.

My Lord, it is the last page but one of Your Lordship's document, right at the bottom:

'C. Proposal of the OKW: At the present moment the disadvantages of repudiating the agreements which have been kept up to now in any case outweigh the advantages by far.

'Just as it was a mistake in 1914 that we ourselves solemnly declared war on all the states which had for a long time wanted to wage war on us, and through this took the whole guilt of the war on our shoulders before the outside world, and just as it was a mistake to admit that the necessary' – note the word 'necessary' – 'passage through Belgium in 1914 was our own fault, so it would be a mistake now to repudiate openly the obligations of international law which we accepted and thereby to stand again as the guilty party before the outside world.

'Adherence to the accepted obligations does not demand in any way that we should have to impose on ourselves any limitations which will interfere with the conduct of the war. For instance, if the British sink a hospital ship, this must be used for propaganda purposes, as has been done to date. That, of course, in no way prevents our sinking an English hospital ship at once as a reprisal and then expressing our regret that it was a mistake in the same manner as the British do.'

That is not very honourable, is it?

JODL: I can only say in reply that this was the sole method which achieved success with the Fuehrer, and by its use success was, in fact, achieved. If I had come to him with moral or purely legal arguments, he would have said, 'Leave me alone with this foolish talk', and he would have proceeded with the renunciation of the Convention; but these things compelled him to reconsider the step and, in consequence, he did not carry it through.

You must after all grant me that at the end of 5½ years I knew best how to achieve good results with him and avoid bad ones. My aim was to achieve success, and I achieved it.

MR ROBERTS: But, you see, you were deploring it there, the fact that you told the world the truth in 1914. In 1914 you said that you regarded treaties only as a scrap of paper. You are saying now, 'What a pity we told the world the truth in 1914. We ought to have told them something untrue, and then we should have, possibly, had a better world reputation.'

JODL: That was an argument which the Fuehrer used frequently. If one repeated his arguments in that form again and again he was more inclined to read and accept one's suggestions. One had to prevent his flinging our proposals to the ground in a fit of rage and immediately decreeing renunciation. That was the approach one had to follow. If one cannot do good openly, it is better to do it in a roundabout way than not at all.

§

Hitler had not governed alone, nor had he come to power without widespread support. Franz von Papen, the former Chancellor, represented a substantial section of German society – reactionary, nationalist and often Roman Catholic – that had welcomed the advent of the Nazis. Even after becoming disillusioned with them, he had stayed in office, continuing to lend the regime some respectability even as those close to him who opposed it were murdered, among them his daughter's fiancé, Baron von Ketteler. At the trial, he argued that what now appeared so clear-cut an issue had, at the time, seemed far more complex. He claimed, like Schacht, that he had best been able to serve Germany's true interests by attempting to influence its leaders from inside the government. When the stakes are high, argued von Papen, the dividing line between right and wrong can seem much less clear-cut. Maxwell Fyfe showed, however, that the defendant had first-hand knowledge of the morality of the methods sanctioned by the Nazi leaders.

Trial transcript, 19 June 1946: A good idea at the time – Franz von Papen explains why he remained in the Government

SIR DAVID MAXWELL FYFE: Herr von Papen, if you, as an ex-Chancellor of the Reich and, as you said yourself, one of the leading Catholic laymen of Germany, an ex-officer of the Imperial Army, had said at that time, 'I am not going to be associated with murder, cold-blooded murder as an instrument of policy,' you might at some risk to yourself have brought down the whole of this rotten regime, might you not?

VON PAPEN: That is possible, but had I said it publicly, then quite probably I would have disappeared somewhere just as my associates did . . .

SIR DAVID MAXWELL FYFE: Defendant, you have heard a number of your co-defendants giving evidence and saying that they didn't know of the terrible repressive measures that were taking place in Germany. You knew very well about these repressive measures, did you not? You knew about the action of the Gestapo, the concentration camps, and later you knew about the elimination of the Jews, did you not?

VON PAPEN: I only knew this much, that in the years 1933 and 1934 political opponents were interned in the concentration camps. I very frequently protested against the methods used in concentration camps. In various cases I liberated people from these camps; but at that time I was quite unaware that murders had even been committed in them.

SIR DAVID MAXWELL FYFE: Well now, just let me take that up. It is good to get down to a concrete instance.

VON PAPEN: Yes.

SIR DAVID MAXWELL FYFE: You remember that at the beginning of 1935 your secretary, Herr von Tschirschsky, was ordered to return from Vienna to Berlin for examination by the Gestapo. Do you remember that?

VON PAPEN: Yes, indeed.

SIR DAVID MAXWELL FYFE: And you remember that he refused to go and he sent you a detailed report of his reasons for not going? Do you remember that?

VON PAPEN: Yes.

SIR DAVID MAXWELL FYFE: . . . And summarising the beginning of it, which would be almost humorous if it did not show such a dreadful state of affairs, your secretary, Herr von Tschirschsky, was arrested simultaneously by two competing groups of Reich policemen, I think the Criminal Police and the Gestapo, and there was a severe danger of Herr von Tschirschsky and some of the police being shot before they could decide who was to take him into custody. But I want you to come to when he is taken into custody . . .

'I spent a few hours like this sitting on the bench. It would make too long a story to give further details of the events which took place during this time. I will therefore restrict myself to the case of the shooting of a well-known personality who was publicly stated to have committed suicide.

'The person in question was brought in under the escort of three SS men and led past us into a cell running parallel to our corridor. The leader of the detachment was an SS Hauptsturmfuehrer, short, dark, and carrying an Army pistol in his hand. I heard the command "Guard the door!" The door leading from our corridor into the other one was shut. Five shots were fired and immediately after the shots the Hauptsturmfuehrer came out of the door with the still smoking pistol in his hand, muttering under his breath, "That swine is settled." Feverish excitement reigned all around; cries and shrieks of terror were heard from the cells. One of the SS men on duty, a comparative youngster, was so excited that he apparently lost all consciousness of the entire situation and informed me, illustrating his remarks with his fingers, that the person concerned had been liquidated by means of three shots in the temple and two in the back of the head.'

You had a pretty good idea of SS and Gestapo methods after Herr von Tschirschsky had given you that report, hadn't you? . . .

Now, that was von Tschirschsky. You told us that Baron von Ketteler was murdered at the end of your time in Vienna . . . Now, the effect of this, the murder of von Ketteler, on you after the experience with von Tschirschsky was that you were ready to take new employment under the Nazi Government in Turkey . . . Why didn't you after this series of murders which had gone on over a period of four years, why didn't you break with these people and stand up like General Yorck or any other people that you may think of from history, stand up for your own views and oppose these murderers? Why didn't you do it?

VON PAPEN: . . . I can understand very well, Sir David, that after all the things we know today, after the millions of murders which have taken place, you consider the German people a nation of criminals, and that you cannot understand that this nation has its patriots as well. I did these things in order to serve my country, and I should like to add, Sir David, that up to the time of the Munich Agreement, and even up to the time of the Polish campaign, even the major powers tried, although they knew everything that was going on in Germany, to work with this Germany.

Why do you wish to reproach a patriotic German with acting likewise, and with hoping likewise, for the same thing for which all the major powers hoped?

SIR DAVID MAXWELL FYFE: The major powers had not had their servants murdered, one after the other, and were not close to Hitler like you. What I am putting to you is that the only reason that could have kept you in the service of the Nazi Government when you knew of all these crimes was that you sympathised and wanted to carry on with the Nazis' work. That is what I am putting to you – that you had this express knowledge; you had seen your own friends, your own servants, murdered around you. You had the detailed knowledge of it, and the only reason that could have led you on and made you take one job after another from the Nazis was that you sympathised with their work. That is what I am putting against you, Herr von Papen.

VON PAPEN: That, Sir David, is perhaps your opinion; my opinion is that I am responsible only to my conscience and to the German people for my decision to work for my fatherland; and I shall accept their verdict.

§

The loquaciousness of von Papen's barrister, Egon Kubuschok, finally exhausted Birkett's patience, prompting him to make some caustic comments in the diary he often wrote up in court while pretending to be taking notes of the trial. Kubuschok was not the first to fall short of the judge's expectations of counsel. In December, a hapless American prosecutor had prefaced a speech with the remark that his knees hadn't knocked so hard since he asked his wife to marry him. Birkett had observed: 'The shocking taste is really almost unbelievable', although his inner kindliness had revealed itself when he asked the young advocate to tea afterwards to give him some calming words of advice. Birkett recorded similarly biting remarks in his journal as the trial finally moved towards its end. He had very high standards; by now he was already dictating advance portions of the judgment, astonishing his secretary with his memory's command of facts.

Norman Birkett: 'A grave and wicked waste of time'

I must record my opinion of Dr Kubuschok, the German counsel for von Papen. My ordeal of the last few days demands it. He is not exactly to be described as a 'wind-bag', because that implies some powers of rhetoric and possibly eloquence. Of these qualities this man is strikingly bereft. He is however a great waster of time, and is highly gifted in the arts of circumlocution. He will never use one word when a dozen will do, and is quite incapable of uttering a simple sentence. Clouds of verbiage, mountains of irrelevance, and oceans of arid pomposity distinguish his every moment in Court, and it is difficult to avoid the extremest forms of irritation with him. I have not avoided it, I regret to say!

He unites with this absence of merit a smug self-complacency, an indifference to ordinary emotions (such as diffidence in taking so much time), and quite obviously is making the most of a situation into which a blind Fortune (blind indeed!) has thrown him. But that this Court should have to suffer under him is a most bitter thing to endure. Incompetence and mediocrity are enthroned and with the despotism associated with power are enjoying their little day. May it soon end!

21 June The witness [Speer] is taken through a great mass of figures dealing with raw materials. The questions themselves are extremely difficult to follow, but they are most fearfully mangled in translation by the worst interpreter the world has ever known.

Oscar Wilde began *De Profundis* by asserting that 'suffering is one long moment' – and the truth of that assertion cannot be better exemplified than in this awful cross-examination, which the Tribunal is compelled to suffer and endure.

I do not think it will be possible to write down a coherent note of this cross-examination. The emotions are too deeply stirred. Irritation, I suppose, is the chief feeling, for not only is the whole proceeding a grave and wicked waste of time, but the illiterate translation is really a torture of the spirit. Time simply stands still, and at the moment at which I write there is almost half an hour to go, thirty minutes of sheer, unadulterated misery.

What a commentary on the greatest trial in history, when the great nations co-operate in concord and unite, and the nations of the world look on!

29 July   Dubost [the French prosecutor] is at the microphone again, making his final speech. He is robust and vigorous: but such is the irony of fate that he is being translated by a stout, tenor-voiced man with the 'refayned' and precious accents of a decaying pontiff. It recalls irresistibly a latecomer making an apology at the Vicarage Garden Party in the village, rather than the grim and stern prosecution of war criminals.

But translators are a race apart – touchy, vain, unaccountable, full of vagaries, puffed up with self-importance of the most explosive kind, inexpressibly egotistical, and, as a rule, violent opponents of soap and sunlight . . .

16 August   I am exceedingly weary today in consequence of a very late night at our party last night and a trifle too much indulgence in 'White Ladies'. Fellow sufferers in this last respect are General Nikitchenko and Colonel Volchkov of the Russian delegation.

I have the greatest difficulty in keeping awake and the documents which are being discussed by Dr Servatius [Sauckel's counsel] are of such surprising dullness that the temptation to sleep is quite overpowering.

§

For many watching the trial, Albert Speer appeared to be the most sympathetic of the defendants. Articulate, spruce and seemingly candid, he had not joined the Government until well after the war had started, although in fact he had been a Nazi Party member since 1931. As Minister for War Production, he had transformed the efficiency of the German munitions industry, but, as he made clear when examined by his advocate Hans Flaechsner, his early admiration for Hitler had come to be replaced by despair, and, when he realised the Fuehrer's determination to prosecute the conflict even at the ruin of the German people, by a plan to assassinate him.

Trial transcript, 20 June 1946: 'I assume my share of responsibility' – the trials of Speer

DR FLAECHSNER: What were your relations with Hitler in regard to your work?

SPEER: My closest contact with him, in my capacity of architect, was probably during the period from 1937 to September 1939; after that, the relationship was no longer so close on account of the circumstances of the war. After I was appointed successor to Todt a closer but much more official working relationship was again established . . .

DR FLAECHSNER: Were you able to carry on political discussions with Hitler?

SPEER: No, he regarded me as a purely technical minister. Attempts to discuss political or personnel problems with him always failed because of the fact that he was unapproachable. From 1944 on, he was so averse to general discussions and discussions on the war situation that I set down my ideas in memorandum form and handed them to him. Hitler knew how to confine every man to his own specialty. He himself was therefore the only co-ordinating factor. This was far beyond his strength and also his knowledge. A unified political leadership was lacking in consequence, as was also an expert military office for making decisions.

DR FLAECHSNER: Then, as technical minister, do you wish to limit your responsibility to your sphere of work?

SPEER: No; I should like to say something of fundamental importance here. This war has brought an inconceivable catastrophe upon the German people, and indeed started a world catastrophe. Therefore it is my unquestionable duty to assume my share of responsibility for this disaster before the German people. This is all the more my obligation, all the more my responsibility, since the head of the Government has avoided responsibility before the German people and before the world. I, as an important member of the leadership of the Reich, therefore, share in the total responsibility, beginning with 1942 . . .

DR FLAECHSNER: Do you assume responsibility for the affairs covered by the extensive sphere of your assignments?

SPEER: Of course, as far as it is possible according to the principles generally applied and as far as actions were taken according to my directives.

DR FLAECHSNER: Do you wish to refer to Fuehrer decrees in this connection?

SPEER: No. Insofar as Hitler gave me orders and I carried them out, I assume the responsibility for them. I did not, of course, carry out all the orders which he gave me.

DR FLAECHSNER: . . . Herr Speer, up to what time did you devote all your powers to obtaining the strongest possible armament and thus continuing the war?

SPEER: Up to the middle of January 1945.

DR FLAECHSNER: Had not the war been lost before that?

SPEER: From a military point of view and as far as the general situation was concerned, it was certainly lost before that. It is difficult, however, to consider a war as lost and to draw the final conclusions as regards one's own person if one is faced with unconditional surrender.

DR FLAECHSNER: Did not considerations arising out of the production situation, of which you were in a position to have a comprehensive view, force you to regard the war as lost long before that?

SPEER: From the armament point of view not until the autumn of 1944, for I succeeded up to that time, in spite of bombing attacks, in maintaining a constant rise in production. If I may express it in figures, this was so great that in the year 1944 I could completely re-equip 130 infantry divisions and forty armoured divisions. That involved new equipment for 2 million men. This figure would have been 30 per cent higher had it not been for the bombing attacks. We reached our production peak for the entire war in August 1944 for munitions; in September 1944 for aircraft; and in December 1944 for ordnance and the new U-boats. The new weapons were to be put into use a few months later, probably in February or March of 1945. I may mention only the jet planes which had already been announced in the press, the new U-boats, the new anti-aircraft installations, et cetera. Here too, however, bombing attacks so retarded the mass production of these new weapons – which in the last phase of the war might have changed the situation – that they could no longer be used against the enemy in large numbers. All of these attempts were fruitless, however, since from 12 May 1944 on our fuel plants became targets for concentrated attacks from the air.

This was catastrophic. 90 per cent of the fuel was lost to us from that time on. The success of these attacks meant the loss of the war as far as production was concerned; for our new tanks and jet planes were of no use without fuel . . .

DR FLAECHSNER: Herr Speer, how was it possible that you and the other co-workers of Hitler, despite your realisation of the situation, still tried to do everything possible to continue the war?

SPEER: In this phase of the war Hitler deceived all of us. From the summer of 1944 on he circulated, through Ambassador Hewel of the Foreign Office, definite statements to the effect that conversation with foreign powers had been started. Generaloberst Jodl has confirmed this to me here in Court . . . In this way he raised hopes that, like Japan, we would start negotiations in this hopeless situation, so that the people would be saved from the worst consequences. To do this, however, it was necessary to stiffen resistance as much as possible. He deceived all of us by holding out to the military leaders false hopes in the success of diplomatic steps and by promising the political leaders fresh victories through the use of new troops and new weapons and by systematically spreading rumours to encourage the people to believe in the appearance of a miracle weapon – all for the purpose of keeping up resistance . . .

DR FLAECHSNER: Generaloberst Jodl has already testified before this Court that both Hitler and his co-workers saw quite clearly the hopelessness of the military and economic situation. Was no unified action taken by some of Hitler's closer advisers in this hopeless situation to demand the termination of war?

SPEER: No. No unified action was taken by the leading men in Hitler's circle. A step like this was quite impossible, for these men considered themselves either as pure specialists or else as people whose job it was to receive orders – or else they resigned themselves to the situation. No one took over the leadership in this situation for the purpose of bringing about at least a discussion with Hitler on the possibility of avoiding further sacrifices . . .

DR FLAECHSNER: Herr Speer, the witness Stahl said in his written interrogatory that about the middle of February 1945 you had demanded from him a supply of the new poison gas in order to assassinate Hitler, Bormann, and Goebbels. Why did you intend to do this then?

SPEER: I thought there was no other way out. In my despair I wanted to take this step as it had become obvious to me since the beginning of February that Hitler intended to go on with the war at all costs, ruthlessly and without consideration for the German people. It was obvious to me that in the loss of the war he confused his own fate with that of the German people and that in his own end he saw the end of the German people as well. It was also obvious that the war was lost so completely that even unconditional surrender would have to be accepted.

DR FLAECHSNER: Did you mean to carry through this assassination yourself, and why was your plan not realised? . . .

SPEER: In those days Hitler, after the military situation conference, often had conversations in his shelter with Ley, Goebbels, and Bormann, who were particularly close to him then because they supported and co-operated in his radical course of action. Since 20 July it was no longer possible even for Hitler's closest associates to enter this shelter without their pockets and briefcases being examined by the SS for explosives. As an architect I knew this shelter intimately. It had an air-conditioning plant similar to the one installed in this courtroom.

It would not be difficult to introduce the gas into the ventilator of the air-conditioning plant, which was in the garden of the Reich Chancellery. It was then bound to circulate through the entire shelter in a very short time. Thereupon, in the middle of February 1945, I sent for Stahl, the head of my main department 'Munitions' with whom I had particularly close relations, since I had worked in close co-operation with him during the destructions. I frankly told him of my intention, as his testimony shows. I asked him to procure this new poison gas for me from the munitions production . . .

Thereupon I had conferences with Hanschel, the chief engineer of the Chancellery, starting in the middle of March 1945. By these discussions I managed to arrange that the antigas filter should no longer be switched on continuously . . . Naturally, Hanschel had no knowledge of the purpose for which I was conducting the talks with him. When the time came, I inspected the ventilator shaft in the garden of the Chancellery along with Hanschel; and there I discovered that on Hitler's personal order this ventilator had recently been surrounded by a chimney 4 metres high. That can still be ascertained today. Due to this it was no longer possible to carry out my plan . . .

Flaechsner moved on to Hitler's command in the last weeks of the war that the earth of the Fatherland be scorched so as to deny it to the enemy, and to punish the German people for their failure in battle. Speer's testimony provided one of the first public insights into the furious despair, even madness, that had reigned inside Hitler's Berlin bunker during the twilight of the Third Reich.

DR FLAECHSNER: Herr Speer, will you briefly elucidate these orders?
SPEER: I can summarise them very briefly. They gave the order to the Gauleiter [district leaders] to carry out the destruction of all industrial plants, all important electrical facilities, water works, gas works, and so on, and also the destruction of all food stores and clothing stores. My jurisdiction had specifically been excluded by that order, and all my orders for the maintenance of industry had been cancelled.

The military authorities had given the order that all bridges should be destroyed, and in addition all railway installations, postal systems, communication systems in the German railways, also the waterways, all ships, all freight cars, and all locomotives. The aim was, as is stated in one of the decrees, the creation of a traffic desert.

The Bormann decree aimed at bringing the population to the centre of the Reich, both from the West and the East, and the foreign workers and prisoners of war were to be included. These millions of people were to be sent upon their trek on foot. No provisions for their existence had been made, nor could it be carried out in view of the situation.

The carrying out of these orders alone would have resulted in an unimaginable hunger catastrophe. Add to this that on 19 March 1945 there was a strict order from Hitler to all Army groups and all Gauleiter that the battle should be conducted without consideration for our own population . . .

During journeys into the most endangered territories, and by means of discussions with my associates, I now quite openly tried to stop the carrying out of these orders. I ordered that the high explosives which were still available in the Ruhr should be dropped down the mines, and that the stores of high explosives which were on the building sites should be hidden.

We distributed submachine guns to the most important plants so that they could fight against destruction. All this, I know, sounds somewhat exaggerated; but the situation at the time was such that if a Gauleiter had dared to approach the coal mines in the Ruhr and there was a single submachine gun available, then it would have been fired.

I tried to convince the local army commanders of the nonsensical character of the task of exploding bridges, which had been given to them, and furthermore by talking to the local authorities I succeeded in stopping most of the evacuation which had been ordered . . .

DR FLAECHSNER: There has been testimony in this courtroom to the effect that the last phase of the war, that is, from January 1945, was justified from the point of view that the nation should be spared unnecessary sacrifices. Were you of that same opinion?

SPEER: No. It was said that military protection against the East would have been necessary to protect refugees. In reality, until the middle of April 1945, the bulk of our last reserves of armoured vehicles and munitions were used for the fight against the West. The tactical principle, therefore, was different from the one it should have been if the fight had been carried out with the aims which have been stated here. The destruction of bridges in the West and the destruction orders against the basis of life of the nation show the opposite. The sacrifices which were made on both sides after

January 1945 were senseless. The dead of this period will be the accusers of the man responsible for the continuation of that fight, Adolf Hitler. The same is true of the ruined cities, which in this last phase had to lose tremendous cultural values and where innumerable dwellings suffered destruction. Many of the difficulties under which the German nation is suffering today are due to the ruthless destruction of bridges, traffic installations, trucks, locomotives, and ships. The German people remained loyal to Adolf Hitler until the end. He betrayed them with intent. He tried to throw them definitely into the abyss. Only after 1 May 1945 did Doenitz try to act with reason, but it was too late.

DR FLAECHSNER: I have one last question. Was it possible for you to reconcile your actions during the last phase of the war with your oath and your conception of loyalty to Adolf Hitler?

SPEER: There is one loyalty which everyone must always keep; and that is loyalty toward one's own people. That duty comes before everything. If I am in a leading position and if I see that the interests of the nation are acted against in such a way, then I too must act. That Hitler had broken faith with the nation must have been clear to every intelligent member of his entourage, certainly at the latest in January or February 1945. Hitler had once been given his mission by the people; he had no right to gamble away the destiny of the people with his own. Therefore I fulfilled my natural duty as a German. I did not succeed in everything, but I am glad today that by my work I was able to render one more service to the workers in Germany and the occupied territories.

Speer then had to deal with a characteristically blunt series of questions from a Soviet prosecutor.

Trial transcript, 21 June 1946: Speer admits to the Russian prosecutor that he has not read *Mein Kampf*

MR COUNSELLOR RAGINSKY: I will remind you of one question, and will you tell me whether or not your answer was put down correctly. It was the question whether you acknowledged that in his book *Mein Kampf* Hitler stated bluntly his aggressive plans for the countries of the East and West and, in particular, for the Soviet Union. You answered, 'Yes, I acknowledge it'. Do you remember that?

SPEER: Yes, that is perfectly possible.

MR COUNSELLOR RAGINSKY: And do you confirm that now?

SPEER: No.

MR COUNSELLOR RAGINSKY: You do not confirm that now?

SPEER: I shall have to tell you that at the time I was ashamed to say that I had not read the whole of *Mein Kampf*. I thought that would sound rather absurd.

MR COUNSELLOR RAGINSKY: All right, we shall not waste time. You were ashamed to admit that, or are you ashamed now? Let us go on to another question.

SPEER: Yes, I cheated at that time.

MR COUNSELLOR RAGINSKY: You cheated at that time; maybe you are cheating now?

SPEER: No.

MR COUNSELLOR RAGINSKY: It does not matter. You worked on the staff of Hess, did you not?

SPEER: Yes.

MR COUNSELLOR RAGINSKY: You worked with Ley?

SPEER: Yes, in the Labour Front.

MR COUNSELLOR RAGINSKY: Yes, the German Labour Front. You had a high rank in the Nazi Party, as you stated here today; you said that today in Court, did you not?

SPEER: No, it was not a high rank; it did not in any way correspond to the position which I occupied in the State.

MR COUNSELLOR RAGINSKY: You had better listen to my questions and then answer them. I repeat; you were collaborating with Hess, and you worked with Ley in the Labour Front. You were one of the leaders of the technicians in the Nazi Party. We will not discuss whether it was a very high rank or not, but you did have a rank in the Nazi Party.

Yesterday, in Court, you said that you were one of Hitler's close friends. You now want to say that so far as the plans and intentions of Hitler were concerned, you only learned about them from the book *Mein Kampf?*

SPEER: I can say a few words in this connection. I was in close contact with Hitler, and I heard his personal views; these views of his did not allow the conclusion that he had any plans of the sort which have appeared in the documents here, and I was particularly relieved in 1939, when the Nonaggression Pact with Russia was signed. After all, your diplomats too must have read *Mein Kampf*; nevertheless, they signed the Nonaggression Pact. And they were certainly more intelligent than I am – I mean in political matters.

MR COUNSELLOR RAGINSKY: I will not now examine who read *Mein Kampf* and who did not; that is irrelevant and does not interest the Tribunal.

The apparent frankness of Speer's admissions and his willingness to accept responsibility masked, however, the grim realities on which his ministerial achievements had been founded. In 1944, when the Allied bombing offensive against German industry reached its height, seven times as many weapons were being manufactured as two years previously. That order of improvement had required an increase of only a third in the number of workers, but most of them were part of a slave army of foreign labour some 7 million strong by the war's end – victims of the demands of German factories, the manpower lost to the Wehrmacht, and the Nazis' belief that a woman's place was at home rather than on the assembly line.

Fritz Sauckel, another of the defendants, had been responsible for press-ganging the labourers needed by Speer but, when cross-examined by Jackson, Speer said that he had known nothing of the appalling conditions under which most had worked, and which had claimed tens of thousands of lives.

Trial transcript, 21 June 1946: 'Guards need something in their hands' – Speer denies that he knew of the conditions under which labourers worked

MR JUSTICE JACKSON: Now there has been some testimony about your relation to concentration camps, and, as I understand it, you have said to us that you did use and encourage the use of forced labour from the concentration camps.

SPEER: Yes, we did use it in the German armament industry.

MR JUSTICE JACKSON: And I think you also recommended that persons in labour camps who were slackers be sent to the concentration camps, did you not?

SPEER: That was the question of the so-called *Bummelanten* and by that name we meant workers who did not get to their work on time or who pretended to be ill. Severe measures were taken against such workers during the war, and I approved of these measures.

MR JUSTICE JACKSON: In fact, in the 30 October 1942 meeting of the Central Planning Board you brought the subject up in the following terms, did you not: 'We must also discuss the slackers. Ley has ascertained that the sick list decreases to one-fourth or one-fifth in factories where doctors are on the staff who examine the sick men. There is nothing to be said against SS and Police taking drastic steps and putting those known to be slackers into concentration camp factories. There is no alternative. Let it happen several times, and the news will soon get around.'

That was your recommendation?

SPEER: Correct.

MR JUSTICE JACKSON: In other words, the workmen stood in considerable terror of concentration camps, and you wanted to take advantage of that to keep them at their work, did you not?

SPEER: It is certain that concentration camps had a bad reputation with us, and the transfer to a concentration camp, or threat of such a possibility, was bound to reduce the number of absentees in the factories right from the beginning. But at that meeting, as I already said yesterday, there was nothing further said about it. It was one of the many remarks one can make in wartime when onc is upset.

MR JUSTICE JACKSON: However, it is very clear – and if I misinterpret you I give you the chance to correct me – that you understood the very bad reputation that the concentration camps had among the workmen and that the concentration camps were regarded as being much more severe than the labour camps as places to be in.

SPEER: That is correct. I knew that. I did not know, of course, what I have heard during this trial, but the other thing was a generally known fact.

MR JUSTICE JACKSON: Well, it was known throughout Germany, was it not, that the concentration camps were pretty tough places to be put?

SPEER: Yes, but not to the extent which has been revealed in this trial.

MR JUSTICE JACKSON: And the bad reputation of the concentration camp, as a matter of fact, was a part of its usefulness in making people fearful of being sent there, was it not?

SPEER: No doubt concentration camps were a means, a menace used to keep order.

MR JUSTICE JACKSON: And to keep people at work?

SPEER: I would not like to put it in that way. I assert that a great number of the foreign workers in our country did their work quite voluntarily once they had come to Germany . . .

MR JUSTICE JACKSON: Now I want to ask you about the recruiting of forced labour. As I understand it, you know about the deportation of 100,000 Jews from Hungary for subterranean airplane factories, and you told us in your interrogation of 18 October 1945 that you made no objection to it. That is true, is it not?

SPEER: That is true, yes.

MR JUSTICE JACKSON: And you told us also, quite candidly, on that day that it was no secret to you that a good deal of the manpower brought in by Sauckel was brought in by illegal methods. That is also true, is it not?

SPEER: I took great care at the time to notice what expression the interrogating officer used; he used the expression 'they came against their wish'; and that I confirmed.

MR JUSTICE JACKSON: Did you not say that it was no secret to you that they were brought in an illegal manner? Didn't you add that yourself?

SPEER: No, no. That was certainly not so.

MR JUSTICE JACKSON: Well, in any event, you knew that at the Fuehrer conference in August of 1942 the Fuehrer had approved of all coercive measures for obtaining labour if they couldn't be obtained on a voluntary basis, and you knew that that programme was carried out. You, as a matter of fact, you did not give any particular attention to the legal side of this thing, did you? You were after manpower; isn't that the fact?

SPEER: That is absolutely correct.

MR JUSTICE JACKSON: And whether it was legal or illegal was not your worry?

SPEER: I consider that in view of the whole war situation and of our views in general on this question it was justified.

MR JUSTICE JACKSON: Yes, it was in accordance with the policy of the Government, and that was as far as you inquired at the time, was it not?

SPEER: Yes. I am of the opinion that at the time I took over my office, in February 1942, all the violations of international law, which later – which are now brought up against me – had already been committed.

MR JUSTICE JACKSON: And you don't question that you share a certain responsibility for that programme for bringing in – whether it is a legal responsibility or not, in fact – for bringing in this labour against its will? You don't deny that, do you?

SPEER: The workers were brought to Germany largely against their will, and I had no objection to their being brought to Germany against their will. On the contrary, during the first period, until the autumn of 1942, I certainly also took some pains to see that as many workers as possible should be brought to Germany in this manner . . .

MR JUSTICE JACKSON: Well, I will ask you about Exhibit 398, which becomes USA-894. I mean Document 398, which becomes Exhibit 894, a statement by Hofer, living in Essen: 'From April 1943 I worked with Lowenkamp every day in Panzer Shop 4. Lowenkamp was brutal to the foreigners. He confiscated food which belonged to the PWs [prisoners of war] and took it home. Every day he maltreated Eastern Workers, Russian PWs, French, Italian, and other foreign civilians. He had a steel cabinet built which was so small that one could hardly stand in it. He locked up foreigners in the box, women too, for 48 hours at a time without giving the people food.

'They were not released even to relieve nature. It was forbidden for other people, too, to give any help to the persons locked in, or to release them. While clearing a concealed store he fired on escaping Russian civilians without hitting any of them.

'One day, while distributing food, I saw how he hit a French civilian in the face with a ladle and made his face bleed. Further, he delivered Russian girls without bothering about the children afterwards. There was never any milk for them so the Russians had to nourish the children with sugar water. When Lowenkamp was arrested he wrote two letters and sent them to me through his wife. He tried to make out that he never beat people.'

There is a good deal more of this, but I will not bother to put it into the record.

Is it your view that that is exaggerated?

SPEER: I consider this affidavit a lie. I would say that among German people such things do not exist, and if such individual cases occurred they were punished. It is not possible to drag the German people in the dirt in such a way. The heads of concerns were decent people too, and took an interest in their workers. If the head of the Krupp plant heard about such things, he certainly took steps immediately.

MR JUSTICE JACKSON: Well, what about the steel boxes? The steel box couldn't have been built? Or don't you believe the steel box story?

SPEER: No, I do not believe it; I mean I do not believe it is true. After the collapse in 1945 a lot of affidavits were certainly drawn up which do not fully correspond to the truth. That is not your fault. It is the fault of – after a defeat, it is quite possible that people lend themselves to things like that . . .

MR JUSTICE JACKSON: Very well. I will ask to have you shown Exhibit D-230. Together with D-230 is an interoffice record of the steel switches, and the steel switches which have been found in the camp will be shown to you. Eighty were distributed, according to the reports.

SPEER: Shall I comment on this?

MR JUSTICE JACKSON: If you wish.

SPEER: Yes. Those are nothing but replacements for rubber

truncheons. We had no rubber; and for that reason, the guards probably had something like this.

MR JUSTICE JACKSON: That is the same inference that I drew from the document.

SPEER: Yes, but the guards did not immediately use these steel switches any more than your police use their rubber truncheons. But they had to have something in their hands. It is the same thing all over the world . . .

The case of Speer is perhaps the most interesting of all those heard at Nuremberg. One wants to ask how such a clever man could have followed such a leader, how he could so willingly have abandoned his sense of good and evil. If we knew the answer to that, we would know a great deal more about how such tragedies repeat themselves. It remains debatable exactly what Speer knew about the camps and those who laboured in his factories. He had, for instance, visited Mauthausen, but claimed never to have been shown anything but healthy inmates. The more pertinent question is probably how much did he want to know. The ignorance that he professed in court of circumstances that closely concerned his area of responsibility certainly presents a contrast with his acute perception of the wider political and military state of the war. Speer, one must assume, was ready to admit the truth when it reflected credit it on him, but more than ready to close his eyes to it when it would not. Simply knowing the difference between right and wrong does not, it seems, guarantee that one will make the better choice between them.

Early July–31 August 1946: Closing speeches

By the start of July, all the cases against the individual defendants, including the absent Martin Bormann, had been concluded. The defence counsel then began to make their closing speeches on behalf of their clients. Many of them used the opportunity to protest at what they viewed as the unlawful nature of the trial, in that it presumed to hold the accused responsible for acts which were carried out by the German state, which were not illegal at the time, and which they had been ordered to perform by others. Jackson, still smarting from the exposure of his inadequacies as a trial lawyer, recovered his reputation in part when he addressed the guilt of those indicted in his own closing speech at the end of July.

Trial transcript, 26 July 1946: Jackson's closing speech for the prosecution

MR JUSTICE ROBERT H. JACKSON (Chief of Counsel for the United States): Mr President and Members of the Tribunal: An advocate can be confronted with few more formidable tasks than to select his closing arguments where there is great disparity between his appropriate time and his available material. In eight months – a short time as state trials go – we have introduced evidence which embraces as vast and varied a panorama of events as has ever been compressed within the framework of a litigation. It is impossible in summation to do more than outline with bold strokes the vitals of this trial's mad and melancholy record, which will live as the historical text of the twentieth century's shame and depravity.

It is common to think of our own time as standing at the apex of civilisation, from which the deficiencies of preceding ages may patronisingly be viewed in the light of what is assumed to be 'progress'. The reality is that in the long perspective of history the present century will not hold an admirable position, unless its second half is to redeem its first. These two-score years in the twentieth century will be recorded in the book of years as one of the most bloody in all annals. Two World Wars have left a legacy of dead which number more than all the armies engaged in any war that made ancient or medieval history. No half-century ever witnessed slaughter on such a scale, such cruelties and inhumanities, such wholesale deportations of peoples into slavery, such annihilations of minorities. The terror of Torquemada pales before the Nazi Inquisition. These deeds are the overshadowing historical facts by which generations to come will remember this decade. If we cannot eliminate the causes and prevent the repetition of these barbaric events, it is not an irresponsible prophecy to say that this twentieth century may yet succeed in bringing the doom of civilisation . . .

The strength of the case against these defendants under the conspiracy Count, which it is the duty of the United States to argue, is in its simplicity. It involves but three ultimate inquiries: First, have the acts defined by the Charter as crimes been committed; second, were they committed pursuant to a Common Plan or Conspiracy; third, are these defendants among those who are criminally responsible?

The charge requires examination of a criminal policy, not of a multitude of isolated, unplanned, or disputed crimes . . .

A glance over the dock will show that, despite quarrels among themselves, each defendant played a part which fitted in with every other, and that all advanced the common plan. It contradicts experience that men of such diverse backgrounds and talents should so forward each other's aims by coincidence.

The large and varied role of Goering was half militarist and half gangster. He stuck his pudgy finger in every pie. He used his SA musclemen to help bring the gang into power. In order to entrench that power he contrived to have the Reichstag burned, established the Gestapo, and created the concentration camps. He was equally adept at massacring opponents and at framing scandals to get rid of stubborn generals. He built up the Luftwaffe and hurled it at his defenceless neighbours. He was among the foremost in harrying Jews out of the land. By mobilising the total economic resources of Germany he made possible the waging of the war which he had taken a large part in planning. He was, next to Hitler, the man who tied the activities of all the defendants together in a common effort.

The parts played by the other defendants, although less comprehensive and less spectacular than that of the Reichsmarschall, were nevertheless integral and necessary contributions to the joint undertaking, without any one of which the success of the common enterprise would have been in jeopardy. No purpose would be served – nor indeed is time available – to review all the crimes which the evidence has charged up to their names. Nevertheless, in viewing the conspiracy as a whole and as an operating mechanism, it may be well to recall briefly the outstanding services which each of the men in the dock rendered to the common cause ...

The zealot Hess, before succumbing to wanderlust, was the engineer tending the Party machinery, passing orders and propaganda down to the Leadership Corps, supervising every aspect of Party activities, and maintaining the organisation as a loyal and ready instrument of power. When apprehensions abroad threatened the success of the Nazi regime for conquest, it was the duplicitous Ribbentrop, the salesman of deception, who was detailed to pour wine on the troubled waters of suspicion by preaching the gospel of limited and peaceful intentions. Keitel, the weak and willing tool, delivered the Armed Forces, the instrument of aggression, over to the Party and directed them in executing its felonious designs.

Kaltenbrunner, the grand inquisitor, took up the bloody mantle of Heydrich to stifle opposition and terrorise compliance, and buttressed the power of National Socialism on a foundation of guiltless corpses. It was Rosenberg, the intellectual high priest of the 'master race', who provided the doctrine of hatred which gave the impetus for the annihilation of Jewry, and who put his infidel theories into practice against the Eastern Occupied Territories. His woolly philosophy also added boredom to the long list of Nazi atrocities. The fanatical Frank, who solidified Nazi control by establishing the new order of authority without law, so that the will of the Party was the only test of legality, proceeded to export his lawlessness to Poland, which he governed with the lash of Caesar and whose population he reduced to sorrowing remnants. Frick, the ruthless organiser, helped the Party to seize power, supervised the police agencies to ensure that it stayed in power, and chained the economy of Bohemia and Moravia to the German war machine.

Streicher, the venomous Bulgarian, manufactured and distributed obscene racial libels which incited the populace to accept and assist the progressively savage operations of 'race purification'. As Minister of Economics Funk accelerated the pace of rearmament, and as Reichsbank president banked for the SS the gold teeth fillings of concentration camp victims – probably the most ghoulish collateral in banking history. It was Schacht, the façade of starched respectability, who in the early days provided the window dressing, the bait for the hesitant, and whose wizardry later made it possible for Hitler to finance the colossal rearmament programme, and to do it secretly.

Doenitz, Hitler's legatee of defeat, promoted the success of the Nazi aggressions by instructing his pack of submarine killers to conduct warfare at sea with the illegal ferocity of the jungle. Raeder, the political admiral, stealthily built up the German Navy in defiance of the Versailles Treaty, and then put it to use in a series of aggressions which he had taken a leading part in planning. Von Schirach, poisoner of a generation, initiated the German youth in Nazi doctrine, trained them in legions for service in the SS and Wehrmacht, and delivered them up to the Party as fanatic, unquestioning executors of its will.

Sauckel, the greatest and cruellest slaver since the Pharaohs of Egypt, produced desperately needed manpower by driving foreign peoples into the land of bondage on a scale unknown even in the ancient days of tyranny in the kingdom of the Nile. Jodl, betrayer of the traditions of his profession, led the Wehrmacht in violating its own code of military honour in order to carry out the barbarous aims of Nazi policy. Von Papen, pious agent of an infidel regime, held the stirrup while Hitler vaulted into the saddle, lubricated the Austrian annexation, and devoted his diplomatic cunning to the service of Nazi objectives abroad.

Seyss-Inquart, spearhead of the Austrian fifth column, took over the government of his own country only to make a present of it to Hitler, and then, moving north, brought terror and oppression to the Netherlands and pillaged its economy for the benefit of the German juggernaut. Von Neurath, the old-school diplomat, who cast the pearls of his experience before Nazis, guided Nazi diplomacy in the early years, soothed the fears of prospective victims, and, as Reich Protector of Bohemia and Moravia, strengthened the German position for the coming attack on Poland. Speer, as Minister of Armaments and Production, joined in planning and executing the programme to dragoon prisoners of war and foreign workers into German war industries, which waxed in output while the labourers waned in starvation. Fritzsche, radio propaganda chief, by manipulation of the truth goaded German public opinion into frenzied support of the regime and anaesthetised the independent judgment of the population so that they did without question their masters' bidding. And Bormann, who has not accepted our invitation to this reunion, sat at the throttle of the vast and powerful engine of the Party, guiding it in the ruthless execution of Nazi policies, from the scourging of the Christian Church to the lynching of captive Allied airmen . . .

The defendants meet this overwhelming case, some by admitting a limited responsibility, some by putting the blame on others, and some by taking the position in effect that while there have been enormous crimes there are no criminals . . .

What these men have overlooked is that Adolf Hitler's acts are their acts. It was these men among millions of others, and it was these men leading millions of others, who built up Adolf Hitler and vested in his psychopathic personality not only innumerable lesser decisions but the supreme issue of war or peace. They intoxicated him with power and adulation. They fed his hates and aroused his fears. They put a loaded gun in his eager hands. It was left to Hitler to pull the trigger, and when he did they all at that time approved. His guilt stands admitted, by some defendants reluctantly, by some vindictively. But his guilt is the guilt of the whole dock, and of every man in it . . .

These men in this dock, on the face of this record, were not strangers to this programme of crime, nor was their connection with it remote or obscure. We find them in the very heart of it. The positions they held show that we have chosen defendants of self-evident responsibility. They are the very top surviving authorities in their respective fields and in the Nazi State. No one lives who, at least until the very last moments of the war, outranked Goering in position, power, and influence. No soldier stood above Keitel and Jodl, and no sailor above Raeder and Doenitz. Who can be responsible for the diplomacy of duplicity if not the Foreign Ministers, von Neurath and Ribbentrop, and the diplomatic handy-man, von Papen? Who should be answerable for the oppressive administration of occupied countries if Gauleiters, protectors, governors, and Kommissars such as Frank, Seyss-Inquart, Frick, von Schirach, von Neurath, and Rosenberg are not? Where shall we look for those who mobilised the economy for total war if we overlook Schacht and Speer and Funk? Who was the master of the great slaving enterprise if it was not Sauckel? Where shall we find the hand that ran the concentration camps if it was not the hand of Kaltenbrunner? And who whipped up the hates and fears of the public, and manipulated the Party organisations to incite these crimes, if not Hess, von Schirach, Fritzsche, Bormann, and the unspeakable Julius Streicher? The list of defendants is made up of men who played indispensable and reciprocal parts in this tragedy. The photographs and the films show them again and again together on important occasions. The documents show them agreed on policies and on methods, and all working aggressively for the expansion of Germany by force of arms.

To escape the implications of their positions and the inference of guilt from their activities, the defendants are almost unanimous in one defence. The refrain is heard time and again: These men were without authority, without knowledge, without influence, without importance. Funk summed up the general self-abasement of the dock in his plaintive lament that: 'I always, so to speak, came up to the door, but I was not permitted to enter.'

In the testimony of each defendant, at some point there was reached the familiar blank wall: Nobody knew anything about what was going on. Time after time we have heard the chorus from the dock: 'I only heard about these things here for the first time' . . .

The defendants have been unanimous, when pressed, in shifting the blame on other men, sometimes on one and sometimes on another. But the names they have repeatedly picked are Hitler, Himmler, Heydrich, Goebbels, and Bormann. All of these are dead or missing. No matter how hard we have pressed the defendants on the stand, they have never pointed the finger at a living man as guilty. It is a temptation to ponder the wondrous workings of a fate which has left only the guilty dead and only the innocent alive. It is almost too remarkable.

The chief villain on whom blame is placed – some of the defendants vie with each other in producing appropriate epithets – is Hitler. He is the man at whom nearly every defendant has pointed an accusing finger.

I shall not dissent from this consensus, nor do I deny that all these dead and missing men shared the guilt. In crimes so reprehensible that degrees of guilt have lost their significance they may have played the most evil parts. But their guilt cannot exculpate the defendants. Hitler did not carry all responsibility to the grave with him. All the guilt is not wrapped in Himmler's shroud. It was these dead men whom these living chose to be their partners in this great conspiratorial brotherhood, and the crimes that they did together they must pay for one by one . . .

But let me for a moment turn devil's advocate. I admit that Hitler was the chief villain. But for the defendants to put all blame on him is neither manly nor true. We know that even the head of the state has the same limits to his senses and to the hours of his days as do lesser men. He must rely on others to be his eyes and ears as to most that goes on in a great empire. Other legs must run his errands; other hands must execute his plans. On whom did Hitler rely for such things more than upon these men in the dock? Who led him to believe he had an invincible air armada if not Goering? Who kept disagreeable facts from him? Did not Goering forbid Field Marshal Milch to warn Hitler that in his opinion Germany was not equal to the war upon Russia? Did not Goering, according to Speer, relieve General Galland of his air force command for speaking of the weaknesses and bungling of the air forces? Who led Hitler, utterly untravelled himself, to believe in the indecision and timidity of democratic peoples if not Ribbentrop, von Neurath, and von Papen? Who fed his illusion of German invincibility if not Keitel, Jodl, Raeder, and Doenitz? Who kept his hatred of the Jews inflamed more than Streicher and Rosenberg? Who would Hitler say deceived him about conditions in concentration camps if not Kaltenbrunner, even as he would deceive us? These men had access to Hitler and often could control the information that reached him and on which he must base his policy and his orders. They were the Praetorian Guard, and while they were under Caesar's orders, Caesar was always in their hands . . .

The fact is that the Nazi habit of economising in the use of truth pulls the foundations out from under their own defences . . . Nor is the lie direct the only means of falsehood. They all speak with a Nazi double talk with which to deceive the unwary. In the Nazi dictionary of sardonic euphemisms 'final solution' of the Jewish problem was a phrase which meant extermination; 'special treatment' of prisoners of war meant killing; 'protective custody' meant concentration camp; 'duty labour' meant slave labour; and an order to 'take a firm attitude' or 'take positive measures' meant to act with unrestrained savagery. Before we accept their word at what seems to be its face, we must always look for hidden meanings . . .

This was the philosophy of the National Socialists. When for years they have deceived the world, and masked falsehood with plausibilities, can anyone be surprised that they continue their habits of a lifetime in this dock? Credibility is one of the main issues of this trial. Only those who have failed to learn the bitter lessons of the last decade can doubt that men who have always played on the unsuspecting credulity of generous opponents would not hesitate to do the same, now.

It is against such a background that these defendants now ask this Tribunal to say that they are not guilty of planning, executing, or conspiring to commit this long list of crimes and wrongs. They stand before the record of this trial as bloodstained Gloucester stood by the body of his slain king. He begged of the widow, as they beg of you: 'Say I slew them not'. And the Queen replied, 'Then say they were not slain. But dead they are . . . ' If you were to say of these men that they are not guilty, it would be as true to say that there has been no war, there are no slain, there has been no crime.

§

Jackson's speech was not well received by those in the dock, noted Gilbert.

Gustave Gilbert: The reaction of the defendants to Jackson's speech

Lunch hour: The reaction of most of the defendants was one of hurt surprise that the prosecution still considered them criminals. Von Papen dropped his mask of polite friendliness in my presence, and denounced the speech. 'That was more the speech of a demagogue than of a leading representative of American jurisprudence! . . . What have we been sitting here for eight months for? The prosecution isn't paying the *slightest* attention to our defence. They still insist on calling us liars and murderers!'

Doenitz dropped his contempt of the hypocritical politicians long enough to agree heartily with von Papen on this issue, since he had also been attacked. He and von Papen supported each other in indignation over Jackson's denunciation.

Schacht joined the discussion, adding his own grievances, and agreeing with the other two. 'I suppose I am expected to tell a man to his face that I am planning to assassinate him! – That was a miserable speech. It had a very low *niveau* [level].' They all agreed that the speech had a very low *niveau*.

Goering reacted with the typical shrug of the shoulders towards evidence that wounded his pride yet left him unable to do anything about it. 'Oh, that was just about what I expected. – Let him call me names as much as he pleases – I didn't expect anything different from him.' He expressed the attitude that sticks and stones will break my bones, but names will never hurt me, without saying so in so many words. However, he found a malicious satisfaction in the fact that his enemies had also gotten it in the neck. 'Anyway, those who kowtowed to the prosecution and denounced the Nazi regime got it in the neck just the same. It serves them right. – They probably thought they would get off cheap that way.'

Goering insinuated that Speer, von Schirach, and Schacht had made a deal with the prosecution to get off easy in exchange for denouncing the Nazi regime. I told him he must surely know that that was out of the question. 'Well, if there wasn't a deal, then they must have expected to get off easy.' I told him that I was convinced that Speer and von Schirach, at least, had made the denunciation out of bitter disillusionment, and had attempted to set the German people straight on the guilt of their leaders.

Goering didn't like that, and defended his own position by contrast to Schacht. 'That's right – at least I'd rather be called a murderer than a hypocrite and opportunist like Schacht. I certainly got off better than he did. – Now the people will say of him, "On the one hand you were a traitor, and on the other hand you stand exposed as a hypocrite just the same." – I'd rather do it my way.' He kept mumbling about Jackson's undignified name-calling, and said that the British prosecution would probably be more dignified. – But, of course, the whole trial is a farce, because the prosecution isn't paying the slightest attention to their defence. I reminded him that the defence will have lasted six months including the organisations, and that they would still have the last word. Goering laughed. 'Unfortunately not – the judges will have the last word.' Then to forestall the impression that he knew he was guilty, he added hastily, ' – And the victors, as I've always told you, are always right.'

§

Jackson was followed by Sir Hartley Shawcross, who paid more attention in his final peroration to answering the defence's arguments on the law governing the proceedings. This, he said, was firmly rooted in international accords signed by Germany, and where it was not, natural justice demanded that civilisation supply the mechanism to turn the undoubted moral guilt of the accused into the legal guilt of a conviction for their crimes.

For a month from the end of July, the cases were heard of the other seven defendants in the trial, the organisations deemed to be tied most closely to the Nazis' crimes. Regime change was all very well, but the fear of the new German leadership was that the blanket conviction of all those who had belonged to such bodies would have grave consequences for the healing process necessary for the rebuilding of the nation. For example, if the OKW was found guilty, what implications might that have for every man who had served under it in the armed forces?

In the event, the judges acted to limit the scope of the prosecution against the OKW. It was soon clear, too, that the Allies had misunderstood the nature of the Reich Cabinet, which despite its name was never a governing body as such, while the SA – the Nazis' thugs in its early years – had faded from view after 1934. The Tribunal also confined proceedings against the Leadership Corps, which notionally transmitted Party doctrine down from the Fuehrer to every parish in Germany, to its four highest ranks.

The guilt of the police and paramilitary organisations was more self-evident. Frederick Elwyn Jones, a future British Lord Chancellor, presented part of the case against the SS, one of whose functions was to perform pseudo-scientific experiments on prisoners as part of Himmler's preoccupation with race. Wolfram Sievers had been head of its Ancestral Heritage Office or Ahnenerbe, which conducted research into the Nazis' theories on Aryan superiority. Jones asked him how exactly it had assembled its ghoulish collection of Jewish skulls.

Trial transcript, 8 August 1946: Collecting skulls for Himmler

MAJOR JONES: Now, that is a letter headed *Das Ahnenerbe*, dated 9 February 1942, marked 'secret'. It is addressed to Brandt, Himmler's adjutant. It is your letter, Witness, is it not, it is your signature at the bottom of it?

SIEVERS: Yes.

MAJOR JONES: I will read it out . . .

'Subject: Securing of skulls of Jewish–Bolshevik commissars for the purpose of scientific research at the Reich University of Strasbourg.

'We have large collections of skulls of almost all races and peoples at our disposal. Of the Jewish race, however, only very few specimens of skulls are available, with the result that it is impossible to arrive at precise conclusions from examination. The war in the East now presents us with the opportunity to overcome this deficiency. By procuring the skulls of the Jewish–Bolshevik commissars, who represent the prototype of the repulsive, but characteristic, subhuman, we have the chance now to obtain scientific material.

'The best practical method for obtaining and collecting this skull material could be followed by directing the Wehrmacht to turn over alive all captured Jewish–Bolshevik commissars to the Feldpolizei [field police]. The Feldpolizei, in turn, would be given special directives to inform a certain office at regular intervals of the numbers and places of detention of these captured Jews, and to give them close attention and care until a special delegate arrives. This special delegate, who will be in charge of securing the material (a junior physician of the Wehrmacht or the Feldpolizei, or a student of medicine equipped with a motor car and driver), will be required to take a previously stipulated series of photographs, make anthropological measurements, and, in addition, determine as far as possible descent, date of birth, and other personal data.

'Following the subsequently induced death of the Jew, whose head should not be damaged, the physician will sever the head from the body and will forward it to its proper point of destination in a hermetically sealed tin can especially made for this purpose and filled with a conserving fluid. Having arrived at the laboratory, the comparison tests and anatomical research on the skull, as well as determination of the race membership and of pathological features of the skull form, the form and size of the brain, et cetera, can be undertaken by photos, measurements, and other data supplied on the head and the skull itself.'

That was the report which you forwarded to Brandt?

SIEVERS: Yes, that was the report of Professor Hirt.

MAJOR JONES: How did the collection of these skeletons from the living proceed?

SIEVERS: I cannot give you the exact details. In earlier interrogations I pointed out that Professor Hirt would have to be asked himself about this matter.

MAJOR JONES: Now, Witness, I want to give you another opportunity of telling the truth. Are you saying to this Tribunal that you do not know what happened with regard to the progress of that collection of skulls and skeletons?

SIEVERS: That may be seen from the report itself. Persons were then assigned for this task by order of Himmler.

MAJOR JONES: Who put the actions into operation; did you have anything to do with it, with the collection of the bodies?

SIEVERS: No, nothing at all, and I do not know either in what way this whole matter developed, since the direct correspondence and the conferences which had taken place previously between Himmler and Hirt are things I know nothing about . . .

MAJOR JONES: . . . You had already been discussing this with Himmler, Witness, had you not? You were his agent for collecting these living men to turn them into skeletons?

SIEVERS: That does not apply in this form. The entire matter covered such a long period of time that I am not able to reconstruct the entire connection on the spur of the moment, as I was concerned only with particulars . . .

MAJOR JONES: Just a moment, Witness. How many human beings were killed to create this collection of skeletons?

SIEVERS: 150 people are mentioned in this report.

MAJOR JONES: That was all you assisted in murdering, was it?

SIEVERS: I had nothing to do with the murdering of these people. I simply carried through the function of a mailman.

§

The case against the organisations finished at the end of August. Then, in one of the compromises made with Continental law, each of the twenty-one men in the dock was allowed to make a short final statement to the court. The first to speak was Goering, whom the prosecution said was complicit in every aspect of the Nazis' conspiracy to wage war with terror. His riposte was that he had only ever been motivated by love of his country.

Trial transcript, 31 August 1946: The second man of the State – Goering's final statement to the court

HERMANN WILHELM GOERING: The Prosecution, in the final speeches, has treated the defendants and their testimony as completely worthless. The statements made under oath by the defendants were accepted as absolutely true when they could serve to support the indictment, but conversely the statements were characterised as perjury when they refuted the indictment. That is very elementary, but it is not a convincing basis for demonstration of proof . . .

The Prosecution uses the fact that I was the second man of the State as proof that I must have known everything that happened. But it does not present any documentary or other convincing proof in cases where I have denied under oath that I knew about certain things, much less desired them. Therefore, it is only an allegation and a conjecture when the Prosecution says, 'Who should have known that if not Goering, who was the successor of the Fuehrer?' . . .

The Prosecution brings forward individual statements over a period of 25 years, which were made under completely different circumstances and without any consequences arising from them at the time, and quotes them as proof of intent and guilt, statements which can easily be made in the excitement of the moment and of the atmosphere that prevailed at the time. There is probably not one leading personage on the opposing side who did not speak or write similarly in the course of a quarter of a century.

Out of all the happenings of these 25 years, from conferences, speeches, laws, actions, and decisions, the Prosecution proves that everything was desired and intended from the beginning according to a deliberate sequence and an unbroken connection. This is an erroneous conception which is entirely devoid of logic, and which will be rectified some day by history, after the proceedings here have proved the incorrectness of these allegations . . .

Mr Jackson stated further that one cannot accuse and punish a state, but rather that one must hold the leaders responsible. One seems to forget that Germany was a sovereign state, and that her legislation within the German nation was not subject to the jurisdiction of foreign countries. No state ever gave notice to the Reich at the proper time, pointing out that any activity for National Socialism would be made subject to punishment and persecution. On the other hand, if we, the leaders as individuals, are called to account and condemned – very well; but you cannot punish the German people at the same time. The German people placed their trust in the Fuehrer, and under his authoritarian government they had no influence on events. Without knowledge of the grave crimes which have become known today, the people, loyal, self-sacrificing, and courageous, fought and suffered through the life-and-death struggle which had broken out against their will. The German people are free of guilt.

I did not want a war, nor did I bring it about. I did everything to prevent it by negotiations. After it had broken out, I did everything to assure victory. Since the three greatest powers on earth, together with many other nations, were fighting against us, we finally succumbed to their tremendous superiority.

I stand up for the things that I have done, but I deny most emphatically that my actions were dictated by the desire to subjugate foreign peoples by wars, to murder them, to rob them, or to enslave them, or to commit atrocities or crimes.

The only motive which guided me was my ardent love for my people, its happiness, its freedom, and its life. And for this I call on the Almighty and my German people to witness.

§

Next to speak was Hess. He began coherently enough, but it soon became clear that all was still not well with his mind.

Trial transcript, 31 August 1946: 'Glazed and staring eyes' – Hess's final statement to the court

I said before that a certain incident in England caused me to think of the reports of the earlier [Soviet show] trials. The reason was that the people around me during my imprisonment acted towards me in a peculiar and incomprehensible way, in a way which led me to conclude that these people somehow were acting in an abnormal state of mind. Some of them – these persons and people around me – were changed from time to time. Some of the new ones who came to me in place of those who had been changed had strange eyes. They were glassy and like eyes in a dream. This symptom, however, lasted only a few days and then they made a completely normal impression. They could no longer be distinguished from normal human beings. Not only I alone noticed these strange eyes, but also the physician who attended me at the time, Dr Johnston, a British Army doctor, a Scotsman.

In the spring of 1942 I had a visitor, a visitor who quite obviously tried to provoke me and acted towards me in a strange way. This visitor also had these strange eyes. Afterwards, Dr Johnston asked me what I thought of this visitor. He told me – I told him I had the impression that for some reason or other he was not completely normal mentally, whereupon Dr Johnston did not protest, as I had expected, but agreed with me and asked me whether I had not noticed those strange eyes, these eyes with a dreamy look. Dr Johnston did not suspect that he himself had exactly the same eyes when he came to me.

The essential point, however, is that in one of the reports of the time, which must still be in the press files on the proceedings – this was in Paris, about the Moscow trial – it said that the defendants had had strange eyes. They had had glazed and dreamy eyes! . . .

THE PRESIDENT [*interposing*]: I must draw the attention of the Defendant Hess to the fact that he has already spoken for 20 minutes, and the Tribunal has indicated to the defendants that it cannot allow them to continue to make statements of great length at this stage of the proceedings.

We have to hear all the defendants. The Tribunal, therefore, hopes that the Defendant Hess will conclude his speech . . .

HESS: . . . The statements which my counsel made in my name before the High Tribunal I permitted to be made for the sake of the future judgment of my people and of history. That is the only thing which matters to me. I do not defend myself against accusers to whom I deny the right to bring charges against me and my fellow-countrymen. I will not discuss accusations which concern things which are purely German matters and therefore of no concern to foreigners. I raise no protest against statements which are aimed at attacking my honour, the honour of the German people. I consider such slanderous attacks by the enemy as a proof of honour.

I was permitted to work for many years of my life under the greatest son whom my people has brought forth in its thousand-year history. Even if I could, I would not want to erase this period of time from my existence. I am happy to know that I have done my duty, to my people, my duty as a German, as a National Socialist, as a loyal follower of my Fuehrer. I do not regret anything.

If I were to begin all over again, I would act just as I have acted, even if I knew that in the end I should meet a fiery death at the stake. No matter what human beings may do, I shall some day stand before the judgment seat of the Eternal. I shall answer to Him, and I know He will judge me innocent.

§

The speeches were made with notable dignity, and perhaps for the only time in the trial allowed the defendants to express themselves without fear of committing a fatal error. That said, they struck the same notes as had been heard continually throughout the proceedings: their own conscience was unblemished; they had only carried out their duty; someone else was to blame. Wilhelm Frick, a former police officer, had been Minister of the Interior for ten years. He had been responsible for silencing opponents of the Nazis by incarcerating them in concentration camps, although he had eventually lost his battle against the advancing influence of Himmler over the security services. From 1943, he had ruled the Czechs.

Trial transcript, 31 August 1946: 'I have a clear conscience' – the final speech of Wilhelm Frick to the court

WILHELM FRICK: I have a clear conscience with respect to the indictment. My entire life was spent in the service of my people and my fatherland. To them I have devoted the best of my strength in the loyal fulfilment of my duty.

I am convinced that no patriotic American or citizen of any other country would have acted differently in my place, if his country had been in the same position. For to have acted any differently would have been a breach of my oath of allegiance, and high treason.

In fulfilling my legal and moral duties, I believe that I have deserved punishment no more than have the tens of thousands of faithful German civil servants and officials in the public service who have already been detained in camps for over a year merely because they did their duty. I feel in duty and honour bound, as a former long-standing public minister, to remember them here in gratitude.

§

Hans Fritzsche, who had disseminated the administration's propaganda, viewed himself as just one more of the Nazis' countless victims.

Trial transcript, 31 August 1946: 'I believed in Hitler' – Fritzsche's final statement to the court

I should not like to waste the great opportunity for the final word in this Trial by enumerating details, all of which can be found in the transcripts and documents. I must turn to the sum total of all the crimes, since the Prosecution alleges that I was connected with all these crimes through a conspiracy.

To this charge I can only say that if I had spread the kind of propaganda in my radio talks of which the Prosecution now accuses me; if I had advocated the doctrine of the master race; if I had preached hatred against other nations; if I had incited people to wars of aggression, acts of violence, murder, and inhumanity; if I had done all that – then, Gentlemen of the Tribunal, the German nation would have turned from me and would have repudiated the system for which I spoke.

Even if I had done this only in disguised form, my listeners would have noticed it and repudiated it.

But the misfortune lies precisely in the fact that I did not advocate all these doctrines which were secretly guiding the actions of Hitler and a small circle which, in the light of the testimony of the witnesses Hoess, Reinecke, and Morgen, among others, is now slowly emerging from the mist in which it was hidden until now.

I believed in Hitler's assurances of a sincere desire for peace. Therefore I strengthened the trust of the German people in them.

I believed in the official German denials of all foreign reports of German atrocities. And with my belief I strengthened the belief of the German people in the uprightness of the German state leadership.

That is my guilt – no more, no less.

The prosecutors have expressed the horror of their nations at the atrocities which occurred. They did not expect any good from Hitler, and they are shattered by the extent of what really happened. But try for a moment to understand the indignation of those who expected good from Hitler and who then saw how their trust, their good will, and their idealism were misused. I find myself in the position of a man who has been deceived, together with many, many other Germans of whom the Prosecution says that they could have recognised all that happened from the smoke rising from the chimneys of the concentration camps, or from the mere sight of the prisoners, and so forth.

I feel that it is a great misfortune that the Prosecution has pictured these matters in such a way as if all of Germany had been a tremendous den of iniquity. It is a misfortune that the Prosecution is generalising the extent of the crimes which are in themselves horrible enough. As against this I must say that if anyone once believed in Hitler during the years of peaceful reconstruction, he only needed to be loyal, courageous, and self-sacrificing to go on believing in him until, by the discovery of carefully hidden secrets, he could recognise the devil in him. That is the only explanation for the struggle which Germany carried on for 68 months. Such a willingness to sacrifice does not grow from crime, but only from idealism and good faith, and from clever and apparently honest organisation.

I regret that the Prosecution has undertaken to generalise the crimes, because it is bound to add still more to the mountain of hatred which lies upon the world. But the time has come to interrupt the perpetual cycle of hatred which has dominated the world up to now. It is high time to call a halt to the alternate sowing and reaping of new harvests of hatred. The murder of five million people is an awful warning, and today humanity possesses the technical means for its own destruction. Therefore, in my judgment, the Prosecution should not replace one hatred by another . . .

It is perfectly possible, perhaps even understandable, that the storm of indignation which swept the world because of the atrocities which were committed should obliterate the borders of individual responsibility. If that happens, if collective responsibility is to be attached even to those who were misused in good faith, Your Honours, I beg you to hold me responsible. As my defence counsel has emphasised, I do not hide behind the millions who acted in good faith and were misused. I will place myself before those for whom my good faith was once an additional guarantee of the purity of purpose of the system. But this responsibility of mine only applies to those who acted in good faith, not for those who originated, assisted in, or knew of these atrocities, beginning with murder and ending with the selection of living human beings for anatomical collections.

Between these criminals and myself there is only one connection: they merely misused me in a different way than they misused those who became their physical victims.

It may be difficult to separate German crime from German idealism. It is not impossible. If this distinction is made, much suffering will be avoided for Germany and for the world.

September 1946: Waiting for judgment

At the start of September, the judges adjourned the court and began the process of agreeing the verdicts. Although the drafting of the judgment – an undertaking that Lawrence largely delegated to Birkett – was already well in hand, the deliberations as to individual guilt proved to be extremely disputatious, and lasted for a month. Hans Fritzsche and the other prisoners found that time began to pass agonisingly slowly.

Hans Fritzsche: 'We wanted to talk . . . '

For us the last few weeks of waiting in our prison cells dragged on unbearably. One day while we were having our usual walk in the courtyard we noticed a supply of timber being delivered at one of the gates and presently we heard the sound of carpenters at work. We were told that a new fence was being erected in the garden behind the prison.

We knew better. It was the gallows which was being put up in the gymnasium, together with a stand for spectators. By listening to the noise of the carpenters' tools we were able to follow the progress of the work.

During those last weeks the American officers did their best to grant us every reasonable wish and we were permitted to meet in groups of three or four; each of us being allowed to issue invitations on two separate occasions to whichever of his fellow-prisoners he chose. No limit was placed on the number of invitations we might accept from other prisoners.

At these meetings the four of us would sit round a table in a special cell put aside for the purpose with guards behind us. Cards and board games were offered us but we never used them; we wanted to talk, and we had in point of fact both good and useful conversations together. Even such outsiders as Streicher and Kaltenbrunner and lone wolves like Frick received their invitations; no one was left without a chance of enjoying at least for once the solace of such a reunion. When our hour was over a guard would shout 'Finished', and there would be the next group waiting at the door.

After long deliberation and laborious preparations the accused were allowed visits from their wives and children. It was not the Commandant who granted us this privilege, but a special order issued by the Tribunal. It was the first opportunity we had had to see our families since the beginning of the trial or, for many of us, since the surrender.

The families were informed by telegram when they were to appear and the respective occupation authorities were instructed to deal with the problems of passports and transportation; while living quarters for the visitors were provided at Nuremberg by the Tribunal. The Russians declared their readiness to join in these arrangements but failed to live up to their promise. Admiral Raeder hoped to see his wife who after being interned with him in Moscow was now living at Luckenwalde, near Berlin. Frau Raeder repeatedly received invitations to come to Nuremberg, and in desperate letters described her efforts to get permission from the local authorities. Finally the Tribunal itself took a hand in the matter and instructed the Inter-Allied Control Council to obtain the necessary permission for her. The Council (which of course included Soviet representatives) officially requested the Russian occupation authorities to grant Frau Raeder the promised facilities, which they readily agreed to do; but still she did not appear. After a time there ceased to be any news from her whatever and she was not heard of again for three years.

It then appeared that the Russians had put her into a concentration camp at precisely the time that they had promised to allow her to visit her husband.

Another prisoner's wife had no difficulty at all in finding her husband. Frau Streicher was able to attend regularly at the prescribed visiting hours, being simply escorted down from another floor of the same prison where she was being held as a witness.

It was heart-rending to see one's next of kin in such a situation, to have to speak to them through glass and wire-netting, and to be unable to help them in their struggle to maintain a bare existence. It was only now that many of us learned of the material plight of our families, who indeed still concealed the full extent of their hardship so as not to add unduly to the burden on the prisoners' minds. In point of fact some of them had to endure what amounted to downright persecution.

During the period they spent in Nuremberg the visiting families were looked after by the two American clergymen who saw to it that the grim atmosphere of the gaol was not too obtrusive. But all physical contact between prisoner and visitor was literally impossible, and the handing over of the most trifling gift, such as a cigarette, out of the question . . .

To describe adequately the emotional impact of these meetings on the prisoners would be impossible; some were hard put to it to maintain their composure and it was on a visiting day that, for the first time, I saw Goering's usual imperturbability forsake him.

On Saturday, 28th September, the visits came to an end, and on Sunday there was deep despondency in all the cells.

On Monday the adjournment was over.

30 September 1946: The verdicts

The trial reached its climax on 30 September. For almost a year, since the revelation of the names of those indicted, the world had watched events unfold, often in anger, sometimes in sheer disbelief. The horrors perpetrated by the Nazi state stood revealed. Now, finally, the arguments about the legitimacy of the proceedings were over, the judges had made up their minds, and the defendants were brought back into the dock. With the waiting world, they prepared to hear their fate, striving hard not to show their fear as all eyes watched them.

Taking it in turns to read the judgment, the Tribunal dealt early on with the argument that they were dispensing victors' justice. It was, they said, an expression of international law existing at the time, and which the Nazis knew they must be breaking when they carried out their invasions. Equally, the law needed to be flexible and to adapt to the needs of a changing world, and in so far as the administration of the trial had required new measures, that was also permissible.

The impression of harmony conveyed by the judgment was, in many places, the result of much compromise. The issue of significance that had most divided the eight judges was the Americans' cherished conspiracy charge, Count One. For the Frenchmen, Falco and Donnedieu de Vabres, to whom the concept of guilt without active participation was wholly novel, the indictment was both highly dubious in law and, since they did not believe there had been a masterplan, not proven in fact either.

Biddle's memoirs provide a unique insight into the judges' discussions, as they tried to find just solutions to many of the dilemmas posed by the botched indictment, the dubious selection of some of the defendants, and the respective political agendas of the members of the Tribunal, notably the Soviets. As Biddle revealed, soon he came to share the French point of view on the conspiracy charge drawn up by Washington, even though the other Anglo-American judges thought this an act of betrayal.

Francis Biddle: 'Reaching our decision on the charges'

The extent of these differences was clearest in our discussion over the counts charging conspiracy. From the beginning Donnedieu de Vabres argued with a good deal of force that these counts should be thrown out. Conspiracy, he said, was a crime unknown to international law. Aggressive war could be recognised as a crime though not specifically embedded in a statute; but you couldn't go much beyond that and create a new crime of conspiracy, not recognised by continental law. Conspiracy violated a fundamental principle of French law, that a crime must be precisely defined. Your English crimes, he continued, are more elastic, flowing from precedent and often clothed with no statute. To the French it was a shocking idea that under the wide range of the English law of conspiracy an individual could be punished. The substantive crime, they insisted, absorbs the conspiracy, which becomes useless once the substantive crime is committed, and we have no need to resort to a theory which involves psychological as well as moral difficulties. The Hitlerian crimes have roots deep in the people, so that we should not dim their sense of responsibility by shifting the blame to the secret plots of a small group. He moved to strike out Count One, the conspiracy charge – to which Falco added that conspiracy was hard to define and difficult to apply. It had neither time nor space. Were there many small conspiracies or one great one? Planning and preparation of a war of aggression were expressly defined as a crime by the Charter, as well as initiating and waging such a war. Was conspiracy to wage war really any different from planning it? Perhaps there was a kind of 'chameleon' conspiracy, the generals like Keitel taking on colour from Hitler, but surely not sitting down with him as fellow plotters, for they reflected his announced will. We should abandon our respective national ideas of criminal law and place ourselves squarely on the facts. This 'collective tendency' violates every rule of individual right. As for you others the choice was a matter of slight technical interest; but of enormous moral value to us.

Nikitchenko, who had become impatient with what he must have considered all this hairsplitting, and who was inclined to consider the French unrealistic theoreticians who wasted the time of men who had a job to do, said, rather tartly, that we were a practical group, not a discussion club. You cannot, he kept repeating, regard this abstractly. Fritzsche, for instance, could not be got if we abandoned the conspiracy count, for his acts in themselves, such as speaking over the radio, were not criminal; and Schacht – Schacht did not wage aggressive war, he joined with the others in conspiring to wage it. Why should we object to this particular innovation? We have allowed others. The Tribunal was not an institution to protect old law and shield old principles from violation. He argued for two hours . . .

But any real difficulty on which we had to focus was not so much any fundamental difference between Anglo-Saxon and continental law, as a determination of where to draw the line. Our law punished conspirators, the French, accomplices: but the result was largely the same. Yet Jackson's theory of conspiracy here involved, dating, as he argued, from the formation of the Nazi Party, and drawing into the net almost anyone who was a German, went too far from any reasonable point of view. The decision must rest on a basic sense of justice in determining the line that divided those who should be held accountable, and those who should not. I was therefore sympathetic to the view of the French, and said so. I would not at present vote any defendant's guilt on the conspiracy charge. I had learned to distrust conspiracy indictments, which in our country were used too often by the Government to catch anyone however remotely connected with the substantive crime. I had seen them resorted to, particularly when I was an Assistant US Attorney in Philadelphia, far too casually, and without any clear sense of responsibility. I remembered criticism of the abuses of the charge of conspiracy made by the Supreme Court. 'So many prosecutors,' said Judge Learned Hand in 1940, 'seek to sweep within the dragnet of conspiracy all those who have been associated in any degree whatever with the main offenders.'

Parker thought that the conspiracy had been proved 'beyond all peradventure' – he liked such old-fashioned phrases, which, when he used them, sounded like the crack of a long whip, tearing the other arguments to shreds. The British were upset by my stand – it was as if I had deserted them. The heart would be taken out, Birkett believed, if we rejected conspiracy. From the beginning the Nazis had planned and worked for war.

My tentative opposition had been somewhat dictated by a sense of the need for compromise, and finally a compromise was reached, and I was assigned the task of putting into words our rather vague agreement.

Despite the lip-service paid by the judges to prior authority and international agreements, all knew that they were operating in an unprecedented context and were making new law. To that end, they had to rely more on common sense than the judgment admitted. Thus, in the interests of reaching agreement the conspiracy count was vastly reduced in scope from its original overarching intention. The 'common plan' was largely ignored as being a charge in itself, and as regarded the other three counts was found relevant just to that to wage aggressive war, and then only from 1937, the date of the Hossbach memorandum. Nonetheless, the judges held that the defence were wrong to claim that a dictatorship was incompatible with the notion of a wider conspiracy. What mattered was not who had directed the plan, but who had gone along with it.

Evidence of the sharp divisions of opinion between the judges on many of the issues can be found in Biddle's candid account of the discussion about Doenitz, who had admitted to breaking international treaties on submarine warfare. He had justified it by the argument that modern conditions of warfare made it impossible to respect the law, proof of which was that the United States Navy had behaved in the same fashion. Biddle accepted this, but the other American judge, John Parker, did not.

Francis Biddle: Divided over Doenitz's guilt

When it came to our making the final judgment on the guilt of Doenitz, Parker and I were in sharp disagreement. There was little in the record, except the unrestricted submarine warfare, on which a finding of guilt could be predicated. Parker's position was that Doenitz had clearly violated the London Agreement; that merchantmen were merchantmen whether armed or not; conditions of modern warfare could not change a treaty. It was just as imperative to warn a merchantman that you were going to torpedo her, if she did not stop and surrender, in the forties as it was in the thirties, when the London Agreement was signed. He admitted that today it might mean the almost instant bombing of the submarine, in answer to a radio call by the merchantman for help. But the law was the law.

There was evidence of shooting down the survivors of one torpedoed merchantman, the *Peleus*, by a German submarine commander; and the prosecution tried hard to tie Doenitz into this but, in the opinion of all of us, without success. But I think it got under Parker's skin, this ruthless machine gunning of sailors clinging to the wreck of the torpedoed ship, adrift in the vast waste of the waters, and to him it was all part of this horrible business. We must not pass it up, or seem to condone it.

Parker hated evil. Sometimes I suspected that he did not believe in it. The atrocities, to his emotions at least, were incredible, even if his mind could accept them. I am sure that even now, after that long cruel page of history was spread out for all to read, based almost entirely on the records of the Germans themselves and on the evidence of German witnesses – I am certain that to many the whole business seems 'grossly exaggerated'.

I was convinced Parker was wrong, and told him so, from every angle and several times, as I wanted to persuade him before we went into conference with the others. I thought we would look like fools if we condemned Admiral Doenitz for doing, towards the end of the war, what Admiral Nimitz had begun when the United States entered it. Finally we agreed to refer the matter to Lawrence, who after having Major Phipps, one of his assistants, brief the point carefully, concluded that my position was sound.

Eventually I voted not guilty; but my three other colleagues thought that there was enough evidence of Doenitz's participation to warrant some punishment . . .

§

The judgment took two days to read, ranging as it did in time across 20 years from the rise of the Nazis through to their acts of war, encompassing both a summary of the evidence and the Tribunal's findings on the scope of the charges. Only on the second day did it begin to address the role of the individual defendants, and to state whether the counts against them had been proved. The moment had come for the accused, including Hans Fritzsche, to hear the court's verdicts.

Hans Fritzsche: Hearing the verdict

As we were taken to our places in the dock we could see that the hall was full to the last seat. Press, radio and newsreels were represented even more numerously than usual; but there was none of the usual bustle of conversation, and even before the Marshal of the Court made his customary plea for silence there was utter quiet.

First came the general summing up which was to precede the verdicts, and in which the entire course of the trial with the main points argued was reviewed. This summary made it fairly clear that on the whole the court had allowed the arguments of the Prosecution, and accepted the evidence of many documents to which the Defence had raised serious and well-founded objections. That night we returned to our prison cells in a very subdued mood. Next morning we were to learn our fate.

On Tuesday we found the court room strangely changed. While there was the same overcrowding and the same respectful silence, the bright lights which for over ten months had shone into every nook and corner of the hall were considerably dimmed. The Tribunal did not wish the prisoners to be photographed at the moment of listening to the verdict.

We were both surprised by such an unexpected show of tact and at the same time astonished by such a lack of reliance in our composure. As a matter of fact the gaps left by absent photographers were well filled by the radio reporters who were all over the place in their little glass cages, broadcasting in every conceivable language. These men carefully watched our every gesture and reported our expressions down to the flutter of an eyelid; which meant for us that we had each of us to, as it were, put on a mask, for we felt we must on no account betray the frightful excitement that had gripped us.

First came the verdict on the indicted organisations which certainly produced some surprise. The Reich Government, the SA, the General Staff, the Supreme Command of the Army and various other bodies were declared not to be criminal. Could that mean, we asked ourselves, that on at any rate some points, the court had after all disregarded the arguments of the Prosecution?

Then it was our turn. We were to remain together in the dock to hear the general judgment of the court as well as the verdict of Guilty or Not Guilty, on the four counts preferred against us; then the sentences would be passed separately, each man who had been found guilty standing alone to hear the nature of his punishment. The eight judges took turns in reading the judgment and verdict on each case.

There was dead silence in the overcrowded hall, as the words Guilty or Not Guilty were announced on count after count. Most of the defendants, as soon as they had heard what concerned them personally, took off their earphones so as not to be distracted while they pondered the meaning of the verdict, in which nothing had been said about the sentence to come.

In the midst of all the verdicts there came the total acquittal of Dr Schacht who accepted it nonchalantly, as is his due. When Papen heard the redeeming word his face flushed for a moment.

As far as my own case was concerned I had deliberately refrained from speculation. I had tried very hard to suppress all emotion, simply registering what was being said. In fact I suppressed my receptivity to such a degree that I even failed to notice when the staff of the court changed shifts and for once neglected my customary nod to one or the other of these long familiar faces.

Suddenly I felt I was being stared at by one of them and looking up I saw an electrician forming a word with his lips which could not be anything but 'Freispruch' (acquittal). I shook my head and shrugged my shoulders. The gesture was repeated and I became worried that it might be observed. I looked around and my glance rested on one of the leading prosecutors who evidently *had* observed the little incident, for he nodded his head as if he wished to confirm the message and moved his lips to form the same German word.

At precisely this moment I heard the court's verdict on my neighbour Neurath who was found guilty on all four counts. The old gentleman was very excited, and I feared he might suffer a stroke so that owing to this temporary preoccupation I heard little of Lord Lawrence's initial remarks about my own case. I only recovered my full capacity of attention when he reached the passage ' . . . not guilty in the meaning of the indictment and to be dismissed by the Marshal of the Court upon the adjournment . . . '

The interpreter who translated these words sat little more than a yard away from me, separated only by a pane of glass. He spoke so softly that I could not hear him except through earphones, yet his voice and the voice of the British judge seemed to me to sound like those trumpets which made the walls of Jericho crumble.

The judges' verdicts surprised nearly everyone in court. Few observers had expected anything but findings of guilt against all the accused, and at best heavy prison terms for those who were not to hang. Instead, von Papen and Schacht were acquitted, largely on the grounds that their involvement had occurred too long before the war itself. Fritzsche, meanwhile, had clearly been a very minor figure in the regime. The others were all found guilty, but not all of them on every charge. Hess, Speer and Sauckel, for instance, were each cleared of two of the four counts against them, von Schirach and Streicher were found innocent of one of two – Count One in both cases – while even Kaltenbrunner and Frick were also acquitted of conspiracy. Only Goering, Ribbentrop, Keitel, Rosenberg, Jodl and von Neurath were convicted on all four counts, while Raeder was found guilty of all three with which he had been charged.

There was one other surprise. The Soviet judges, acting under orders for Moscow, had demanded that there be no acquittals, and when they found themselves unable to persuade the rest of the Tribunal, filed a dissenting judgment. Nikitchenko, it is said, had to ask his fellow judges to help him write it, there being no precedent for a dissenting judgment in the Soviet courts.

Early October 1946: The sentences

One by one, those found guilty were brought back into court to receive their sentences. Goering, wearing a suit that had become increasingly loose during the course of the trials, had trouble with his headphones. When they were repaired he put them on to hear the sentence of death. Ribbentrop was white with fear, but dignified. Kaltenbrunner received his sentence with a small bow to the bench. But Hess slapped a guard as he tried to hand him his headphones, which he refused to wear. As the accused returned to their cells, Gilbert was on hand to assess their reactions to their fate.

Gustave Gilbert: 'Death – by hanging!'

While the convicted defendants were getting ready to be called to hear their individual sentences, I talked to the acquitted defendants, Schacht, von Papen, and Fritzsche, as they packed their belongings and moved to cells on the third tier.

Fritzsche was so unnerved and overcome, he seemed to lose his balance and almost fell over as though he were dizzy: 'I am entirely overwhelmed,' he whispered, ' to be set free right here, and not even be sent back to Russia. That was more than I had hoped for.' He was glad that the Tribunal had realised that unlike Streicher he had not incited hatred.

Von Papen was elated and quite obviously surprised. 'I had hoped for it, but did not really expect it.' Then, with a gesture of compassion for von Neurath, he took out of his pocket an orange he had saved from lunch, and asked me to give it to von Neurath. Fritzsche asked me to give his to von Schirach. Schacht ate his own orange.

Then the convicted defendants came down one by one after hearing their sentences. It was my duty to meet them as they returned to their cells. I asked each one what the sentence was.

Goering came down first and strode into his cell, his face pale and frozen, his eyes popping. 'Death!' he said as he dropped on the cot and reached for a book. His hands were trembling in spite of his attempt to be nonchalant. His eyes were moist and he was panting, fighting back an emotional breakdown. He asked me in an unsteady voice to leave him alone for a while.

Hess strutted in, laughing nervously, and said that he had not even been listening, so he did not know what the sentence was – and what was more, he didn't care. As the guard unlocked his handcuffs, he asked why he had been handcuffed and Goering had not. I said it was probably an oversight with the first prisoner. Hess laughed again and said mysteriously that he knew why. (A guard told me that Hess had been given a life sentence.)

Ribbentrop wandered in, aghast, and started to walk around the cell in a daze, whispering, 'Death! Death! Now I won't be able to write my beautiful memoirs. Tsk! Tsk! So much hatred! Tsk! Tsk!' Then he sat down, a completely broken man, and stared into space . . .

Keitel was already in his cell, his back to the door, when I entered. He wheeled around and snapped to attention at the far end of the cell, his fists clenched and arms rigid, horror in his eyes. 'Death – by hanging!' he announced, his voice hoarse with intense shame. 'That, at least, I thought I would be spared. I don't blame you for standing at a distance from a man sentenced to death by hanging. I understand that perfectly. But I am still the same as before. If you will please only – visit me sometimes in these last days.' I said I would.

Kaltenbrunner's clasped hands expressed the fear that did not show in his insensitive face. 'Death!' he whispered, and could say no more.

Frank smiled politely, but could not look at me. 'Death by hanging,' he said softly, nodding his head in acquiescence. 'I deserved it and I expected it, as I've always told you. I am glad that I have had the chance to defend myself and to think things over in the last few months.'

Rosenberg sneered agitatedly as he changed into his prison overalls. 'The rope! The rope! That's what you wanted, wasn't it?'

Streicher smiled a crooked smile. 'Death, of course. Just what I expected. You all must have known it all along.'

Funk watched the guard unlock his handcuffs in simpering bewilderment. Then he walked around the cell with bowed head, mumbling, as if he couldn't quite grasp it. 'Life imprisonment! What does that mean? They won't keep me in prison all my life, will they? They don't mean that, do they?' Then he grumbled that he was not surprised at Fritzsche's acquittal, but was surprised that they let Schacht and von Papen off – very surprised.

Doenitz didn't know quite how to take it. 'Ten years! Well – anyway, I cleared U-boat warfare. Your own Admiral Nimitz said – you heard it.' He said he was sure his colleague Admiral Nimitz understood him perfectly.

As Raeder came into the cell block, he asked the guard at the gate in a high-pitched voice, in a desperate attempt to be casual, whether they were going walking this afternoon. He limped to his cell, and, as I approached, signified that he did not want to talk. I did not enter his cell, but asked him through the portal what his sentence was. 'I don't know. I forget.' He said, waving me away. (A guard told me he had been given life imprisonment.)

Von Schirach's face was grave and tense as he marched to his cell, head high. 'Twenty,' he said, as the guard unlocked the handcuffs. I told him his wife would be relieved to know that he had not received the death penalty, which she had feared. 'Better a quick death than a slow one,' he answered. He asked what the other sentences were so far and seemed to agree that each one was about what he had expected.

Sauckel was perspiring and trembling all over when I entered his cell. 'I have been sentenced to death!' he sputtered. 'I don't consider the sentence fair. I have never been cruel myself. I always wanted the best for the workers. But I am a man – and I can take it.' Then he started to cry.

Jodl marched to his cell, rigid and upright, avoiding my glance. After he had been unhandcuffed and faced me in his cell, he hesitated a few seconds, as if he could not get the words out. His face was spotted red with vascular tension. 'Death – by hanging! That, at least, I did not deserve. The death part – all right, somebody has to stand for the responsibility. But that – .' His mouth quivered and his voice choked for the first time. 'That I did not deserve.'

Seyss-Inquart smiled, but the crack in his voice belied the casualness of his words. 'Death by hanging.' He smiled again and shrugged his shoulders. 'Well, in view of the whole situation, I never expected anything different. It's all right.' He asked if they would still get tobacco, then apologised for being so trivial at a time like this.

Speer laughed nervously. 'Twenty years. Well, that's fair enough. They couldn't have given me a lighter sentence, considering the facts, and I can't complain, I said the sentences must be severe, and I admitted my share of the guilt, so it would be ridiculous if I complained about the punishment. But I am glad that Fritzsche got off.'

Von Neurath stammered, 'Fifteen years.' He could hardly talk, but was touched by von Papen's orange.

Frick shrugged, callous to the end. 'Hanging. I didn't expect anything different.' He asked about the others and I told him there were eleven death sentences, including his own. 'So. Eleven death sentences. I figured fourteen. Well, I hope they get it over with fast.'

When Goering collected himself enough to talk, he said that he had naturally expected the death penalty, and was glad that he had not got a life sentence, because those who are sentenced to life imprisonment never become martyrs. But there wasn't any of the old confident bravado in his voice. Goering seems to realise, at last, that there is nothing funny about death, when you're the one who is going to die.

Goering, Ribbentrop, Keitel, Jodl, Rosenberg, Frick, Seyss-Inquart, Sauckel, Kaltenbrunner, Frank and Streicher, together with the absent Bormann, were all sentenced to hang. Raeder, Funk and Hess received life imprisonment, while Speer and von Schirach were given 20-year terms, and von Neurath and Doenitz 15 and 10 years respectively.

Many of the sentences were, to say the least, perplexing. No reasons were given, and thus no indication as to why Sauckel should be condemned to death, while Speer – whose demands had driven Sauckel's campaign to seize labour – should be spared. Presumably his refusal to carry out Hitler's scorched-earth policies and his apparent contrition had counted for much with the Tribunal. The death sentence given to Streicher was barely justified by any concrete harm he had caused, and can only have been based on the judges' personal revulsion of his character and a feeling that the Jews must be avenged. He was the defendant most obviously convicted of the new offence of a crime against humanity, his incitement to racial hatred.

Given what we know of Biddle's refusal to punish Doenitz over submarine warfare, the 10-year sentence given him for his notional application of the Commando Order seems rather as if the other judges had later tried to even the score. That Keitel and Jodl should hang is more comprehensible, given their part in distributing Hitler's reprisal orders, although Jodl was posthumously exonerated by a denazification court. Von Papen and Schacht, however, were not – their acquittals had astonished many in Germany – and though acquitted at Nuremberg they were later sentenced to eight years' hard labour in a German prison, though this was reduced on appeal. Fritzsche, too, served three years after being convicted at a denazification trial. He died soon after being released from gaol. Von Papen re-entered politics, without success, but the opportunistic Schacht did rebuild his career in finance, notably as an adviser to the Egyptian Government of Colonel Nasser.

Within a few days, the judges had left Nuremberg for the homes that some had not seen for more than a year. Biddle and Parker received the thanks of President Truman, then gradually eased into retirement. Lawrence was ennobled, much to the chagrin of Birkett, who had to wait another twelve years before receiving a peerage himself. Rudenko rose to become Chief Prosecutor of the Soviet Union, and later presented the case against Gary Powers, the downed U-2 pilot. His compatriots, however, seemed to vanish into thin air. Many of the other judges had become friends with Nikitchenko, but despite their sending letters and presents to Moscow in the months that followed, no reply ever came.

§

Some questioned what value the trial had, what effect it would have on the German people, whom opinion polls suggested had little trust in the objectivity of the process. Among those who tested the water was the American war correspondent Martha Gellhorn.

Martha Gellhorn: 'Hitler really was not so bad'

The night before the verdict we decided to escape the cracked rubble that is Nuremberg. We would drive out into the countryside, which is sweet and richly green, and find a village and a pub and a meal and some beer. In Ansbach a boy offered to guide us to a café. He was tall and blond, twenty years old, with charming manners and blue eyes and white teeth. We invited him to eat with us.

We have talked to many Germans since the early days of entering this country with the Army. I remember the very beginning when white sheets of surrender hung from every window and no one was a Nazi, and oddly enough vast numbers of Germans were half Jew and everyone had hidden a Communist, and all were agreed that Hitler was a monster.

Then, six months later, I remember that had changed and we heard how even during the worst period of the war they had butter and coal and clothes to wear and now (with an accusing look at us) there were none of those things. I remember my German driver eating a large white-bread sandwich and telling me bitterly that everyone was starving. But listening to this handsome boy in Ansbach was probably the most melancholy experience of all.

He had been a soldier since he was sixteen, in the Panzer grenadiers, which means that he was top-notch quality by German standards. He had been wounded three times, had fought against the English at Caen and on the Russian front. He said quite simply that Germany made war because England was ready to attack her. The Allied bombings, he said regretfully (for he did not wish to hurt our feelings), were not correct; they could not be forgotten: What did innocent women and children have to do with war?

'Then why do you suppose the German air force bombed Warsaw and London and Coventry first?' we asked. He was puzzled by this, but said there was probably a reason. He went on to remark that this talk about the concentration camps was exaggerated and propaganda; he had seen people returning from 'protective custody' to this very town and they were fat and sunburned.

There must have been some look in our eyes which stopped him, for he changed the subject by saying that it was wrong to kill the Jews, it was a mistake. On the other hand, said the boy, you could not help hating the Jews because they never did any real work. In his life he had only seen Jews changing money in a tricky way. Now the Jews were returning to this town, and German families had to give them back their houses and sit in the street; no one spoke to the Jews.

Life was very hard nowadays, and there was little to eat. Of course you could buy whatever you liked on the black market. The black market was run by foreigners and notably by all these Poles. The Poles, he said, got many extra pairs of shoes from UNRWA and sold them and so grew into rich black marketers.

The Hitler Jugend, he opined, had been a fine organisation; they were given trips and concerts; they were taught culture. In the worst year of the war in Germany, everyone had everything he needed, but look at them now.

'Didn't you get all the things, the food and the clothes and all the little niceties, from Poland and France, Belgium and Holland?' my colleague inquired.

'No,' said the boy proudly, 'from Germany.'

'Nuts!' said my colleague, who was beginning to feel sick.

At the end of the war, the boy continued, people hated Hitler because he had lost the war; but now they were beginning to see that Hitler really was not so bad, for things were much worse than when he had been running Germany. As for these trials, said the boy, Goering had been following ideals, he admitted it, he had been trying to do his best for Germany. The generals and admirals obeyed orders and should not be tried at all. But Funk, who had wept on the witness stand, was not a real German and whatever happened to him was all right. Anyhow, of course, the Allies would do whatever they liked at this trial since they had won the war.

When we left, the boy looked at us with hurt eyes, for he saw that he had not made a favourable impression though he had been so friendly and tried so hard to help us understand Germany.

I visited various responsible Germans, asking their opinion of the Nuremberg trial. There is no use in reporting those dreary interviews. One respectable businessman suggested that I consider Nuremberg, bombed flat, and Hiroshima, wiped out. Apparently, he said, what the victors do is all right; only the vanquished are bad. The upshot of those conversations was that since the Allies had won the war they could hold a trial if they liked, but why didn't they just shoot the defendants without endless talk? The German people were sick of all these trials.

It took forty-seven minutes on the afternoon of 1 October to deliver sentence on the twenty-one German leaders. After it was over, an empty, stunned feeling in the courtroom, the judges filed out, the room was quiet, the trial was over, justice had been done. Justice seemed very small suddenly. Of course it had to be, for there was no punishment great enough for such guilt.

§

In the last few days of his life, Joachim von Ribbentrop made some brief notes about the court and the death sentence it had passed on him. To the end, he felt that Germany, and its erstwhile rulers, had been unfairly victimised.

Von Ribbentrop's complaint

The Nuremberg trial carries neither legal nor political conviction, for the following reasons:

Only the victorious Powers were represented on the Court, which was interested in securing convictions. They were judges in their own cause, which conflicts with the very conception of law.

The convictions were based on a statute that had been enacted *ex post facto*; this violated another fundamental legal principle: no punishment without a law.

The alleged 'conspiracy' was clearly proved untrue at the trial, but even so there were convictions on this count.

Another thing was proved. Assuming Germany's action against Poland to have amounted to 'aggressive war', then the Soviet Union was an accomplice. Russia having been a co-aggressor, no Russian judge was qualified to pass judgment on an alleged crime of which his own state was guilty. History will therefore come to the conclusion that the court was improperly constituted. Quite apart from the question of 'aggressive war', the evidence at Nuremberg has revealed that the causes went back much farther, namely to Versailles.

The defence had no fair chance to defend German foreign policy. Our prepared application for the admission of evidence was not allowed. I was refused permission to describe the decisively important developments leading up to the war. Half of the 300 documents which the defence had prepared were not admitted, without good cause being shown. Witnesses and affidavits were only admitted after the prosecution had been heard; most of them were rejected. For instance, statements by some policeman or private individual who had served on a Government commission were admitted as official evidence, but correspondence between Hitler and Chamberlain, reports by ambassadors and diplomatic minutes, etc., were rejected. Only the prosecution, not the defence, had access to German and foreign archives. The prosecution only searched for incriminating documents and their use was biased; it knowingly concealed exonerating documents and withheld them from the defence. In cross-examination tricks and so called 'surprise documents' were used; there was no fair chance to give a considered reply.

The defendants are not responsible for the atrocities. Those who committed them, or were responsible for them, are dead. This applies, in particular, to the killing of the Jews, which, as was clearly proved at the trial, was kept absolutely secret and was not known to the defendants. Meanwhile, the other side, especially the East, has committed atrocities against Germans which are in no way less terrible than the killings of Jews. Judges who are citizens of states which committed or tolerated such atrocities – especially after the war, cannot be conceded the right to judge Germans.

Every German who is convicted as a result of political justice is an obstacle to the reconciliation which is so urgently needed between the German and Western nations. The Soviets will reap the benefit; for, not without reason, these trials are regarded as an American business.

15/16 October 1946: Retribution

The date of their execution was kept secret from the condemned men, but by the night of 15 October it had become common knowledge that the hangings were scheduled for the early hours of the next day. It was to be Burton Andrus's final duty at Nuremberg, but as he recalls here, he had not counted on the determination of Goering to take centre stage once more.

Burton Andrus: Goering's last triumph

It was 'lights out' in the row of condemned cells. Now only a pale glow illuminated the men lying in their beds. The guards watched through the cell-door peep-holes as the eleven lay wide awake or tossed and turned uneasily on their bunks. For the timing was no longer a secret; they knew for certain that the hangings would start after midnight.

Hermann Goering had been in earnest conversation with Chaplain Gerecke about the possibility of communion. However, because Goering had repeated his disbelief in the Scriptures and persisted in his rejection of Christ to the end, Gerecke had been forced to refuse him. Sadly Gerecke stood up, said good night to Goering and left the cell. Goering, with about an hour left before his cell-light was dimmed, sat at his table and began to write.

Finally he folded the paper and made his way across to his toilet in the corner. A few minutes later he ponderously returned to his bunk, climbed under the bedclothes but remained wide awake, his hands lying – conforming with the regulations – outside the blankets. He stared up at the whitewashed ceiling, thinking. The sentinel leaning against the door did not take his eyes from the peep-hole.

But Goering had already accomplished his last cunning act on earth. Sitting on the toilet with only his legs and feet visible from the peep-hole, enjoying the only privacy allowed in his waking or sleeping life, he had taken something either from the toilet pan or from his anus, and put it in his mouth. In Goering's cheek nestled a tiny glass bulb vial. The moment he bit the glass and the cyanide flowed into his mouth he would be dead.

It was 10.45 pm. His mouth held shut, making a narrow slit between his still flabby cheeks, Goering glanced over to the cell peep-hole, his eyes meeting those of the guard. Then, with a sudden clamp of his jaws, he bit hard on the glass. The potassium cyanide rushed into his mouth and flowed down his gulping throat. In a quick convulsion, which forced a gurgle from his throat, Goering's life had almost gone.

The guard saw the convulsion and heard the rattling gurgle. He yelled along the corridor to the other guards and at the same time unbolted the cell door, hurling it open. As other guards and an officer raced into the cell, his eyes stared up glassily to the ceiling. The Reichsmarshal was dead.

Chaplain Gerecke had been in the guard-room when a guard rushed in. 'Come on, Chaplain! Goering's having a fit!' I was with the Quadripartite Commission going over the last details of the executions which were scheduled for just under three hours' time. We ran along the corridor, Gerecke getting to Goering's bunk just before me. He leaned down and whispered scripture into the man's ear, but it could never have been heard. Goering was already turning green. The blankets had been dragged from him, exposing black silk pyjama trousers, his toes curling down towards the soles of his feet. They had always been misshapen from the use of over-tight boots. One arm, in a pale-coloured pyjama jacket with blue spots, hung down. His eyes were shut.

One of the guards – or Gerecke – handed me a single folded sheet of paper. 'It was on his bunk,' he said. I took it, gave orders for each prisoner to be told what had happened and doubled the watch on them. Then I took the paper, unread, along to the Commission office, where the suicide investigation would almost immediately begin. I did not even try to read that note because if I had, it could have led to 'prejudice'. As Goering was in my charge when he died, I would be the man held responsible for the happening.

I then gave orders for the doctors to assemble at the cell and to await the Quadripartite Commission, which was on its way. The Commission had given instruction, immediately they had heard of Goering's suicide, that all the rest awaiting execution should be handcuffed. Accordingly I had each man manacled to his guard, leaving the right hand free to eat the midnight supper which was about to be served.

Then I consulted a doctor and got his opinion as to the cause of death. The Commission authorised me to notify the eight official press witnesses, who had been locked up together in a room in the jail, of all the known facts of Goering's death. I was ordered to summon all the reporters from nearby Faber Castle as fast as transportation could bring them.

When we gave the news later to the other pressmen there was a panicky rush for telephones. At least one man had written a 'forward' story, describing Goering's hanging with the rest. The paper was caught before it went on the New York streets, but Goering's action must have cost them thousands of dollars. To all questions I could only reply: 'Goering is dead. He committed suicide by poisoning himself. The Quadripartite Commission is investigating. I have no further details.'

§

A small number of journalists had been selected by lot to witness the executions. Kingsbury Smith was their lone American representative at the last act of the drama.

Kingsbury Smith: Thirteen steps to the scaffold – a witness to the execution

Hermann Wilhelm Goering cheated the gallows of Allied justice by committing suicide in his prison cell shortly before the ten other condemned Nazi leaders were hanged in Nuremberg gaol. He swallowed cyanide he had concealed in a copper cartridge shell, while lying on a cot in his cell.

The one-time Number Two man in the Nazi hierarchy was dead two hours before he was scheduled to have been dropped through the trapdoor of a gallows erected in a small, brightly lighted gymnasium in the gaol yard, thirty-five yards from the cell block where he spent his last days of ignominy.

Joachim von Ribbentrop, foreign minister in the ill-starred regime of Adolf Hitler, took Goering's place as first to the scaffold.

Last to depart this life in a total span of just about two hours was Arthur Seyss-Inquart, former Gauleiter of Holland and Austria.

In between these two once-powerful leaders, the gallows claimed, in the order named, Field Marshal Wilhelm Keitel; Ernst Kaltenbrunner, once head of the Nazis' security police; Alfred Rosenberg, arch-priest of Nazi culture in foreign lands; Hans Frank, Gauleiter of Poland; Wilhelm Frick, Nazi minister of the interior; Fritz Sauckel, boss of slave labour, Colonel General Alfred Jodl; and Julius Streicher, who bossed the anti-Semitism drive of the Hitler Reich.

As they went to the gallows, most of the ten endeavoured to show bravery. Some were defiant and some were resigned and some begged the Almighty for mercy.

All except Rosenberg made brief, last-minute statements on the scaffold. But the only one to make any reference to Hitler or the Nazi ideology in his final moments was Julius Streicher.

Three black-painted wooden scaffolds stood inside the gymnasium, a room approximately thirty-three feet wide by eighty feet long with plaster walls in which cracks showed. The gymnasium had been used only three days before by the American security guards for a basketball game. Two gallows were used alternately. The third was a spare for use if needed. The men were hanged one at a time, but to get the executions over with quickly, the military police would bring in a man while the prisoner who preceded him still was dangling at the end of the rope.

The ten once great men in Hitler's Reich that was to have lasted for a thousand years walked up thirteen wooden steps to a platform eight feet high which also was eight feet square.

Ropes were suspended from a crossbeam supported on two posts. A new one was used for each man.

When the trap was sprung, the victim dropped from sight in the interior of the scaffolding. The bottom of it was boarded up with wood on three sides and shielded by a dark canvas curtain on the fourth, so that no one saw the death struggles of the men dangling with broken necks.

Von Ribbentrop entered the execution chamber at 1.11 a.m. Nuremberg time. He was stopped immediately inside the door by two Army sergeants who closed in on each side of him and held his arms, while another sergeant who had followed him in removed manacles from his hands and replaced them with a leather strap.

It was planned originally to permit the condemned men to walk from their cells to the execution chamber with their hands free, but all were manacled immediately following Goering's suicide.

Von Ribbentrop was able to maintain his apparent stoicism to the last. He walked steadily toward the scaffold between his two guards, but he did not answer at first when an officer standing at the foot of the gallows went through the formality of asking his name. When the query was repeated he almost shouted, 'Joachim von Ribbentrop!' and then mounted the steps without any sign of hesitation.

When he was turned around on the platform to face the witnesses, he seemed to clench his teeth and raise his head with the old arrogance. When asked whether he had any final message he said, 'God protect Germany,' in German, and then added, 'May I say something else?'

The interpreter nodded and the former diplomatic wizard of Nazidom spoke his last words in loud, firm tones: 'My last wish is that Germany realise its entity and that an understanding be reached between the East and the West. I wish peace to the world.'

As the black hood was placed in position on his head, von Ribbentrop looked straight ahead.

Then the hangman adjusted the rope, pulled the lever, and von Ribbentrop slipped away to his fate.

Field Marshal Keitel, who was immediately behind von Ribbentrop in the order of executions, was the first military leader to be executed under the new concept of international law – the principle that professional soldiers cannot escape punishment for waging aggressive wars and permitting crimes against humanity with the claim they were dutifully carrying out orders of superiors.

Keitel entered the chamber two minutes after the trap had dropped beneath von Ribbentrop, while the latter still was at the end of his rope. But von Ribbentrop's body was concealed inside the first scaffold; all that could be seen was the taut rope.

Keitel did not appear as tense as von Ribbentrop. He held his head high while his hands were being tied and walked erect toward the gallows with a military bearing. When asked his name he responded loudly and mounted the gallows as he might have mounted a reviewing stand to take a salute from German armies.

He certainly did not appear to need the help of guards who walked alongside, holding his arms. When he turned around atop the platform he looked over the crowd with the iron-jawed haughtiness of a proud Prussian officer. His last words, uttered in a full, clear voice, were translated as 'I call on God Almighty to have mercy on the German people. More than 2 million German soldiers went to their death for the fatherland before me. I follow now my sons – all for Germany.'

After his black-booted, uniformed body plunged through the trap, witnesses agreed Keitel had showed more courage on the scaffold than in the courtroom, where he had tried to shift his guilt upon the ghost of Hitler, claiming that all was the Fuehrer's fault and that he merely carried out orders and had no responsibility.

With both von Ribbentrop and Keitel hanging at the end of their ropes there was a pause in the proceedings. The American colonel directing the executions asked the American general representing the United States on the Allied Control Commission if those present could smoke. An affirmative answer brought cigarettes into the hands of almost every one of the thirty-odd persons present. Officers and GIs walked around nervously or spoke a few words to one another in hushed voices while Allied correspondents scribbled furiously their notes on this historic though ghastly event.

In a few minutes an American Army doctor accompanied by a Russian Army doctor and both carrying stethoscopes walked to the first scaffold, lifted the curtain and disappeared within.

They emerged at 1.30 a.m. and spoke to an American colonel. The colonel swung around and facing official witnesses snapped to attention to say, 'The man is dead.'

Two GIs quickly appeared with a stretcher which was carried up and lifted into the interior of the scaffold. The hangman mounted the gallows steps, took a large commando-type knife out of a sheath strapped to his side and cut the rope.

Von Ribbentrop's limp body with the black hood still over his head was removed to the far end of the room and placed behind a black canvas curtain. This all had taken less than ten minutes.

The directing colonel turned to the witnesses and said, 'Cigarettes out, please, gentlemen.' Another colonel went out the door and over to the condemned block to fetch the next man. This was Ernst Kaltenbrunner. He entered the execution chamber at 1.36 a.m., wearing a sweater beneath his blue double-breasted coat.

With his lean haggard face furrowed by old duelling scars [in fact, the result of a car accident], this terrible successor to Reinhard Heydrich had a frightening look as he glanced around the room.

He wet his lips apparently in nervousness as he turned to mount the gallows, but he walked steadily. He answered his name in a calm, low voice. When he turned around on the gallows platform he first faced a United States Army Roman Catholic chaplain wearing a Franciscan habit. When Kaltenbrunner was invited to make a last statement, he said, 'I have loved my German people and my fatherland with a warm heart. I have done my duty by the laws of my people and I am sorry my people were led this time by men who were not soldiers and that crimes were committed of which I had no knowledge.'

This was the man, one of whose agents – a man named Rudolf Hoess – confessed at a trial that under Kaltenbrunner's orders he gassed 3 million human beings at the Auschwitz concentration camp!

As the black hood was raised over his head Kaltenbrunner, still speaking in a low voice, used a German phrase which translated means, 'Germany, good luck.'

His trap was sprung at 1.39 a.m.

Field Marshal Keitel was pronounced dead at 1.44 a.m. and three minutes later guards had removed his body. The scaffold was made ready for Alfred Rosenberg.

Rosenberg was dull and sunken-checked as he looked around the court. His complexion was pasty-brown, but he did not appear nervous and walked with a steady step to and up the gallows.

Apart from giving his name and replying 'no' to a question as to whether he had anything to say, he did not utter a word. Despite his avowed atheism he was accompanied by a Protestant chaplain who followed him to the gallows and stood beside him praying.

Rosenberg looked at the chaplain once, expressionless. Ninety seconds after he was swinging from the end of a hangman's rope. His was the swiftest execution of the ten.

There was a brief lull in the proceedings until Kaltenbrunner was pronounced dead at 1.52 a.m.

Hans Frank was next in the parade of death. He was the only one of the condemned to enter the chamber with a smile on his countenance.

Although nervous and swallowing frequently, this man, who was converted to Roman Catholicism after his arrest, gave the appearance of being relieved at the prospect of atoning for his evil deeds.

He answered to his name quietly and when asked for any last statement, he replied in a low voice that was almost a whisper, 'I am thankful for the kind treatment during my captivity and I ask God to accept me with mercy.'

Frank closed his eyes and swallowed as the black hood went over his head.

The sixth man to leave his prison cell and walk with handcuffed wrists to the death house was sixty-nine-year-old Wilhelm Frick. He entered the execution chamber at 2.05 a.m., six minutes after Rosenberg had been pronounced dead. He seemed the least steady of any so far and stumbled on the thirteenth step of the gallows. His only words were, 'Long live eternal Germany,' before he was hooded and dropped through the trap.

Julius Streicher made his melodramatic appearance at 2.12 a.m.

While his manacles were being removed and his hands bound, this ugly, dwarfish little man, wearing a threadbare suit and a well-worn bluish shirt buttoned to the neck but without a tie (he was notorious during his days of power for his flashy dress), glanced at the three wooden scaffolds rising up menacingly in front of him. Then he glared around the room, his eyes resting momentarily upon the small group of witnesses. By this time, his hands were tied securely behind his back. Two guards, one on each arm, directed him to Number One gallows on the left of the entrance. He walked steadily the six feet to the first wooden step but his face was twitching.

As the guards stopped him at the bottom of the steps for identification formality he uttered his piercing scream: 'Heil Hitler!'

The shriek sent a shiver down my back.

As its echo died away an American colonel standing by the steps said sharply, 'Ask the man his name.' In response to the interpreter's query Streicher shouted, 'You know my name well.'

The interpreter repeated his request and the condemned man yelled, 'Julius Streicher.'

As he reached the platform, Streicher cried out, 'Now it goes to God.' He was pushed the last two steps to the mortal spot beneath the hangman's rope. The rope was being held back against a wooden rail by the hangman.

Streicher was swung around to face the witnesses and glared at them. Suddenly he screamed, *'Purim Fest 1946.'* (Purim is a Jewish holiday celebrated in the spring, commemorating the execution of Haman, ancient persecutor of the Jews described in the Old Testament.)

The American officer standing at the scaffold said, 'Ask the man if he has any last words.'

When the interpreter had translated, Streicher shouted, 'The Bolsheviks will hang you one day.'

When the black hood was raised over his head, Streicher said, 'I am with God.'

As it was being adjusted, Streicher's muffled voice could be heard to say, 'Adele, my dear wife.'

At that instant the trap opened with a loud bang. He went down kicking. When the rope snapped taut with the body swinging wildly, groans could be heard from within the concealed interior of the scaffold. Finally, the hangman, who had descended from the gallows platform, lifted the black canvas curtain and went inside. Something happened that put a stop to the groans and brought the rope to a standstill. After it was over I was not in a mood to ask what he did, but I assume that he grabbed the swinging body and pulled down on it. We were all of the opinion that Streicher had strangled.

Then, following removal of the corpse of Frick, who had been pronounced dead at 2.20 a.m., Fritz Sauckel was brought face to with his doom.

Wearing a sweater with no coat and looking wild-eyed, Sauckel proved to be the most defiant of any except Streicher.

Here was the man who put millions into bondage on a scale unknown since the pre-Christian era. Gazing around the room from the gallows platform he suddenly screamed, 'I am dying innocent. The sentence is wrong. God protect Germany and make Germany great again. Long live Germany! God protect my family.'

The trap was sprung at 2.26 a.m. and, as in the case of Streicher, there was a loud groan from the gallows pit as the noose snapped tightly under the weight of his body.

Ninth in the procession of death was Alfred Jodl. With the black coat-collar of his Wehrmacht uniform half turned up at the back as though hurriedly put on, Jodl entered the dismal death house with obvious signs of nervousness. He wet his lips constantly and his features were drawn and haggard as he walked, not nearly so steady as Keitel, up the gallows steps. Yet his voice was calm when he uttered his last six words on earth: 'My greetings to you, my Germany.'

At 2.34 a.m. Jodl plunged into the black hole of the scaffold. He and Sauckel hung together until the latter was pronounced dead six minutes later and removed.

The Czechoslovak-born Seyss-Inquart, whom Hitler had made ruler of Holland and Austria, was the last actor to make his appearance in this unparalleled scene. He entered the chamber at 2.38½ a.m., wearing glasses which made his face an easily remembered caricature.

He looked around with noticeable signs of unsteadiness as he limped on his left clubfoot to the gallows. He mounted the steps slowly, with guards helping him.

When he spoke his last words his voice was low but intense. He said, 'I hope that this execution is the last act of the tragedy of the Second World War and that the lesson taken from this world war will be that peace and understanding should exist between peoples. I believe in Germany.'

He dropped to death at 2.45 a.m.

With the bodies of Jodl and Seyss-Inquart still hanging, awaiting formal pronouncement of death, the gymnasium doors opened again and guards entered carrying Goering's body on a stretcher.

He had succeeded in wrecking plans of the Allied Control Council to have him lead the parade of condemned Nazi chieftains to their death. But the council's representatives were determined that Goering at least would take his place as a dead man beneath the shadow of the scaffold.

The guards carrying the stretcher set it down between the first and second gallows. Goering's big bare feet stuck out from under the bottom end of a khaki-coloured United States Army blanket. One blue-silk-clad arm was hanging over the side.

The colonel in charge of the proceedings ordered the blanket removed so that witnesses and Allied correspondents could see for themselves that Goering was definitely dead. The Army did not want any legend to develop that Goering had managed to escape.

As the blanket came off it revealed Goering clad in black silk pyjamas with a blue jacket shirt over them, and this was soaking wet, apparently the result of efforts by prison doctors to revive him.

The face of this twentieth-century freebooting political racketeer was still contorted with the pain of his last agonising moments and his final gesture of defiance.

They covered him up quickly and this Nazi warlord, who like a character out of the days of the Borgias, had wallowed in blood and beauty, passed behind a canvas curtain into the black pages of history.

The corpses were photographed to scotch future rumours that any of them still lived, and the bodies were then cremated (though not, as legend later had it, at Dachau). Their ashes were scattered in a river.

§

The seven defendants who had been condemned to imprisonment – Raeder, Funk, von Neurath, von Schirach, Doenitz, Speer and Hess – passed their terms as the sole inmates of Spandau Prison, Berlin. One by one they were released – some early as their health declined – except for Hess, who because of Soviet opposition to his being freed was destined to spend the remainder of his life in jail. He was found dead there in 1987, having committed suicide at the age of 92.

Albert Speer was freed in 1966, and died in London in 1981. While in Spandau, he wrote his memoirs in an attempt to come to terms with his haunted past.

Albert Speer: An attempt at understanding

Today, a quarter of a century after these events, it is not only specific faults that burden my conscience, great as these may have been. My moral failure is not a matter of this item and that; it resides in my active association with the whole course of events. I had participated in a war which, as we of the intimate circle should never have doubted, was aimed at world dominion. What is more, by my abilities and my energies I had prolonged that war by many months. I had assented to having the globe of the world crown that domed hall which was to be the symbol of the new Berlin. Nor was it only symbolically that Hitler dreamed of possessing the globe. It was part of his dream to subjugate the other nations. France, I had heard him say many times, was to be reduced to the status of a small nation. Belgium, Holland, even Burgundy, were to be incorporated into his Reich. The national life of the Poles and the Soviet Russians was to be extinguished; they were to be made into helot peoples. Nor, for one who wanted to listen, had Hitler ever concealed his intention to exterminate the Jewish people. In his speech of January 30, 1939, he openly stated as much. Although I never actually agreed with Hitler on these questions, I had nevertheless designed the buildings and produced the weapons which served his ends.

During the next twenty years of my life I was guarded, in Spandau prison, by nationals of the four powers against whom I had organised Hitler's war. Along with my fellow six prisoners, they were the only people I had close contact with. Many of them mourned loved ones who had died in the war – in particular, every one of the Soviet guards had lost some close relative, brothers or a father. Yet not one of them bore a grudge toward me for my personal share in the tragedy; never did I hear words of recrimination. At the lowest ebb of my existence, in contact with these ordinary people, I encountered uncorrupted feelings of sympathy, helpfulness, human understanding, feelings that bypassed the prison rules . . . On the day before my appointment as Minister of Armaments and War Production I had encountered peasants in the Ukraine who had saved me from frostbite. At the time I had been merely touched, without understanding. Now, after all was over, I once again was treated to examples of human kindness that transcended all enmity. And now, at last, I wanted to understand. This book, too, is an attempt at such understanding.

Summaries

The charges

Count One – The Common Plan or Conspiracy: Participation as a leader, organiser or accomplice in the joint plot to commit the other three counts.
Count Two – Crimes against Peace: Planning or waging a war of aggression.
Count Three – War Crimes: Violation of the laws and customs of war, including ill-treatment of civilians in occupied territory, murder of prisoners of war, and the killing of hostages.
Count Four – Crimes against Humanity: Murder, extermination, enslavement and persecution on political or racial grounds of any civilian population, before or during the war.

The defendants, their individual charges, summary of the judgments, the verdicts and sentences

Hermann Goering (b. 1893): The most prominent Nazi after Hitler, and his designated successor from 1939 until 1945. Head of the Luftwaffe, and economic supremo in the late 1930s.
Counts One and Two: Goering was charged by Hitler with expanding Germany's armed might. He was present at the Hossbach conference, was the ringleader of the Anschluss, threatened to bomb Prague so as to effect the annexation of the Sudetenland, and led the Luftwaffe in the attack on

Poland and the aggressive wars that followed. His objection to the invasion of the USSR was merely for strategic rather than moral reasons. He was second only to Hitler as the moving force for war.

Counts Three and Four: As the Plenipotentiary for the Four Year Plan, Goering issued directives forcing prisoners of war to work in the armament industry, and directed the spoliation of conquered territory. He persecuted the Jews, principally to confiscate their property and to curtail their economic activities. His own admissions are enough to condemn him.

Verdict: Guilty on all four counts.

Sentence: Death.

Rudolf Hess (b. 1894): Until his flight to Britain in 1941, Hess was Deputy Leader of the Nazi Party.

Counts One and Two: As Hitler's Deputy and Reichminister without Portfolio, overseeing all legislation, Hess was active in the preparation for war. He urged the German people to make sacrifices to pay for rearmament, using the phrase 'Guns instead of butter'. He was in touch with the Nazi Party in Austria, then banned, during the period leading up to the Anschluss, and signed a decree absorbing the Czech Sudetenland, and later parts of Poland, into the Reich. He publicly defended Germany's aggression, and blamed England for provoking the invasion of Poland.

Counts Three and Four: There is evidence to suggest that Hess knew of war crimes in the East, and that he proposed discriminatory laws against the Jews and Poles, but the evidence is insufficient for a finding of guilt. Though exhibiting signs of mental abnormality, Hess is capable of defending himself and was sane at the time of the acts now charged against him.

Verdict: Guilty on Counts One and Two.

Sentence: Life imprisonment.

Joachim von Ribbentrop (b. 1893): Germany's Foreign Minister, 1938–45.

Counts One and Two: Von Ribbentrop had been aware of Hitler's threats against Austria and told the British Government that Germany had not presented Austria with an ultimatum. He participated in the aggressive plans against Czechoslovakia, and had sought Italian support for a European war in the event that one was caused by the invasion of Poland. He misled the British as to the Germans' intent with regard to Poland immediately before the attack.

Ribbentrop had also known of the plans to invade Norway, Denmark, the Low Countries, Greece, Yugoslavia and Russia.

Counts Three and Four: The German officials in control of Denmark and Vichy France were ultimately responsible to von Ribbentrop, who also urged the Italians to be ruthless in their governance of Yugoslavia and Italy. He ordered German representatives in Axis satellite countries such as Hungary to hasten the deportation of the Jews. He took part in meetings at which it was agreed that captured Allied airmen should be lynched and that a captive French general should be murdered. Given his knowledge of the plans for war, von Ribbentrop's defence that he believed Hitler wanted peace does not ring true. Instead, he shared Hitler's aims and ideology.

Verdict: Guilty on all four counts.

Sentence: Death.

Wilhelm Keitel (b. 1882): Chief of Staff of the High Command of the Armed Forces, the Oberkommando der Wehrmacht (OKW).

Counts One and Two: Keitel put military pressure on Austria before the Anschluss, and initialled Hitler's plans to invade Czechoslovakia. He took part in the preparation for the other invasions that followed and signed orders for the attacks. He opposed that against the Soviet Union for military reasons, and as a breach of the pact with the Soviets, but nonetheless countersigned the plans for Barbarossa.

Counts Three and Four: Keitel affirmed the Commando Order issued by Hitler even though he thought it illegal. He complied with the ruthless treatment of Soviet POWs and with the liquidation of the Polish intelligentsia. He gave orders for reprisals against civilians, and allowed their arrest and execution without trial. He testified that he had protested to Hitler about many of these issues, but had ultimately obeyed the orders as the commands of his superior. This cannot mitigate such shocking crimes.

Verdict: Guilty on all four counts.

Sentence: Death.

Ernst Kaltenbrunner (b. 1903): From 1943, Chief of the Reich Main Security Office (RSHA), which controlled the Gestapo, the SD – the SS's security agency – the civil police and later the Abwehr (military intelligence), as well as the administration of the concentration camps.

Count One: As head of the SS in Austria, Kaltenbrunner intrigued against the Government, and his men entered the Chancellery building to pressurise the Austrian President while Seyss-Inquart was putting the final touches to the preparations for the Anschluss. But the Charter does not define that annexation as a war, and there is no evidence to suggest that Kaltenbrunner took part in plans to wage such wars.

Counts Three and Four: Kaltenbrunner led the RSHA when it was engaged in a widespread programme of war crimes and crimes against humanity. He knew of the conditions in the concentration camps and his office transmitted orders for executions there that originated from Himmler. The organisations over which he presided murdered prisoners of war, captured commandos, Jews, Soviet Commissars and civilians in occupied territories. They practised torture and recruited slave labour. A section of the RSHA supervised the Final Solution. Kaltenbrunner was aware of the crimes being committed by the RSHA and took part in many of them.

Verdict: Guilty on Counts Three and Four.

Sentence: Death.

Alfred Rosenberg (b. 1893): The Nazi Party's philosopher, arguing that it was the destiny of the German nation to dominate Europe and that the Jews were a lesser race, and Minister for the Occupied Eastern Territories from 1941.

Counts One and Two: Rosenberg, who had charge of the Nazis' relations with like-minded organisations outside Germany, was one of the originators of the plan to invade Norway, an idea prompted by his contacts with Quisling. He helped to formulate the policies by which the Occupied Eastern Territories were administered.

Counts Three and Four: Rosenberg was responsible for the system of organised plunder of other nations' cultural treasures. From 1941, he was the supreme authority for the Eastern Territories and knew of the brutal treatment to which they were subjected. His subordinates were engaged in the mass killing of Jews, and he himself proposed that when hostages were to be shot Jews should be used. He also approved of the shipment of labour, including young boys, to the Reich.

Verdict: Guilty on all four counts.

Sentence: Death.

Hans Frank (b. 1900): Minister of Justice from 1933, and Governor-General of Poland, 1939–44.

Count One: The evidence offered does not show that Frank was connected with the plan to wage war.

Counts Three and Four: As Governor of Occupied Poland, Frank administered a policy intended to destroy that country as a nation. There was widespread killing of those likely to resist German domination. The economic demands made were out of all proportion to the country's resources. Millions of native Jews were exterminated. It may be true that Frank was not the originator of all the crimes committed by his Government, but he was a knowing participant in the terror it practised.

Verdict: Guilty on Counts Three and Four.

Verdict: Death.

Wilhelm Frick (b. 1877): Minister of the Interior, 1933–43, then Protector of Bohemia and Moravia.

Counts One and Two: Frick was largely responsible for the internal suppression of opposition to the Nazis within Germany, as well as the repression of the Church, trade unions and Jews. He was only concerned with domestic administration before the Anschluss, and was therefore not involved in the common plan, but he did sign legislation incorporating Austria and parts of Poland into the Reich. He was also involved in the administration of Bohemia and Moravia (the Czechs), Holland, Norway and other territories through his officials.

Counts Three and Four: Frick's work formed the basis of the Nuremberg Laws designed to eliminate the Jews from many aspects of German life. They paved the way for the Final Solution. He forced Germanisation on parts of Austria and Poland. He supervised the euthanasia programme against the sick and aged. As Reich Protector of Bohemia and Moravia after 1943, he had restricted personal authority but bears general responsibility for the acts of terrorism carried out there, based on policies of which he had full knowledge.

Verdict: Guilty on Counts Two, Three and Four.

Sentence: Death.

Julius Streicher (b. 1885): Editor of the anti-Semitic weekly *Der Stuermer* and focus of the anti-Jewish movement in the 1930s.

Count One: Streicher was never within Hitler's inner circle and there is no evidence he was involved in the common plan to wage war.

Count Four: Streicher was known as 'Jew-baiter Number One', and preached hatred against the Jews for 25 years. Week after week, he infected the German mind with anti-Semitism and incited the German people to persecution. From 1938, he was calling for the annihilation of the Jewish race, intensifying his exhortations during the war even though he knew of mass murders of Jews. His incitement to extermination constitutes a crime against humanity.

Verdict: Guilty on Count Four.

Sentence: Death.

Walther Funk (b. 1890): Minister of Economics, 1937–45.

Counts One and Two: Funk was not a leading figure in the plans for war before 1939, and his activity in the economic sphere was supervised by Goering. He did, however, participate in the economic preparation of some wars, notably the invasions of Poland and the Soviet Union.

Counts Three and Four: Funk had participated in discrimination against the Jews while at the Ministry of Propaganda and had made a speech defending the Kristallnacht riots. In 1942, he agreed to receive gold and jewels from the SS at the Reichsbank, and either knew or closed his eyes to the fact that this was the property of those murdered in the camps. He seized the reserves of the Czech and Yugoslav central banks, and knew of the programmes of forced labour. He was, however, never a dominant figure in his spheres of activity, which is a mitigating fact.

Verdict: Guilty on Counts Two, Three and Four.

Sentence: Life imprisonment.

Hjalmar Schacht (b. 1877): Minister of Economics, 1934–7.

Counts One and Two: Schacht was an active supporter of the Nazis and played an important role in the rearmament programme from 1933, using the Reichsbank's facilities. As Minister of Economics he organised the German economy for war, utilising such measures as stockpiling and exchange control. By 1937, however, he had been supplanted by Goering, who advocated an expansion of the munitions programme that Schacht regarded as unviable in economic terms. Rearmament is not criminal under the Charter, nor was Schacht part of the inner circle that planned the invasions. The prosecution implies that, with his knowledge of Germany's finances, Schacht ought to have understood the significance of Hitler's frantic rearmament, but that necessary inference has not been established beyond a reasonable doubt.

Verdict: Acquitted.

Karl Doenitz (b. 1891): Commander of Germany's U-boat fleet, 1935–43, then Commander-in-Chief of the Navy. President of the Reich, May 1945, as Hitler's successor.

Counts One and Two: Although Doenitz built and trained the U-boat arm, at that stage he was just a line officer who did not participate in the conspiracy to wage war. He did, however, later wage aggressive war, leading the principal arm of the German fleet and taking sole charge of its strategy. Although by April 1945 he knew that the war was lost, he urged the Navy to fight on, and ordered the Wehrmacht to continue the war in the East for a week after he became head of state in May. This, he said, was so as to allow the civilian population to be evacuated.

Count Three: Doenitz was accused of ordering his submarines to practise unrestricted warfare against merchant shipping, including neutral ships, contrary to the international Naval Protocol of 1936. He argued that, contrary to treaty, British merchant ships had been armed by the Admiralty, were giving information by wireless and had been ordered to ram submarines. In the circumstances, Doenitz's conduct against British shipping was not a violation of the law, but the sinking of neutral ships was.

The Tribunal is also of the opinion that it has not been shown that Doenitz ordered the deliberate killing of shipwrecked survivors, but that he did breach the Protocol by ordering them not to be rescued, notwithstanding the dangers that might pose to submarines. That said, given how naval warfare was conducted by the British and US navies, the sentence on Doenitz is not assessed on the grounds of his breaches of the law on submarine warfare. Doenitz knew of the Commando Order and permitted it to remain in force when he became Commander-in-Chief of the Navy. He also advised Hitler that if the Geneva Convention were to be renounced it should be done without warning.

Verdict: Guilty on Counts Two and Three.

Sentence: Ten years' imprisonment.

Erich Raeder (b. 1876): Commander-in-Chief of the Navy, 1935–43.

Counts One and Two: Raeder rebuilt the German Navy and accepts that he violated the Versailles Treaty by so doing. He was present at the Hossbach conference, though claims the speech was a device by Hitler to spur the Army to rearm faster. The idea of invading Norway was first his, although he maintains this was to forestall the British. He received directives about other invasions, although he was opposed to that against Russia, favouring a Mediterranean policy and the defeat of Britain as priorities.

Count Three: Like Doenitz, Raeder is charged with carrying out unrestricted submarine warfare contrary to the London Protocol of 1936. The Tribunal makes the same finding with respect to him as it does for Doenitz. Raeder knew of and passed on the Commando Order, leading to the shooting of two British commandos by the Navy in 1942.

Verdict: Guilty on all three counts.

Sentence: Life imprisonment.

Baldur von Schirach (b. 1907): Head of the Hitler Youth, 1933–40.

Count One: Using physical violence, von Schirach took over all groups that competed with the Hitler Youth. He used the organisation for pre-military training, subjecting its members to an intensive programme of Nazi propaganda. From 1938, the Hitler Youth was the primary source of recruits for the SS. But despite the movement's warlike activities, von Schirach was not involved in the planning of any wars of aggression.

Count Four: As Gauleiter of Vienna, von Schirach participated in the deportation of Jews to the camps.

Verdict: Guilty on Count Four.

Sentence: 20 years' imprisonment.

Fritz Sauckel (b. 1894): Plenipotentiary for Labour Mobilisation, 1942–5.

Counts One and Two: The evidence has not established that Sauckel was sufficiently connected with the common plan or with the waging of aggressive war.

Counts Three and Four: From 1942, Sauckel was given charge of the exploitation of the labour resources of occupied territories. His commissioners despatched some five million workers to the Reich, few of them voluntarily, transporting and then treating them with brutality. Sauckel was aware of the ruthless methods employed to obtain this slave labour, although he did not advocate cruelty for its own sake. His attitude was to extract the maximum possible degree of work at the lowest possible cost.

Verdict: Guilty on Counts Three and Four.

Sentence: Death.

Alfred Jodl (b. 1890): Chief of the Operations Staff of the High Command of the Armed Forces, 1939–45.

Counts One and Two: Jodl reported directly to Hitler on operational matters and was the actual planner of the conduct of the war. His staff plans were used to exert military pressure on Austria and to provide the pretext for the intervention in Czechoslovakia. He was involved in the timing of the attacks on Western Europe and the Balkans. Plans for the invasion of Russia were drawn up a year before it began, and Jodl initialled 'Case Barbarossa'.

Counts Three and Four: Jodl signed the covering memorandum to the Commando Order, although he testified that he was opposed to it. In 1944, he ordered the evacuation of northern Norway and the burning of 30,000 homes so as to deny help to the Russians. His defence was that he was bound by the orders of his superior, Hitler. Participation in crimes such as these has never been required of a soldier.

Verdict: Guilty on all four counts.

Sentence: Death.

Franz von Papen (b. 1879): Chancellor of Germany, 1932, and Deputy Chancellor, 1933–4.

Counts One and Two: In June 1934, von Papen was arrested following the purge of the SA and two of his associates were murdered. Notwithstanding this, in July, on the day after the assassination of the Austrian Chancellor Dollfuss, von Papen accepted the post of Minister to Austria. There he worked to undermine the Government and to strengthen the position of the local Party in order to bring about the Anschluss, the union of the two countries. Intrigue and bullying, however, are not crimes under the Charter, and there is no evidence he was a party to the plans to occupy Austria by force or that he agreed with such a step when it was taken.

Verdict: Acquitted.

Arthur Seyss-Inquart (b. 1892): Chancellor of Austria, 1938–9, Deputy Governor of Poland, 1939–40, Reich Commissioner of Occupied Holland, 1940–5.

Counts One and Two: Seyss-Inquart took part in the last stages of the intrigue that brought about the occupation of Austria, and became its Chancellor because of the Germans' threats of invasion. When President Miklas resigned rather than sign the law making Austria a province of Germany, Seyss-Inquart took his functions, as Reich Governor. He had Jews deported to the East and political opponents sent to camps.

Counts Three and Four: In Poland from September 1939, and in Holland from May 1940, Seyss-Inquart governed territories occupied by aggressive war. He knew of the start of the AB action under which Polish intellectuals were murdered. In the Netherlands, he applied terror, such as the shooting of hostages, and sent forced labour to Germany. He supervised the deportation of 120,000 Dutch Jews to Auschwitz. It is true that some of the excesses were carried out by units that reported to Himmler, and that he successfully opposed the scorched-earth orders at the end of the war. But he was a knowing participant in war crimes and crimes against humanity.

Verdict: Guilty on Counts Two, Three and Four.

Sentence: Death.

Albert Speer (b. 1905): Minister for Armaments and Production from 1942, and Hitler's favoured architect.

Counts One and Two: The Tribunal is of the opinion that Speer's activities do not amount to the planning of wars of aggression. He became head of the armament industry well after the wars had been commenced, and his activities were solely in aid of the war effort as other productive enterprises were.

Counts Three and Four: The evidence relates entirely to his participation in the slave labour programme. This was administered by Sauckel, but it was Speer who transmitted to him estimates of the numbers of workers needed, whom he knew would be supplied under compulsion. Speer also made use of forced labour in his role as head of the Todt Organisation, which constructed such projects as the Atlantic Wall and military highways. He was not directly involved in cruelty to labourers but urged that drastic action be taken against suspected malingerers. His system of 'blocked labour' did keep many workers in their home countries, producing goods for German industry, and he was

one of the few to tell Hitler openly that the war was lost. At personal risk, he took steps to prevent the implementation of the scorched-earth policy.
Verdict: Guilty on Counts Three and Four.
Sentence: 20 years' imprisonment.

Constantin von Neurath (b. 1873): Foreign Minister, 1932–8, and Protector of Bohemia and Moravia, 1939–41.
Counts One and Two: Von Neurath played an important role as Foreign Minister in the reoccupation of the Rhineland in 1936, and took part in the Hossbach conference, although he testified that Hitler's statements that day caused him to have a heart attack. He resigned soon after, but despite knowing the regime's plans he retained a relationship with it as a Minister without Portfolio. He took charge of the Foreign Office at the time of the Anschluss, and participated in the negotiations at Munich.
Counts Three and Four: As Reich Protector for Bohemia and Moravia from March 1939, von Neurath instituted an administration similar to that of Germany in a territory occupied by aggressive action. All opposition was outlawed and anti-Semitic laws introduced. Many prominent Czechs were imprisoned and died in camps. Von Neurath claimed that the repression was carried out by forces reporting to Himmler, and in mitigation he did intervene for the release of Czech prisoners. He effectively resigned in September 1941 by going on indefinite leave after being told he was not acting harshly enough.
Verdict: Guilty on all four counts.
Sentence: 15 years' imprisonment.

Hans Fritzsche (b. 1900): Head of the Home Press Division, Ministry of Propaganda, 1938–42, Head of the Radio Division, 1942–5.
Count One: Fritzsche, as head of the Home Press Division, held a daily press conference to deliver the directives of the Propaganda Ministry to 2,300 newspapers. He instructed the press how certain issues, such as the Jewish problem or the invasion of Poland, should be covered. Yet he had no control of the formulation of propaganda and was merely a conduit for his superiors' directives. Again, as head of the Radio Division from 1942, he was subject to Goebbels' supervision. He never attained sufficient stature to attend the planning conferences which led to war.

Counts Three and Four: The prosecution asserted that Fritzsche encouraged the commission of war crimes by deliberately falsifying news, but he was never sufficiently important to originate propaganda campaigns. His speeches were anti-Semitic, but never urged extermination of the Jews. If he spread false news, it was because he believed it true, and his aim was never to incite atrocities, only to arouse popular sentiment in favour of Hitler and the German war effort. He was not a participant in the crimes charged.
Verdict: Acquitted.

Martin Bormann (b. 1900): Head of the Party Chancellery from 1941, replacing Hess. Tried in absentia.
Count One: Bormann gained ready access to the Fuehrer's conferences only from 1941, as head of the Party Chancellery, and was not therefore a party to the initial conspiracy to wage war.
Counts Three and Four: From January 1942, Bormann had control over all laws and directives issued by Hitler. He placed all Party agencies at the disposal of Himmler's resettlement programme, and he knew of the plans for mass killings in Russia. He was extremely active in the persecution of the Jews; in 1943, he signed a law withdrawing the protection of the courts from them and placing them under the jurisdiction of the Gestapo. He was prominent in the slave labour programme, and authorised the use of firearms against recalcitrant prisoners of war. In 1944, he removed jurisdiction of POWS from the OKW and gave it to the SS. He was responsible for the campaign to lynch captured Allied airmen. Evidence of his death is not conclusive and the Tribunal is prepared to try him in absentia.
Verdict: Guilty on Counts Three and Four.
Verdict: Death.

Robert Ley (b. 1890): From 1933 Leader of the Labour Front, the only trade union allowed by the Nazis. Ley committed suicide after being indicted but before the trial commenced.

Gustav Krupp von Bohlen und Halbach (b. 1870): Chairman of the gigantic family firm of munitions manufacturers. The indictment against Krupp was dismissed by the judges early in the trial on the grounds of his senility. The company had been run by his son Alfred for most of the war.

The indicted organisations and a summary of the judgments

The Reich Cabinet: By arraigning the Reich Cabinet, the Four Powers intended to catch as a group the 48 men who had held ministerial office under Hitler, including those who were also individual defendants, together with any other members of the Secret Defence Council and the Council of Ministers.

The prosecution has named as a criminal organisation the Reich Cabinet, consisting of members of the ordinary cabinet after 1933, the Council of Ministers for the defence of the Reich and the Secret Cabinet Council. The Tribunal is of the opinion that there should be no declaration of criminality because it is not shown that after 1937 it ever really acted as a group (and the Secret Cabinet Council never met at all) and because the group of persons charged is so small that members could be conveniently tried in proper cases. Individual members were involved in the conspiracy to wage war, but as individuals. When Hitler disclosed his aims at the Hossbach conference, it was not to the Cabinet. No Cabinet order authorised the invasion of Poland. Perhaps 23 members of the group remain to be brought to trial, and those who are guilty should be.
Verdict: Not criminal.

The Leadership Corps of the Nazi Party: The hierarchical organisation through which the Nazis distributed their orders and ideology, from the ministers via the *Gauleiter* – provincial bosses – down to the *Blockleiter* on virtually every street. The numbers indicted were potentially huge, as the Corps had more than 600,000 members, but at a local level they had not wielded much authority nor committed grave crimes, and in the event the prosecution confined itself to bringing suit against its upper ranks.

The Leadership Corps was the official organisation of the Nazi Party, run by Hess and later by Bormann. The machinery of the Corps was used for the dissemination of propaganda and to keep a detailed check on the political attitudes of the German people. This was not criminal, but it was also used for illegal Germanisation measures in those parts of occupied territories, such as in Poland, Lithuania, France and Yugoslavia, that were incorporated directly into the Reich. It was involved in the persecution of the Jews, for instance to keep public opinion quiet about their treatment, and it was involved in the administration of slave labour and the mistreatment of prisoners of war.

Verdict: Criminal, at the level of *Kreisleiter* (county head) and above.

The Gestapo: The Gestapo (from *Geheime Staatspolizei* or 'secret state police') was created in 1933 by Goering, then Minister for Prussia, as an expansion of that province's political police. It was soon taken over and turned into a national force by Himmler, who placed it under the authority of his own SS. Working free of legal restraints, the Gestapo became an instrument of repression and terror, albeit one much more dependent on denunciations than on detection, and it was closely involved in the execution of partisans and the murder of Jews.

The SD (*Sicherheitsdienst*): The SD was the Party's security and intelligence service, created by Himmler and led by Heydrich until his assassination in 1942. Like much of the Nazis' apparatus, it duplicated many of the functions of the official state security bodies, such as the Abwehr – military intelligence – which it eventually swallowed in 1944. Its agents were involved in sabotage and espionage, and helped mount the purge against the SA in 1934.

The prosecution presented the cases of the Gestapo and SD together because of their close working relationship. Under Heydrich from 1939 they were consolidated into one unit, the RSHA, with seven offices, among them Amt IV for the Gestapo and Amt III for SD activities within Germany. There was close co-ordination and much interaction between the two bodies, and with the Criminal Police and the SS and Wehrmacht at times, such as in the Einsatzgruppen. The Gestapo detained political prisoners and sent them to the camps, while both organisations participated in the deportation of the Jews. Members took part in the torture and execution of civilian populations in occupied territories, and in the secret deportations to Germany under the Nacht und Nebel edict. They also enforced the 'Bullet' decree (Action Kugel), and murdered prisoners of war.

Verdict: Criminal, with the exception of clerical and stenographic staff.

The SA: The brown-shirted thugs of the Nazi Party in the 1920s and 1930s, originally recruited from former soldiers to act as bodyguards at public meetings. Under Ernst Roehm, the *Sturmabteilung* (Storm Division) grew vastly in strength and in political ambition. In 1934 Hitler broke it in the Night of the Long Knives, using the SS to execute the SA's leadership. Although it remained associated with the Party in the minds of foreigners, it thereafter had no role beyond occasional demonstrations of force and civil defence duties.

In the early days of the Nazi movement, the SA was the Party's 'strong arm'. By the end of 1933, it numbered four and a half million men, organised on military lines and used to fight street battles against opponents. After the Party came to power, it was used to intimidate Jews. The atrocities committed by its ruffians in the early 1930s were not, however, part of a plan to wage aggressive war, and it cannot be said that later its members generally participated in criminal acts.
Verdict: Not criminal.

The SS: The *Schutzstaffel* (Defence Unit) originated as Hitler's personal bodyguard, but grew greatly in size and evolved into the Party's military and racial elite.

The SS was originally established as an elite unit of the SA, but was given separate status after taking part in the Roehm Purge of the SA in 1934. By 1939, it was almost a quarter of a million strong. During the war, the Waffen SS, the armed units that grew from it, numbered 580,000 men, under the tactical command of the Army. About a third of its number were conscripts after 1940. SS units participated in the steps leading up to war, for instance being used in occupying the Sudetenland. There is evidence that the shooting of unarmed prisoners was general practice in some Waffen SS divisions. Units of the Waffen SS were used in the exterminations in the East in the guise of combating partisans. The SS was responsible for the guarding and administration of concentration camps. Terrible experiments were performed there. Units participated in the Einsatzgruppen massacres of Jews and in that of the Jews in the Warsaw Ghetto. An attempt was made to keep some of its activities secret, but the slaughter was so widespread that it must have been commonly known.
Verdict: Criminal, aside from those conscripted who did not participate in crimes.

The General Staff and High Command of the German Armed Forces: The prosecution's initial belief was that the war had been driven by the militarism of the German officer corps, which was also credited with having helped to plan the war crimes committed by soldiers, especially in the East. Many Germans were worried that the indictment of the OKW signalled in effect a proxy trial of the entire armed forces.

According to the indictment, this group consists of about 130 officers who held certain positions in the military hierarchy between 1938 and 1945. They were commanders-in-chief of one of the three services, or chiefs of staff, or held office in the OKW – the High Command – which in a sense was Hitler's personal staff. The Tribunal does not find that they were an organisation, and indeed no serious effort was made so to assert. They were only an aggregation of those who happened to hold high rank in a certain period. Those joining this group cannot have known they were joining a criminal organisation, as no such organisation existed before the indictment was drawn up. These men have, however, been a disgrace to the profession of arms, and they have made a mockery of obedience to orders. They were a ruthless military caste, and where guilty of crimes should be brought to trial as individuals. *Verdict:* Not criminal.

The judges of the International Military Tribunal

United Kingdom of Great Britain and Northern Ireland
Lord Justice (Sir Geoffrey) Lawrence, President
Mr Justice (Sir Norman) Birkett, Alternate Member

United States of America
Justice Francis Biddle
Judge John Parker, Alternate Member

France
Professor Henri Donnedieu de Vabres
Counsellor Robert Falco, Alternate Member

Union of Soviet Socialist Republics
Major-General Iona Nikitchenko
Lieutenant-Colonel Alexander Volchkov, Alternate Member

Prosecution Counsel

United States of America
Chief Prosecutor
Mr Justice Robert H. Jackson

Executive Trial Counsel
Colonel Robert G. Storey
Mr Thomas J. Dodd
Associate Trial Counsel
Mr Sidney S. Alderman
Brigadier-General Telford Taylor
Colonel John Harlan Amen
Mr Ralph G. Albrecht
Assistant Trial Counsel
Colonel Leonard Wheeler, Jr
Lieutenant-Colonel William H. Baldwin
Lieutenant-Colonel Smith W. Brookhart, Jr
Commander James Britt Donovan
Major Frank B. Wallis
Major William F. Walsh
Major Warren F. Farr
Captain Samuel Harris
Captain Drexel A. Sprecher
Lieutenant-Commander Whitney R. Harris
Lieutenant Thomas F. Lambert, Jr
Lieutenant Henry K. Atherton
Lieutenant Brady O. Bryson
Lieutenant Bernard D. Meltzer
Dr Robert M. Kempner
Mr Walter W. Brudno

United Kingdom of Great Britain and Northern Ireland
Chief Prosecutor
Sir Hartley Shawcross
Deputy Chief Prosecutor
Sir David Maxwell Fyfe
Leading Counsel
Mr G.D. Roberts
Junior Counsel
Lieutenant-Colonel Mervyn Griffith-Jones
Colonel H. J. Phillimore

Major Frederick Elwyn Jones
Major J. Harcourt Barrington

France
Chief Prosecutors
M. François de Menthon
M. Auguste Champetier de Ribes
Deputy Chief Prosecutors
M. Charles Dubost
M. Edgar Faure
Assistant Prosecutors
M. Pierre Mounier
M. Charles Gerthoffer
M. Delphin Debenest
M. Jacques B. Herzog
M. Henry Delpech
M. Serge Fuster
M. Conslant Quatre
M. Henri Monneray

Union of Soviet Socialist Republics
Chief Prosecutor
General Roman Rudenko
Deputy Chief Prosecutor
Colonel Y.V. Pokrovsky
Assistant Prosecutors
State Counsellor of Justice of the 2nd Class, L.R. Shenin
State Counsellor of Justice of the 2nd Class, M.Y. Raginsky
State Counsellor of Justice of the 3rd Class, N.D. Zorya
Chief Counsellor of Justice, L.N. Smirnov
Colonel D.S. Karev
Lieutenant-Colonel J.A. Ozol
Captain V.V. Kuchin

Defence Counsel

Defendant	Counsel
Hermann Goering	Otto Stahmer
Rudolf Hess	Guenther von Rohrscheidt (to 5 February 1946) Alfred Seidl (from 5 February 1946)
Joachim von Ribbentrop	Fritz Sauter (to 5 January 1946) Martin Horn (from 5 January 1946)
Wilhelm Keitel	Otto Nelte
Ernst Kaltenbrunner	Kurt Kauffmann
Alfred Rosenberg	Alfred Thoma
Hans Frank	Alfred Seidl
Wilhelm Frick	Otto Pannenbeeker
Julius Streicher	Hans Marx
Walther Funk	Fritz Sauter
Hjalmar Schacht	Rudolf Dix
Karl Doenitz	Flottenrichter Otto Kranzbuehler
Erich Raeder	Walter Siemers
Baldur von Schirach	Fritz Sauter
Fritz Sauckel	Robert Servatius
Alfred Jodl	Franz Exner and Hermann Jahreiss
Martin Bormann	Friedrich Bergold
Franz von Papen	Egon Kubuschok
Arthur Seyss-Inquart	Gustav Steinbauer
Albert Speer	Hans Flaechsner
Constantin von Neurath	Otto Freiherr von Luedinghausen
Hans Fritzsche	Heinz Fritz
Reich Cabinet	Egon Kubuschok
Leadership Corps of Nazi Party	Robert Servatius

SS and SD	Ludwig Babel
	Horst Pelckmann
	Carl Haensel
	Hans Gawlik
SA	Georg Boehm
	Martin Loeffler
Gestapo	Rudolf Merkel
General Staff and High Command	Franz Exner (to 27 January 1946)
	Hans Laternser (from 27 January 1946)

Acknowledgments

The author and publishers wish to thank the following for permission to use copyright material:

Carlton Books for material from Franz von Papen, *Memoirs*, trans. by Brian Connell, Andre Deutsch (1952) pp. 561–3;

Curtis Brown Ltd, London, on behalf of the Estate of the author for material from H Montgomery Hyde, *Birkett*, Hamish Hamilton (1964) pp. 503–4, 504–5, 516, 519, 520, 521. Copyright © H Montgomery Hyde, 1964;

Doubleday, a division of Random House, Inc, for material from Francis Biddle, *In Brief Authority* (1962) pp. 376, 379–81, 453–4, 466–8. Copyright © 1962 Francis Biddle;

Alexander Matthews, literary executor of the Estate of the author, for material from Martha Gellhorn, *The Face of War* (1988) pp. 229–32. Copyright © 1988 Martha Gellhorn;

William Neave on behalf of the Estate of the author for material from Airey Neave, *Nuremberg*, Hodder & Stoughton (1978);

Select Bibliography

Andrus Burton, *I Was the Nuremberg Jailer* (New York; Coward, McCann & Geoghegan, 1969)

Benton, Wilbourn, and Georg Grimm, *Nuremberg: German Views of the War Trials* (Dallas; Southern Methodist University Press, 1955)

Biddle, Francis, *In Brief Authority* (Garden City, NY; Doubleday, 1962)

Calvocoressi, Peter, *Threading My Way* (London; Duckworth, 1994)

Conot, Robert, *Justice at Nuremberg* (New York; Harper & Row, 1983)

Davidson, Eugene, *The Trial of the Germans* (New York; Collier Books, 1966)

Doenitz, Karl, *Ten Years and Twenty Days* (Cleveland; World Publishing, 1959)

Fritzsche, Hans, *The Sword in the Scales* (London; Alan Wingate, 1953)

Gaskin, Hilary, *Eyewitnesses at Nuremberg* (London; Arms and Armour, 1990)

Gellhorn, Martha, *The Face of War* (London; Hart Davis, 1959)

Gilbert, G.M., *Nuremberg Diary* (New York; Signet, 1947)

Goldensohn, Leon, *The Nuremberg Interviews* (New York; Vintage, 2004)

Harris, Whitney, *Tyranny on Trial* (Dallas; Southern Methodist University Press, 1954)

Hyde, H. Montgomery, *Birkett* (London; Hamish Hamilton, 1964)

Jones, Elwyn, *In My Time* (London; Weidenfeld and Nicolson, 1983)

Kelley, Douglas M., *22 Cells at Nuremberg* (New York; Greenberg, 1947)

Kalnoky, Ingeborg, *The Witness House* (London; New English Library, 1974)

Kilmuir, Lord (David Maxwell Fyfe), *Political Adventure* (London; Weidenfeld and Nicolson, 1964)

Marrus, Michael, *The Nuremberg War Crimes Trial 1945–46* (New York; St Martin's, 1997)

McMillan, James, *Five Men at Nuremberg* (London; Harrap, 1985)

Neave, Airey, *Nuremberg* (London; Hodder and Stoughton, 1978)

Overy, Richard, *Interrogations* (London; Viking, 2001)

Papen, Franz von, *Memoirs* (London; Andre Deutsch, 1952)

Persico, Joseph E., *Nuremberg: Infamy on Trial* (New York; Viking, 1994)

Ribbentrop, Joachim von, *The Ribbentrop Memoirs* (London; Weidenfeld and Nicolson, 1953)

Shawcross, Hartley, *Life Sentence* (London; Constable, 1995)

Schacht, Hjalmar, *Account Settled* (London; Weidenfeld and Nicolson, 1948)

Smith, Bradley F., *Reaching Judgment at Nuremberg* (New York; Basic Books, 1977)

Speer, Albert, *Inside the Third Reich* (London; Weidenfeld and Nicolson, 1970)

Taylor, Telford, *Anatomy of the Nuremberg Trials: A Personal Memoir* (Chicago; Quadrangle Books, 1992)

Tusa, Ann, and John Tusa, *The Nuremberg Trial* (London; Macmillan, 1983)

West, Rebecca, *A Train of Powder* (New York; Viking, 1955)

Index

Note: Page numbers in *italics* indicate entries in the Summaries.